W9-CFW-414

SPIN

underground
u.s.a.

under

the bes

ground u.s.a.
f rock culture coast to coast

**introduction by
Craig Marks**

**edited by
Duncan Bock**

**illustrations by
Gary Panter**

VINTAGE BOOKS
a division of Random House, Inc.
New York

A Vintage Original, September 1997
First Edition

Copyright © 1997 by Camouflage Associates, A Partnership

All rights reserved under International and Pan-American Copyright
Conventions. Published in the United States by Vintage Books, a division of
Random House, Inc., New York, and simultaneously in Canada by Random
House of Canada Limited, Toronto.

The Library of Congress Cataloging-in-Publication Data
Underground U.S.A./Spin; introduction by Craig Marks; edited by Duncan
Bock; illustrations by Gary Panter.
p.   cm.
Includes index.
ISBN: 0-679-75575-6
1. Rock music—United States—Guidebooks. 2. Popular culture—United
States—Guidebooks. I. Bock, Duncan. II. Spin (New York, N.Y.)
ML3534.U5   1997   97-2597
917.304'929—dc21
CIP
MN

Random House Web address: http/www.randomhouse.com/
10 9 8 7 6 5 4 3 2 1

Balliett & Fitzgerald, Inc.
Editors: Duncan Bock, Chris Mitchell, Tom Dyja
Design: Howard Slatkin and Susan Canavan
Associate Editor: Maria Fernandez
Copy Editors: Nanette Maxim, Ted Botha
Proofreader: Andrew Beaujon
Assistant Editor: Doug Gillison
Editorial Assistants: Ben Welch, Margaret Hanscom

con-

tents

introduction

Unlike, say, major-league baseball or the movie industry, rock 'n' roll is a geographically democratic enterprise. Throughout its 40-plus-year history, rock's heroes and antiheroes have been as likely to emerge from America's small towns and second-tier cities as they have from the twin axes of New York and Los Angeles. Cities like Memphis and Seattle are indelibly linked to their sonic legacy, and vice versa; rock 'n' roll is nothing if not a reflection of place, and there's no better way to trace the character of a city than through its musical traditions.

But what you can learn about a city using rock 'n' roll as your tour guide encompasses much more than just club listings or infamous adresses ("blah blah choked on vomit at this spot, 1969"). By valuing rock 'n' roll not just as a music but as a lifestyle—one that eschews traditional middle-class aesthetics in favor of a commitment to bohemia's underground glories—you can discover an alternate version of a city that few residents will even know and even fewer travel books ever bother with.

It's with this in mind that we bring you *underground u.s.a.*, a 20-city guide to an American splendor rarely promoted. All 20 of the selected cities share at least one thing in common: They're contributors to the current vitality of American rock 'n' roll and offer their young visitors an underground nexus of pleasures that revolve around the notion that you don't have to spend lavishly in order to have a lavish good time. You'll hardly ever find a thriving music scene that doesn't allow its practitioners to live as artists on the cheap, and so this book allows you to live as they do, through the insider expertise of writers—alternative-newspaper contributors, indie musicians, underground-food columnists—who know their towns' tattoo parlors and comic stores, surf shops and burrito joints, dive bars and dance clubs, well, intimately.

As a sometime rock journalist whose vocation entails spending, say, a couple of days in Providence on the trail of the latest would-be rock stars, I find myself posing the same kind of question to locals time and time again: where's the best record store, the best Thai restaurant, the best used-book shop, the best jukebox? And in fact, the "locals" are often as clueless as I am; their idea of "best" often translates into most expensive, or most popular, or most convenient, none of which is a substitute for that particular accolade: "Best." It's a subjective superlative, of course, but if you're hoping to glean the essence of a city in a short period of time, you need someone to be able to separate the great from the not-so, the authentic from the wannabe, the magical from the trying-too-hard. In keeping, you'll find the entries in *underground u.s.a.* grouped around such unlikely headings as "Best barbecue from an oil drum," "Best Tiki lounge," and "Best plastic clothes," among many. Live music venues, cheap eats, skate parks, dyke bars, techno clubs: they're all in *underground u.s.a.*, as up-to-the-moment as possible, and they'll open up the secret folds of the 20 cities included in a manner both handy and detailed.

Whether you're hounding rock stars, road-tripping around the country, or scouting for a place to settle down, *underground u.s.a.* offers insightful, tailored information for such a discerning bohemian as yourself. So what are you waiting for? America's hidden charms await.

Craig Marks
Executive Editor
SPIN

underground
u.s.a.

atlanta/
athens

by Jeff Clark

"Atlanta, home of Southern lifestyle, family values, and the womb of 20th-century, spiritual, liberation music!"
— Andre, *OutKast*

"Peace and tranquility...but sometimes suckers try you."
— Big Boi, *OutKast*

Underground Atlanta is often dismissed as a chicken shack full of grits 'n' biscuits and not much else. Frankly, if you've ever had good grits and homemade biscuits, you'd know there could be worse fates. While Atlanta may be best known as the antiseptic capital of the New South, home to Coke, Turner, and too many conventions, it does have its signature shacks of hip-hop and rock— small-time scenes and labels in the Southeast's biggest city. In fact, Atlanta's underground is so diverse, encompassing both a huge black college population and assorted off-center rock and folk crowds, it's hard to pin down a trademark sound. Is Atlanta typified by the redneck underground country/rockabilly/surf hybrid that thrives at Little Five Points' Star Bar or the glitzy R&B and hip-hop industry that's enjoyed high-profile status since artists and producers like Babyface, Dallas Austin, and Keith Sweat moved their operations here? Is it the scruffy Southern-fried album rock of the Black Crowes, Drivin' 'N' Cryin', and Collective Soul or the eccentric sounds that come out of low-rent Cabbagetown south of downtown? Is it the post-Indigo Girls acoustic strummings of Decatur, due west of the city, or the wacko jammings of landmark musician Colonel Bruce Hampton's various musical units? Or is it not found in Atlanta at all, but still simmering in the slacker collegiate town of Athens, an hour's drive away? Yes, to all of the above, and more.

While the Athens music scene is not nearly as hopping as it was a decade ago, when R.E.M. and the B-52's had made it an alternative music mecca, folks like Vic Chesnutt keep it interesting. Atlanta's never really had a musical day in the sun, but there's always been great outsider stuff going on—which connects to the music industry's lack of presence here. Sure, all the major labels have marketing and distribution offices in Atlanta, but that's about the extent of it, aside from urban players like LaFace and Rowdy. Otherwise, it's smaller regional operations like Long Play Records (home to Southern Gothic street poets Smoke and sultry singer Kelly Hogan), Half-Baked (post-minimalists Bob and confrontational art-terrorists Pineal Ventana), and Worrybird (female power-punk trio Catfight).

Producer Brendan O'Brien (Pearl Jam, Stone Temple Pilots) and Indigo Girl Amy Ray get medals of honor for channeling their homegrown success back into the community by starting their own record labels. O'Brien's 57 Records has championed the tough power-pop of 3 lb. Thrill, while his smaller Shotput imprint has concentrated on weirder fare from the Hampton Grease Band (an early '70s Zappa-esque outfit led by the aforementioned Bruce Hampton) and introspective guitarist Glenn Phillips. Likewise, with an eclectic list of releases that includes titles by bluesy songstress Michelle Malone, quirky Danielle Howle (from nearby Columbia, South Carolina), and the scuzz-wave Rock*A*Teens, Ray's Daemon Records gives an outlet to some of the more unclassifiable—but certainly not unlistenable—music the region has been producing in the '90s.

If Atlanta's underground music environment is as diverse, cliquish, and segregated as any other big city's, one Daemon release from 1994 seems to sum up the we'll-try-anything spirit that locks these disparate communities together: Under the direction of drummer Michael Lorant of eclectic popsters Big Fish Ensemble, scores of players from the underground rock, acoustic, and R&B scenes came together to recreate a charmingly low-key but ultimately faithful production of the Rice/Webber warhorse *Jesus Christ Superstar*. That such a bizarre, unassuming circus—which was performed live in Atlanta, Austin, and Seattle over the course of the following year—evoked so much humor, tragedy, and pure joy stands as a testament to the power of Atlanta's outrider music fringes.

So as you're shuffling through the shops and clubs of Atlanta looking for some token of *the cool*, don't be surprised if you don't find it. Atlanta's been watered down and refurbished like other cities, with much of its homegrown flavor swept away in the flurry, but its underground denizens remain a steadfast class of their own. And with them, it's more an attitude than a fashion, more an offbeat way of life than an obvious trend. No, Atlantans ain't bumpkins (he said with a toothless drawl) but on the other hand, the real world you'll find here—if you look hard enough—is nothing like what you'll see on MTV. Wouldn't have it any other way. Now, pass me the damned grits!

lay of the land
Atlanta

For all of downtown Atlanta's convention-fueled sterility and the homogenous mall-sprawl of the outer burbs, the tattered circle in between has much to offer the independent-minded young scamp. It's just a matter of deciding how bohemian you're gonna be. In the upscale **Buckhead** neighborhood, due north of downtown, perfectly tanned and coifed young princesses in Beamers and Lexuses zoom straight for the valet parking in the bustling shopping district by day, while drunk suburbanites cruise the myriad spiffy bars and dance clubs by night.

If you (like Atlanta's never-ending stream of conventioneers) want outright sleaze, Atlanta probably has more strip clubs per capita than any other city in the nation. Take a jaunt down **Cheshire Bridge Road**, where nude strip clubs, lingerie modeling "jack shacks," S&M danceterias, and gay gift shops do business among an odd array of ethnic restaurants, antique shops, and fortune-tellers. Or, if you have something more sedate yet urban in mind, try the **Virginia-Highland** neighborhood, just northeast of downtown, where old brick-and-hardwood-floor apartments are within walking distance of some of the city's best cafes, coffee shops, bars, and galleries.

By contrast, the old, eccentric **Cabbagetown** neighborhood due east of the city seems almost lost in time, although recent renovations have upgraded the living conditions. It's almost like a barefoot small Southern town in itself, complete with overall-wearing oldsters who've lived there all their lives and have no intention of moving, sonny. The rent's cheap, it's close to all the good clubs, and there ain't no suburban high school punks cluttering the sidewalks.

If you want to get at the true hub of Atlanta's freak scene, you have to go to **Little Five Points**, a little south of the Highlands. The central triangle here—surrounded by an array of colorful eating joints, secondhand clothes boutiques, and scrappy rock clubs—can be like the parking lot at a Phish show. Except that in addition to tie-dyed Hackysack stoners, you also get the dreadlocked rastas, green-Mohawked punkers, black-haired Goths, hardcore skins, drunks, vagrants, and young suburban wanna-bes who aren't sure just what they wanna be yet. Imagine all of the above asking you for change at once under a ceiling of discarded sneakers hanging from telephone lines. Lemme hear you say "alternative"!

As for nightlife, here are some tips: Club shows usually start around 10:30 P.M., with many lasting well past 2 A.M. Last call for alcohol is 4 A.M. every night except Saturday night (Sunday morning), when 3 A.M. will get you thrown out on the sidewalk. You aren't allowed to bring drinks out of these establishments, either. A few after-hours places are allowed to stay open well past sunrise, all of them catering to the dance-till-you-drop crowd.

Athens

Despite recent growth, Athens (approximately 60 miles northeast of Atlanta) still typifies the small Southern college town, with cheaper rent and a slower pace. Except during the slow summers, the students enrolled at the University of Georgia swarm the downtown area—nearly doubling Athens' population during the school year—making for a roving party wherever you wander. The town is centered around a six-square-block area right next to the university, filled with stores, clubs, bars, and restaurants. College Avenue has wide sidewalks, giving it a town-square feel where cafes put tables outdoors and students wheedle away long afternoons. There are some incredibly beautiful houses and, of course, some great bars. And yeah, you'll occasionally see an R.E.M.-er hanging around. Just don't bug 'em, o-tay?

getting from a to b

As it's kind of spread out, **Atlanta** is a car-oriented city, although a convenient and recently completed bicycle trail now cuts across the metro area. As for buses and subways, MARTA provides both, and while it's handy if you're going anywhere near the rail stations, trains and buses stop running shortly after midnight and don't start up again till around 5. If you want a taxi, you can usually get one at any hour, but they rarely stop for you on the street. You usually need to call one of the cab companies—Checker Cab *(404/351–1111)* or Yellow Cab *(404/521–0200)* are two—and request a ride, then wait between five and ten minutes for it to show up. On the other hand, **Athens**, 60-or-so miles northeast of Atlanta, is a good walking town, as most of what you'll want is in or close to the quaint central city blocks, referred to as in-town.

sources

To find out what's going on, the best source in Atlanta is alternative weekly *Creative Loafing*. This free paper covers politics, local issues, film, food, theater, etc., but the music section is its largest, with a full nightly listing of venues and bookings. Athens' free weekly *Flagpole* is

smaller, and it suffers from an unreasonable degree of hometown boos-
terism, but if you want to know what's going on, it's the source of choice.

clubs

Atlanta

Best place to drink until you see Elvis: If you think you see
Lenny and Squiggy smoking Camels outside the **Star Community Bar**
(437 Moreland Ave. NE, 404/681–9018), don't worry, you haven't
entered a bad sitcom (well, not exactly). Rockabilly chic is rising again,
and this nifty club, housed in a defunct bank, is Atlanta's headquarters
for what's known locally as the redneck underground, a new generation
of Southern rockers who gag on MTV and corporate-rock culture. These
back-to-basics greasers like roots music—and it doesn't matter whose
roots. They'll take country crooners, surf guitar, swing, or other pre-1964
pop. In addition to floor-packing locals like Subsonics and Kelly Hogan,
the Star Bar is a popular stop for touring acts like Southern Culture on
the Skids, Rosie Flores, and Flat Duo Jets, all of whom turn the small
red room into a spontaneous hoedown. This is where folks like Steve
Earle and Jason Ringenberg hang out when they pass through town,
drawn by the colorful characters, the cheap Pabst Blue Ribbon, and the
majestic Elvis shrine—a loving monument to the King housed inside (of
course) the former bank's vault. If you need a break from the manic festivities, venture downstairs to the Little Vinyl Lounge, where master bartender Mike Geier will stir you up a cocktail while you gawk at the incredible selections on the jukebox: Frank, Hank, and the Left Banke, they're
here. Just don't play "Crazy" by Patsy Cline—it's a dead giveaway for
tourists.

Best nudie rock club: Forget Stone Mountain and the CNN Center!
The only Atlanta tourist attraction that keeps packing 'em in year-round
is the city's astounding number of nude dance clubs. You can go spend
$100 of your hard-earned cash at the Club Taj-Mahal in Marietta on the
northwest side of town or at the Cheetah on Spring Street downtown, but
for those on a lower budget, the **Clermont Lounge** *(789 Ponce De Leon
Ave. NE, 404/874–4783)* can't be beat. Sure, it's a seedy little dive, and
the haggard, seen-better-days dancers don't look like they're having fun.
You got a problem with that? Partly due to the unapologetically low-rent
interior, with wood paneling and '70s nudie magazines on the walls, and
partly because it has offbeat bands like Smoke playing every Thursday
night (until someone in the upstairs hotel complains), the Clermont is a

notorious hangout for local music types looking for trouble. Lounge mascot Blondie, a Tina Turner look-alike with an assortment of blonde wigs and outrageous outfits, often reads her poetry between bands, then crushes a few beer cans between her bosoms. So, make Russ Meyer proud: Join toothless street people and young punks for a night of bottom feeding, and remember that quality is in the eye of the beholder.

Best outdoor mosh pit: While the dungeonesque inside of the **Masquerade** *(695 North Ave. NE, 404/577–8178)* might not be the ideal place to slam to your favorite band (too much noise from the disco downstairs—nearly every band complains about it onstage), the backyard Masquerade Music Park is the only entirely general admission outdoor venue in town. Meaning, when the Ramones or Rollins Band plugs in, the place turns into one huge pool of sun-drenched human movement. If you don't mind being a bit farther back (this place is relatively small, only a few thousand can fit inside), there's usually room to sprawl out on the grass and laugh at everyone.

Best acoustic club: Due east of Atlanta ten minutes by car is the small burg of Decatur, the unofficial home of Atlanta's acoustic scene. **Eddie's Attic** *(515-B N. McDonough St., Decatur, 404/377–4976)* is the big club catering to the singer/songwriter, and remains a popular hangout for hopeful young Joni Mitchells and James Taylors. Eddie doesn't like rock 'n' roll all that much, but every now and then he lets a good band plug in. In this second-floor hideaway in a downtown building, you'll have two rooms to choose from, either music and bar inside, or a tent-covered open-air deck where you can watch TV and drink beer. When they're in town, Indigo Girls like to hang out here, and occasionally get up and play, sending the politically correct crowd into an earnest swoon.

Best punk-rock house parties: Welcome to the '90s. Atlanta doesn't have any more unreconstructed punk clubs, especially ones for the underagers. Most, like the famous and much-missed Wreck Room, have either shut down or changed formats; the unforgettably named Somber Reptile is now a blues and BBQ joint. So, what do some enterprising kids do but book their favorite bands in their own homes! With publicity via fliers and word of mouth, the parties at squatlike dwellings that go by names like "Driver Dome" and "i defy" compete with real clubs for attendance and sheer youthful enthusiasm. Beer is frowned upon; raucous slam pits form in basement band rooms; and four or five acts play per bill, ranging from local unknowns to touring acts with one 7-inch out that are also unknown unless you read *Maximum Rock 'n' Roll* cover to cover. In the interest of public safety, we're not going to give out addresses or phone numbers for these; but suffice to say that if you're in the city and you keep up with the scene, you'll know about them. Check for fliers at indie record stores like **Criminal Records** and **Wax 'n' Facts** (see Shopping), or at restaurants like **Tortillas** or **Fellini's Pizza** (see Dining).

Best dance tracks: As in any self-respecting urban mecca, Atlanta's club kids move from place to place with the ferocity of a swarm of locusts: Chew it up, spit it out, and move on. Still, the in-towner It people's choice of the moment, **MJQ** *(551 Ponce De Leon Ave., NE, 404/ 724–9096)*, seems destined for longevity, if only because there's none of the off-putting sterility that dooms most dance halls. Instead, MJQ looks like a cross between a European discotheque and a mid-'60s love pad. People come to hang out and mingle as much as to sway to the beat; little dens and couches wait in the back for taking it easy. Some of the best DJs in town spin here, with the sounds covering everything from acid jazz and disco to lounge and soul. Cover charges seem to be arbitrary. If the door-man has seen you before and you don't look like a geek, you can usually waltz in—assuming you can find the place. There's no sign out front, and it occupies the basement of an old hotel. Occasionally, local bands like the dreamy pop group Seely, and '60s-soul and '50s-beat-jazz-inspired Cicada Sings, play.

Best butch and femme dance club: The **Otherside** *(1924 Piedmont Rd., 404/875–5238)* is a mostly lesbian dance club along a stretch of road packed with nude-dancing emporiums and fast-food huts. While relatively sizable, it's a sociable, low-key joint offering musical theme nights for hip-hop, house, retro, even country music (complete with line dancing). Gay males patronize the Otherside regularly, and straights will feel at home as well. Local femme-friendly bands like Lift and Viva La Diva play live on weekends.

Best after-hours dance club: At 4 A.M. on Sunday morning, **Backstreet** *(845 Peachtree St. NE, 404/873–1986)* is more happening than any club in the city. Why? Last call in most clubs and bars is 3 A.M. on Saturday nights (4 any other night), but there are a handful of dives allowed by the city to operate at all hours. Only a few late-night licenses exist; they are passed from one tavern owner to the next for big bucks. The centrally located (not far from the Fox Theatre), trilevel Backstreet is probably the most popular of its kind. It's mostly gay at any other hour, but the after-hours crowd includes all manner of flotsam and jetsam—breeder, bi, and otherwise. At the bar, you'll find the normal assortment of drug addicts, drag queens, and strippers tying one on after a long night at work, while the dance floor is a flurry of more energetic vampires. Backstreet's Friday and Saturday midnight drag shows are a hoot. After Atlanta's favorite hometown girl RuPaul made it big and moved to New York in the late '80s, every drag diva in town thought she was the one. You be the judge.

Athens

Best rock club, hands down: Don't plan on seeing an unannounced R.E.M. show at Athens' **40 Watt Club** *(285 Washington St., Athens, 706/549–7871)*. Ever since Peter Buck divorced Barrie (who runs the joint) and moved to Seattle in 1992, R.E.M. has stopped this time-honored, off-tour ritual. Still, the 40 Watt remains the area's finest all-purpose rock club. A stripped-down room with a long bar on the right, pool tables on the left, and a stage in middle, it's small enough and friendly enough to book the better local acts like Jack Logan and Man Or Astroman?, yet large enough to cram in national headliners (some of whom skip over nearby Atlanta). Thanks to tickets that are 20 to 25 percent cheaper than in the big city, many savvy Atlanta scenesters make the one-hour drive to see bands here even when they're booked for Atlanta two nights later. An adjacent record store stocks most of the 7-inches and CDs from the Athens bands on the stage, plus the 40 Watt offers occasional movies and disco nights to break up the monotony. In the summer it's hotter than hell inside, but that's where the cases of cold beer behind the bar come in.

bars

Atlanta

Best neighborhood dive: Despite its bourgeois moniker, the **Euclid Avenue Yacht Club** *(1136 Euclid Ave. NE, 404/688–2582)* is just an unassuming little watering hole that acts as "ye olde meeting place" for kaleidoscopic Little Five Points. This old brig hauls in a catch of regulars that includes punks, college kids, rednecks, slackers, and shifty old men. Every Sunday afternoon the place is wall-to-wall with leather-and-chain-clad bikers and the street outside is lined with freshly polished Harleys. Maybe the laddies are all coming from church services. The ranks include weekenders and club riders. Whatever their reason, it's easy to see why the Yacht Club is a worthy stop. With its folk-art-meets-maritime decorations, it's a comfortable dive, famous for kosher dogs and a generous selection of microbrews. If you live in the neighborhood, you'll surely see someone you know; if not, you'll be babbling with newfound cronies by last call.

Best blues bar: While it might not bring in the big-name blues acts that the more established **Blind Willie's** *(828 N. Highland Ave. NE, 404/873–2583)* lands, the funky **Northside Tavern** *(1058 Howell Mill Rd. NW, 404/874–8745)* offers a more laid-back Louisiana juke-joint atmosphere. The free gumbo on Thursday nights adds to the community spirit, while local acts like good-time house band Mudcat, Slim Fatz, and old-time blues belter Cora Mae Bryant entertain on most other nights. It's near Georgia Tech and a few neighborhoods where the rent's so cheap they might as well pay you to live there; thus, you're likely to share the pool tables and back courtyard with a motley assortment of oddballs.

Best cheap taps: At the **Austin Avenue Buffet** *(918 Austin Ave. NE, 404/524–9274)* the cold Bud and Miller draft is oh-so-cheap it's no wonder local country and redneck underground bands like to plug in here. This fun neighborhood spot looks like a double-wide trailer decorated with tin beer signs. It has a kitchen but you never see anybody eating here. A lot of people come to this out-of-the-way country drinking shack not just to get a drink, but because it's a hangout destination in itself. Some say the early closing time of 10 P.M. is a drawback, but that just gives you more time to stagger up the street to Little Five Points for more trouble.

Athens
Best art-student bar: You want fancy imports and microbrews? Sit down. The **Globe** *(199 N. Lumpkin St., corner of Clayton and Lumpkin streets, Athens, 706/353–4721)* is a popular drinking trough for UGA's art-student crowd, as it carries lots and lots of beer and has an upstairs gallery where the work of local artistes is displayed. It doubles as a film and performance space where you can see work by Athens indie filmmakers and occasionally hear local bands. Meanwhile, if beer ain't your thing, the Globe also has a full stock of wine, scotch, and bourbon. Better take a taxi home.

food/coffee
Atlanta
Best pizza: Fellini's Pizza *(six locations, the busiest being in Little Five Points at 422 Seminole Ave. NE, 404/525–2530)* has been the day job for

a laundry list of Atlanta rock 'n' rollers. No fewer than three Black Crowes flipped pies here before going big time: Vocalist Chris Robinson and drummer Steve Gorman were both fired, while Chris's guitar-slinging brother, Rich, was robbed at gunpoint his first day on the job and never returned. Other notable Georgia musicians who paid the rent via Fellini's include Tim Nielsen (bass, Drivin' 'N' Cryin'), Chan Marshall (vocals/guitar, Cat Power), Ruthie Morris (guitar, Magnapop), and Anne Richmond Boston (former vocalist, Swimming Pool Q's). But besides wondering whether the freak ringing you up will be the next Michael Stipe, the primary reason to patronize Fellini's, which itself is operated by prominent Atlanta musician and studio owner Clay Harper (ex-vocalist for the Coolies), is the tasty pizza, always tangy and delectable. Some folks say the quality has dropped since it expanded to multiple locations, but some folks like to make fun of the Black Crowes, too.

Best guacamole: Tortillas *(774 Ponce De Leon Ave. NE, 404/892–0193)* is also notable for its roster of local musicians on the employee list; but again the real reason to come here is the San Francisco–style Mexican food. The burritos are big and bursting with beans; the quesadillas melt in your mouth; and the chips-and-guac is downright spiritual. The primary beef everyone seems to have with Tortillas, besides the ever-fluctuating operating hours, is the Cokes— seved in tiny 8-ounce bottles. Best to pass up the hometown potion and swill a beer instead. It's a meeting house for the shaved skull and no-animal-products locals—get gig fliers or drummer-wanted ads here or just get in touch with the youth.

Best bulk barbecue and beans: If it's a stinkin' helping of barbecue 'n' beans you're after, **Fat Matt's Rib Shack** *(1811 Piedmont Ave. NE, 404/607–1622)* has the cure for what ails ya. No doubt this is the most popular 'cue joint in town, especially with the music crowd. Grab plenty of napkins, because you'll need them—it's not a place for daintiness. Local blues bands make some noise after the sun goes down (as if there's any room for them), and there's also an adjacent Chicken Shack that excels at, well, chicken. It's got wooden picnic tables inside and outside, great for spreading out your mess.

Best after-hours greasy spoon: The sign outside the **Majestic Food Shop** *(1031 Ponce De Leon Ave. NE, 404/875–0276)* reads FOOD THAT PLEASES, and a more accurate motto there's never been. Otherwise known to locals as the Majestic, this is the quintessential greasy spoon, a late-night landmark since 1929, with waitresses who look like Aunt Bea after escaping from prison, yummy vittles that slide down a little too easily, and plenty of bizarre sights to keep your bleary eyes occupied. It's a human zoo in the wee hours, when the place is bustling with punks, poets, cops, hippies, club casualties, and freaks of every size and smell. The Majestic is open 24 hours a day, but the food only seems to taste right at 4 A.M.

Best fast food: The counter help and fry cooks at the **Varsity** *(61 North Ave. NW, 404/881–1706)* speak an odd language all their own, but you probably would too if you had to clean the grease traps at this bilevel monument to clogged arteries. Chili dogs, onion rings, burgers, shakes—you can get them inside or have a smiling company representative bring your order to your parked car. Everyone from Bill Clinton to the Go-Go's has chowed down at the Varsity, and the place was recently immortalized in the Brenda Starr comic strip. How alt.rock can you get?

Athens
Best soul-food shack: If it wasn't for R.E.M.'s *Automatic for the People* album, probably none of us would even have heard of **Weaver D's** *(1016 E. Broad St., Athens, 706/353–7797)*. Of course, ever since that album carried Weaver's slogan for its title, his shack has been hyped and exploited to no end, just like Mr. Howard Finster's once-magical Paradise Garden; but hell, we're not proud, so let's join this bandwagon! First of all, this is excellent Southern soul food—especially the fried chicken, okra, black-eyed peas, and mashed potatoes with gravy. There's lots of R.E.M. memorabilia on the wall, plus articles on the restaurant itself. The old picnic tables in the dining area are invariably packed during lunch hour, and that happened before all the attention, too. The locals know how good this place is.

Best veggie outpost: R.E.M.'s Michael Stipe remains a ubiquitous presence around Athens, especially at a pair of veggie restaurants. Stipe owns the building that houses **The Grit** *(199 Prince Ave., Athens, 706/543–6592)*, a good choice for all but the staunchest carnivores. Its selection is vast and varied, and it has a boho feel. The food is positively delicious: Try the quesadillas, the black-bean chili, or the "Golden Bowl" (an all-inclusive concoction of hummus, brown rice, tofu chunks, and more). The Sunday brunch omelettes are also quite popular but plan on waiting for a table if you come for brunch. And, yeah, they even serve grits. Just don't volunteer to dine outside unless you enjoy inhaling exhaust, as the building is on one of the busier streets in Athens. The Grit is next to an organic grocery store.

Runner-up: The Stipe-owned **Guaranteed** *(167 E. Broad St., Athens, 706/208–0962)* is for the vegans among us. No dairy products here, pal. Instead, hunker down over the tasty sandwiches, wheatberry burgers, salads, fresh fruit juice, and nondairy shakes. The blueberry pancakes are simply wonderful. Both restaurants draw townies and students alike and feature the work of local artists on the walls.

Best 24-hour coffeehouse: Decorated in haphazard "found art" style, and percolating with the free-flowing strains of hot jazz, **Jittery Joe's** *(243 Washington St., Athens, 706/548–3116)* is bohemian enough to appeal to downtown locals but close enough to the University of Georgia campus to attract a lot of students. As does nearly everyone in Athens, co-owner Keith Kortemeier plays in a band (the Martians). He has absolutely no experience in the coffeehouse business and is driven instead by sheer enthusiasm, common sense, and his worship of the Butthole Surfers. The sofas are comfy, it's open all-the-freakin'-time, and the java's good, too.

shopping

records

Atlanta

Best indie store, period: While other area record stores may excel in size, or used or vinyl selections, **Criminal Records** *(466 Moreland Ave. NE, 404/215–9511)* in Little Five Points takes the prize for best all-around selection of indie-rock CDs and general Gen-X pop-culture flatulence. The underground comix selection is among the best in the city, as is its assortment of zines (check out local favorite *Baby Sue*) and rock books (like most of Henry Rollins's 2.13.63 product). An integral part of the scene, it frequently ties into club shows and has national and local acts playing live inside the store or in the parking lot. The young staffers have a sniffy music-nerd attitude—in a good way. They'll make you feel like an idiot if you don't buy anything on Teenbeat, but they'll take your money anyway.

Best vinyl: Located just down the block from Criminal Records, **Wax 'N' Facts** *(432 Moreland Ave. NE, 404/525–2275)* is probably Atlanta's best-known post-punk record shack. If it's vinyl you're looking for, this is your place—it still carries tons of it, used and new, with lots of imports. This is the former home of the defunct Atlanta New Wave label DB Recs, so you can often find some of its old junk lying around (Pylon singles, Uncle Green albums, etc.), plus CDs, posters, T-shirts, and selected magazines. You say it's cluttered? Haven't you ever been in an independent record store?

Phattest dance tracks: In Midtown, **Earwax Records** *(1052 Peachtree St. NE, 404/875–5600)* appears from the outside to be just another abandoned urban building, complete with garish graffiti adorning the walls; even though it might not look like much, this is one of the best spots in town for the latest hip-hop. The staff here knows what's up; several are local DJs, and they exhibit their expertise by spotlighting their favorites on the inside walls. Almost entirely vinyl, the majority of the R&B, jazz, and reggae in the racks is used, but the store carries an extensive selection of new rap, dance, and hip-hop 12-inches. There are a few CDs in the front hangout area, plus hats and paraphernalia. Local and national urban and hip-hop music acts like Outkast and Organized Confusion are known to drop in and check it out.

Athens
Best one-stop record shop: According to local lore, Peter Buck first met Michael Stipe while Buck was working at **Wuxtry** *(197 E. Clayton St., Athens, 706/369–9428)* in the late '70s ... which is not the only (or even the best) reason to visit this ramshackle little store, a longtime fixture for fans and bands in the Athens music scene. The main room holds all the new (nonused) records, tapes and CDs, including lots of 7-inch singles from current Athens faves like Servotron and Olivia Tremor Control. Next door is a store for used CDs and tapes, while upstairs, Bizarro Wuxtry stocks comix and tons of used vinyl. And yeah, many current Athens musicians continue to work behind the counter, perhaps hoping to sell a Patti Smith album to their future lead singer.

books

Atlanta
Best out-of-print books: There doesn't seem to be a whole lot of order to **A Cappella Books** *(1133 Euclid Ave. NE, 404/681–5128)*, but if you come in looking for something fascinating or strange, you will surely walk out with at least one new tome. Its forte is hard-to-find, out-of-print titles, but basically shopping here is like rummaging through a

voracious book-lover's old attic. The staff is cool—they know how to read and do it often.

Best books: The local franchise **Oxford Books** *(Buckhead location, 360 Pharr Rd. NE, 404/262–3333; Sandy Springs, 6320 Roswell Rd. NW, 404/364–3040)* is a bookworm's paradise, especially for those searching out something not on the *New York Times* bestseller list. Oxford carries things the big chain stores have never even heard of. The Buckhead outlet offers numerous spots to sit and read, plus a small upstairs cafe that is overpriced but tailor-made for meeting intelligent people of the opposite sex; the other location is a tad smaller. Both have humongous newsstands with many out-of-town newspapers, separate comix and games sections, and lots of celebrity readings and book signings.

Athens

Best used and rare books: If it's a gargantuan selection of books at bargain-basement prices you're after, try the **Jackson Street Bookstore** *(260 N. Jackson St., Athens, 706/546–0245)*. Here, on the old wood floors and ceiling-high bookshelves, you'll find the largest selection of used books in Athens, plus many rare collectible books from the early 20th century. A really good place for Lit majors searching for hard-to-find volumes, Jackson Street Bookstore carries academic texts, lots of dictionaries, and has a huge fiction and biography selection.

Runner-up: For local authors, the small **Blue Moon Books** *(282 E. Clayton St., Athens, 706/353–8877)* offers about the best selection in town, although it specializes in spiritual/occult and gay/lesbian topics. It stocks both new and used, and with the closing of a couple other small stores recently, Blue Moon is one of the best non-chain outlets in Athens.

clothes

Atlanta

Best vinyl skirts: Looking for that special something for tonight's big night out? Say, a pink-fur bra? A fluorescent-green vinyl skirt? Some polka-dot boots with four-inch heels? Or maybe a gold-sparkle Elvis jumpsuit? Whatever your (bad) taste desires, it's likely **The Junkman's Daughter** *(464 Moreland Ave. NE, 404/577–3188)* will have it or get it. While wacky apparel is this store's raison d'être, it's also a one-stop for all things tacky. You'll find old games, retro jewelry, tin toys, dolls, books, collectibles, and novelty knickknacks. If you need a gift for that special punk-rock girl or guy, Junkman's Daughter is screaming for your parents' money. It has an equally cool location in Athens, **The Junkman's Daughter's Brother** *(458 E. Clayton St., Athens, 706/543–4454)*.

Best secondhand duds: Specializing in hand-me-downs from the late 1800s through the 1960s, **Stefan's Vintage Clothing** *(1160 Euclid Ave. NE, 404/688–4929)* will keep you in half-century-old stitches. The bulk of its stock comes from the later decades, so there's lots of '50s bowling shirts and '60s paisley. It's a mandatory stop for the campier element of the local music scene, and much of the fun lies in wondering what schmuck last wore the plaid slacks and purple smoking jacket you just purchased. Chances are he bought it from a vintage store across town last month. It's pretty picked over but you can find bargains, and the selection is always changing.

Runner-up: Right down the street in Little Five Points, **Wish** *(447 Moreland Ave. NE, 404/880–0402)*, specializes in over-the-top '70s wear, from wide-collared polyester tops and Wonder Woman T-shirts to kitschy Elton John eyewear and vintage metal lunch boxes. You'll also find some flashy higher-end club wear, as the beat of throbbing disco music pumps through the sound system.

Athens
Best used rags: The long, warehouselike **Potter's House** *(434 Prince Ave., Athens, 706/543–8338)* has a room with a huge mountain of used clothing, officially dubbed the "Rag Pile," where you can jump in, fill a shopping bag full of mix 'n' match castaways, and walk out several hours later only $5 poorer. One assumes that not springing for such luxuries as racks and hangers allows for such steals, but whatever the reason, this is a tad cheaper—and face it, more fun—than sifting through yet another Salvation Army. It's an all-encompassing thrift store, meaning you can also find anything from china to baby strollers, from wicker furniture to weird old albums.

et cetera

Atlanta
Best recycled junk: Co-owned by Emily Saliers of Indigo Girls, **Common Pond** *(996 Virginia Ave. NE, 404/876–6368)* is a neat little shop in Virginia-Highland that crosses Martha Stewart *objet* fetishism with environmental awareness. It's got all the pomo furnishings and gadgets you've dreamed of, from organic dry goods to pet toys. Recycled is the material of choice, from the gimmicky (purses made out of old

license plates) to the practical (nifty clothes, linens, and toys). A few items seem kinda pricey, but where else are you going to find a notebook made from scrap computer boards?

body alterations
Atlanta
Best tattoos: Tornado Tattoo *(464-A Moreland Ave. NE., 404/524–0009)* has Little Five Points covered—literally. The skin art experts agree: Ask for artist Gary Yoxen, a big, hairy, tattoo-soaked veteran of several Atlanta punk and hardcore bands, and a master of the ink needle. He looks like he'd gladly break your neck, but deep down he's just a sweetheart. Trust us.

Best piercing: Most tattoo parlors in Atlanta also offer body piercing (Tornado does), but if you want a joint that specializes in skin jewelry, the best bet is **Piercing Experience** *(1654 McLendon Ave. NE, 404/378–9100)*. The folks here will gladly shoot holes in just about any body part you desire. The staff are already fully adorned in shiny studs and rings; they don't make you feel like an idiot, and damned if they don't take Visa and MasterCard too.

hotel/motel
Atlanta
Best rock stops: If you're going by averages, the most likely place a well-known touring band will stay while in Atlanta is the **Ritz-Carlton Hotel** in Buckhead *(3434 Peachtree Rd. NE, 404/237–2700)*. It boasts all the usuals: large rooms; a well stocked bar; great restaurant; proximity to shopping, nightlife, strip clubs, and a main highway—all that plus major-label prices (ranging from $155 for the smallest room to $1,050 for the largest top-level suite).

Best mid-range deal: The Wyndham Hotel Midtown *(125 10th St. NE, 404/873–4800)* offers the convenience of a great central location. You can walk to Piedmont Park, as well as several bars, clubs, and restaurants; there's a subway station a block away; and anything else is an affordable, short cab or bus ride. The decent prices range from $79 to $129. Lots of bands stay here if they can't stomach Buckhead, which is to say, lots of bands stay here. It's nice—the rooms aren't huge, and it's basically what you'd get at any good cosmopolitan Marriott or

Holiday Inn. Also, it's perfect for May's annual Music Midtown Festival, when the land across from the Wyndham is the site of a three-day, multi-act musical free-for-all.

Best dive: If you want to get some shut-eye in a place so seedy the late GG Allin felt compelled to write a song about it, the **Clermont Hotel** *(789 Ponce De Leon Ave. NE, 404/874–8611)* is just the ticket for fun, fun, fun. Heck, while every Hyatt and Marriott in Atlanta was booked years in advance, there were *plenty* of rooms available at the Clermont during the Olympics! Growled GG in the classic "Hotel Clermont": "The room stinks, the towels aren't fluffed, so fuck you! Die, fuckin' die!" Such is a typical night here. Rates begin at $55.85 for a double. Added bonus: The basement houses one of Atlanta's smallest but most colorful nude dancing clubs, and local (occasionally national) bands play here every Thursday night.

local wonders

Atlanta

Best picnic with dead people: The 88-acre **Oakland Cemetery** *(248 Oakland Ave., 404/688–2107)* is Atlanta's largest and most historic grave site, the final resting place for *Gone With the Wind* author Margaret Mitchell, golf legend Bobby Jones, and 2,500 Confederate soldiers. Since 1850, more than 40,000 bodies have been buried here; many have been commemorated with majestic statues and mausoleums. It's spooky and beautiful, a great place for a leisurely stroll and a picnic lunch.

Best drive-in: Once as American as hot rods and apple pie, the drive-in theater has plummeted in popularity since the heyday of Cheech and Chong. Atlanta is no exception. But one Southern Gothic experience not to miss is the **Starlight Drive-In** *(2000 Moreland Ave. SE, 404/627–5786)*. One of only two left in the city, it offers not only the best selection for your money (six screens, first-run flicks!), but also the best atmosphere for snuggling, if only out of trepidation: It's located next to a cemetery, across the street from some of Atlanta's most rundown apartments, and a half mile from a U.S. Penitentiary.

Athens

Best Frisbee tossing: Every spring, the Frisbees come out in full force in Athens, and whether you're in some sort of competitive league or just wanting a little recreation under the sun, every park and field in town is swarming with the flying discs. The large green grounds of the **Lyndon House** (*293 Hoyt St., Athens, 706/613–3623*), an old two-story house doubling as a publicly funded arts center and gallery, are a prime spot for this ritual, as well as any other outdoor recreation that doesn't require too much organization. In addition to the open field, two baseball diamonds are on the grounds. There's talk the Lyndon House will soon be expanding into a larger arts center, which is great for art, but it will likely take away much of the surrounding land. Enjoy it while you can.

transmissions

Atlanta

Best college radio: What used to be a predictable, run-of-the-mill college radio station has improved by leaps and bounds since 1994; and now Georgia State University's **WRAS (88.5 FM)** is one of the more exciting music stations in the South. After finally giving up competing with the bland, commercial alternative beast, 99X (99.7 FM), student-run Album 88, as it's called itself since the '70s when it was AOR, went for broke and actually started playing interesting underground music you really couldn't hear anywhere else in town. Nearly every cool band that passes through town stops by for an on-air performance at the 100,000-watt outlet, which can be heard in some parts of Athens (Stereolab and Girls Against Boys are among the bigger-name recent guests). Some of the better specialty shows Album 88 offers are *Stereo Odyssey*, Sundays from 4 to 6 P.M. (a hodgepodge of great rock 'n' roll from the '60s through the '90s with no limits, the way radio should be); *Big Band Jump*, Sundays from 11 A.M. till noon (hosted by Don Kennedy, an Atlanta broadcaster for decades); and *Outer Limits*, Wednesdays from 10 P.M. to midnight (garage psychedelia and beyond).

Best eclectic: While WRAS has an identifiable postpunk rock sensibility, Georgia Tech's **WREK (91.1 FM)** prides itself on being completely unpredictable. Its rotation includes the usual underground indie rock, but ventures further, mixing in reggae, blues, jazz, classical, world music, and more. Its specialty shows offer some focus, including *Destroy All Music*, Wednesdays 8 to 9 P.M. (noise, electronic, and experimental); *Live at WREK*, Tuesdays 10 to 11 P.M. (local bands play live for an hour); and *WREKage*, Fridays from 10 P.M. to 2 A.M. (the heaviest metal in town).

Best country: Forsyth County's **WMLB (1170 AM)** might well be called Atlanta's only country radio—the only one that matters, anyway. The low-wattage daytime-only outlet can't even be heard in south and central Atlanta, but for those who can pick it up, the mix of old (Hank Williams, Johnny Cash) and new Americana (Junior Brown, Tish Hinojosa) is like a transmission from heaven. It's hoping for a power boost and perhaps an FM band, but here's hoping if it gets more powerful it won't lose its small-town charm (livestock-on-the-loose news flashes are not unheard of). Would that rock radio could be this personable.

Best hip-hop: Only in its second year, Hot 97 **(WHTA, 97.5 FM)** has taken the city's African-Americans by storm with its tough dose of street-level rap and hip-hop. Atlanta's large concentration of predominantly black colleges has helped Hot 97 make its mark quick. Ironically, the station's general manager is a middle-aged white lady.

austin

by Jason Cohen

"Ever since I first came to Austin, there have been many good musicians to play with and good people to listen. That may not sound like much, but to a musician it's everything."
— **Junior Brown**

A ustin has long been considered the cultural oasis of Texas: the only hospitable city for hippies, eggheads, and artists in a state full of big hair, big oil, and big pickups. It is both the intellectual (the University of Texas, or UT) and political (the state government) center of the state, which means lots of bookstores and lots of entertainment. It also means jostling for barstool space with lots of jarheads and bureaucrats. And, this being Texas, the hippies, artists and eggheads drive pickups too.

In the '90s, Austin has become a city at war with itself. The cheap, easy living that was the hallmark of this artsy college town is no longer a reality. For better or for worse, there's actually an economy (with enough high-tech and software concerns that the term "Silicon Prairie" gets thrown around). For longtime Austinites, it's mostly for worse, as the local government tries to figure out, with little success, how to evolve as a city and still be cool. Prosperity and expansion have begun to spoil the natural resources that make the area so welcoming: Barton Springs, the natural pool that's right in town, is frequently shut down due to pollution, and both Lake Austin and Lake Travis can be overrun with speedboats and wave riders. A crowded city also means rising rents, and when that happens, aspiring musicians and wandering UT postgrads can no longer survive on spouses, day jobs, pawn shops, and guest lists.

The musicians are still here, however—they are to Austin as the screenplay is to Hollywood, with every busboy thumbing through the "bass player wanted" ads. The city officially bills itself as the Live Music Capital of the World, and backs it up with 70 different music venues—

pretty amazing for a burg of 500,000. This national reputation is further enhanced by the South by Southwest Music and Media Conference. Now in its tenth year, the annual mid-March affair has expanded to include a film festival and a multimedia confab. It's nirvana for music lovers, but it's not necessarily the best time to experience Austin for the sake of Austin.

Legendary locals include Janis Joplin, Roky Erickson, Willie Nelson and Stevie Ray Vaughan, whose tacky statue on the shores of Town Lake has become a local landmark right up there with the Texas Tower (y'know, sniper Charles Whitman's old haunt). More recently, Austin had its time as the New Athens or the Old Seattle or whatever you wanna call it, with mid-'80s bands like the Wild Seeds, the True Believers, the Reivers, Glass Eye, and the only survivor of that bunch, the continuingly amazing Texas Instruments, who finally gave in to legal pressure and changed their name to the Instruments in 1996. That scene still has a legacy, as producers (John Croslin of the Reivers, Brian Beattie of Glass Eye) and grown-up solo artists (Michael Hall of the Wild Seeds, Kathy McCarty from Glass Eye, and Alejandro Escovedo from the Troobs). But the town's greatest contribution has turned out to be its slightly earlier vintage punk scene: influential bands like Scratch Acid, the Big Boys, and of course, the Butthole Surfers, who continue to forge ahead as a band and as individuals—guitarist Paul Leary is a successful producer, drummer King Coffey is a record-company mogul, and Gibby is … well, a Gibby.

lay of the land

Austin's neighborhoods are tiny, and mostly residential. As far as commerce and entertainment goes, there are only a few areas to get familiar with: Campus, Downtown, and Everywhere Else. Campus, of course, consists of the University of Texas, which is bordered on the west by Guadalupe Street, a.k.a. "The Drag." Downtown's main thoroughfare is Congress Avenue. To the east is 6th Street, the official club and entertainment district. To the west is a burgeoning warehouse area that features, well, more clubs and entertainment. Everywhere Else includes everything from the funky treasures of the East Side and South Austin to the suburban shopping malls to the west and north. Austin's "city limits" are quite large, but the central city itself is a manageable 40 blocks or so. The heart of downtown is bisected by Town Lake, which is both a fine place to paddleboat and a body of water you would never, ever want to fish in. Town Lake is also known as the Colorado River, though that doesn't mean you'll end up in the Grand Canyon if you head downstream.

getting from a to b

Public transportation in Austin consists entirely of buses, which is just fine, though the city is small enough that a bike works too. If neither of those options sound appealing, fear not—wherever you're going, the cab fare won't be more than ten bucks. Try **Roy's** (*512/482–0000*) if you want to replicate the opening scene of *Slacker*, though **American/ Yellow/Checker** (*512/472–1111*) is the largest company, and damn well ought to be with that unwieldy postmerger appellation. If renting a car is an option, do it—you'll get around the city that much more easily, but more important, you can get away—to the various swimming holes, barbecues, scenic spots, and Old West towns that are anywhere from 30 minutes to two hours away (and San Antonio is only 90 miles down the road). Parking is more of a problem than it used to be, but it's there, if not for nothing than for three or four bucks. Do be sure to obey the TOW ZONE signs in front of dark, seemingly dormant businesses; the local towing companies will be happy to take your 50 dollars even though the accountant's office didn't really need its parking lot at 1 A.M. on Friday.

sources

For 15 years, the free weekly *Austin Chronicle* has been the place to go for club listings, local political coverage, and all other strains of art, culture, and life. Ken Lieck's "Dancing About Architecture" remains the music scene's equivalent of a town crier, while political writer Daryl Slusher left to become a city council member (after a close call in a mayoral race) in 1996. Meanwhile, for just a couple of years, the daily *American-Statesman* has published a weekly entertainment supplement, "XLEnt." It began as a blatant *Chron*nabe, but nevertheless offers good writing and an equally voluminous batch of listings. Both publications are in the Web game: the *Chronicle* is at http://www.auschron.com and the *Statesman* at http://www.Austin360.com. Statewide mag *Texas Monthly* has a site at http://www.texasmonthly.com, while relative newcomer *Citysearch*, at http://www.citysearch.com, includes Austin in its corporate game plan.

A few final thoughts—or commands—to live by:

1) Forget what you learned in Spanish class: if you don't say "Gwad-ah-LOOP" for Guadalupe Street or "MAN-chack" for Manchaca Road you'll reveal yourself as an outsider.
2) Don't try to party with Gibby. You can't handle it.
3) Don't move here.

clubs

Home of the blues: It doesn't look like much from the outside: a square wood building with a tiny parking lot that appears as if foreclosure either hit yesterday or will tomorrow. But **Antone's** *(213 W. 5th St., 512/474–5314)* is probably the most hallowed blues club in the country—even Isaac Tigrett and Dan Aykroyd would have to agree. Despite several changes of address, this Austin institution has been going for 21 years, spawning both a record label and a record store along the way. Besides serving as a launching pad for such artists as Lou Ann Barton, the Fabulous Thunderbirds, Stevie Ray Vaughan, Marcia Ball and, of course, the ubiquitous Antone's house band (Sarah Brown, Derek O'Brien, Kaz Kazanoff, and others), the club has been a home away from home for all the blues greats, past and present, still going and no longer with us, including James Cotton, Lazy Lester, Buddy Guy, and just about everyone else. If the words "jam session" turn you off, stay away. But in a town where "blues" can often be synonymous with "bar band," Antone's is the real deal. The club's history has included several locations; in early '97, after a long run near the UT campus, it relocated to the heart of downtown.

Best place to get discovered by a big indie label: The **Blue Flamingo** *(7th St. & Red River, 512/469–0014)* is the city's finest underground punk-rock haven, but it is also a drag bar, owned and operated by a strapping personality who goes by the name of "Miss Laura." Crack and sex get traded on a nearby street corner (even though the Austin Police Department is less than a block away), while after sundown, local bands cram side by side into the front window space and flail away through a shitty P.A. Fortunately, they're the kind of bands for whom sonic quality is not generally an issue. The night that Matador Records honcho Gerard Cosloy made his visit a few years back, he caught a set by a new group called Spoon; a couple of years later they made their debut CD for Matador.

Best two-stepping action: Ideally, a great Texas dance hall should be located in the middle of nowhere, serving as the only social center in towns like Luckenbach or Bandera. But within Austin's city limits, the **Broken Spoke** *(3201 S. Lamar Blvd., 512/442–6189)* is the best sawdust floor in town. Acts like fiddler Alvin Crow and cowboy songwriter Chris Wall split the difference between danceability and credibility; needless to say, you won't find any Achy Breaky line-dancing here. Best of all, the gals are happy to take the lead—and do the asking—as much as the guys are.

Runner-up: Not precisely in the middle of nowhere, but close enough, **Gruene Hall** *(1281 Gruene St. in New Braunfels, 60 miles south of Austin, 210/606–1281)* is the venue of choice for such Texas music names as Robert Earl Keen, Jimmie Dale Gilmore, and Tish Hinojosa.

Best happy hour: Cheap drinks are easy to come by at 6:30 P.M.; but **The Continental Club** *(1315 S. Congress Ave., 512/441–2444)* delivers more bang for the buck by offering quality, free happy-hour music two hours a night, from local heroes like uncategorizable chanteuse Toni Price or loungeabilly specialists Rocket 69 (sadly, the club's marquee attraction, blues pianist Grey Ghost, finally passed on at the age of 93 in '96). Lots of other clubs have picked up on the trend, but there's no place quite like the Continental, a sweaty, friendly joint, big on tattoos and pompadours, that delivers country, blues, and rockabilly with equally feverish energy. Later at night, the Continental has bigger acts for a cover charge. Regulars include Junior Brown, Monte Warden, Kelly Willis, and Wayne Hancock. You surely don't want to miss the annual Buck Owens and Elvis Presley birthday celebrations.

Best outdoor jazz (and cigars): While the clientele can be unrecognizably upscale and the atmosphere comes dangerously close to that dreaded lounge-revival vibe, **Cedar Street** *(208 W. 4th St., 512/708–8811)* couldn't be any lovelier a choice for a sultry, moonlit night of martinis, tobacco, and saxophones. This sunken, tree-lined atrium offers music seven nights a week, with local jazzmen like Elias Haslanger, Kyle Turner, and Jon Blondell rounded out by various R&B and country soul groups.

Best neon sign: When the **Electric Lounge** *(302 Bowie, 512/476–FUSE, 3873)* burned to the ground in 1993, only one piece of the place survived: the big red neon script that gives the stage an unnatural glow. Not everyone loves it—some bands prefer to turn it off, and a member of the Muffs actually smashed it. The sign survived; will we be able to say the same about the Muffs? With or without neon, the Lounge has become Austin's top venue for moderately successful touring bands (e.g., Vic Chesnutt, Ben Folds Five, Throwing Muses), as well as Austin groups like Sincola or Spoon, that are big enough (or on the road enough) to only play in town once a month instead of twice a week (exceptions: the Asylum Street Spankers, a fixture every Wednesday, and the excellent countrified and country-fried acoustic-rock band the Gourds, who might have to pay rent here if they weren't getting paid to play). There's also a separate, couch-lined area, the Elbow Room, that's a good place to hang, while early evenings offer up art, poetry slams, and subterranean theater.

Best cover charge: An Austin institution that grew out of a Houston institution, **Emo's** *(603 Red River, 512/477–EMOS, 3667)* main attraction used to be the free admission to all of its shows, including those of touring bands like Rocket From the Crypt or L7. The club has since begun charging two dollars (more for underage fans—punishment for not spending their bucks on booze), but that's still a pretty good deal, and an improvement in some ways, because now the people who are only there to scam and drink don't clutter up the music room with indifference and nonstop chatter. At its beginning, Emo's was known as the main lair of People in Black, when piercings and leather actually seemed odd in Austin. These days the crowd is more diverse, though with the grunge and punk-oriented CD jukeboxes and Frank Kozik artwork (both original paintings and dozens of posters) on the walls and ceilings, there's little doubt what the Emo's aesthetic is. The club has dominated the local scene to the point that there's a band called the FuckEmo's; the only hitch is that they gig there regularly now.

Best hangout disguised as a rock club: One problem with the "Live Music Capital of the World" is that there's too much live music and not enough places to just hang out drinking Shiner and playing pool. **Hole in the Wall** *(2528 Guadalupe St., 512/472–5599)* is the only spot that does both, combining a real here-comes-a-regular vibe (especially before sundown) with half a dozen pool tables and the most eclectic assortment of bands in the coziest music room in town.

Best place to catch rising bands: Liberty Lunch *(405 W. 2nd St., 512/477–0461)*, a half-outdoor, half-indoor rectangle, has been the site of some of Austin's most memorable shows, by the likes of Nirvana, My Bloody Valentine, and Sonic Youth. Besides the fine sightlines, the Lunch has the friendliest staff in town, a roomy outdoor alcove, and just enough ceiling fans to keep things tolerable on July nights. Honorable mention: Once they've gotten too big for the Lunch but aren't quite ready for arenas, you'll find the out-of-town headliners at sibling venues the **Austin Music Hall** *(2nd & Nueces, 512/263–4146)* or the **Backyard** *(13101 Hwy. 71, 512/263–4146)*. The former is indoors, while the latter is a starlit natural amphitheater; both provide great sightlines and good acoustics in the 2,500-plus category.

Best cowboy/cowgirl gay clubs: No, these aren't "theme" clubs—this is Texas, partner. **5th Street Station** *(505 East 5th St., 512/478–6065)*, for boys, offers steak dinners and two-step lessons amid the karaoke nights and drag shows. For girls, there's one of the largest clubs in Texas, the **Rainbow Cattle Company** *(305 West 5th St., 512/472–5288)*. As the name would suggest, the place has a thing for meat—bring your own steak for grilling every Thursday.

bars

Best brewpub: Texas has only allowed brewpubs to exist since late 1993, and the **Waterloo Brewing Company** *(401 Guadalupe St., 512/477-1836)* was the first Austin establishment to take advantage of the new law. Others soon followed suit, but in this case first remains best, largely because of the Waterloo Weizen (wheat beer). Ed's Best Bitter and the lighter Clara's Clara are also fine choices, particularly during the happiest of all happy hours: pints are $1 from 5–6 P.M. Outdoor seating, upstairs pool tables, and a meat-and-potatoes menu (literally and figuratively) that's more than adequate.

Best English pub: Dog and Duck *(406 W. 17th St., 512/479–0598)* 28 beers on tap, including five lagers, 13 ales, one malt, one pilsner, one porter, one stout, and three weizens, along with shepherd's pie, fish and chips, a suitably hearty interior, and a friendly bunch of bar and kitchen men, including some of your favorite local musicians.

Best escape from live music: Sometimes it seems like Austin has a special law that says you can't consume alcohol without also being exposed to a singer/songwriter—even the most patently nonmusical establishments attempt to draw bigger crowds with live entertainment. Not so the **Cedar Door** *(910 W. Cesar Chavez St., 512/473–3712)*, a multiroom, multioutdoor-decked spot tucked away between the shores of Town Lake and the retro-futuristic glare of the local electric company offices. The place is cozy enough to be a neighborhood bar, but big enough that everybody goes there. The only thing you'll get with your booze is conversation, or introspection if you prefer to drink alone.

Best "Twin Peaks" ambience: Carousel Lounge *(1110 E. 52nd St., 512/452–6790)* Believe it or not, the very category is a cliché, simply because it's too true—everyone who takes in the Carousel's soft-colored lights, old lady bartenders and, of course, the titular merry-go-round hovering behind the bar invariably wonders when Kyle McLachlan or the backwards-talking dwarf might appear. Instead, they get the marvelous musical stylings of blind pianist Jay Clark on Friday and Saturday nights. Come here too often and it becomes kitsch, but in small doses the Carousel is genuine and surreal.

Best margarita: Straight-up or on the rocks, the tequila renaissance has given us sipping shots, margs disguised as martinis, and heavenly concoctions featuring upscale liqueurs and overpriced agave. But if you're looking for a tasty, tangy old-fashioned Cuervo, lime, and Triple Sec combo, the **Texas Chili Parlor** (*1409 Lavaca, 512/472-2828*) makes a XX margarita that's almost as potent as its con carne. Prefer them fruity and frozen? As *Texas Monthly* food critic Patricia Sharpe once put it, "You're an adult. You don't drink frozen margaritas."

Runner-up: But for the kid in you, **Baby Acapulco** (*1628 Barton Springs Rd, 512/474-8774, also with North and Southeast locations*) can't be beat, with multiflavored fruit selections (from mango to berry to an indeterminate blue color) that are ultrasweet and deceptively potent—the restaurant frequently enforces a two-drink limit.

Best martyrs to Austin's music-scene history: Campus-area establishments the **Texas Showdown** (*2610 Guadalupe St., 512/472-2010*) and the **Crown and Anchor** (*1109 San Jacinto St., 512/322-9168*)—a no-frills bar and a voluminously stocked beer-only joint, respectively—are usually so crammed with college kids that you may as well hang out at a frat party. However, the Showdown is prized by regulars (who keep their beer mugs hanging on hooks) and UT types alike, while the Crown and Anchor tops off its enormous on-tap selection with amazing salty brown french fries. The old-timers will be happy to tell you how the Showdown used to be Raul's—the acknowledged birthplace of the Austin punk scene—while the Crown was better known as New Sincerity linchpin the Beach. So drink a toast to music scenes past.

food/coffee

Best 3 A.M. fare: Equating the two may disturb those with a definite preference, but the **Magnolia Cafe** (*2304 Lake Austin Blvd., 512/478-8645; 1920 S. Congress Ave., 512/445-0000*) and the **Kerbey Lane Cafe** (*3704 Kerbey Lane, 512/451-1436; 12602 Research Blvd., 512/258-7757; 2700 S. Lamar Blvd., 512/445-4451*) are both healthy, versatile, superlatively tasty 24-hour stalwarts. You'll find everything from chicken sandwiches and vegetable platters to black beans with rice and Austin's signature breakfast dish, *migas* (eggs scrambled with corn tortillas, cheese, and peppers). Magnolia stands out for its home fries (overdressed with various cheeses, salsas, and veggies), while Kerbey Lane gets the edge for its fruity, thick-yet-light pancakes (in buckwheat, buttermilk, or gingerbread varieties). Perfect when you've just closed a bar; also perfectly fine for actual breakfasts, lunches, and dinners (with an expanded entrée selection).

Runner-up: If you'd rather pass over that granola-friendly cafe atmosphere for a true countertop greasy spoon, **Star Seeds** *(3105 N I-H 35, 512/478–7107)* is the only place in town (besides Denny's or IHOP) that fits the bill.

Best cheap eats: Tamale House *(best location at 5003 Airport Blvd., 512/453–9842; also at 2218 College Ave. and 2825 Guadalupe St.)* is the "Breakfast of the Underemployed." Forget about Taco Hell—here you'll find rice and egg, bean and egg, egg and potato, and various other breakfast-taco permutations all available for—really!—four bits each. Chorizo, bacon, and the like cost a bit more. Good *migas*, lunch items, and, of course, tamales as well.

Best breakfast tacos: There's something about the way **Guero's** *(1412 S. Congress Ave., 512/447–7688)* fries together its potatoes, eggs, and whatever else (bacon, chorizo, cheese, even chicken)—the tastes and textures intermingle so seamlessly, like an omelette or a tart. And the rest of Guero's menu contains excellent food that straddles the line between Tex-Mex and interior Mexican, with fine $10 entrées and great creamy beans (both refried and charro) that are entirely lard- and pork-free.

Best barbecue sauce: It's 40 minutes out of town, but there's always a wait for tables at the **Salt Lick** *(Camp Ben McCullough, 512/858–4959)*, a Hill Country restaurant that draws weekly regulars from four counties, as well as a steady stream of tourists and, during the South by Southwest conference, oodles of music-biz weasels. They do great brisket, good ribs, and divinely inspired sausage, but what sets the Salt Lick apart is the sauce, an Asian-inspired (the restaurant's owners are Hawaiian) tomato-free concoction that's sweet and tangy, with hints of vinegar and orange. It's good on just about everything, as you'll find out once you've brought a half a dozen bottles home.

Runner-up: A more traditional, pepper-and-tomato-based sauce can be found at **Stubb's** *(801 Red River, 512/480–0203)* a Lubbock-born institution that opened for business in Austin as a restaurant and music venue in 1996.

Best barbecue meat: Sauce, schmauce, true barbecue purists would say, and at the **Kreuz Market** in Lockhart *(40 miles south on Route 183 to 208 Commerce St., 512/398–2361)* they not only do away with the dressing, but also the sides—no beans or coleslaw here. Monotheism is the name of the game, and that single god is meat. Shoulder, brisket, sausage, even prime rib, all served on butcher paper.

Runner-up: Funky, hippie-ish and conveniently located (with late-night hours) just around the corner from Antone's (see "Clubs"), **Ruby's** *(512 W. 29th St., 512/477–1651)* primary attraction is its organic meat, especially the chunky fall-apart-tender brisket. Other wicked highlights include the barbecue beans, which come spicier than most chili bowls, and the home fries sautéed with peppers, cheese, and onions.

Best upscale Mexican: Manuel's *(310 Congress Ave., 512/472–7555)* redefines the Austin-Mexican (as opposed to Tex-Mex) food experience. On the one hand, it's as simple as using black beans instead of pintos, white cheese instead of orange and fresh peppers instead of pickled ones. On the other hand, it's as complicated as a molé sauce with herbs and spices, or corn chowder, or crabmeat tacos.

Runner-up: **Fonda San Miguel** *(2330 W. North Loop, 512/459–4121)* offers very similar fare, with a lush, authentically kitschy Mexican decor and what might be the most decadent Sunday brunch in town.

Best place to take your vegetarian friends when you aren't one: Threadgill's *(6416 N. Lamar Blvd., 512/451–5440, with a downtown location at Congress Avenue and Barton Springs Street that opened in the fall of '96)* gave Janis Joplin her start, was Jimmie Dale Gilmore's permanent musical residence for several years, and is owned by Eddie Wilson, who previously ran the legendary Austin venue Armadillo World Headquarters. But while music, history, and the cool neon-lit art deco diner setting are nice, the reason that Threadgill's is always packed is the food. Proceed directly to the chicken-fried steak—served with cream gravy, mashed potatoes, and lots of veggies (seconds on veggies are free!). You can get chicken-fried chicken, but don't think it's any healthier, and be forewarned, ham-stuffed black-eyed peas and garlic cheese grits are considered vegetables around here. That being the case, non-meat-eaters will have to avoid the southern-cooked items; however, they'll still find plenty of fresh pickings—in fact, the three-item vegetable plate is almost as popular an option as the chicken-fried meats. Before every meal you'll get succulent homemade breads that are rich and flaky enough to make buttering superfluous (everybody does it anyway).

Runner-up: If you'd like to avoid the cardiac trauma unit, or if you need an unsullied vegetarian experience, **Mother's** *(4215 Duval St., 512/451–3994)* is the place.

Best espresso (as seen in *Slacker*): Quackenbush's *(2120 Guadalupe St., 512/472–4477)* was serving up lattes and Americanos long before Austin got its first Starbucks (along with a slew of independently owned coffee joints). With lots of tables, plus a card shop and an obscure movie-screening room upstairs, this campus-area hangout is the closest that Austin gets to Berkeley; it's the only place to spend an afternoon pondering poststructuralist essays, or perhaps that graduate student with the nose ring in the corner.

Runner-up: In terms of pure quality of brew, Quack's has been beaten out by **Little City**, which roasts its own beans, makes excellent sandwiches, and has both downtown *(916 Congress Ave., 512/476–2489)* and campus *(3403 Guadalupe St., 512/467–2326)* locations. Also worth noting is **Insomnia** *(2222 Guadalupe St., 512/474–5730)*, which is open 24 hours and makes a mean banana-espresso shake.

Best coffee: For years, **Ruta Maya** beans have been grown in Chiapas, Mexico, roasted in Austin, and consumed with breakfast at local restaurants like Magnolia or Guero's. Now, two coffeehouse locations *(218 W. 4th St., 512/472–9638; 2222 Rio Grande St., 512/322–0922)* let you go straight to the well of strong, dark, thick coffee—not for the faint of heart or the caffeine-shy. The 4th Street location is also a cigar emporium; both spots offer low-key live music and ultralate hours.

shopping

records

Best all-around record store: Located right in the heart of downtown, **Waterloo Records** *(600 N. Lamar Blvd., 512/474–2500)* carries everything, and while that also means it can come up short in extremely specific musical categories (i.e., if your passion is techno, or old blues records, there are better places to go) the place is amiably and knowledgeably staffed, well stocked, and amazingly large for an independently owned store. They still have a sizable vinyl section, and their in-store performances, featuring both local and national acts (as well as free beverages) are the best.

Best record store where "alternative" really means something: The inventory at **33 Degrees** *(2821 San Jacinto St., 512/476–7333)* probably isn't much bigger than the average SPIN reader's personal collection. Nevertheless, this campus-area crevice has taste to make up for its size, with a fierce, microcosmic love of the obscure and avant-garde (garage-punk singles, reissued Faust or Sun Ra CDs).

Runner-up: **Sound Exchange** *(21st & Guadalupe streets, 512/476–2274)* is the only store in town with a full commitment to independent music, including a wide-ranging stock of CDs, vinyl, 7-inches, and imports and an attitudinal staff that truly knows their stuff.

Best used CDs: Used is all they do at **Duval Discs** *(4101 Guadalupe St., 512/459–0737)*, and what's amazing is that you can almost always find the most current hits in stock, all for ten bucks or less.

Runner-up: **Technophilia** *(504 W. 24th St., 512/477–1812)*, in the heart of campus, covers the same territory, from brand-new releases to whatever catalog items Austin's residents decided to purge from their homes that week.

Best retro: Vinyl lives at **Antone's Records** *(2928 Guadalupe St., 512/322–0660)*, which is located right across the street from its namesake. As you would expect, the store (and its expert salesclerks) is particularly strong on blues, folk, country, and jazz.

Best atmosphere: The walls of **Stashus Mule** *(3701 Guadalupe St., 512/451–4808)* include shrines to R.E.M. and the Replacements, plus multiple rows of collectibles ranging from '60s rock treasures to rare '80s 7-inchers (Big Black's "Heartbeat," anyone?). The rest of the store's inventory includes new wave (just how many import singles did Julian Cope release?), as well as new releases, with equal room for vinyl and CDs. It's like shopping in someone's personal record collection.

Best hip-hop: Located in an outdoor mall next to a giant international supermarket, **Music Mania** *(3909 N. I-H 35, 512/451–3361)* doesn't look like much, but it's the only store in Austin that specializes in hip-hop and R&B. When Tupac went down, this is where the faithful gathered.

Best dance: What do Austin's DJs do during the day? Well, after they wake up, most of the good ones moonlight (daylight?) at **Alien Records** *(501 W. 15th St., 512/477–3909),* where you can find everything from Chemical Brothers import singles to Marshall Jefferson 12-inches and original local cassettes.

books

Best underground bookstores: Fringeware *(2716 Guadalupe St., 512/323–0039)* is a haven for fanzines, underground books, and other oddities. **Desert Books** *(1904 Guadalupe St., at basement level, 512/ 322–9771)* offers your basic collection of transgressive literature and marginalized intellectualism.

Runner-up: Also worth a look is **Booksource** *(13729 Research Blvd, 512/258–1313; and Westgate Mall, 512/891–9588),* a suitably messy, sprawling haven for books, comics, and records.

Best local chain: You know all those giant Barnes & Nobles that keep popping up in your town? Well, Austin claims to have invented those things, in the form of the local **Bookstop** chain *(4001 Lamar Blvd., 512/452–9541, with three other locations).* Bookstop was ultimately purchased by Barnes & Noble and used as a blueprint for its "superstore" concept. And while Barnes & Noble doesn't discount like it used to, Bookstop still has its Reader's Choice program, earning members savings of anywhere from ten to a whopping 40 percent.

Best geek hangout: Can't fans of "The X-Files," Raymond Chandler, Bruce Sterling, and James Ellroy get along? Well, they can at **Adventures in Crime and Space** *(609-A W 6th St., 512/473–2665),* a mystery and sci-fi haven that also stocks a generous amount of horror, fantasy, true crime, fanzines, and graphic novels. The musty, deceptively large storefront is divided into four little libraries: new and used sci-fi, and new and used mystery. You'll also find rarities, the odd bit of memorabilia, and "nonfiction" UFO books from the '50s.

Best nonreligious specialty bookstore: Despite its famous liberalism, you wouldn't believe how many Christian bookstores Austin has. New Agers are well represented too. Then, on the progressive side, there's **Bookwoman** *(918 W. 12th St., 512/472–2785)*. Austin's feminist bookstore offers everything from cultural histories and political tracts to "herotica" and fiction. The place is perfectly welcoming to customers with the wrong chromosome too.

Runner-up: **Lobo** *(3204-A Guadalupe St., 512/454–5406)* is part bookstore, part gift shop, and entirely geared toward the gay and lesbian community.

clothes

Best vintage: More like a theme park than a retail establishment, **Lucy in Disguise With Diamonds/Electric Ladyland** *(1506 S. Congress Ave., 512/ 444–2002)* is an excessive wonderland of elegance, tackiness, and glamour. It is both a costume shop and a vintage clothing store, which means jewelry, masks, antique formal wear, headdresses, boas, and long gloves, in a confluence of styles that runs the gamut from Liberace to Janis Joplin.

Runner-up: **Flipnotics** *(1603 Barton Springs St., 512/322–9011)* has new and used threads, both cutting edge and classic, as well as a coffee bar and a performance space.

Best junk shop: And we mean junk in the nicest possible way—the proprietors of **Under the Sun** *(5341 Burnet Rd., 512/453–8128)* call it that for a reason: they have everything. Which is to say, tchotchkes, collectibles, and antiques, as well as recycled Levi's, vintage clothing, furniture, and used albums. 'Cause if you're gonna buy those hip-huggers you might as well get an old Sweet album to go with 'em.

Best new women's clothes: Austin is not a major city (it's only the fourth largest burgh in the state), and that being the case, serious shoppers may find that it lacks some basic amenities, like upscale department stores (no Barneys or Bloomie's here) or designer boutiques. **Emeralds** *(624 N. Lamar Blvd., 512/476–3660)* is one of the few exceptions in the latter category, offering women's shoes and clothing in the $50–$300 price range that includes major labels like Anna Sui, as well as small European and domestic designers. Cool knickknacks and housewares too.

et cetera

Best gallery: The owners of **Yard Dog Folk Art Gallery** *(1510 S. Congress Ave., 512/912–1613)* travel all over the American South rounding up "outsider" art. The store's roster includes the famous Finster family, as well as untrained unknowns like Lammar Sorrento, who paints vivid, colorful portraits of legends like Robert Johnson and Roy Orbison. At least one art-school veteran, Mekon and Waco Brother Jon Langford, is also a regular exhibitor, with his cowboy and country-music paintings.

Best thing you'd never see in California: Smokers *(1805 Airport Blvd., 512/469–9822 and 5335 Airport Blvd., 512/419–7611)* is not your ordinary tobacconist. It's a drive-thru cigarette store, no bigger than a Fotomat booth. You'll still have to find a place that will let you smoke 'em in public, though.

Best flea market: People still live cheap in Austin, and that means used furnishings, hidden antiques bargains, recycled bedding, and so on, all easily found at the monthly **City Wide Garage Sale**, where people come from all over town to buy and sell their wares. Cruise up down the aisles of the rickety Austin Coliseum (Riverside Drive, one block east of Lamar Boulevard) and you'll find both prosaic household items and true treasures; it's also much easier than moving from front lawn to front lawn every Sunday.

Best punk/hippie/druggie collisions: **Planet K** *(1516 S. Lamar Blvd, 512/443–2292, with two other locations)* and **Oat Willie's** *(617 W. 29th St., 512/482–0630; 1931-C E. Oltorf, 512/448–3313)* are both remnants of early-'70s Austin (the Cosmic Cowboy, Armadillo years), updated for the '90s. These so-called subculture stores function as head shops (a personal favorite, found only in the South: tins of Skoal and Copenhagen, hollowed out for weed storage), as well as oddball gift shops that carry comics, piercing accoutrements, political books, greeting cards, and other psychedelic tchotchkes.

Best shortcut to Mexico: The best way to buy Mexican crafts, gifts, and folk art is to get in your car and head for the border; you'll save many pesos that way too. But if you can't leave the states, **Tesoros** *(209 Congress Ave., 512/479–8341)* has a lovely, haunting collection of jewelry, religious artifacts, and Day of the Dead iconography.

body alterations

Best piercing: It's a lingerie boutique, it's a piercing parlor ... It's **Forbidden Fruit**, and whether you're after silks, oils, and lace or leather, metal, and rubber, it's one-stop shopping for the sensual and the daring. Four locations: 2001 Guadalupe St. *(512/478–8542)* and 101A East N. Loop *(512/453–8090)*, with a downtown store at 512 Neches St. *(512/478–8358)* and tattoos and piercing around the corner at 513 E. 6th St. *(512/476–4596)*.

Best custom tattooists: The folks at **Perfection** *(4205 Guadalupe St., 512/453–2089)* do nothing but original work, with each artist specializing in particular styles. Chris has a flair for Eastern motifs; one of his most memorable jobs was a full-body sequence of Tibetan, Thai, and Japanese Buddhist themes.

Runner-up: **River City** *(500 E. 6th St., 512/476–8282)*, is Austin's oldest, best-known tattoo shop, for both custom and prefab designs. They also do piercings.

hotel/motel

Best record-company weasel habitat: The height of high-class hotels in downtown Austin is the **Four Seasons** *(99 San Jacinto Blvd., 512/478–4500)*. As a result, it's the only place where A&R guys and marketing mavens flex those expense accounts, especially during South by Southwest, when the late-night bar scene is a schmoozer's heaven (or hell). Imagine one of those overchatty New York or L.A. band showcases, without the band. Still, it's as top of the line as you'd expect from a Four Seasons, with the occasional movie-star sighting, 24-hour room service, and a fine in-house restaurant, Shoreline Grill, which does indeed offer a view of Town Lake. Rates begin at $175 for a double.

Runner-up: At the **Driskill** *(604 Brazos, 512/474-5911)*, you give up some of the amenities, but what you get in return is a glorious old downtown building that's filled with character—it's both ornate and slightly faded. You never know, maybe LBJ slept in your room 40 years ago. Rates begin at $105.

Best getaway: The **Dabbs Railroad Hotel** *(112 W. Burnet Rd., 915/247–7905)*, in Llano (in the Hill Country about 40 miles west of Austin), is so named not because it's next to the railroad, but because it *was* the railroad. Or at least, a train station, and one of the guest rooms still has the red stoplight to prove it. With fewer than a dozen rooms, minimal amenities, and absolutely zero trendiness despite the fact that everyone knows about it, this is the ideal spot for a rustic weekend of solitude. Though beware—the walls are rather thin, so your neighbor might be able to hear you practicing that solitude. In the morning there's breakfast just like the railworkers used to eat: biscuits, gravy, and industrial-strength coffee.

Best lo-fi accommodations: There's plenty of chain motels off of I-35, but for a cheap, centrally located, tolerable place to sleep, the **Austin Motel** *(1220 S. Congress Ave., 512/441–1157)* is the ticket. Every touring indie rock band should stay there—if they don't have friends in town, that is. Instead of Denny's, Waffle House, or the Kettle, you can dine on the fine, funky Mexican fare of El Sol y La Luna next door. And believe it or not, suites are available, and some of the rooms have Jacuzzis—you can't say that about Motel 6. Most important, you'll never struggle with that dangerous merge from the frontage road to the Interstate. Rates begin at $46.

Runner-up: If your AYH dues are paid up, the local **Youth Hostel** is a mere half mile from downtown *(2200 S. Lakeshore Blvd., 512/444–2294)*.

local wonders

Best Hill Country drive: "Texas never whispers," Pavement once declared, and that's because it's flat, brown, and airless—all horizon and no land. Except that it's not true, at least, not when it comes to the Hill Country. Yep, this area, which surrounds Austin to the west and south (snaking as far down as San Antonio) is filled with things rolling, green, and (yes) dusty. It's a mix of unspoiled ranchland, half-inhabited small towns, and tourist attractions. Take Route 290 west of Austin and after passing through LBJ's birthplace, Johnson City (which isn't even named after him) you'll end up in Fredericksburg, an antiques-laden German village that's about two hours away. After a little shopping, head north on Route 965 for 20 minutes, and you'll end up in the hiker's haven of **Enchanted Rock** *(800/792–1112)*, the state's most crowded park. And that's just the tip of the iceberg: Head south, and you can hit the ranchland attractions of Kerrville (also home of the famous summer folk festival), the Guadalupe River views of Hunt, and the watering holes (the kind that are indoors) of Bandera, the so-called Cowboy Capital of the World.

Best swimming hole: Barton Springs *(Zilker Park, two miles east of Congress Avenue on Barton Springs Road, 512/476–9044, $3 admission)* is Austin's defining landmark; the man-made but naturally fed pool is *the* gloriously cool antidote to a whole summer of Texas days, while the park, with its contiguous hike-and-bike trail, is the place for all other strains of outdoor activity. The springs is the dominant symbol of Austin's identity crisis. As it closes occasionally due to fecal contamination, while pollutant-heavy golf courses and condo complexes pop up all around the watershed, it has become the rallying point for Austin's struggle against development.

Runner-up: **Hamilton Pool**, a natural spring-fed swimming hole *(13 miles southwest of Austin, just off of Highway 71, 512/264-2740, $2 admission)* is well worth the 30-minute trip. About the same distance is **Hippie Hollow** *(Comanche Trail, two miles off 620)*, another favorite, not so much for its cliffs, hiking, or access to Lake Travis, as for its reliable proliferation of intoxicants and naked people.

Most lovable mascot: In 1996, Austin got itself a minor-league hockey team, the Ice Bats. Of course, no such thing exists in nature, but Austin just can't get enough of its real bat colony, the one that flees the confines of the Congress Avenue Bridge every night at sunset, momentarily transforming the sky into a black cloud of blind, insect-seeking, squeaking rodents. Everybody should see it at least once. The banks of Town Lake fill up with gawkers every night around happy-hour time; a merchandising boom has even sprung up around the little creatures. The bats head to Mexico for the winter, so the show's only on in spring, summer, and fall.

transmissions

Best noncollegiate college-radio station: The University of Texas–owned **KUT (90.5 FM)** completely shuts out its student constituency, but this professionally operated station still proffers a quirky, high-powered blend of divergent music programming, thoughtful culture-vulture interviews, and essential NPR fare. John Aielli has reigned over the li'l-bit-of-everything program "Eklektikos" *(Monday–Friday, 6–11 A.M.)* for years, while Paul Ray's "Twine Time" *(Saturdays, 7–9)* is the best jazz/blues/R&B party you can have in your living room, short of getting King Curtis as a houseguest.

Best time-share: UT also operates **KVRX**, your basic adventurous, underground college-radio station, except that it shares the **91.7 FM** spot with the community-run outlet **KOOP**. It took years for the stations to get going (and agree to share), but now that they have, Austin gets two radio stations for the price of one, with dozens of musical-specialty shows (from garage rock to lounge to "alternative" country), plus lots of local public-affairs programming and national political fare from Pacifica.

Best metaphor for the graying of Austin's scene: 1973, 1978, and 1983 were all very good years for Austin music, which means the town is now full of 35- to 50-year-old country, blues, and postpunk fans who never go out anymore. They do listen to the radio, though, and **KGSR (107.1 FM)** is there for them. It's had a Texas-centric approach since 1990, helping to create a format (now known in radio-biz parlance as "adult alternative"), in which Wilco, James Carter, Willie Nelson, Sting, and Robyn Hitchcock all coexist. Now if they'd only kick out Sting.

boston

by Matt Ashare

"Boston has great record stores and great bands coming to town all the time. It's weird, but even with all that, I rarely go out."
— **Lou Barlow**, *Sebadoh*

"I can spend hours and hours in the Starr Bookshop in Harvard Square looking for a new focus for my obsessiveness. They have hundreds of crazy and beautiful old books in there."
— **Tanya Donelly**

The River Charles, which separates Boston from Cambridge, still flows thick with that dirty water immortalized by the Standells back in 1968. The band wasn't from Boston, but the secondhand garage-rock it was peddling somehow defined the raucous rumble that emanated from the city's sweaty underground at a time when Cambridge's Harvard Square was still revered as a folk-music haven. Three-chord romps defined the "Bosstown" sound, and you can still hear an echo of it when Mono Man (a.k.a. Jeff Conolly) brings his Lyres to the Rat in Boston's Kenmore Square and starts pounding out the chords to "Soapy" for the thousandth time, screaming something incoherent into a dented microphone.

Boston never really turns its back on the past, but the hub of the city's rock scene has moved away from Boston proper, across the Charles to Cambridge. Along with Lou Barlow and his two bands, Sebadoh and Folk Implosion, the Cambridge club scene is home to the Dambuilders, Matador labelmates Come and Helium, Morphine, ex–Throwing Muse Tanya Donelly, Buffalo Tom, as well as women in rock Tracy Bonham, Mary Lou Lord, and Jennifer Trynin. The Cars' Synchro Sound studio on Boston's Newbury Street has long been eclipsed by Cambridge's Fort Apache, home to the hotshot production team of Sean Slade and Paul Q. Kolderie (Hole, Radiohead, Buffalo Tom, Dinosaur Jr.).

Still, it's hard to separate the old from the new in Beantown. With its Colonial heritage and Old World ethnic neighborhoods, Boston has always had one foot planted firmly in the past. But the hordes of college students who invade the city every year and the fortresslike high-tech firms that now dot the same Route 128 Jonathan Richman immortalized a generation ago in "Roadrunner" are both elements of that bridge to the 21st century Bill Clinton is so fond of conjuring. Cultures mix and mingle: Irish bars turn into art-student hangouts, rebellious college grads settle down and start their own businesses, and an underground thrives in the close-knit confusion.

This cultural collision may help explain why the city's pop scene has had a less-than-cohesive "sound" since the Standells era. In the '70s you had Aerosmith and J. Geils looking back to the blues for inspiration while Tom Scholz and his band Boston made some of the slickest, most technologically advanced basement tapes in the history of rock. Then the Cars arrived with some of-the-moment, Warholian new wave. The '80s brought into play the opposing forces of the revered post-punk outfit Mission of Burma and the ridiculed synth-poppers 'til Tuesday, the regular-guy schtick of the Del Fuegos and the art-punk weirdness of the Pixies and Throwing Muses, as well as the singular merchandizing empire of New Kids on the Block. And for every band that made a national impact in the '80s, there were dozens of might-have-beens that are still revered locally.

In the '90s, the Hub has produced and supported indie-rock heroes Sebadoh, Top 40 alt.rockers Letters to Cleo and Tracy Bonham, ska-punk sensations the Mighty Mighty Bosstones, pop songwriters Evan Dando and Juliana Hatfield, and hard-to-classify guitarless trio Morphine. And that's really just scratching the surface of a scene that doesn't show any signs of slowing down, and probably won't unless people stop going to Harvard, or MIT, or Boston College, or Boston University, or Northeastern, or ....

lay of the land

Cambridge is north and west of Boston, directly across the Charles River. Starting with the Cambridge areas nearest downtown Boston, MIT and Kendall Square come first, then, continuing northeast, there is **Central Square** where, drawn by rent control, ample parking, and the emergence of one of the most unlikely rock venues imaginable—a Middle Eastern restaurant known simply as the Middle East—rockdom and its cohorts have pitched camp. Within a three-block radius are enough dance floors, cozy bars, relaxed restaurants, and online coffeehouses to keep your evenings booked for months. Further west, **Harvard Square** is more Village-like, with its mix of vintage clothing and record and book stores, dyed-hair punks and hippy street musicians, and cultural institutions like the Brattle Theatre and American Repertory Theatre. Keep going west and you'll hit Tufts.

Boston is just as compact. Directly across the Harvard Bridge from MIT is Boston University, Kenmore Square, and Fenway Park. On **Lansdowne Street**, just opposite Fenway, you'll find a row of giant, corporate-looking clubs—including Aerosmith's own Mama Kin—where, depending on the night, you can either dance to house music, check out a touring national act, or watch *Melrose Place*. True Fenway-area rockers tend to hang out at the nearby Rat in Kenmore Square or a few blocks away at the Linwood Grille, a big dive bar that features local bands on weekends. To the east is the ritzy Back Bay area. If you're just looking to hang out or to kill an afternoon window-shopping and people-watching, Back Bay's **Newbury Street** is still the closest thing Boston has to New York's Fifth Avenue, with a Tower Records and Newbury Comics peddling CDs on one end and the Ritz and the Boston Common selling civility on the other. Upper-income club rats tend to coalesce at trendy nightspots on **Boylston Street**. Cupping around the eastern end of the Commons are most of the historic parts of the city—Beacon Hill, the Italian North End, and theme parky Quincy Market. Come back around for Downtown and the financial district, Charlestown, the Combat Zone, home of all the Hub's X-rated activities, and the gentrified South End. East of the South End is *very* local South Boston.

getting from a to b

Driving in Boston and Cambridge is as bad as it gets outside of the Third World. You might think that with some of the brightest engineering minds on Earth teaching and studying at Harvard and MIT, the city would've had some sensible planning. But thanks to the network of cow paths and pastures that once defined the city's landscape, the urban infrastructure tends to defy logic. There simply is no grid; traffic signs are baffling at best and often misleading.

There is, however, a decent public transportation system, the **MBTA** (always referred to as the T), which can, with a little finessing, get you where you're going. The different T lines are color-coded: Red gets you from downtown Boston to Cambridge, Green takes you from downtown Boston to Allston, Brookline, and Newton, and Blue will get you from the airport into town. But counterintuitive logic comes in handy when using the T. For example, the Green Line has one branch that goes up Beacon Street and another that goes up Commonwealth Avenue, two parallel roads that run down the middle of the city. You might think the "B" line would run on Beacon Street and the "C" on Commonwealth Avenue, but, in fact, the opposite is true. Ah yes, and though clubs stay open until one or two in the morning, the T only runs until 12:45 A.M. So always bring cab fare—call Yellow Cab *(617/547–3000)* or Checker Cab *(617/497–9000)* if you can't flag one—a car, or a friend with cab fare or a car. And be warned: Boston drivers will cut you off for no reason, make irrational U-turns, run red lights and stop signs, and otherwise violate the law in remarkably blatant fashion. It's bred in the bone, so to speak, so don't take it personally.

sources

You'll find the most up-to-date and easy-to-use Boston-area club listings in the city's largest alternative weekly, the *Boston Phoenix*. The *Phoenix*, which comes out Thursdays, also features excellent arts criticism and comprehensive coverage of the local scene. It's $1.50 at the newsstand and most convenience stores, but a free edition is delivered to most area college campuses. You can also find most of the paper on the Web, at bostonphoenix.com.

Also on Thursdays, the daily broadsheet, *The Boston Globe*, carries its "Calendar" section, an insert that includes the occasional scene report, as well as listings that are heavily slanted toward family-type events. (Much of the same information is available at the Globe's boston.com Web site.) The Globe's music section comes out Fridays, as does the local scene report by the city's tabloid newspaper, *The Boston Herald*.

Boston's always had a healthy zine underground, and almost every club in town has a good assortment of freebies to choose from. One of the longest-running is the *Noise*, which mixes irreverent gossip with reviews of local shows and releases.

clubs

Best rock club: It's not the pumpkin kibi, the falafel sandwiches, or even the belly dancers on Wednesday nights that draws full houses at **Middle East** *(corner of Mass Ave. and Brookline St., 617/864–EAST)*, the Cambridge restaurant where Patti Smith and an entourage of Michael Stipe, Tom Verlaine, and Thurston Moore dropped by for a snack during Smith's '96 comeback tour. The food and the dancers are just fine, but the top-line booking is what's made the Middle East the number one club for Boston rockers. Owned and operated by Lebanese brothers Joseph and Nabil Seder, the Middle East was just a restaurant until the late '80s, when a couple of local scenesters starting booking rock shows in an isolated back room on weeknights. By 1991, the back room was rocking seven nights a week and a large abandoned bowling alley in the basement next door was transformed into a 500-plus-capacity venue. Now, on any given night of the week, you might find national acts like Luscious Jackson or the Mighty Mighty Bosstones packing them in downstairs; up-and-coming indie rockers like Brainiac or the Delta 72 sweating it out upstairs; some jazzbos jamming upstairs in a side room known as the "Bakery"; and Morphine's Mark Sandman picking at a plate of french fries in the restaurant. The Middle East also has the only 2 A.M. liquor license in the area, which means it's open on Thursday, Friday, and Saturday nights for at least an hour after the rest of Cambridge has shut down. Most shows are 18- or 19-and-over, they don't usually sell out in advance, and the cover's mostly under $10.

Best Plan B: Right next door to the Middle East, **T.T. the Bear's Place** *(10 Brookline St., 617/492–BEAR)* caters to the same alternarock scene. Sure, it's a bit of a rivalry, but that helps make Central Square a destination of choice. The nice thing about T.T.'s is the stage is on one side and there's a hangout area on the other, so you can sit out a set if you want and even play a little pool. Weeknights are mostly audition nights for local bands, which means they're hit-or-miss. But weekend headliners are almost always strong: Paul Westerberg played his first Boston-area solo gig here, as did Son Volt.

Best bet on a Monday night: Tucked away on a residential side street in Central Square, the **Green Street Grill at Charlie's Tap** *(280 Green St., 617/876–1655)* is where the local scenesters gather on Monday nights for fine cheap food, perfectly mixed drinks, and live music that ranges from the smooth lounge stylings of the local outfit Lars Vegas and the funk grooves of the Hypnosonics (a horn-driven side project led by Morphine's Mark Sandman) to the countrified rock of former Scruffy the Cat leader Charlie Chesterman. The Tap, as it's often called, or Green Street, as it's also known, is a popular hangout and an excellent restaurant any night of the week. It has the unassuming look of a neighborhood bar, its Caribbean-influenced food and draught-beer selection are exceptional, and its jukebox cranks out a reliably satisfying mix of R&B, jazz, funk, and soul. On Mondays, you pick from one of four entrees on a reduced-price ($8.95) menu that's weighted toward comfort food like roast beef with mashed potatoes but always features a Caribbean pepper pot or pasta dish. Then at about 10:30 P.M., the band comes on for its first set. Order another bottle of wine for your table and don't even think about going home 'til it's Tuesday.

Best place to get spanked: Greater Boston's naughty leather- and latex-clad boys and girls descend on Central Square's **Man Ray** *(21*

Brookline St., 617/864–0400) every Friday night for dancing and, well, socializing. That can mean anything from watching techno-erotic videos on the club's many monitors to cheering on an S&M fashion show to simply comparing tattoos and body piercings. Any night of the week, Man Ray is defined by its black, Batcave-like interior, but the atmosphere's a little tamer on Saturdays, when the whips-and-chains crowd mingles with less fetishistic fans of house, techno, and trance music. Wednesday night is Gothic industrial, and Thurday is "Campus," a night for gay men and their friends.

Best Eurotrash girls (and boys): Cracker's David Lowery could have ended his search for the Eurotrash girl of his dreams years ago if he'd only known about **M-80** *(967 Commonwealth Ave., 617/562–8800)*. The ostensibly members-only dance club, which is nestled right in the heart of Boston University, caters to the city's large population of wealthy foreign students, who all seem to have access to daddy's platinum Amex card and a shiny new Mercedes. It also happens to be an adjunct of the **Paradise Rock Club**, one of the city's long-standing generic venues for national touring acts with at least one radio hit under their belts. So on a Friday or Saturday night you might find indie-rockers from a Luna or Sebadoh show sharing bathroom space with the Armani-clothed offspring of foreign magnates, which is always an interesting sight. Paradise shows tend to end before midnight so the Eurotrash crowd can have the run of the place.

Best living history of local punk: One of the stops on any historic tour of Boston rock would have to be the **Rathskeller** *(528 Commonwealth Ave., 617/536–2750)* in Kenmore Square. Several generations of punk rockers have lined up outside the sweaty basement club to see everyone from Big Black to Black Francis. Back in the '80s, the Rat was the grungy heart of the local rock scene, a place where your feet stuck to the floor, the toilets barely flushed, and everyone paid their dues, including R.E.M. and U2. That was when Taang! Records, the punk label that launched the Mighty Mighty Bosstones, Lemonheads, and Gang Green, was still in town. These days the Rat tends to cater more narrowly to the punk-rock/heavy-metal crowd, and on days when one of Epitaph or Lookout's finest is in town or when Gang Green plays a reunion show, the spiked hair and leather jackets on the sidewalk in front of the club can bring back memories of the good old days—when moshing was called slam-dancing and being a punk meant not being on MTV, dammit.

Best place to get in free after the game: Offering free admission to Red Sox ticket-stub holders after games hasn't helped **Mama Kin**'s *(36 Lansdowne St., 617/536–2100)* standing in the local rock community. Aerosmith opened the club hoping to give something back to the city it calls home, and they spared no expense. The band's song titles are carved into one of the massive bars, the sound systems in both of the club's live-music rooms are state of the art (and often a little too loud), and there's even an upstairs space for acoustic shows and local theater productions (the Lansdowne Street Playhouse). Unfortunately, the jocks often overshadow the rock, which doesn't make Mama Kin a particularly comfortable hangout. (When Aerosmith decided to play some club shows in 1995, they did one night each at Mama Kin and the Middle East—and that pretty much says it all.) Parking can also be a problem, especially during the school year, when students flock to Lansdowne Street to engage in their mating rituals at the strip's other clubs and maybe even to catch a glimpse of Steven Tyler at Mama Kin. They never do.

Best queen scene: For years, **Jacques** *(79 Broadway, 617/426–8902)*, in the predominantly gay Bay Village enclave of Boston, was home to the city's most flamboyant cross-dressers. Then the club's sleazy cool started to attract more adventurous members of the rock scene. And finally a balance was struck between the queens and the scenesters: On weekends, local bands trade sets with lip-synching impersonators like Zola, and on weeknights you can grab a beer no matter how you're dressed. Rick Berlin, a piano-playing cabaret dude with an alternative edge, plays solo on most Sunday nights. And there's even a pool table.

bars

Best no-frills bar: The local rock scene has a strange habit of seeking out the most unlikely places to call its own, and Allston's **Model Cafe** *(7 N. Beacon St., 617/254–9365)* is one of them. Once a no-frills Allston neighborhood restaurant with high-backed wooden booths, meat loaf specials, and a full-service bar that catered to thirsty old men in the evenings, the Model started getting hip in the early '90s, as far as anyone can surmise, simply because it wasn't on the beaten path. The bigger weekend crowds inspired the owners to bring in lower-backed booths, a pool table, and a CD jukebox, and there was even a live-music series that lasted a few months. Now it's an almost indispensable hangout with cheap beer and very little attitude. It gets crowded, especially on Sunday nights, when weekend warriors show up to trade battle stories.

Best South End hangout: The South End's **Delux Cafe** *(100 Chandler St., 617/338–5258)* used to be a low-key, out-of-the-way bar for neighborhood regulars. But when **Anchovy's** *(433 Columbus Ave., 617/266–5088)*, a popular nearby Italian restaurant-bar, started overflowing with a bristling crew of young, hard-drinking hipsters, the Delux stepped in (after changing its name from Joie de Vivre) as another South End option. Rotating exhibits of works by local artists and walls decked out in all manner of American kitsch—from old album covers and Elvis busts to plastic dinosaurs and an illuminated Santa Claus—give the Delux a decidedly bohemian feel. An impressive, ever-changing menu of hearty contemporary fare, which can include anything from chicken quesadillas to curry-fried rice, is served until 11:30 P.M. and cooked in a remarkably small kitchen.

Best last call: For years now, **J.J. Foley's** has been known to have the latest last call in town. Both Foley's, that is. The Foley's in the South End *(117 E. Berkeley St., no phone)* gets an older, mostly male, and mostly Irish crowd of heavy drinkers—and it's not in the best neighborhood. The one nestled in the heart of downtown Boston *(21 Kingston St.)* is where you'll find many of the city's art-damaged rockers hanging late on weekend nights—if you can find it, that is. The bar is on a side street in a maze of confusing one-ways sandwiched between Chinatown, the Downtown Crossing shopping area, and Boston's small but teeming Combat Zone. It has no listed phone number, just a pay phone inside by the rest rooms. But you can usually spot it from either end of Kingston Street by looking for a lot of bikes chained to the fence, the grates, and the light posts outside. The Irish guy at the door won't let anyone in after 2 A.M., but the bartenders tend to let last call slip for those already inside.

Best place to read *Dubliners* at the bar: There have always been and always will be heated arguments about what's the best Irish bar in Boston and which one serves the best pint of Guinness. In Jamaica Plain, the **Brendan Behan** *(378 Centre St., 617/522–5286)* lives up to its literary legacy by hosting the occasional author's reading. It also brings in a well-rounded crowd of young and old neighborhood types and folks from all over town who come to soak up the Joycean vibes. There are pictures of major Irish literary figures on the walls, including the bar's namesake, and a steady supply of some of the best-poured pints of Guinness in town. And there's occasional music at night, either of the Irish or of the folk-rock variety.

Best scorpion bowl: If you like scorpion bowls, then you've probably never met one you didn't like after the first quart or two. But what sets the fruity, rum-laced concoctions at the **Hong Kong** *(1236 Mass Ave., 617/864–5311)* apart from the rest is location, location, location. The Hong Kong is one of the few places in Harvard Square where you can grab a drink and a pu pu platter without feeling like you're surrounded by college students. That may just be a result of the room's poor lighting, or its Polynesian-kitsch atmosphere, or the fact that the Hong Kong's bright-pink exterior tends to scare off the less adventurous. The restaurant actually has three floors of dining, with gold-painted wood partitions on the first floor, an oddly brew-pub-styled bar on the second, and a comedy club on the third. Whichever floor you choose, the scorpion bowls come in a giant communal trough. And believe me, there's plenty of alcohol in there.

Best place to get juiced: The sound of the giant juicer at the **Other Side Cosmic Cafe** *(407 Newbury St., 617/536–9477)* has a tendency to drown out all conversation. But at least you know you're getting fresh carrot and wheat-grass juice. You can also order a beer at this quirky yet comfortable hangout, whose duct-taped vinyl booths and chic recycled decor debuted in the early '90s to cater to slackers and grungesters alike. If you're underage, the Other Side is a decent substitute for night-clubbing. If you're over 21, then it's a healthy alternative.

Best jazz bar: If Boston has a reputation in the jazz world, it's for producing fusion technicians like Pat Metheny, not gutsy, street-level players. So, true to the stereotype, the city's two premiere jazz clubs, **Scullers** *(400 Soldiers Field Rd., 617/562–4111)* and the **Regattabar** *(Charles Hotel, Cambridge, 617/661–5000)*, are a bit sterile in terms of atmosphere—they're both hotel bars, for chrissake. But **Wally's** *(427 Mass Ave, 617/424–1408)* is a wonderful departure from the norm. A South End neighborhood hangout with one of the more racially mixed clienteles you'll find in greater Boston, Wally's is a small, smoky, and usually rather crowded establishment that features mainly local jazz artists six nights a week. Even Berklee College of Music kids, who sometimes show up here to play a set, sound more soulful in this setting.

food/coffee

Best beef on the bone: Last time we checked, Massachusetts was miles away from the country's barbecue belt. But someone must have forgotten to tell that to the owners of **Redbone's** *(55 Chester St., Somerville, 617/628–2200)*. Slow-cooked, smoked pork ribs are nothing special in this day and age—even chic restaurants sometimes feature them—but good barbecued beef ribs are still hard to find outside Texas. Everything's good at Redbone's, from the baby backs to the yams and greens to the pecan pie, but the Fred Flintstone–size beef ribs are amazing. Expect the wait for a table in the bustling dining room to take up to 20 minutes, time you can pass at the bar enjoying a wide selection of microbrews on tap and a gallery of signed photos from some of the blues cats who've dropped in before playing down the street at the rootsy club **Johnny D's** *(17 Holland St., 617/776–9667)*.

Best use of garlic: One of the Boston area's best-kept secrets is a small Spanish restaurant in Somerville named **Dalí** *(415 Washington St., 617/661–3254)*, which specializes in tapas and an unabashedly bold use of garlic. You can think of tapas as continental Europe's answer to dim sum, or just as an opportunity to eat sublime appetizers all night without having to order an entree. Though a good number of the tapas on Dali's menu are garlicky, the restaurant is also one of the more romantic places in town. Just bring some breath mints, or drink plenty of sangria, or make sure neither one of you goes solo on the garlic soup.

Best chicken-fried steak: If you're not worried about your cholesterol count, and you want to eat diner food cooked to a tee, **Bob the Chef** in Boston's South End is your guy. Sit at the counter so you can watch the food cook the old-fashioned way: with hot oil on metal. Bob's *(604 Columbus Ave., 617/536–6204)* gets a mix of locals and others who've traveled far and wide for the old-world atmosphere and hearty food. The chicken-fried steak is terrific, but then so is the chicken-fried chicken. Breakfast is always a treat, though you'll have to wait for space on weekends. One thing you won't have to do is drop a lot of cash.

Best dry-rubbed pork: Chris Schlesinger learned a valuable lesson from the revered barbecue philosophers of Memphis and North Carolina: You don't need bucketloads of sauce to make great barbecue. Dry rubbing some spices on the meat and then slow-cooking it is really the way to go. That's how they do it at Schlesinger's **East Coast Grill** *(1271 Cambridge St., 617/491–6568)*, a bright, bustling establishment in Cambridge's Inman Square that is heartily devoted to the thrill of the grill. (Even the light fixtures are made out of grill parts.) And Schlesinger didn't stop at dry-rubbing pork, smoking ribs and brisket, or grilling meats. The Grill serves up one of the best pieces of seared, sushi-quality tuna in town, great grilled-veggie salads, and even a tempting, grilled little-neck clams appetizer. It's also worth saving some room for dessert.

Best sorbet: If you can't handle a heavy dessert at the East Coast Grill, take a little walk around the block until you end up right next door at **Christina's Homemade Ice Cream** *(1255 Cambridge St., 617/492–7021).* There have been ice cream rivalries in Boston since the days when a local guy named Steve introduced the world to the trendy idea of Heath Bar mix-ins. But Christina's has moved on to a whole new level of artistry in frozen desserts with its tantalizing array of exotic sorbets. Mango, papaya, cranberry, and kiwi are some that have gotten raves.

Best after-hours grease: There's something about a greasy burger or a butter-saturated cheese omelet that hits the spot after a night of clubbing. Sure, the surgeon general doesn't recommend it, but sometimes you just have to make like Homer Simpson and let your stomach do the talking. And that's why God invented places like **Dolly's** *(382 Highland Ave., Somerville, 617/628–0888),* a deco-ish, pink-and-black diner that doesn't even open until 11 P.M. and closes at 4 A.M. weekdays, 5 A.M. weekends. The trick to getting a table or counter space at Dolly's is to arrive a little before two, when the after-hours hordes descend. But even if you have to wait for a table, there's usually plenty of human drama unfolding to keep you entertained, whether it's a lovers' quarrel, some cabbies arguing about the best route to Logan, or a drunk guy spilling coffee in his lap.

Best caffeine rush: The "Black Death," a concoction that features six shots of espresso in a tall pint glass, is not recommended for novices. But if you're a heavy coffee drinker and it's going to be a long night, there's really no better legal way to get wired than ordering one of these potent brews at the **Liberty Cafe** *(497B Mass Ave., 617/492–9900).* The Liberty sits in the middle of club world in Central Square, so on Wednesday nights you might catch suburban Goth kids in the bathrooms taking off the clothes mommy made them wear out of the house and putting on something more comfortable for Goth night at Man Ray. Most other nights, the Liberty caters to a crowd of underage kids and caffeine-hungry refugees from the Middle East and T.T.'s, which are both across the street.

Best French and Cambodian cuisine: Dining at the **Elephant Walk**, which has two locations in the Boston area, is like getting two restaurant experiences in one. On the left side of the menu, you've got your French fare—top-notch, nouvelle cuisine–type food, including perfectly prepared duck and chicken entrées and tantalizing desserts. The right side of the menu features traditional Cambodian food from poulet phochani to banana-flower salad, as well as curries that beat just about any Thai restaurant in town. The original Elephant Walk *(70 Union Sq., Somerville, 617/623–9939)* has more Southeast Asian character (i.e., bamboo furniture) than the newer one *(900 Beacon St., 617/247–1500)* in Brookline. But the food is great at both.

shopping

records

Best rare records: You probably didn't know there was a burgeoning psychedelic-rock scene in the Southern Hemisphere during the '60s and early '70s. Or that the recorded artifacts of a Chilean outfit named Aguaturbia's Psychedelic Drugstore are prized finds for discriminating vinyl collectors. But that only makes browsing the racks at **Twisted Village** *(12 Eliot St., 617/354–6898)* in Harvard Square more of a kick. The store, which is run by two avant-rock musicians turned record collectors turned entrepreneurs—Kate Biggar and Wayne Rogers—specializes in hard-to-find oddities, from Blind Willie McTell blues records and Martin Denny exotica to contemporary imports of CDs from Japanoise masters like Keiji Haino. The store does carry a range of new and used indie-rock releases, so, yeah, you can get the latest Pavement on vinyl. Be sure to gape at the first pressing of *The Velvet Underground & Nico* that hangs on the wall behind the register and ask if there are any in-store avant-rock shows coming up on the weekend.

Best big b.p.m.s: Boston doesn't have a dance club that caters directly to the rave crowd, so if you're looking for the scoop on upcoming all-night raves, record stores are your best bet. **Biscuithead** *(93 Mass Ave., 617/247–3268)* and **Boston Beat Imports** *(1108 Boylston St., 247–2428)* are the two most popular hangouts for the baggy-pants DJ set, and both shops carry a full selection of domestic and imported trip-hop, jungle, ambient, acid jazz, and whatever the latest techno permutation happens to be. Biscuithead also features DJ accessories and custom-mixed tapes. If those two don't have the imported dance track you're chasing, check out the **Vinyl Connection** *(23 Huntington Ave., 617/536–2560)*, which doesn't even dabble in cassettes or CDs.

Best alt.rock accessories: The local CD chain **Newbury Comics** has always specialized not just in supplying the discs that provide the soundtrack for youth rebellion, but in offering all the extras as well—from ANARCHY IN THE UK T-shirts and safety-pin earrings in the early '80s to Urban Decay and Hard Candy lipsticks, Beavis and Butt-head trading cards, and a full rack of fanzines in the '90s. Comic books are also one of the chain's mainstays, and you can usually find a good selection of new releases on vinyl at most of the stores. The original location *(332 Newbury St., 617/236–4930)* in Boston and the Harvard Square store *(36 JFK St., 617/491–0337)* are the best in terms of post-punk atmosphere—i.e., the ratio of indie-rockers to frat boys is more favorable. And both are right down the street from a **Tower Records** *(360 Newbury St., 617/247–5900; 93 Mt. Auburn St., 617/876–3377)*, for convenient comparison shopping.

books

Best pulp fiction: You'll find mystery novels at just about all the major bookstores in the Boston/Cambridge area. But if you're looking for someone who not only specializes in whodunits, but actually lives them, then you've gotta drop by on Kate at **Kate's Mystery Books** *(2211 Mass Ave., 617/491–2661)*. Located in a house in Porter Square, Cambridge, Kate's is a shrine to 20th-century pulp fiction, from Jim Thompson's *The Grifters* to the latest hard-boiled creation of Andrew Vachss as well as the harder-to-find sort. The store also features regular readings by local and national mystery writers. If you're in town over the summer, drop by and see if Kate will be leading her suspense-filled "mystery walks" anytime soon.

Best hard-to-reach books: The shelves at **Avenue Victor Hugo** *(339 Newbury St., 617/266–7746)* are stacked so high with used classics that you need a footstool to browse. That's only part of the fun of this Newbury Street landmark, which has always been known for having an extensive selection of science fiction on hand. Really, though, you can find used books on just about anything at Avenue Victor Hugo—just ask the guy behind the counter where to look.

Best coed comics: At **Million Year Picnic** in Harvard Square *(99 Mount Auburn St., Cambridge, 617/492–6763)*, there always seem to be just as many girls as boys flipping gingerly through the pages of the latest

DC, Marvel, and indie comic books. Maybe that's because the tiny basement store tends to de-emphasize the testosterone-charged escapism of spandex-clad superheroes in favor of giving top billing to more adventurous imprints like the Vertigo Verite line. In other words, if you're looking for the latest installment of *Too Much Coffee Man*, *The Preacher,* or *Jinx*, look here. The store also carries an extensive selection of foreign, small-press, and adults-only comics. There's even a healthy section of back issues.

clothes

Best clothing by the pound: Bargain hunting is a New England tradition, bred in the bones of any true Yankee. And for years now, frugal housewives have been descending on downtown's **Filene's Basement** *(426 Washington St., 617/542–2011)* to claw at cut-rate suits and dresses. For the younger generation of thrill-seeking penny-pinchers, a store called the **Garment District** *(200 Broadway, Cambridge, 617/876–5230)* has become the place to shop, not just for its selection of secondhand everything—flannel shirts, Brooks Brothers buttondowns, used vinyl, Dr Martens, baby-doll dresses, and fake pearls—but because every day you get a chance to buy piles of less-select clothing for just a buck a pound. The deal works best if you're an early riser, because most of the good stuff gets weeded out in the first hour. The rummaging starts at 9 A.M. weekdays and at 7:45 A.M. Saturdays and Sundays. The Garment District also carries Gen-X accessories like Manic Panic lipstick, nail polish, and hair dye, 8-track tapes, sunglasses, jewelry, and sometimes even artist's canvas for $2 a pound.

Runner-up: For those of you who'd rather not pick through dresses, the **Closet Upstairs** *(233 Newbury St., 617/267–5757)* is a reasonable alternative for more carefully culled used women's clothes.

Best used blues: Otto, the finicky proprietor of **Gumshoe**, a cozy shop in Jamaica Plain *(40 South St., 617/522–5066)*, doesn't carry just any old clothing. He hunts down the cream of the crap, so to speak, salvaging '70s-style Levi's cords and leather jackets, real Hawaiian shirts, and old-style, zipper-front Levi's blue jeans that can sometimes fetch startling sums. Check out the back room for vintage china, clocks, and fans. And look overhead for Otto's great collection of cool old lamps.

Best leather pants: It's a good bet the folks at **Vanson Leathers** *(213 Stoughton Tpk., Stoughton, 617/344–5444)* had real bikers in mind when they decided to open their plant/showroom in the suburb of

Stoughton. So the owners were probably pretty amused when twenty-something grungesters started showing up in their parents' cars to browse the racks of custom-designed jackets, pants, and bodysuits. Vanson offers absolute top-quality utilitarian leatherwear—none of that fancy Eurojunk. Its quality standards mean most jackets will run you at least $400. But for rockers who haven't gotten their major-label advances yet, Vanson also has a whole room of cut-rate overstock where you can get jackets and pants for as little as $100.

et cetera

Best space-age bachelor-pad junk: New England is antique country but, of course, the coolest old stuff isn't all that old. No, the coolest treasures are the futuristic spoils of the '50s, '60s, and '70s—we're talking Paul McCobb desks and Heywood-Wakefield dressers; bakelite jewelry and vinyl bowling-ball bags; General Electric fans and classic steel toasters; suave cocktail shakers and Jetsons-style reading lamps. If you're just looking to browse the best (i.e., expensive, European, mid-century designs), check out **Machine Age** (354 Congress St., 617/482–0048), a downtown storefront showroom that carries everything from giant vintage European living-room sets to tiny domestic knickknacks from the '50s. The store's in a loft-intensive part of town and has the feel of a SoHo gallery.

Runner-up: For better deals, a less expansive selection, and a friendlier atmosphere, check out **NV53** (1700A Mass Ave., Cambridge, 617/661–8463), between Harvard and Porter Squares.

Best Godzilla toys: Corporate America was so busy lamenting Japanese automakers' world dominance in the 1980s that it never stopped to notice toy manufacturing was the industry in which Tokyo really had the edge. You'll find proof of Japan's superiority in the Godzilla toys and action figures scattered among the *Godzilla* movies, Frank Kozik posters, and Zippo lighters at **Day-Old Antiques** (1644 Mass Ave., Cambridge, 617/354–1999). Thanks to the poster-art and a small but excellent used-vinyl section, this small store caters to an interesting mix of rock types and sci-fi nerds.

Best glow-in-the-dark condoms: There are always a few Beavis and Butt-head types giggling on the street outside **Condom World** (332 Newbury St., 617/267–7233). But their kind rarely go inside, because Condom World is one of the only stores in town where you can't buy a pack of condoms and pretend you're not. If you're buying anything at Condom World, you're buying condoms, because that's all they carry. Of course, they do offer an unusually wide variety....

Best leather and lace: You can't miss the whips and masks in the window at Cambridge's **Hubba Hubba** *(932 Mass Ave., 617/492–9082).* What's nice about the place is it's not located in a sleazy section of town, so its clientele isn't all that intimidating. The store carries enough basic black to keep the Goth crowd happy, and plenty of serious leather, rubber, and vinyl restraining devices for performance-minded S&M folks.

body alterations

Best piercing: Boston has never exactly been on the cutting edge of the body-mutilation trend, so the piercing experts at **Rites of Passage** *(107 Brighton Ave., Allston, 617/783–1918)* haven't had to put up with too much competition. Not that being the only real game in town has compromised the standards at this modern-primitive stronghold. Rites of Passage offers the best of both worlds—real tribal artifacts on the walls, and the best in Western sterilization techniques. And the service staff has also dabbled in branding and other forms of body scarring.

Best tattoos: Not in Boston, that's for sure. Someday a grassroots campaign may overturn the statute that forbids tattooing on Massachusetts soil. But for now, it's illegal to get a tattoo in Boston, Cambridge, or any other part of the Commonwealth. Unless you're willing to risk a hefty fine, wait until you're out of state to implant ink in your flesh.

Best Manic Panic dye jobs: For those times when getting your hair to shine an unnatural magenta is a must but you're tired of staining your cuticles and your forehead along with it, **E C O Centrix** *(30 Newbury St., 617/ 262–2222)* is the way to go. The other upscale boutiques in the neighborhood might frown on outré tints, but not this salon.

Runner-up: If you're on the other side of the river in Cambridge, the coolly named **Judy Jetson** salon *(1765 Mass Ave., 617/354–2628)* also has Manic Panic colors.

hotel/motel

Best stargazing: The **Ritz-Carlton** *(15 Arlington St., 617/536–5700)* used to be the preferred accommodation for visiting celebs. But these days the best place to spot the Rolling Stones or U2 when they're in town is at the four-star **Four Seasons** *(200 Boylston St., 617/338–4400)*. Built in the mid-'80s and located on the edge of Boston Common, the Seasons doesn't have the old-world, old-money charm of the Ritz—it's a thoroughly modern, sleekly designed complex. But, hell, it's good enough for Mick. Rates begin at $405 for a double.

Best HoJos: Most national-level, major-label touring acts who haven't quite hit the big time end up playing at one of the Lansdowne Street clubs. So on any given night of the week you can expect a couple of giant tour buses to pull up in front of one or both of the **Howard Johnson**s that flank Kenmore Square. They're relatively cheap and conveniently located too. One's at 575 Commonwealth Ave. *(617/267–3100)*, with nicer rooms and rates that run from $90 to $175 for one person; the other's at 1271 Boylston St. *(617/267–8300)*, with slightly cheaper rates that run from $70 to $150.

Best brownstone accommodations: If you want the feel of living in a Boston brownstone for just a couple of nights, the **Copley Inn** *(19 Garrison St., 617/236–0300)* offers affordable bed-and-breakfast-style accommodations (without the breakfast) in a 21-unit brownstone downtown. You get a room with a double bed, your own phone number and voice mail, and a fully functional kitchenette for between $75 and $105, depending on the season.

local wonders

Best tunes on the dunes: If it's summertime and you're up for a little road trip, it's usually worth the hour-plus drive on Route 3 to Cape Cod for a little ocean-side rockin' at the **Wellfleet Beachcomber** *(Cahoon Hollow Beach, Wellfleet, 508/349–6055)*. Located at the bottom of a long, winding road that's a lot less daunting on the way down than it is on the way up at the end of the night, and set atop a giant dune overlooking the beach, this tiny shack imports some of Boston's best bands every summer for what can, and often do, turn into unforgettable nights of partying. Beachcomber alumni include Letters to Cleo, Come, the Dambuilders, and even out-of-towners like Dick Dale and C.J. Chenier. On weekend nights there's usually a bonfire on the beach after the show, so you might want to pack a cooler of cold ones in the trunk. Beachcomber gigs are always listed in Boston papers like the Phoenix. And there are cheap hotels if you're looking to spend the night. Call ahead for rooms, but be warned: The Sunday drive back from the Cape can mean fighting some hellish traffic.

Best rotary: In other parts of the country they're called traffic circles. In Boston, where they are more numerous than anyplace else in the world, we call them "rotaries," and they are clearly designed to intimidate, confuse, and otherwise unnerve even the most experienced drivers. Basically, a rotary is an interchange where automobiles are forced to merge on and then off of a circular section of road. And they are guaranteed to bring out the cutthroat competitive driver in even your grandmother. One of the best is located where Storrow Drive meets the downtown expressway (Rte. 93)—and one of the great things about it is you can stand on the footbridge overhead and witness some of the cruelest driving maneuvers ever imaginable. The best action starts around 3:30 P.M. and continues until 7. Bring earplugs.

Best religious experience: Boston may be home to some of the oldest churches in America, including the one where Paul Revere hung his lanterns, but it's also got one of the largest, scariest statues of the mother of God. The **Madonna Queen National Shrine** *(111 Orient Ave., East Boston, 617/569–2100)* not only features a 50-foot metal rendering of the Lady herself (which was floated over from Italy in the 1950s) and a very high kitsch factor, it also offers a decent hilltop view of the city. Located across the street from a stern-looking Catholic school and protected behind eight-foot-high gates, the statue is circled by walls that feature relief carvings of all 12 stations of the cross. All in all, it would have made a perfect location for an early Madonna video. Open daily from 10 A.M. until 7 P.M.

Best midnight skinny-dipping: Actually, it's illegal to swim at **Walden Pond** *(Rte. 126 in Concord, about 20 minutes from the city; 508/369–3254)* after sunset, and the agency in charge of the place where Henry David Thoreau penned his classic *Civil Disobedience* really doesn't take kindly to people who break the rules. But you can usually just park your car and sneak in a five-minute swim before the cops show up (not that we're urging anyone to break the law). The officers are usually thoughtful enough to turn on their blue and white lights before they start their search. As long as you get dressed, plead ignorance, and say, "Yes, sir," they probably won't give you a hassle. Otherwise, Walden Pond is a great place for a legal daytime swim during the summer, or for a meditative walk through 300 acres of woods.

There are fish and turtles in the pond, a bathroom/changing-room, and even a full-size replica of Henry David's cabin located near the reservation's entrance off Route 126.

transmissions

Best wake-up call: Being a big college town, Boston has always been strong on the left of the dial. **WMBR (88.1 FM)**, MIT's commercial-free station, edges out the competition, the strongest of which are Emerson's **WERS (88.9 FM)** and Boston College's **WZBC (90.3 FM)**, by offering one of the coolest and most diverse morning lineups of indie-rock in town. The long-running "Breakfast of Champions" show (8–10 A.M.) features everything from garage punk to New Zealand–style drone pop. And then the "Late Risers Club" picks up with a mix of current and classic indie rock from 10 A.M. until noon.

chapel hill/ raleigh/ durham

by Mac McCaughan and Andrea Reusing

"Dip's Country Kitchen is the first place I go when I get back to town. It serves the best and cheapest Southern food in Chapel Hill." — **Eric Bachmann,** *Archers of Loaf*

Nobody should be surprised by the joyful guitar noise blasting from what's known as North Carolina's Triangle. With three major southern universities within 20 minutes of each other, what do you expect? If you put a bunch of youths in a town where there's not much to do (when you're in and out of school, who thinks about school all that much?), give them two radio stations that spew forth the latest from North Carolina and beyond (WXYC and WXDU, see Transmissions), and a caravan of punk-rock tour vans stopping on their way from D.C. to Atlanta, these kids are going to rock. And since the early '80s, Chapel Hill, Raleigh, and Durham have done just that, producing a steady stream of underground sound, from Corrosion of Conformity's white-hot hardcore to the Archers of Loaf's beautifully croaking indie pop.

If the cities were farther apart, each would remain a fundamentally obscure college town with some good eats and clubs, much like Champaign, Illinois, or Columbia, Missouri. The towns are different enough to deserve individual inspection, but taken together the region has a volatile chemistry. Every March, basketball fever sweeps the area, often pitting Duke, U.N.C, and N.C. State against each other in the Atlantic Coast Conference, and even if frat brothers with their faces painted blue freak you out, this part of the county—home turf for Michael Jordan and Grant Hill—is as good a place as any to get involved in an intense pickup game. While locals will put down their basketballs or bus trays and carpool from Chapel Hill to Raleigh at the drop of a dime to see a good gig, it's generally considered a pain to drive the whole 20 miles from Durham to the Vertigo in Raleigh just for a bite to eat. Likewise, locals tend to stick to their own bars when juicing up.

Of the three towns, Chapel Hill is the most welcoming to dropouts, do-it-yourselfers, and other malcontents. Some people say it's easy to live in Chapel Hill, others that it's just easy to get stuck. A small, leafy town on a hill—hence, its name—it exists for one reason only: the University of North Carolina, the oldest state institution in the country, founded in 1795. With over half the town made up of students, living's cheap (though getting pricier), and Chapel Hill's more laid-back than its neighboring towns. State Capital **Raleigh**'s business is government, while **Durham** is the home of Duke University and the dying tobacco industry. Durham still smells of it—the odor hits you as soon as you get out of your car downtown. When you hear people refer to "Moo U.," they mean the area's third big university, N.C. State in Raleigh, an agriculture and tech school. The nickname has been kept alive, of course, by sneering Duke and U.N.C. students.

In contrast to Durham and Chapel Hill, the Raleigh music scene was about hardcore punk rock. In the early Reagan years, speed demons like No Labels, Corrosion of Conformity, and the Stillborn Christians played an endless series of matinees (sometimes opening for touring heavyweights like the Minutemen or JFA) and house parties, recording the first North Carolina hardcore compilation, a 7-inch called "Why Are We Here?" on No Core Records. Of these bands, only Corrosion of Conformity is chugging along—still heavy, but without the Mach speed and insanity they perfected on their second record, *Animosity*.

It says something about the student population of Duke University, which fancies itself the Harvard of the South, that Durham has never been able to support a rock club. The Duke Coffeehouse hosted early hardcore shows by bands like the Ugly Americans, and over a decade later it still fights the good fight on some nights, hosting acts ranging from moody New York noisemakers Versus to avant-garde violinist Tony Conrad. But unlike a nightclub, the Coffeehouse is a space, relying on the university, not a loyal following of concertgoers, to pay the rent.

From Durham it's a brief drive to the small-town streets of Chapel Hill, home of some imaginary guitar-rock, power-pop, or punk revival that either began in 1989 or last week, depending on which magazine you read. Merge Records (founded by the present author, Mac McCaughan, and Laura Ballance) debuted in the summer of 1989 as a tiny seven-inch-single label along with Superchunk (then Chunk), a tiny punk-rock band. Other people all over the country were doing the same thing (and probably with the same inspirations: Dischord, SST, Sub Pop, K), but the advantage here was in the D.I.Y. tradition and the broad base of like-minded musicians already firmly in place.

Locals tend to emphasize some sort of inherent difference in "Raleigh bands" versus "Chapel Hill bands," but early Merge bands like Erectus Monotone (fractured, clattering pop), Polvo (detuned, Eastern-leaning guitars over tricky rhythms), and Superchunk came out of a unified late-'80s scene based in both Raleigh and Chapel Hill. Durham spawned Jettison Records and bands like the howling, disjointed Blue Green Gods and Blue Chair at around that time. Mammoth Records (now a division of a major label) has been headquartered in Carrboro, a town just west of Chapel Hill, for some time.

One note about the liquor laws in North Carolina: An establishment may only serve liquor or wine if it is a restaurant or a private club, so as a barfly you may end up drinking a lot of beer (see below for places that'll pour you a stiff one).

lay of the land

In the state capital, Raleigh, the downtown looks like it did in the '50s. **Hillsborough Street** runs west from the downtown government buildings all the way to the heart of the N.C. State campus. Some of the most interesting neighborhoods lie between these two hubs of activity: **Boylan Heights** (mythologized by local pop classicists the Connells in a song of the same name) is full of huge old homes, many of them now divided into apartments. Thriving young businesses—like Tannis Root Productions, silkscreeners of rock tees for everyone from Mudhoney to Yoko Ono, and Barefoot Press, which has printed countless seven-inch sleeves and posters for bands and labels all over the country—have started here, taking advantage of the cheap rents, and in the process have brought life to the area. Raleigh is often seen as the most redneck (though it's no Charlotte) of the three towns, and though some here play up the cracker angle just to dig at the other, more milk-fed collegiate towns, Raleigh is also the least homogeneous—bigger, most racially mixed, most surprising—city in the Triangle.

Though it often seems that a sold-out crowd at Chapel Hill's Cat's Cradle could keep Durham's cigarette manufacturers afloat for years, the last major factory (Liggett & Meyers) shrinks every year. With its always-visible chapel tower, Duke's West Campus is all Gothic architecture, slate walkways, and massive green quadrangles. A couple of miles away, toward downtown, **East Campus** is less bucolic but the home of two Durham cultural beacons: the student-run radio station, WXDU (88.7 FM), and the Duke Coffeehouse. The hippie-ish **Ninth Street**

shopping district has more bookstores than you can shake a stick at, as well as a few decent cafes and boutiques. Durham's the most confusing place to drive around, but getting lost here can be fun.

In "uptown" Chapel Hill you can walk anywhere you need to go, and **Franklin Street** is the equivalent of Hillsborough Street in Raleigh and Ninth Street in Durham—only it's many times more Main Street U.S.A. Heading west from campus on Franklin Street, it's only about two minutes before you'll cross the proverbial tracks into **Carrboro**. You may not notice that you've left Chapel Hill, but Carrboro is where many have moved to get away from the crowds of students that flood into town every year. It's cheaper to live in Carrboro because you can't walk to campus, and most blocks are still full of impressive old homes that date back to the mill era. **Pittsboro**, 14 miles to the south of Chapel Hill, in Chatham County, and historic **Hillsborough**, 10 miles to the north, are nearby towns that warrant snooping around.

In between the three towns is a well-kept compound known as Research Triangle Park—RTP to locals—a sprawling research and development center shared by behemoths like IBM and pharmaceutical giant Glaxo-Wellcome. A cause of the rising population throughout the area, the massive RTP workforce now jams the highways at rush hour—just like in the big city you're thinking about moving here to escape from.

getting from a to b

You need a car to get around the Triangle. Public transportation is sadly lacking, and though they've been talking about some sort of train/monorail/space shuttle between the three towns for years, you're best off renting a car if you didn't drive here in the first place. Highway 15-501 connects Durham and Chapel Hill, and it's about 10 miles between the two. I-40 runs from Raleigh, through RTP, and on to Chapel Hill (and then on to Amarillo and L.A., if you're so inclined), with exits for Durham as well. Rush hour is a headache on both of these. City maps are well worth picking up, as only Raleigh's layout approximates a navigable grid, and that's just downtown.

Late at night there are plenty of cabs to take your inebriated self home, but you have to call them (or have the last watering hole of the evening do it for you). If you're in Raleigh, try Yellow Cab *(919/832–1821)*; Tar Heel Cab serves Chapel Hill *(919/933–1255)*.

sources

For daily news, Raleigh's *The News and Observer* is pretty useful, but it's also easy to find a *New York Times* at a newsstand. There are two free weeklies available, for movie and concert listings, previews, and reviews: The *Spectator* and the *Independent*. Either one is perfectly good for listings. The *Independent* is a good read, with extensive coverage of state and local politics, social issues, arts, reliable entertainment picks, and fairly trustworthy movie and music reviews. Look for the *Spectator* and the *Independent* at record stores, restaurants, and movie theaters.

Zinewise, the Triangle is always in flux—you never know which have stopped publishing altogether and which are just late paying the printer. There are a couple of consistent standouts: the newsprint *Preparation X* offers a sarcastic take on America by surveying locals on embarrassing stories, leaving music-writing to the massive indie-rock/free-jazz/avant-garde tome called *Tuba Frenzy*. New ones are popping up and disappearing all the time, so just keep an eye out at the record stores. For a huge selection of national and local magazines and newspapers, check out **The Newsstand** *(302 E. Main St., Carrboro, 919/942–4920)*, and for a paper and a fountain soda uptown in Chapel Hill, **Jeff's Confectionary** *(125 E. Franklin, Chapel Hill)* seems as old as the university itself.

Online, there's a local rock chat room where you can learn more than you ever cared to know about the scene (alt.music.chapel-hill), and both Merge (www.mrg2000.com/merge/) and Mammoth Records (www.mammoth.com) have their own Web sites.

clubs

Chapel Hill

Best rock club-as-institution: The **Cat's Cradle** *(300 E. Main St., Carrboro, 919/967–9053)* has been synonymous with live music in Chapel Hill for over 25 years. A convenient stop between D.C. and Atlanta for touring bands, the Cradle has also achieved a national profile: As long ago as 1986, Sonic Youth name-checked the club in a *Village Voice* interview. Though the soft-spoken owner of the last ten years, Frank Heath, attributes the uncanny longevity of the club to things like "luck" and "having a good name," the Cradle is a mecca because it has given a tiny town like Chapel Hill legendary shows by everyone from Sun Ra to the Dream Syndicate, Richard Thompson to Redd Kross. And the locals revere the club for it. Of course, mersh success stories like Pearl Jam and the Black Crowes (then R.E.M. wannabes Mr. Crowe's Garden) plugged in at some point. It's as though the Cradle supports the community, not the other way around. Some of the most fabled shows are the sweaty early-'80s dance parties that featured local ska heroes the Pressure Boys and rockabilly legends Flat Duo Jets. When indie-rock faves like the Archers of Loaf or Polvo pack the place now, it's simply what one expects from the area's best, favorite rock club.

Best go-go cage: When the Cat's Cradle moved to its current cavernous space in Carrboro, there was no medium-size venue for rock in Chapel Hill for a while. **Local 506** *(506 W. Franklin St., Chapel Hill, 919/942–5506)* soon filled that gap. The stage is small and looks as though it may be swallowed by the silver ductwork winding around its edge, but the sound has gotten better over the last couple of years and the go-go cage attached to the stage is often occupied by inebriated locals dancing madly to the strains of popular Chapel Hill hip-shakers like Pipe, Zen Frisbee, and the Family Dollar Pharaohs. This club is also the site of the yearly garage-rock invitational known as Sleazefest, unofficially hosted by the local band Southern Culture on the Skids. Unlike many Chapel Hill nightspots that feature live music, Local 506 serves hard liquor, which explains why there are so many volunteers for the cage. Unfortunately, 506 is unusually smoke-filled, even for a rock dive, and your eyes may ask to leave before your ears are ready.

Best intimate rock club: The **Lizard and Snake Cafe** *(110 N. Columbia St., Chapel Hill, 919/929–2828)* is a recent, welcome addition to the Chapel Hill roster. It has a good location, right uptown, and feels intimate. You used to be able to watch bands from outside, through the giant plate-glass windows on Columbia Street, while you decided whether or not to pay. A velvet curtain draped over the same windows has greatly improved the once-harsh live sound and prevents such cheating, though when the cover is usually between $2 and $5, shouldn't you just spring for it? A Mexican restaurant by day, the Cafe hosts live rock at least four nights a week, ranging from the three local kids you never heard of to a sneak show by popular townies like Pipe. It also hosts genuinely choice touring bands too obscure to fill the Cat's Cradle, recent visitors including Lois, Epic Soundtracks, Mark Eitzel, Richard Buckner, and Mark Robinson. Rock works here, but more delicate music fares better with the small P.A.

Durham

Best dance club: The **Power Company** *(315 W. Main St., Durham, 919/683–1151)* is one of only a handful of dance clubs in the area and its loyal membership gives it a comfortable feel. The flashy sound, lights, and lasers setup is impressive, the dance floor large and multitiered. The club has a steady following of regulars who come from all parts of the triangle. The ratio of women to men is high for a gay club and although most of the regulars seem to know each other, the mood isn't cliqueish. Admission and drinks (liquor is available, since the Power Company is technically a private club) are surprisingly cheap. Musically, house is pretty much the constant, occasionally interspersed with techno or novelty hits, like the high-energy klezmer-house hybrid popular last week.

Raleigh

Best place to go deaf: In the early to mid-'80s, the **Brewery** *(3009 Hillsborough St., Raleigh, 919/834–7018)* was the only club in the area to consistently host touring hard-core and punk-rock bands (Saccharine Trust, Black Flag, Husker Du, and every other early SST band you can think of), and, more important, was a (small) stage for local HC pioneers like Corrosion of Conformity, No Labels, and the Stillborn Christians. For Sunday matinees, punk rockers from as far away as Richmond and Atlanta packed the small club—and the parking lot between bands. A second flowering of the Raleigh music scene, around 1986, saw even more nontraditionally wacked bands like the Angels of Epistemology, Days Of, and the Black Girls use the Brewery as a home base of sorts, and local music is still represented well here. The sound has always been fair-to-good, but the disappointing thing about the Brewery these days is that the marquee out front rarely shows any sign of the adventurous booking that once made the club an exciting place to lose your hearing.

bars

Chapel Hill

Best postshow drink: Upscale restaurant by day, **Henry's Bistro** *(403 Rosemary St., Chapel Hill, 919/967–4720)* comes alive at night, when crowds of scenesters pack the bar and spill out onto the patio to wait for that bourbon that they're sure someone owes them. The kitchen goes into late-night mode at 10:30, and an order of olive bread (toasted baguette topped with olives and melted smoked mozzarella) or a burger au poivre might be what you need after a couple hours' exploration of the beer list. Standouts include the local beer Weeping Radish; Cooper's sparkling ale, from Australia; and Duvel, from Belgium. If you went to see a band at the Cradle, and that girl or guy you saw earlier at Pepper's (see food, below) and now have a crush on went to see a band at Local 506, this is the best place to casually bump into them later. The atmosphere is friendly, but not very well ventilated, so try to get a table outside, weather permitting.

Best Saturday morning Bloody Mary: Spring Garden *(111 E. Main St., Carrboro, 919/929–2708)* is probably Carrboro's oldest bar. It occupies an odd brick structure that resembles the Flatiron building in New York City, coming to a point where Weaver and Main streets split, and the bar inside is accordingly V-shaped, with the bartenders trapped in the middle. They serve food (the veggie burger is okay), but the crowd is here mainly for the microbrews on tap and the generously portioned mixed drinks. A spicy Bloody Mary in a pint glass with a celery stalk could be just the thing to make you forget about the hard living you did last night at the Cradle. It's also a big nightspot with a beer list; since it's down the street from the Cradle, people will stop by for a shot of bourbon between acts.

Raleigh

Best neighborhood bar: Southern liquor laws discourage the type of hard-liquor, old-man bars that dot northern urban centers. In the Triangle, folks tend to drink liquor and wine in restaurants, and beer everywhere else. Bill Mooney looked to places like Philly and Jersey City for models when conceiving the **Stingray Room** *(1620½ Glenwood Ave., Raleigh, 919/828–9993)* and has created a place where people go to hang out, have a cocktail, and listen to good music on the juke. The snazzy two-wheeler you pedaled as a kid is the bar's namesake, and old bikes vie for space on the walls with the backs of dismantled yet still-glowing pinball machines that you (or your parents) used to play. Down on the floor, the functional pinball machines (most recently Dirty Harry and Elton John) create a racket, as do the balls cracking on three pool tables. The crowd is a late-night one, and the makeup is equal parts postshow hipsters, restaurant employees just off work, and neighborhood regulars. To get around North Carolina's blue laws, the Stingray Room is officially a private club, however, nonmembers can be admitted as guests.

Best afterwork martini: At the top of the stairs at the **Rockford** *(320½ Glenwood Ave., Raleigh, 919/821–9020)*, take a right and grab a stool at the expansive mahogany and copper bar. It's a cool, quiet place to spend an hour in the late afternoon, and the booze they offer matches the classy, renovated feel of this old brick building, with more than a few single-malt scotches and single-barrel bourbons. The Rockford's pride is in its martini: icy, generously poured, with liquor and olives both of high quality. Appetizers like the crab cakes or baked brie are good drinking companions. Actually, in North Carolina, "happy hour" is illegal, so don't limit yourself to the late afternoon for this type of activity. The Rockford serves meals (lunch and dinner), but the restaurant is a bit sterile compared to the comfortable bar. A good place to feel anonymous, but not somewhere to camp out for a bender.

Best topless bar: As much a place to go out for a night of drinking with friends as a place for skeezy ogres to gawk at topless dancers, the **Foxy Lady** *(1817 Capital Blvd., Raleigh 919/833–5886)* is a casual hangout where there's a wait for the pool tables and catcalls are absent. Though a few men seem zombified at the edge of the stage, the dancing seems almost incidental. Scenesters drink Bud from cans, and the dancers casually rap with regulars between table dances (there are no lap dances in North Carolina).

food

Chapel Hill

Best Southern cooking: Founded by Mildred "Dip" Council, **Dip's Country Kitchen** *(405 West Rosemary St., Chapel Hill, 919/942–5837)* has a motto—"put a little South in your mouth"—that exactly describes their duty in Chapel Hill. Dip's has churned out regulation Southern fare (country ham, fried chicken, barbecue, and sweet-potato pie) with a consistent, if sometimes surly, hand for the past ten years. There are always a bunch of fresh vegetables to choose from, and the vegetables that contain meat (greens cooked with pork) are clearly marked, something of a rarity in the meat-centric South. The chicken and dumplings is the standout dish—with tender meat, rich gravy, and rolled dumplings that are so light you can swallow them whole.

Best triggerfish fajitas: Proprietor and minor-league baseball extremist (there's a countdown-'til-first-game-of-the-season on the wall) Phil Campbell has managed to create a warm, popular Tex-Mex haven in an unlikely location: the corner of a decrepit Chapel Hill strip mall. The **Flying Burrito** *(746 Airport Rd., Chapel Hill, 919/967–7744)* has been dishing out its hearty burritos—the Flying Chicken, the Flying Vegetarian, etc.—to an almost cultish following of students and locals for over a decade. The large standard menu includes huevos rancheros, barbecued chicken and ribs, and the more distinctive Bull City Burrito (with sauerkraut) and Flyin'

Mayan Burrito (black beans and sweet potatoes). Helpings are huge and prices are low, but if you're willing to spend a bit more, head for the blackboard specials.

Runner-up: For mushy refritos and thick cheesy enchiladas, as delicious as they are bad for you, and the best (frozen) margaritas in town, check out the family-run and festive **El Rodeo** *(1404 E. Franklin St., Chapel Hill, 919/929–6566; 2404 Wake Forest Rd., Raleigh, 919/833–1460; 905 W. Main St., Durham, 919/683–2417).*

Best slice: The Chapel Hill phone book contains at least 20 listings for pizza restaurants, but few specialize in slices. **Pepper's Pizza** *(127 E. Franklin St., Chapel Hill, 919/967–7766)* offers calzones, stromboli, and whole pies, but it's the slice (and rock 'n' roll atmosphere) that sets this place apart. Pepper's sits at what is basically the geographical center of town, so turnover is high at the barstool seating up front, and the booths and tables in back are often packed.

Best late-night hangout: **Time-Out Restaurant** *(133 W. Franklin St., Chapel Hill, 919/929–2425)* specializes in grease, but as the only joint open all night in a town full of beer-swilling college students, it has a loyal following. Huge biscuits and fried chicken under bright fluorescent lights are the order of the evening. If you spent all your money on brew, a Bucket of Bones (just what it sounds like) will only cost you about a buck. The walls are hung with photos of U.N.C. star athletes past and present making the "time out" signal, and it appears that the alumni remain faithful: When Michael Jordan's in town, a late-night visit by the famous Tarheel is not unusual.

Runner-up: Another late-night (but not all-night) institution is **Hector's** *(201-A E. Franklin St., 919/942-9420)*, serving "Greek" food (the "Greek" Grilled Cheese is a tasty dose of dairy) "until the line is gone"—usually around 3 A.M.

Best shrimp and grits: Fifteen years ago, the now famous, late Bill Neal and partner Gene Hamer founded the restaurant **Crook's Corner** *(610 West Franklin St., Chapel Hill, 919/929–7643)* in the former space of a cement-floored barbecue shack of the same name. Today, Crook's is the most beloved restaurant in Chapel Hill, if not the Triangle, a huge deal for a public not known for its love of dining out. Most of the year, Crook's looks as much like a garden as it does a restaurant; its perimeter is packed with wildflowers and grasses and the covered patio is enclosed by rows of tall bamboo. The menu is seasonal, with a few consistent items like the Cajun Ribeye steak, the Jalapeño-Cheddar Hush Puppies and Neal's classic Shrimp and Grits—a big plate of fresh North Carolina shrimp, bacon, scallions, and tomatoes over cheese grits (that could convince the most grit-shy eater). Crooks is not cheap (dishes average $12 to $15, with some specialties peaking at $18), but there are many inexpensive appetizers and salads on the menu and they have the best burger and fries in town.

Durham

Best no-frills seafood: On the protein front, the South inspires thoughts of barbecue pits, not clambakes. However, in the Triangle you're only two hours from the coast. Fresh local seafood is available in many restaurants, but **Fishmonger's** *(806 West Main St., Durham, 919/682–0128)*, also a seafood market, trusts its fish enough to serve it simply. Seating is communal (long picnic tables), and in the heat of summer the ceiling fans hardly cool the large dining room, but you're here for the seafood—not the conversation—and at lunch the oysters will make you forget about these minor problems. Steamed or raw, they'll cost you a paltry $2 for a half dozen (they are served at dinner, too, but not this cheap). A printed warning on the menu warns that your dinner could "take a little longer than you are used to"—it often does—so take this opportunity to work your way down the lengthy beer list.

Best barbecue: Bullock's Barbecue *(3330 Wortham, Durham, 919/ 383–3211)* doesn't serve appetizers—that would only be a distraction. The people who line up at the front door nightly (often as far as the parking lot) are hungry, and Bullock's sees no reason to prolong their suffering. The menu is huge, but it basically boils down to three things— barbecue, fried chicken, and Brunswick stew (traditionally a one-pot hunter's meal of game, often squirrel—at Bullock's it's pork). The all-you-can-eat, family-style dinner includes this trifecta plus hush puppies and coleslaw for $7.50. Family-style dining is an all-or-nothing proposition. The whole table must order it, presumably so as not to tempt the would-be grazer. Despite the oddly '80s pastel decor, there's a distinctly Southern, multigenerational family feel to the place. Waitress to a packed table of Duke law students: "Finish this up, shug, so I can get you some more."

Raleigh

Best faux diner: The **Vertigo Diner** *(426 McDowell St., Raleigh, 919/832–4477)* mixes nouvelle cooking with retro diner decor, and the result is a sincere down-home mix. Menu favorites include house-made shrimp and salmon ravioli; coriander-crusted rare tuna on greens and shaved fennel; and smoked pork loin with a tart sauté of cabbage and apples. This downtown space was a classic coffee shop in its previous life (down to the series of U-shaped Formica counters with low chrome-and-vinyl stools); when the new owners moved in, almost all they had to do was dim the lights and tack up the new drink specials.

Best Vietnamese summer roll: Located in the suburban sprawl of North Raleigh, **Far East** *(Brentwood Square Shopping Center, Raleigh, 919/872–7489)* is one of the Triangle's few great Asian dining experiences. Nearly all of the diners are Vietnamese, and many come from as far away as Greensboro and Richmond. Husband-and-wife team Hung and Mia run the show in the kitchen and they are happy to advise unfamiliar diners. On weekends, the small storefront dining room fills up early (there is usually a line by 11:00 A.M.) and most tables enjoy morning coffee and appetizers before moving on to the special weekend dishes, like whole fried "salty fish" with lemongrass and Near East pancake, a tender, perplexingly yellow crêpe filled with fresh shrimp and bean sprouts. Most dishes are served with a stack of fresh greens, including Vietnamese cilantro, Thai basil, and mint.

Best rectangular burger: The **Char-Grill's** *(618 Hillsborough St., Raleigh, 919/821–7636)* look is so meta–burger stand (huge plate-glass windows, boxy silver roof) that its almost surprising to find that it's actually a thriving business, not a project of a '50s Architecture Preservation Society. From the order window, you can see your burger (officially called a "hamburger steak") pass through all stages of its creation. The only menu changes since 1959 have been the recent addition of a grilled chicken sandwich and a garden salad. Come for a messy, satisfying hamburger and a milk shake so thick that it hurts your face if you drink it with a straw.

shopping

records

Chapel Hill
Best new CDs: Until recently, **Schoolkids Records** had always been the hip record (now CD—the only vinyl here is the seven-inch variety) store in Chapel Hill; it was certainly the oldest independently owned shop of its kind in the Triangle. Situated in an ancient building in the cen-

ter of town and famous for its surly staff (pop-punk locals Small wrote a song about "the nasty little chick down at the record store") but impeccable taste, it seemed like the end of an era when the neon sign for **Monster Records** *(118 E. Franklin St., Chapel Hill, 919/929–7766)* went up in the old Schoolkids window. But it appears that Monster is committed to providing the kind of smartly stocked shelves that Schoolkids was once famous for; and it possibly has a kinder, gentler staff.

Runner-up: The **Record Exchange** *(128-C E. Franklin St., Chapel Hill, 919/933–6261)*, located a block away, has fanzines and a wide selection of used discs to complement a tasteful-but-slim new selection.

Best jazz on vinyl: Roots *(118-A E. Main St., Carrboro, 919/969–8827)* is a recent entry into the overcrowded Triangle music market, but the location (downtown in quickly growing Carrboro) and focus (jazz, folk, blues—what the name implies) set this store apart from the CDs-and-a-few-seven-inches crowd. Owner Gerry Williams left his business of 18 years, Orpheus Records in D.C.'s Georgetown, for a change of scenery, and ended up filling a niche. He carries what he likes (what he describes as "everything from Sebadoh to the Carter Family"), and what he likes is mostly jazz. Jazz on vinyl is hard to find around here, and the used section at Roots usually spans everything from Ellington to Archie Shepp to completely obscure '70s free jazz.

Best used new wave vinyl: Owner Barry Blanchette reckons that his used vinyl sells so well because many music-loving folks, in the mid-to-late-80's rush to go digital, missed out on great albums by bands like Christmas and the Close Lobsters, and now they want to make up for lost time. **Nice Price Books** *(100 Boyd St., Carrboro, 919/929–6222; 3106 Hillsborough St., Raleigh, 919/829–0230; 3415 Hillsborough Rd., Durham, 919/383–0119)* is certainly the place to do it. Of course, it sells books, too. The interesting if haphazard array of used fiction can yield some cheap gems, and the labyrinthine back room is packed with used paperback mystery and romance—but thumbing through the records will keep you busy for hours. New wave rules here; it's as though a good college radio station unloaded their entire library straight into the bins.

Durham
Best indie labels: When **Poindexter Records** *(718 Ninth St., Durham, 919/286–1852)* opened in 1985, teenage New-Wavers rejoiced at the existence of an independent record store in Durham; there were none, though Chapel Hill and Raleigh had both been home to Schoolkids for

years. Owner Jack Campbell had previously managed a Schoolkids, and in the 11 years since, Poindexter's has carved a unique niche in the now-happening stretch of Ninth Street. It's worth stopping by for Poindexter's out-there jazz selection and fanzine-dream indie-rock stock. The staff is more laid back than anywhere else in the Triangle, and probably won't ridicule you for asking whether the Blue Humans can be found in Jazz or Rock.

books

Chapel Hill

Best afternoon in a bookstore: In the **Bookshop** *(400 W. Franklin St., Chapel Hill, 919/942–5178)*, tight alcoves of floor-to-ceiling used books radiate from a central aisle stretching back as far as you can see into the dim-yet-cozy store. The fiction is the best used selection in town, and includes beautiful (reasonably priced) first editions by contemporary authors like Nicholson Baker, V.S. Naipaul, and Duke professor Ariel Dorfman, as well as perennials like Graham Greene and Nabokov.

Runners-up: If you don't have bookstore burnout, the **Avid Reader** *(462 W. Franklin St., Chapel Hill, 919/933–9585)*, just down the street, has fewer titles and slightly more collector-oriented prices, but is worth a look. The lefty in you will want to cross Franklin for **Internationalist Books** *(405 Franklin St., Chapel Hill, 919/942–1740)*, a Chapel Hill institution that carries mostly political reads, as well as Che Guevera T-shirts.

Best comic books: With superheroes regularly gracing the big screen these days, it may have been a while since you've seen your favorite freaks in print. Whether you're a hard-core *X-Men* collector or looking for the latest Chris Ware book from Fantagraphics, the best place to geek out in the Triangle is the **Second Foundation Bookstore** *(136 E. Rosemary St., Chapel Hill, 919/967–4439)*. Though the comics-and-cards industry has gone mall, this 15-year-old store has a browsing, friendly bookstore feel—not everything's under glass.

Durham

Best cheap back issues of *Granta*: Bookstores in college towns are about as common as Phish T-shirts, but the venerable **Book Exchange** *(105–109 W. Chapel Hill St., Durham, 919/682–4562)* stands apart. Housed in a hulking brick building at the Five Points intersection of downtown Durham, it quietly goes about its business (as it has since 1933) in quite an unusual way. Most of the three stories of floor-to-ceiling books are organized not by author, title, or subject, but by publisher. The Book Exchange makes an effort to amass complete catalogues of the publishers they stock, including defunct houses. Random browsing may seem intimidating, but if prompted, employees practically insist upon guiding you through the stacks, casually pointing out the treasure-filled shelves (many hand-built by the original owner, the late Mr. Marley, who once shaved a very drunk William Faulkner on a U.N.C. lawn) that haven't been touched or repriced in years. It's not unusual to find a 1975 copy of *A Confederacy of Dunces* at its original price next to a current, $25 edition.

clothes

Chapel Hill

Best bowling shirts: Vintage clothing stores are often packed with beautiful gabardine shirts and Jackie O. dresses that only Jackie O. could afford. **Time After Time** *(414 W. Franklin St., Chapel Hill, 919/942–2304)* carries such things, as well as rackfuls of cords, varsity jackets, and stuff you can't believe anyone wore once. But the prices are more Salvation Army than New York's Antique Boutique, which means you can stock up on tacky clothes for cheap. Turnover is good—those purple flares you're looking for may come in next week.

Durham

Best old winter jackets: PTA thrift shops are scattered throughout the Triangle, but always seem to have just been picked over by a crowd of youths sharing your tastes in everything. **Thrift World** *(3205 Chapel Hill Rd., Durham, 919/490–1556)* occupies an old supermarket space, which gives you some idea of the volume. The housewares and furniture are more misses than hits, but the racks of somebody's outgrown wardrobe usually hold a few items to fit you, whether it's that brown wide-wale corduroy sailor's coat for next winter, a classic London Fog James Dean number, or a worn-out red T-shirt commemorating N.C. State's 1983 NCAA basketball championship.

Raleigh

Best shopping-as-lifestyle: At **Beanie + Cecil** *(Cameron Village, 412 Daniels St., Raleigh, 919/821–5455)*, a bloodless sorority girl shops for something funky with her mother ("$175 for terrycloth?") while the young blonde shopkeeper concentrates on striking the right balance of chilly and aloof. She stocks Kate Spade, Cynthia Rowley, Calvin Klein (CK), Isaac Mizrahi (ISAAC), and Comme des Garçons (the scent), making her shop the closest thing to Barneys in the Triangle. For a slightly more pro-letarian, but less plush, experience, try **Uniquities** *(Cameron Village, 150 Daniels St., Raleigh, 919/832–1234; also at 452 W. Franklin St., Chapel Hill, 919/933–4007)*, where a bargain-minded shopper can find sale-priced Elizabeth Wayman or Nicole Miller and miles of Pucci knockoffs.

et cetera

Chapel Hill

Best balms: The only **Burt's Bees** *(Carr Mill Mall, Carrboro, 919/510–8720)* store carries the full line of Bert's skin care goodies at about 30 percent cheaper than you could find them at your local health-food store. A less contrived Body Shop, Burt's Bees was founded in Maine and is now based in Raleigh. Products include Farmer's Friend Hand Salve, Lemongrass Insect Lotion, and the ever-popular Burt's Beeswax Lip Balm.

Best useless gems: Twenty minutes south of Chapel Hill is the arty-yet-staid town of Pittsboro, where locals enjoy good antiques shopping and a surfeit of local craftmakers. **Beggars and Choosers** *(38 Hillsborough St., Pittsboro, 919/542–5884)* has three floors of furniture, clothes, and tchotchkes, lovingly curated. There's usually enough to go around, even for the inept shopper. So lovingly that she almost always refuses to haggle—prices are firm, but generally fair.

Runner-up: Two doors up the street from Beggars and Choosers is **52 Hillsborough** *(52 Hillsborough St., Pittsboro, 919/542–0789)* a small multidealer store that makes up for mainly useless furnishings and bric-a-brac with a small but gem-filled book collection.

Raleigh

Best mod plastic furniture: Park Place Antiques *(135 E. Martin St., Raleigh, 919/821–5880)* has taken over nearly a block's worth of real estate in an up-and-coming section of downtown Raleigh and filled the old building with stuff ranging from pricey antiques with a capital A to plain old useless hand-me-downs. Downstairs you'll find room after room of random but cool junk like metal plant stands and Russell Wright dinnerware, sold by different dealers, at uniformly reasonable prices. Upstairs, however, the '50s and '60s are in full force: Entire Formica dining-room sets, wacky lamps, and kidney-shaped coffee tables will make you wish you'd brought a bigger car. This stuff is priced toward the collector, but it's quite cheap compared to what you'd pay for similar mod gear in a big city.

Best leather 'n' latex one-stop shopping: Innovations *(517 Hillsborogh St., Raleigh, 919/833–4833)* is three tasteful fetish shops under one roof, catering to today's polymorhpous perverse Southern-fried rockers ... and housefraus. The mastermind behind this swanky emporium owned a store in Boston for 11 years before setting up shop in the Triangle. Innovations sells custom-made leather and jewelry (earrings, navel rings, jackets, chaps). A separate business inside the store, **Piercing by David** is proud to have offered body alterations when piercing was a fetish, not a fad. David's card lists a phone number for emergencies. Through a separate entrance in back is **GUMMI**, an upscale latex boutique, where a corset will run you $325. Your choice of latex lubricant or talc is provided in the dressing room.

body alterations

Chapel Hill

Best tattoos: Choice Peach *(304-E West Weaver St., Carrboro, 919/932–9888)* takes the idea of custom tattoos seriously. One customer was given five consultations before the big day. Total cost: $40. Billed as North Carolina's only all-custom-tattoo parlor, Choice Peach may also be North Carolina's only codependent tattoo parlor, catering to those who know they like tattoos but don't know of what. There are no prefab designs: Either bring one with you or the inker/owner will work one out for you. All work is done by appointment; however, browsing is possible.

Raleigh

Best hair salon: Cherry Bomb *(127 Newbern Place, Raleigh, 919/ 755–0555)* is hidden in a graceful historic brownstone near the statehouse in Raleigh, orginally built in 1917 as lodgings for state legislators. A combined hair salon and art gallery, Cherry Bomb puts on about 15 shows a year (usually by locals), while offering $28 cuts for the Triangle's finickiest hipsters. The art is hat installations, iron works, and handmade books; the cuts range from simple trims to as far out as you want.

hotel/motel

Chapel Hill

Best motel if you're on the lam: The **Tar Heel Motel** *(1312 N. Fordham Blvd., Chapel Hill, 919/929–3090)* is a long, low, brick, all-the-rooms-have-a-view-of-the-highway kind of place that makes you feel like you're meeting someone else's wife in a B movie. It's fairly cheap (around $46 per room).

Raleigh
Best hotel for a drink: The cylindrical **State Capital Holiday Inn** *(320 Hillsborough St., Raleigh, 919/932–0501)* is visible from pretty much anywhere in Raleigh proper, yet impossible to use as a landmark when you're lost, as it looks the same from all sides. It varies from your basic Holiday Inn in a couple of ways: because the hotel (built in '63) is round, the rooms are shaped like slices of pie, and there's a cheesy lounge on top called the Top of the Tower, with the best drinking-view of Raleigh. It only rotates if you sit in the bar long enough, according to the manager. Centrally located but not especially cheap: $69 for the cheapest double, and rates go up from there during peak seasons (graduation week, etc.).

local wonders

Chapel Hill
Best chainsaw-wielding folk artist: **Clyde Jones**'s work graces several local establishments (a few sculptures in and around Crook's Corner Restaurant, a painting in Wellspring Grocery), and local voodoo-rockers Southern Culture on the Skids have enshrined him in song, but to know the world of Clyde Jones you must go there. Take Highway 15-501 South to the tiny, Jones-centric town of Bynum (6 miles south of Chapel Hill), where this celebrated artist lives among his "critters"—animals made with Clyde's chainsaw from raw lumber and recycled junk. You can walk unharmed through his yard, among floundering sharks, 20-foot-tall giraffes, and multiheaded reindeer. His house is muralized on all sides and hung with weather-beaten but vibrant paintings and photos of Jones with his young fans. Jones's work is not for sale, but he might instruct you on the finer points of constructing a giant penguin.

Durham
Best lo-fi drive-in: The **Starlite Drive-In** *(2523 E. Club Blvd., Durham, 919/688–1037)* sign looks a lot like you would imagine it would, and its towering pink neon letters welcome you with a loud hum and occasional crackling noises. Movie fare is of the big-budget-but-bad variety, but if you're bored at least you can watch the stars. If the attendants in the snack bar seem a bit paranoid, it might have something to do with the gun shop that is also housed there (or the concealed-

weapons licensing courses they sponsor). The speaker you attach to your window may be original (it sounds 40 years old), but on weeknights you will have your choice of parking spot if privacy is a consideration.

transmissions

Best stations to hear Minxus follow Mingus: It's hard to imagine the state of the music scene around here if UNC's **WXYC (89.3 FM)** and Duke's **WXDU (88.7 FM)** hadn't been blowing out the left side of the dial for the last 15 or 20 years. Where else would high-school kids sick of the Allmans and Floyd have heard the Jam, Black Flag, the Replacements, or the Minutemen? Both stations trumpeted local music long before everyone's cousin had a seven-inch in the stores, and the bands give back with regular benefits. Both are eclectic and enjoyably obscure. But where WXDU is (basically) indie rock slanted during the day, with great jazz from 5 to 8 P.M. weeknights, and features even more block programming on weekends (country, women's music, etc.), WXYC is basically free-form, so you're more likely to be jarred by some sort of be bop/indie pop/techno/tabla-music combo while cruising around with the radio on. WXYC recently broke broadcast ground when they became the first radio station anywhere in the world to simulcast their signal over the Internet, so now you can hear the new Spatula single in Singapore.

chicago

by Cara Jepsen

"Though there's no doubt that 'Chicago as the next Seattle' is nothing more than a media construct, there is a lot of great music here." — **Chris Holmes,** *Yum-Yum*

Chicago will always have to answer for foisting the Cryin' Shames, Styx, Survivor, and Chicago on the rest of the world. In the anonymous *Blues Brothers* days before Chicago gained a dubious reputation in *Billboard* as the "next Seattle," it was always better to say you were from Chicago than to actually live here. To cite one reason: In 1979, drive-time shock jock Steve Dahl sponsored a "Disco Demolition" during a White Sox doubleheader. Spurred on by the sight of burning disco albums in the outfield, beery fans went berserk, leaving the field too damaged for baseball. Adding insult to injury, in those days Chicago hadn't yet learned how to rock hard—an ironic state in a city known for innovation in other kinds of music.

From the amplified blues of Muddy Waters, Howlin' Wolf, and Buddy Guy to the '60s South Side experimental jazz collective that brought the world Henry Threadgill, Fred Anderson, Anthony Braxton, and Joseph Jarmon, Chicago has had a heavy tradition of pushing boundaries. If the Second City helped kill disco, it also repaid the world with house music. At clubs like the Warehouse, DJ Frankie Knuckles and a fabulous gay black underground gave new meaning to dance fever with an unheard of 100 thumping-and-pounding beats per minute. And by the mid-'80s things had changed for the better on many fronts: The Bulls drafted Michael Jordan in 1986, the same year that Northwestern graduate Steve Albini put out Big Black's definitive buzz-saw-guitar-and-drum-machine album *Atomizer*.

More traditional punk bands like Naked Raygun and less traditional synth wall-of-sound machines like Al Jourgensen's Ministry played their own versions of merciless, hard-edged assault music for jackbooted punks. At gigs, slammers circled around a scary mass of bodies in the middle of the pit called skinhead island. Labels like Touch and Go (for punks) and Wax Trax! (for industrial and dance) were putting out great bands like Butthole Surfers, Big Black, Urge Overkill, and Front 242, and a few stellar record shops, like the old Lincoln Park storefront of Wax Trax!, served as focal points for a small scene where everybody knew everybody. By the time one-half of Texas's Scratch Acid had relocated to Chicago to form the Jesus Lizard, local glamour boys Urge Overkill were perfecting their arena-rawk-star schtick at gigs in clubs like the Cubby Bear. Liz Phair recorded her *Exile in Guyville* album at producer Brad Wood's now famous Idful Studio. Meanwhile, a renaissance in underground comix found its home here, with heavyweights like *Eightball*'s Dan Clowes (since decamped to Berkeley) and the enigmatic Chris Ware. Suddenly, everybody wanted to be in Chicago, and *Billboard* published its "next Seattle" article.

In the wake of a subsequent major-label feeding frenzy, more bands, famous and otherwise, have relocated here, including the Mekons, Poi Dog Pondering, and Syd Straw. And Chicago's scenesters uphold their reputation as a particularly bitchy and factional group. The minute Urge Overkill got big, a bike messenger began methodically to stalk Blackie O, Nash, and King at their favorite night haunts, documenting the project in her own—admittedly hilarious in its strange obsessiveness—anti-Urge fanzine, *The Stalker*. Even though the locals may pull together for benefits to help a favorite club like **Lounge Ax** in a legal battle, if Veruca Salt's new record races up the charts, everyone badmouths the band behind its back for not paying dues. Just ask Billy Corgan. If Chicago was once so out of it it may as well have been in Nebraska, the secret's out now.

lay of the land

Chicago is flanked on the east by Lake Michigan and on the west by a vast sprawl of faceless suburbs where local Waynes and Garths have developed their own ingrown scenes. The lake's shoreline runs almost the entire length of the city, and from Lake Shore Drive you can catch views of some of the city's stunning architecture on Michigan Avenue. The heart of Chicago's deserted-at-night downtown is called the **Loop**, after a circle of elevated train tracks; the nearby Sears Tower was for a while the tallest building in the world. The Chicago River separates the Loop from Michigan Avenue's swank retail mile. Downtown also includes areas to the west and north of the bending river; **River North** has a lot of trendy restaurants (including Michael Jordan's) and galleries.

Legendary for its failed public-housing experiments and the electric blues spawned in 43rd Street clubs like the Checkerboard Lounge, Chicago's **South Side** is also home to well-groomed middle-class neighborhoods like Kenwood, where Louis Farrakhan lives, and **Hyde Park**, a leafy university neighborhood near the University of Chicago that has a few good bookstores and bars.

The heart of Chicago's bar and club scene, however, is on the **North Side**. Over the past decade, the city's underground center has moved from the North Side's Lake View and Wrigleyville (still home of important clubs like the **Metro** and many collegiate reggae party clubs) to Polish and Latin **Wicker Park**, where it's slowly spreading west and south, following the cheap rent. In the Wicker Park heyday, cartoonists Gary Leib, Terry Laban, Archer Prewitt, and Dan Clowes used to get together Thursday nights at the coffeehouse Earwax (see Dining) to draw free-form comics. The locus of WP is the intersection of **Milwaukee** (an old Native American trading route), **Damen**, and **North** avenues; and the area's coffee shops, bars, and theater and music venues continue to attract the unwashed, pierced lumpen hardcores. The focus of '70s counterculture, **Lake View** is still hugely popular and has some worthwhile hangouts, including coffee shops and premier blues bars on Halsted and Lincoln avenues—though, residentially, it has been overrun by milk-fed Big-10 graduates on the fast track to urban professionalism. To the south and east on Clark Street, **Boy's Town**, the city's latest gay area, has its own thriving cafe scene.

getting from a to b

There are two important things to remember when getting around Chicago: The first is that Lake Michigan is always to the east; the second is the phone number of the Regional Transportation Authority's Travel Information Center: 312/836–7000. The center operates almost around the clock (4:45 A.M. to 1:15 A.M.) and its representatives know exactly how to get from here to there using mass transit. The city has an excellent bus and elevated train system (most lines run all night and trips cost $1.50 plus 30 cents for a transfer), and CTA maps are supposedly available at all stations, but the maps can be hard to come by. Cabs are easy to flag downtown, though you might have a tough time further out. Try Yellow *(312/TAXI–CAB)* in a pinch.

Chicago is eminently more drivable than cities like Boston and New York. Street parking is not unheard of, even downtown. But a word to the wise: Drivers here tend to be slow but reckless—a lethal combination—so drive defensively. Cyclists have a friend in City Hall (Mayor Daley, that is): There are sturdy racks located throughout the city.

The streets themselves are laid out in an easy-to-understand grid pattern. Point zero is downtown at Madison and State streets. Everything west of State has a "West" in the address; everything north of Madison has a "North" in the address (the same goes for east and south). For example, 1600 N. Lake Shore Drive is 16 blocks north of Madison. It's worthwhile to purchase a map, since most list block numbers as well as street names. If, however, you're going somewhere by car and get lost, pull over and call WGN radio's 24-hour Traffic Help Line (312/527–1522). It's staffed by people who know how to get you out of a jam quickly.

sources

The first place to look to find out what's going on is *The Reader*, the city's oldest and fattest free arts weekly (it's also the one that spawned the *Readers* you'll find in other towns). *The Reader* has the most extensive music listings and personal ads (the "None of the Above" category is particularly worth a look), as well as reviews of bands, plays, art exhibits, and films. It hits the stores Thursday evenings. Beware, though: Shows chosen as "Critics' Choices" tend to sell out.

The scrappy *NewCity* tabloid, the city's other alternative weekly, hits the stands Wednesday and can give you a leg up on what's happening. While listings aren't as extensive as the *Reader*'s, its writers do a better job of covering garage and metal.

Windy City Times, which comes out Thursdays, is the primary gay weekly publication, but the weekly booklet *Nightlines* also has extensive listings, particularly for lesbian-oriented activities.

The two major dailies are relatively mainstream. The working-class *Sun-Times* devotes more space to cultural events, but *Tribune* rock critic Greg Kot's reviews and stories tend to be in-depth and right on the money. Both papers have Friday sections that list upcoming events, but the alternative weeklies' listings are better.

Online, *The Reader* has a big Web site (www.chireader.com) with help wanted ads, a hefty chunk of the paper's music section, and a link into apartment listings—meaning you can get a date and place to crash before setting foot in the city. The *Tribune* Web site (www.chicago.tribune.com) includes a neighborhood-by-neighborhood guide to shops, restaurants, museums, and beaches. *NewCity*'s features and listings—including Extra Raw, a daily local music update—are at www.newcitynet.com.

clubs

Best rock club: "Reservoir Dog" Tim Roth has visited, and Counting Crow Adam Duritz was standing on the sidewalk outside when a drunk driver almost ran him down...but if **The Empty Bottle** *(1035 N. Western Ave., 773/276–3600)* is home to anyone, it's the up-and-coming bands who hang out, gig, and, often, work behind the bar here. The five-year-old L-shaped club is also schmooze central for local unhygienic rock journalists and their prey. What attracts them all is the Bottle's cheap drinks and great booking: The club pulls such acts as the Flaming Lips, the New Bomb Turks, Kim Salmon and the Surrealists, and the Grifters—who, by the way, played 1996's Empty Bottle Prom as a '70s cover band called the Pump Action Retards. Rawk bands play most nights, though Wednesdays are known for some of the best jazz programming in town. Sunday is dub DJ night, another local scenester extravaganza, where members of post-rock bands as Tortoise and Rome work the cross fade. There are couches to lounge on, a separate room for pool and pinball, three resident cats, and **Bite**, an inexpensive restaurant next door that stays open late. No wonder it's hard to even get to the bar on weekends, thanks to gill-to-gill crowds of zine producers in soccer T-shirts.

Best club night: "If there are any freaks in town, they show up for gay night," says one satisfied Crobar regular. Sure enough, Sunday's GLEE (Gays, Lesbians, Everyone's Equal) Club Nights at **Crobar** *(1543 N. Kingsbury St., 312/413–7000)* bring out ravers in three-stripe Adidas and nylon, club kids with ski goggles and fairy wands, not-to-be-touched drag queens, and even Bulls rebounder-cum-pogoer Dennis Rodman shooting the shit with his equally freaky pals. Apart from the circus, the real attraction of this industrial-style club is the music. For years, long-time Chicago DJs Ralphi Rosario, Teri Bristol, and Earl Pleasure have spun tribal house from the booth located high above the center of the dance floor. Just don't come on the wrong night, or you'll end up in the middle of white-faced Goth kids (Thursdays), an industrial dance party (Wednesdays), or, worst of all, amateur night (Fridays and Saturdays).

Best gay disco: The relatively new **Rhumba** *(3631 N. Halsted Ave., 773/975–6622)* is a semi-fancy Brazilian restaurant when the night is young. But after dinner on weekend nights the tables and chairs disappear and the space turns into **Fusion**, a gay dance club much like Vortex, the club that anchored the site for six years before the owners decided to try the Brazilian restaurant thing. Like its predecessor, Fusion features hotshot DJs spinning the most current club music and guest appearances by jocks like Carlos Petruz and Buc. Unfortunately, Vortex's famed foam parties (imagine how little clubgoers might wear when given the chance to dance knee-deep in foam) are a thing of the past. Fusion is open till 4 A.M. on Fridays, 5 A.M. on Sundays.

Best coffeehouse club: Matching La-Z-Boy recliners and a wood-burning stove dominate the main room of **Uncommon Ground** *(1214 W. Grace St., 773/929–3680)*, a colorful, comfortable coffeehouse where folk, rock, and funk acts hit the stage and play to a packed house on weekends. Indeed, several of the more popular live acts made it onto an *Uncommon Ground* CD sampler, including Jeff Buckley, who performed at the joint before he made it big and the coffeehouse itself physically expanded. The food—veggie sandwiches, apple cornmeal pancakes, gazpacho—is still as comforting as ever. And the coffee's good too.

Best jazz jams: The South Side's **New Apartment Lounge** *(504 E. 75th St., 773/483–7728)* looks like the cocktail lounge connected to a '70s disco—mirrored ceiling, mirrored walls, plenty of blue and Brady orange. But every Tuesday night for the past 15 years, aging sax master Von "Vonski" Freeman and his colleagues have turned a cubbyhole next to the door into a makeshift stage and kicked out some of the coolest jazz in town. Before you make the trip, take a minute to put on some decent clothes: The mostly African-American regulars dress up for the event, and the pasty U of C students who show up later look decidedly out of place. There's no cover, but bring some cash so you can order a few drinks to show your appreciation.

Best restored speakeasy: Al Jolson, Eddie Cantor, and Sophie Tucker all headlined shows at **The Green Mill Jazz Club** *(4802 N. Broadway Ave., 773/665–8400)* in the early part of the century. But the dark, smoky landmark in multiracial Uptown is perhaps best known as one of Al Capone's favorite hangouts. During the '20s, Capone henchman "Machine-gun" Jack McGurn gained 25 percent ownership in the club after "convincing" singer Joe E. Lewis—by cutting his tongue (see the Sinatra flick, *The Joker Is Wild*)—to keep his act at the Mill. That, and Prohibition, brought in Al Capone and his cronies; they'd sit at a booth where they could keep an eye on both doors and myth has it they had hidden escape doors leading to a tunnel in the basement. Things are bit a mellower today, though the city's most famous nightclub has lately had enough with-it entertainment going on to get by without the nostalgia. Marc Smith's Sunday night Uptown Poetry Slam is a loud performance art Gong Show where performers tend to reveal too much about themselves (personally, sexually) and are either applauded or harassed and booed off stage. Music varies by the night, with each act bringing in a different crowd.

Best blues club: Most white-shirted tourists flock to well-known North Side clubs to hear the music that made Chicago famous. But the locals (and the occasional visiting foreign dignitary—Czech Republic President Vaclav Havel made it his first stop in a 1994 visit to Chicago) know that **Rosa's Lounge** *(3420 W. Armitage Ave., 773/342–0452)* is worth a trip to Logan Square, a neighborhood where young artists and musicians are moving in on a previously poor white and Latino stronghold. Tony Manguillo, a former drummer in Junior Wells's band, has owned the club with the tiny stage and long bar since 1985, shortly after he followed the band to Chicago from his native Italy. The club is definitely a family affair: Manguillo's mother, Rosa, works behind the bar, and Manguillo, who does all the booking, gets behind the drum kit Monday and Thursday nights. Regular acts include old-school local Lurrie Bell, Sugar Blue, and—you guessed it—Junior Wells.

Runner-up: For bigger blues acts, hit the **Checkerboard Lounge** *(423 E. 43rd St., 773/624–3240)* on the South Side, where the audience is mostly black and locals often sit in on jam sessions. What's not to like at a club where a fading sign on the wall warns band members who smoke or drink that their pay will be docked?

Best rising bands: When it opened in the mid '80s, **Metro** *(3730 N. Clark St., 773/235–0605)* was one of the few places that booked up-and-coming rock bands for all-ages shows. Nirvana played the comfortable, ornate bilevel theater before making it big, and over the years it's also been a home away from home to the Dead Kennedys, Sonic Youth, Smashing Pumpkins, the Pixies, PJ Harvey, and Ween. More recently, acts like Beck, Sick of It All, and Meat Beat Manifesto have hit the Metro's stage. Late shows at the club feature lesser-known artists and tend to go on very, verrry late. Three or four little-known, often local bands play 18-and-over shows regularly on Wednesday nights. Between bands, drinking age patrons can visit **Smart Bar** *(773/549–4140)*, the recently remodeled dance club downstairs.

Best all-ages hangout: Chicago's home stage for punk bands who would otherwise be stuck in their parents' garage, the **Fireside Bowl**

(2646 W. Fullerton Ave., 773/486–2700) has become so popular that it now avoids publicity. The bookers still have their ears to the ground, landing legit draws like Bikini Kill, MDC, and Huggy Bear as well as tomorrow's big acts. Fireside is an operational and decrepit bowling alley that looks like it saw its best days in the '50s. Sightlines suck and the vibe is a bit like a punk-rock sock hop, but shows are all-ages and usually just $5. If you're over 21, you can drink at the adjacent bar; if not, there's always bowling. Shows often start at 7:30 P.M.

Best dance club (for everybody): Since it opened in 1983, **Berlin** *(954 W. Belmont Ave., 773/348–4975)* has been known for its DJs and constantly changing themes and decor; the club is more cabaret than anything else, with huge murals, distressed walls, and chandeliers. You never know what you'll encounter on a given night. Tuesdays and Thursdays are generally boys' nights, and the girly Women's Obsessions nights (featuring female go-go dancers) happen the first and third Wednesdays of the month. There's New Wave night, Danceteria night, and Disco Wednesdays. But two of the best draws are amateur drag night—a hilarious contest the first Sunday of each month—and The Artist Formerly Known As Prince night, held in conjunction with The Artist Formerly Known As Prince national fan club, which brings in the "nicest and most polite crowd" the club has ever seen, according to the owners. Berlin is near the Belmont El as well as a gaggle of late-night eateries; its cover is cheap ($2 to $3), and it stays open later than most bars (4 A.M. on weekdays, 5 on Saturdays).

Best reliable scene: There's nothing like a friend in hard times. Among the bands who've played the **Lounge Ax** *(2438 N. Lincoln Ave., 773/525–6620)*, co-owners Sue Miller and Julia Adams are known for playing by the rules and providing beer, a bed (there's a cot in the club's bowels), and a shoulder to cry on. And some great acts have passed through since 1987—Boss Hog, the Dirty Three, the Geraldine Fibbers, Reverend Horton Heat, Jonathan Richman. But a noise complaint from a denizen of the fast-gentrifying Lincoln Park neighborhood has recently brought the license of Miller and Adams's ragged, comfortable club into question, forcing the duo to begin hunting for a new venue. Their past niceness was rewarded by 1996's *Lounge Ax Defense and Relocation Compact Disc* (Touch and Go), a benefit compilation that featured unreleased tracks from Shellac, the Mekons, Sebadoh, and Guided by Voices. A series of benefit shows followed, giving the owners a nest egg for their upcoming move. Until then, though, you can catch Adams pouring drinks behind the bar, and Miller sneaking out of the club with her baby gear in tow (she and Jeff Tweedy of Wilco/Uncle Tupelo fame are proud parents of a son).

Best hip-hop: "If a place lasts more than two months, it's a surprise," notes one local scenester. The hip-hop scene is constantly in flux; most stuff happens on a weekly basis at different clubs. The best place to get a handle on what's happening any given day is **Gramaphone Records** (see Shopping), the city's primary dance-music record shop. The most consistent hip-hop event (i.e., it's lasted several months) happens Mondays at the **Elbow Room** *(2871 N. Lincoln Ave., 773/549-5549)*, a smoky, low-ceilinged basement club on the city's North Side that also books rockabilly and hard rock. Hosted by MCs Spo and Dirty M.F., Mondays are a combination of short performances by both large and small acts, and DJs including acid jazz king and Liquid Soul member Jesse de la Peña, who also coordinates the event.

Best dyke disco: The glitzy **Paris Dance** *(1122 W. Montrose Ave., 773/769-0602)* harks back to the reign of disco, when clubs were all about neon, airbrushed murals, mirrors, and DJ booths that overlooked the dance floor. Paris is updated a bit—the 12-year-old club has video monitors, and there's a pool table and coffee bar. But it is, essentially, a disco. For girls. Which, if you're lucky, means you'll be hit on in a very nonthreatening way. Depending on which night you come, you'll dance to salsa (Fridays), Motown (Thursdays), or something else (weekends). If you're in town for Pride Day in July, stop by and join the 7,000 people who fill the club's parking lot after the parade.

bars

Best rock bar: Delilah's *(2771 N. Lincoln Ave., 773/472-2771)* is the result of a makeover that turned Chicago's top smelly punk dive, Crash Palace, into a tasteful, intimate bar with paintings on the wall. (The Palace was the landmark bar where members of Urge Overkill got into a fistfight with a testy grrrl bike messenger who soon after launched the caustic anti-Urge fanzine *The Stalker*.) These days things are more sedate, with the occasional record release party packing the romantically lit room. Delilah's is known for its selection of whiskeys and DJs. Monday is punk-rock night, Wednesday is country and western, and Sunday is when you're most likely to spot a local rock star DJing—more often than not it's Urge's Blackie O (now that Jim Ellison is dead and Liz Phair is a mom).

The Psychotronic Film Society shows free films upstairs on Saturdays at 6 (themes include blaxploitation, Sinatra, and kung fu).

Best bar with DJ: At first glance the **Artful Dodger** *(1734 W. Wabansia Ave., 773/227–6859)* looks like a typical Chicago dive with its tin ceiling, long bar, and room in back. Enter that room, though, and you'll be treated to earsplitting music spun by a DJ (genre varies by night) and psychedelic murals activated by the black lights above. To really enjoy the back room though, you need to go to the bar and order either an Aqua Velva or a Purple Haze. The first is a pint-size tequila-based drink that has a green light stick in it, and the latter is a fruity vodka drink that glows purple. Once you have one of those in hand, everyone will stare at you and you'll either feel important, stupid, or paranoid. Ignore those feelings and dance, or have a go at the Pierce Brosnan/007 pinball machine. There's a DJ every night but Tuesday. Weekend jocks specialize in dance music—minus techno—and during the week you can hear everything from country, rock, jazz, and '70s funk to hip-hop, depending on who's spinning.

Best old Chicago bar: For a real taste of old-timey Chicago, the **Zebra Lounge** *(1220 N. State St., 312/642–5140)* has it all—a sing-along piano bar (after 9:30 P.M.), zebra-skin wallpaper, an older clientele, and bartenders named Dick and Peter. Sure, *Crime Story* got there ahead of you, but that show's long gone and no one watched it anyway. The Zebra's been around 60 years, and it'll certainly outlast the creepy Margarita Night barnyards nearby.

Best one-nighter: Normally a mixed bar with videos, the tiny **Closet** *(3325 N. Broadway Ave., 773/477–8533)* shifts gears once a month for Bang Yer Head Night, when DJ Chandra and bartender/"Hostess from Hell" Pate (a blonde, pierced presence-and-a-half) take over, dispensing Jell-O shots, White Castle sliders, toys, and temporary tattoos to a healthy mix of lesbians, gays, and straights. When patrons tire of the squirt gun fights and Russ Meyer videos, Pate lines 'em up for beer bongs. Or, in the summer, she pulls out a hose for an impromptu wet T-shirt contest. Meanwhile, Chandra works the tables with a choice selection of rock, metal, and the occasional alternatune. Call ahead to put the next Bang Yer Head Night on your calendar.

Best girl bar where boys are welcome: Just a stone's throw from Little Vietnam in ethnically diverse Uptown sits **Big Chick's** *(5024 N.*

Sheridan Rd., 773/728–5511), a beautifully designed bar that attracts a mixed crowd, from boy couples to women's softball teams to black, white, Pakistani, and Native American hetero locals stopping by for a cold one after work. Owner Michelle Fire's fine art collection—which includes works by Tony Fitzpatrick, Diane Arbus, and Jimmy Suddith—adorns the bar's pink walls, and her eclectic taste is also reflected in a jukebox that contains 45s from the Henry Mancini Orchestra, 6, Joan Jett, Salt-N-Pepa, AC/DC, and Rose Royce. There's a pool table, a small beer garden in back, and a second art-laden room where DJs spin on weekends. If you have an attitude, leave it in the car: This is a very unpretentious, friendly place. If you're low on funds, go on a summer Sunday afternoon, when Big Chick's holds a free barbecue in back.

Best jukebox: European polka hits, Leonard Cohen, the Jesus Lizard, Elmore James, Tav Falco, and Tricky share space on the CD jukebox at **Tumin's** *(2159 W. Chicago Ave., no phone)*. On weeknights the long, thin dive with the pool table in back is populated by longhairs and close-cropped, tattooed guys; many work as bike messengers by day, which perhaps explains why the place is also known as Bill's Alcohol Abuse Center. It's located in the Ukrainian Village, a low-rent area bordering Wicker Park.

Best punk dive: The walls of **Club Foot** *(1824 W. Augusta Blvd., 773/489–0379)* are covered with a veritable history of Chicago punk, stuff culled from the collections of longtime scenesters Chuck Uchida and Lauree Rohrig, owner of the bar. Hanging near the front door is a green satin jacket from O'Banion's Pub, the city's first punk bar, and the rest of the exhibit rolls out time-capsule evidence of just about every band that preceded Smashing Pumpkins. It's all easy to see, too, since it's off the beaten path, the bar is often empty. If that's not enough to pull you in, there are tons of old toys, live DJs every night (their taste usually veers toward old punk), a pool table, a collection of postcards from local penis sculptress Cynthia Plastercaster, and an excellent sound system.

food/coffee

Best 3 A.M. quesadillas: Mexican polkas play on the jukebox and the mood is upbeat at **El Chino** *(1505 N. Milwaukee Ave., 773/772–1905)* whatever the hour. The friendly waitresses speak limited English, but offer chips and salsa just for sitting down. Or, if you still have your stomach, there's Coronas with lime, plus passable versions of the usual Mexican fare—tostadas, burritos, and quesadillas. On weekends, the doors don't close until 4 A.M., which leaves plenty of time to enjoy the picture-window views of pierced drunkards stumbling toward their cars after the Wicker Park bars close. If you tire of nachos, you can grab some fries a block north at **Wicker Dog**, on the corner of North, Damen, and Milwaukee avenues.

Best macrobiotic plate: The food needs flavor, the waiflike service is slow, the seats are hard, yet the **Chicago Diner** *(3411 N. Halsted Ave., 773/935–6696)* has attracted the likes of Madonna, Boy George, Emo Phillips, Indigo Girls, Emilio Estevez, and Def Leppard. Why? Because this small North Side diner has long been one of the few places in this town of butchers and meat packing that caters to vegan, macrobiotic, and other special diets. The buckwheat pancakes and mac plate are tops, but the best deal is the hearty scrambled tofu deluxe with cornbread—just make sure you order a side of salsa with it (for flavor).

Best diner grub: The **Diner Grill** *(1635 W. Irving Park Rd., 773/248–2030)* was once a favorite haunt of North Side bohemians. But times changed. Rents went up, the kids moved south to Wicker Park (or "the East Village"), and the Diner Grill went back to being what it was— a 13-stool, old-school diner with cheap grub and salty regulars. Created in 1937 when two trolleys were welded together to form a modest, box-like structure, the place has been in the same family for about 40 years. You'll still see the occasional aging rocker ambling in for a late-night omelette (the grill's 24-hour day is convenient that way). The real draw is the show put on by the three DIY grillman/cashier/waiter/raconteurs who run the joint; they're quick with the comebacks and always have a story to tell. Two 25-cent-per-song mini-jukeboxes on the counter have everything from George Jones to K.C. All that, plus you can try your luck at Illinois' Lotto game.

Best South Indian vegetarian: It's a bit off the beaten path, located up north on Devon Avenue in the middle of Chicago's Indian community, but the spicy South Indian cuisine at the all-veggie **Udupi Palace** *(2543 W. Devon Ave., 773/338–2152)* is definitely worth the trip. The noisy restaurant is almost always crowded with Indian families eating expertly cooked giant (bigger than your head and neck combined) paper masala *dosai* crepes and traditional items like *samosas*, *poori*, and vegetable *biryani*. The service is solicitous, the food inexpensive, and there's no corkage fee.

Best breakfast: The hearty comfort food is what has brought Liz Phair, Oprah Winfrey, Michael Jordan, Morton Downey Jr., Veruca Salt, and the Sex Pistols through the doors of **Wishbone** *(1001 W. Washington St., 312/850–2663)*. Breakfast favorites at this barnlike operation on the near West Side include inventive fusion dishes like corn cakes with red pepper sauce, and crab cakes with red eggs served with salsa and black beans. If that doesn't whet your appetite, try dinner, which features fried chicken, bean cakes, collard greens, mashed sweet potatoes, and sautéed spinach. The star-studded Wishbone sits just across the street from Oprah's Harpo Studios (coincidence?); for a more intimate meal, visit the original Wishbone at 1800 W. Grand Avenue *(312/829–3597)*.

Best fried chicken to go: The late Harold P. Pierce opened the first **Harold's Chicken Shack** in 1950 and once offered delivery service via a white Cadillac decorated in papier-mâché to look like a roaster. Today there are scores of the clean red-and-white franchises dotting the South Side (including an easily accessible one at 53rd St. and Woodlawn Avenue in Hyde Park). Servers take your order from behind a thick plate of bulletproof glass, and the goods are delivered through a revolving plastic tray. The chicken is excellent (it's from Pierce's original recipe and cooked to order), and the not-very-PC sign out front depicts a black man with a hatchet chasing a chicken. Though not shown on the sign, catfish, perch, and giblet (gizzard and liver) dinners are also served, and excellent sauces come on the side, including a kickin' extra hot. There's also a Harold's downtown, at 636 S. Wabash Avenue (773/362–0442), and another on the North Side at 4701 N. Sheridan Road (773/784–9299).

Best coffeehouse: The bulletin board in the front of Wicker Park's **Earwax** *(1564 N. Milwaukee Ave., 773/772–4019)* is papered with apartments to share, bass players needed, and yard sales not to be missed. The friendly but often slow staff serves up inexpensive but undistinguished greens, wheat burgers, and giant iced coffees. But Earwax's Indian tapestry tablecloths, circus decor, and large, comfortable booths make it a great place in which to read and watch the Wicker Park irregulars, most of whom appear to be in need of a shower—or Prozac. Upstairs, the cafe runs a popular, offbeat video, record, and magazine shop.

shopping

records

Best DJ store: Small-but-important **Gramaphone Records** *(2663 N. Clark St., 773/472–3683)* is Chicago's best source for dance, rap, and house music. Along with new and used vinyl (there's a vinyl listening station in back), Gramaphone carries custom tapes by local and national DJs such as Derrick Carter (prog-house), Terry Mullen (prog-house/trance), and Oscar McMillan (vocal/house).

Best used CDs: Chicago has a couple of **Reckless Records** stores, outlets of the London-based chain, with overwhelming stock that can be dangerous if you don't have a list of what you're looking for—it's too easy to make impulse buys when you run across that Orange Juice record you were looking for in 1992. A better place to start, for CDs at least, is the **Evil Clown** in Wrigleyville/Lake View *(3418 N. Halsted Ave., 773/472–4761)*, where you can listen to the Bongwater disc before committing. The Clown has new and used Gothic, ambient, trip-hop, industrial, and alternative rock, as well as blues, jazz, and soundtracks. It's a good place to find imports and small-label acts.

Best Goth and industrial: Faith and the Muse? Switchblade Symphony? Haujobb? Wumpscut? If these bad boys make you want to squeal like a pig, it's time to trip across Wrigleyville/Lake View to the aptly named **Armageddon** *(711 W. Belmont Ave., 773/244–0666)*, which deals only in Gothic and industrial. Its pale-faced, black-haired staff can tell you exactly where the Goth scene is going down that night.

Best hard-to-find records: You won't find top-40 hits at Wicker Park's **The Quaker Goes Deaf** *(1937 W. North Ave., 773/252–9334)*. This clean, comfortable shop is full of imports, indie records, and CDs that are truly obscure—so obscure, in fact, that most have explanatory tags. Take a release by Borbetomagus: "Two saxes and an electric guitar do battle for the throne of avant-noise/jazzdom." If that doesn't win you over, the store also has a CD-listening station. The Quaker also buys records and offers a search service.

Runners-up: Another good shop, a few miles north in Evanston, is **Vintage Vinyl Records** *(925 Davis St., Evanston, 847/328–2899)*, which specializes in rare and out-of-print mint-condition records and experimental import releases. For the widest selections of seven-inch records by Chicago bands, tiny **Blackout Records** *(3729 N. Southport Ave., 773/296–0744)* in Lake View wins hands down.

Best jazz and blues: For jazz, blues, R&B, and gospel on both CD and vinyl, the **Jazz Record Mart** downtown *(444 N. Wabash Ave., 312/222–1467)* has the largest selection in town. The jam-packed store has literally hundreds of thousands of records (even 78s!) and CDs, with selections ranging from the straight-ahead vintage jazz of Bix Beiderbecke to the latest Marsalis release, from Honey Boy Edwards to Magic Slim. The staff—musicians, DJs, and music freaks—is unpretentious and knowledgeable.

books

Best bookstore: Located in the basement of the beautiful, Gothic Chicago Theological Seminary on the University of Chicago campus, the **Seminary Cooperative Bookstore** *(5757 S. University Ave., 773/752–4381)* has more than 100,000 titles and boasts the largest selection of books on the humanities in the nation. Packed to its low rafters with books, books, books, it looks and feels like a place where university-style learning and the written word are still held sacred. And it really is a co-op: For a $30 share, members receive a lifetime discount of 10 percent. But you don't need to be a member to shop there or enjoy signings or readings by authors as un-Gothic as Sister Souljah and humorist Mark Leyner.

Runners-up: If specialty genres are what you're looking for, the Seminary co-op has a branch nearby called **57th Street Books** *(1301 E. 57th St., 773/684–1300)* that carries science fiction, cookbooks, and children's books. Also nearby is arguably the city's best selection of used books, at **Powell's Bookstore** *(1501 E. 57th St., 773/955–7780)*.

Best comix and zines: The underground-only **Quimby's Queer Store** *(1328 N. Damen Ave., 773/342–0910)* near Wicker Park carries thousands of zines, from 25-cent Xerox-and-staple jobs to ones about to make the jump to "real" magazine status like *Bust*, *Ben is Dead*, and *Cake*. They also carry small-press comics from Fantagraphics, Kitchen Sink, and others, as well as rare books dealing with tattooing, body piercing, underground film, and alternative sex, such as Head Press Magazine's *Critical Vision: Random Essays and Tracts Concerning Sex, Religion and Death* and *Torture Garden*, a collection of photos from the London Fetish Club. A hot hangout for forlorn-looking single men.

clothes

Best vintage: If you're looking for a '40s double-breasted tuxedo jacket or an authentic '20s gown, the place to go is **Flashy Trash** *(3524 N. Halsted Ave., 773/327–6900)*. The front of the store has the latest in poly T-shirts, plastic purses, neat watches, and skimpy dresses by designers like Todd Oldham, Star 69, Trip, Insane, and Jocko. In back you'll find timeless gems that date to the turn of the century. The sales staff is helpful without being cloying and will help you decide which long gloves, costume jewelry, or vintage shoes go with your new outfit.

Best rock boutique: Roseanne and her assistants once exited the **99th Floor** *(3406 N. Halsted Ave., 773/348–7781)* with four garbage bags full of merchandise. Airbrushed tour buses often pull up in front of this tiny Wrigleyville/Lake View rock boutique, so that glam rock stars can spree on the latest in high-end British men's and women's fashions—and we mean way beyond Nana, honey. Yeah, you'll pay for it, but at least it won't fall apart after the first wash.

Runner-up: **The Alley** *(858 W. Belmont Ave., 773/525–3180)* has lower-end merchandise, often American knockoffs of 99th Floor, but it's the best place in town for civilians to buy the sturdy leather jackets worn by Chicago's finest. New ones go for under $200, but it's worthwhile to shell out the extra $50 to get a used one that's been purchased from an honest-to-God cop. These have a cool patch on the shoulder, but more important, they're authentic. The Alley also carries novelty, parody, and rock T-shirts; platform Mary Janes and thigh-high boots (underground shoes being the shop's specialty); pants, skirts, and zip-front dresses in patent leather; hair dyes; and everything else you need to look like an angry young punk.

Best thrifting: Chicago's rapidly expanding local chain, **Village Discount Outlets**, has rack upon rack of clothes, dirty children's toys, cracked dishes, knobless appliances, and used mattresses. Skip the junk, go for the clothes. The easiest-to-get-to branch is at 2855 N. Halsted Avenue *(773/388–4772)*. If you have patience you can find wheat among the chaff, like a mint-condition white Austrian wool cape, circa 1966, or perfectly worn Levis flares for $3 to $6.

Best rave wear: Always a few important steps ahead of Urban Outfitters is **Aero/Untitled** *(2701 N. Clark St., 773/404–0650)*. Just two doors down from Gramaphone Records, it's actually three stores in one, all smelling of incense. Shop one, called Little Sister, specializes in tiny T-shirts, vinyl skirts, and labels like Lush, Dollhouse, and Tasty. Shop two, Untitled, carries baggy, casual menswear from Fuct, Mecca, and Pervert. Prices rocket when you hit the back of the store—Aero—where the racks are full of higher-end items from Diesel and Mossimo. The store also has bags, lighters, sunglasses, tapes by local and Detroit house DJs, and whatever else is popular this week. Oh, and a live DJ spins records on Saturdays.

et cetera

Best '70s gewgaws: Looking for an MC Hammer doll or a vintage GI Joe? Tiny **Flashback Collectibles** *(3450 N. Clark St., 773/929–5060)* is piled to the rafters with everything that made a '70s childhood worthwhile. From Paul Michael Glaser posters to Twister T-shirts, from HAVE A NICE DAY pillows to Hamburgler glasses, the selection of posters, dolls, T-shirts, Viewmasters, key chains, lunch boxes, and other paraphernalia is unbeatable.

Best guitar shop: If you want to avoid the corporate anonymity of buying an ax at the North Side's Guitar Center, **Specimen Products** *(1728 W. Division St., 773/489–4830)* offers a great way to fight back. Proprietor Ian Schneller, a sculptor and musician (he's in the local band Falstaff), makes one-of-a-kind guitars for a discerning clientele that includes Red Red Meat, the Cocktails, and Tar. They aren't cheap (prices start at $1,000), and custom jobs take a while to complete (two to six months); but Schneller's handmade, usually fretless instruments have a sound quality and visual charisma that can't be matched. If Frank Lloyd Wright made guitars, they would have the clean lines and lack of superfluous ornamentation of a Schneller ax. A few models are usually available for purchase at the store, which triples as the creator's workshop and living quarters. Bonus point: Schneller also makes cellos and violins.

Best enlightened adult toys: Cupid's Treasures *(3519 N. Halsted Ave., 773/348–3884)*, a giant, pink-walled sex shop, politely serves Chi-town's gay, lesbian, straight, bi, and curious populations. It's got one of the city's largest dildo collections, and leather, latex, and vinyl goodies for guys 'n' gals. Men's panties? Thigh-high boots? You got da right place, pal. A non-sleazy atmosphere and a friendly, nonjudgmental male and female staff are pluses.

Best street fair: People selling junk out of the back of their cars used to vie for space with established businesses in the old days of the gritty, 120-year-old Maxwell Street Market. But in 1985, the University of Illinois helped push the Sunday market a half-mile east from its traditional seedy site at Maxwell and Halsted to a fancier location at Canal Street between Taylor and Depot streets. The result (open 7 A.M. to 3 P.M. Sundays, 312/744–9088) is a smaller, gentler working-class market with more police and bathrooms, fewer hucksters, and less porn, junk, garbage, and crime. It has less character, too, but as time goes on it seems to get a little closer to what it once was. You can still enjoy an open blues jam, now based underneath the viaduct in the middle of the market near 13th Street. And you can still find cheap art, tube socks, knives, bicycles, shoes, used books, and tools.

body alterations

Best full-body-care salon: What can't you retouch at **Milio's** *(3205 N. Clark St., 773/549–1461)*? When "Partridge Family" wiseacre-cum-radio shock jock Danny Bonaduce decided to have his station's logo tattooed on his hinder, he went to Milio's. The immodest redhead had the dirty deed done right smack in the middle of the salon. The sky's the limit at Milio's! Grab a tall cool one at the salon's juice bar and consider the possibilities: hair dyes, braids, piercing, tattooing, and designer and custom-made clothes. The hip, down-to-earth staff also excels at traditional haircuts, highlights, manicures, pedicures, and waxing. (The DePaul University cheerleaders once spent a morning at Milio's getting bikini waxes in a back room.) If that's not enough to recommend it, the 20-year-old salon is also a favorite among the city's transvestites, cross-dressers, and drag queens. Warning: You need to be 21 (and prove it) to alter your body with ink in Chicago.

Best custom ink: The purists at **Guilty and Innocent Productions** *(3105 N. Lincoln Ave., 773/404–6963)* refuse to bow to fashion. No Celtic tattoos, no "Mom" or "Winona," either. Instead, nationally known artists Guy Aitchison and Kim Saigh work directly with their clients to create custom-only designs—meaning the two are often booked up months in advance. On a recent day at the clean, airy studio, Aitchison was putting a detailed marine scene on a fisherman who had flown in from Florida while Saigh colored in another client's sci-fi character. Piercer Mike Leatherman, one of the best in the city, rounds out the trio; it's a little bit easier to get in to see him. The reception area is also a store. On display is a small but carefully chosen selection of barbells and hand-carved jewelry, as well as T-shirts and prints of Aitchison's fanciful paintings.

Best cheap hair salon: Don't let the casual attitude and comfortable, slightly disheveled setting fool you, **Big Hair** *(2012 W. Roscoe St., 773/ 348–0440)* is the poor boy and girl's luxury salon. The going rate for a cut is $8—it's not Supercuts either—for everything from summer buzzes to Louise Brooks Goth kid 'dos to shags to, yes, mohawks. Ever-friendly owner and stylist Patty Bekker and her staff will also tease, spray, and style your hair for special nights out; they do color and perms too. Great magazines and loud music, from Meat Beat Manifesto to Donna Summer. Who said bouffant?

hotel/motel

Best rock hotel: Guests are no longer allowed to dye their hair in the sinks, and the police are starting to ticket tour buses that park in front, but the Lincoln Park North **Days Inn** *(646 W. Diversey Ave, 773/525–7010)* still has a reputation for being the place where mid-size rock stars spend the night. The who's who includes the Breeders, Sonic Youth, Belly, Juliana Hatfield, Lemonheads (Juliana and Evan did not stay at the same time, thank you), Mazzy Star, Matthew Sweet, Arrested Development, the Fall, Blur, and Sheryl Crow. Nary a day goes by without a rock band staying here, and, fortunately, rates are low enough ($79 to $104 for a double) that the rest of us can afford it, too.

Best Wicker Park B&B: Wicker Park is still the most happening neighborhood in Chicago, and its own comfortable bed-and-breakfast, **The House of Two Urns** *(1239 N. Greenview Ave., 773/235–1408)*, is not far from ground zero: the intersection of Milwaukee, Damen, and North avenues. Book ahead of time: There are only three rooms. The amenities do the comforts of home one better—you're greeted with slippers and a robe, cable TV, a hair dryer, and a continental breakfast complete with fresh-baked scones. Rates start at $65 per couple per night, $50 if you're single.

Best cheap bunk: It's appropriate that a stone hobo bathes in the fountain outside of the clean, modern **Chicago International Hostel** *(6318 N. Winthrop St., 773/262–1011)*, where a bed goes for $13 a night. Most rooms in this 125-bed hostel have six to eight beds, which means you'd better know how to share space. Pluses: kitchen access, showers, a TV-free lounge, and no chores. You're also fortuitously located on a quiet street in East Rogers Park on Chicago's far North Side. That puts you near Loyola University, several coffee shops, and Lake Michigan beaches. The hard part is figuring out when to check in (7–10 A.M. or 4 P.M.–2 A.M.) and what to do with yourself when they kick you out (10 A.M.–4 P.M.) every day.

local wonders

Best parking-lot blues jam: The stage is set up against a brick wall, the neighborhood is not for the squeamish, and the parking lot where the audience stands may have been paved during the first Daley administration. But the blues you'll hear at the **Fish Market open jam sessions** are far more authentic than what you'll pay to hear at some famous North Side blues clubs. For more than 15 years, musicians from all over the city, sometimes the world, have gathered on summer weekend nights to share the stage at an empty lot at Kedzie Street and Jackson Boulevard across from the Delta Fish Market. Word of mouth draws blues fans of all shapes and sizes—babies, children, hipsters. And that neighborhood mom next to you might become a heartbroken songbird the moment she hops on stage. The whole show's free, but when the hat's passed for donations you'd do well to show your appreciation.

Best lake view: Lake Michigan keeps the city cool in summer and warm in winter. Despite the proximity of busy, noisy Lake Shore Drive, the lakefront is crammed with bike paths, parks, museums, beaches, and even a golf course. You can view the lake from many spots, but the best place to see it is on the North Side at **Cricket Hill** near **Montrose Beach** (*Montrose Ave. at Lake Shore Drive, 312/747–2200*). Climb to the top of the small hill (one of the city's few; it's made of landfill) and you'll see Montrose Harbor, Montrose Beach (one of the city's most racially integrated), and a vista with blue water on three sides. Look south and you'll see the city skyline.

transmissions

Best soul radio: Vintage soul and R&B from the '60s and '70s are the hallmarks of Dusty Radio (**WGCI, 1390 AM**), one of the few stations in the world that'll play the Temptations and Boz Scaggs side by side. On-air dedications, unusual giveaways, and the scratchiness of its weak AM signal only add to the station's magic. Richard Pegue, a local musician, DJ, producer, and legend, hosts a long-running Saturday Night Dusties Party that's not to be missed.

Best college station: Northwestern University's 5,000-watt, **WNUR (89.3 FM)** is the area's best-known college station, with its state-of-the-art studios and regular CMJ reports, but it's Northeastern Illinois University's scrappy 100-watt **WZRD (The Wizard, 88.3 FM)** that wins the prize for truly alternative programming—unfortunately, the station's weak signal means you have to be on the city's North Side to hear it. The freeform, all-the-time station features student DJs forbidden to say their names on the air (that would take away from The Wizard's collective identity), and who follow Throbbing Gristle with Mingus. One DJ recently mixed an old *Dr. Demento* show with acid jazz. The Wizard is also the local outlet for the offbeat program *Hour of Slack* as well as *Negativeland* and *Pacifica News*.

Best late-night blues show: It's the witching hour, plus the music, that lends a timeless appeal to Steve Cushing's syndicated **Blues Before Sunrise (midnight Saturday to 5 A.M. Sunday on WBEZ, 91.5 FM)**. The show combines selections from Cushing's collection of 78s, 33s, and CDs, straddling hep harmony, gospel, and deep Mississippi Delta Blues—from Ma Rainey to Blind Willie McTell to the King Cole Trio. Most important, Cushing never ventures into amplified Albert Collins territory.

columbus

by Ron House

"James Thurber once said 'Columbus is a town in which almost anything is likely to happen and in which almost everything has.' He must have been sniffing his Magic Marker that day."
— **Marcy Mays,** *Scrawl*

Until recently, artists and other presumed hipsters survived adolescence in Columbus just to leave it, returning only to dry out or to bury relatives. Things have changed. Columbus is a '90s boomtown, growing fat off its service industries yet painfully insecure about its big-league status. Having survived a minimal bout in the early '90s, the city should be as happy for what it isn't as for what it is. Low rent, many jobs, and a growing music scene give Columbus a feel that Chicago or New York will never have.

Home of the nation's single largest campus in Ohio State University, this is nothing if not an instant youth market. OSU's Buckeyes were mostly known for beer buckets and football until they rioted against the Vietnam War in 1970, and the campus ushered in sex and drugs by hosting the national Weather Underground orgies. Many original hippies are still active and help organize Columbus' best three-day party, the Comfest, in late June. Too bad they like a lot of feeble music, mostly of the white-boy funk and Deadhead reggae variety.

The first inklings of a punk scene went unnoticed when Cleveland legends the Electric Eels played here (behind chicken wire) in 1974. Record stores and poster boards started reflecting the New Wave revolution in 1977. Great shows by the Ramones, Patti Smith, and the Dead Boys led to the formation of many new bands and eventually one great nightclub, Crazy Mama's. Only Mark Eitzel, ex–American Music Clubber, of the early scene, would dump Columbus and find greater glory in more glittery towns.

Aided by a promoter intent on losing money, Stache's shed its cosmic country trappings and began booking bands in the early '80s, helping create an indie-rock network. Local bands like Great Plains, Scrawl, Royal Crescent Mob, and the Gibson Brothers honed their chops by opening up for the likes of the Minutemen and Meat Puppets, and then went on to make small waves nationally by releasing records on prestigious labels like Homestead and Rough Trade. Scrawl was dubbed the "spiritual grandmothers of the Riot Grrls" by *USA TODAY*. And Jon Spencer found the dirt in roots music by apprenticing with the Gibson Brothers.

Since 1990, Hometown labels Datapanik and Anyway have provided a springboard for a whole slew of bands punkier and more lo-fi than their predecessors. The New Bomb Turks added smarts and style to a ramalama buzz-saw sound, creating a devoted fan base in Europe and other punk hotbeds. Gaunt followed close behind, distinguishing itself with leader Jerry Wick's neurotic and idiosyncratic songwriting. Thomas Jefferson Slave Apartments (my band), Bassholes, Moviola, and the Yips are just a few of the other bands who've carved a niche nationwide. Raves became a rage in 1992, when over a thousand maniacs attended all-night sessions at the venerable Valley Dale Ballroom. White-collar suburban types and frat kids made clubs like 700 High and Paradigm wild if temporary rave successes. The scene reached its, uh, apotheosis when the massive Mekka debuted in the summer of '95. There's been some decline since, but the hard-core kids survive, with guerrilla clubs called things like Virtual Overdrive touting "funkadelia" nights on leaflets all over High Street.

The rise of scene-based record company scrutiny (thanks, Nirvana) and the huge profits created by the compact disc market have also wrought massive changes in Columbus music. In one week alone in August 1996, five bands released albums on national labels: Monster Truck 005 on Sympathy, Big Back 40 on Polygram, Scrawl on Elektra, New Bomb Turks on Epitaph, and Mike Rep on Anyway/Revolver. That four out of five of these records are great says this scene won't wilt under the national spotlight.

Columbus is also home to numerous eccentric musicians oblivious to national scrutiny. Take Jim Shepard, the mastermind behind seminal band Vertical Slit and current outfit V3. His lengthy discography (on labels like American, Thrill Jockey, and Siltbreeze) is a catalog of elegance gone decadent, progressive in that anglophilic/John Cale/'70s sense. Columbus' best example of an artist dedicated (or crazy) enough to live for his art, Shepard can be spotted in any number of High Street watering holes. You should buy this guy a cold one—make it a Foster's, not a Bud.

lay of the land

Flat and gridlike, Columbus is fundamentally a one-street town. **High Street** is the city's spine, nerve center, and heart. It runs the length of the city, starting in its humble, rural south, quickening through the touristy German Village and self-explanatory Brewery District, then hitting downtown at Broad Street, where the newly remodeled State Capitol lords over it all. The main drag proceeds north through the galleries and restaurants that make up the booming **Short North** (the name, like the area, was appropriated from those of Appalachian descent), slackens squalidly between Fifth and Eleventh Avenues, only to run smack into **Ohio State** and its attendant craziness until Hudson Street. The best exits for campus off Interstate 71 (north of I-70) are Eleventh Avenue and Hudson Street. North of campus, beginning at Arcadia Street on High Street, is **Clintonville**, a cool neighborhood of '40s-era A-frames and duplexes popular with baby boomers and lesbians. North of that is where the rich people and their suburban lackeys live. Other areas of note include **Grandview**, a restaurant hotbed just west of town, across the **Olentangy River**. **Old Town East** (east of I-71 downtown) is a predominantly black neighborhood of old mansions in various states of repair. It's great for driving around. Some may find the area east of High Street between Fifth and Fifteenth dangerous.

getting from a to b

Columbus is fundamentally a driving town, although it's easy to maneuver on foot if you confine yourself to one neighborhood. Parking on campus is something locals complain about, but in comparison to New York or Chicago, it's cake. Tow trucks are a reality in some areas, so check the signs. Buses go up and down High Street fairly frequently weekdays and cost $1.10. Cabs are more phoned than hailed. Try Yellow Cab at 614/444–4444.

sources

Thanks to the wonderful cash cow of 1-900 ads, Columbus now supports three weekly papers. The *Other Paper* is the easygoing tweaker of the establishment's nose. It's funny, professional, and features the most comprehensive concert coverage. Reviewer John Petric loves to bash easy targets like Hootie and the Blowfish. The old-timer *Alive* has witnessed a revival of late, with some good investigative coverage, and Kevin Wolfe writes weekly about great bands like Cornershop and Stereolab. All have good listings and should be read with coffee and a pinch of salt. *Moo* is the scene's monthly cheerleader, where local artists receive the attention they feel they deserve nationwide. Craig Regala may be the city's most unique writer, welding a Lester Bangs/Stooges vision of rock history with a post-feminist tough-man facade. The newsprint tabloid has a cute little contest question section (Worst Album by a Major Artist?) and a great listings section that covers most of the Midwest.

The online fanzine *Cringe* (treadway@mps.ohio-state.edu.) is an e-mail foray into scene info/gossip that occasionally emerges onto the printed page. Editor Joel Treadway claims *Cringe* is the sum of its contributors, but the zine still bears his contrarian imprint. Bands like Hairy Patt are in its pantheon, while the New Bomb Turks receive only peripheral coverage. It's quirky and funny in spots. Cute bass players (male or female) are important criteria.

clubs

Best unknowns: Everybody knows that this country now has more bands than unwed mothers, and you can bet our government is not going to do anything about it. **Bernie's Distillery** *(1896 N. High St., 614/291–4127)* has addressed the problem, bless its soul. The cover charge for this funky basement bistro is never more than $2, and frequently it's free. If the first band is Assmaster 2000 and they really suck, you can always leave without feeling cheated, your beer money still intact. Or you can make your way to the deli side of the bar and drink and complain about the band, a favorite custom of the locals. There are usually three bands a night, and most of Columbus' local favorites like Hairy Patt and Flying Saucers play there regularly, so it may be worth your while to stick around. If you're in a band, the Distillery is a fun club to play because the minimal stage is right on top of the first row of tables, and all you need is a crowd of 50 or so to get a real body-rubbing, sweat-sharing scene going. Beck played there after "Loser" was a hit, but most people didn't get within two blocks. Out-of-town unknowns frequently appear and surprise the cynical cognoscenti (Number One Cup and Harry Pussy, to name a couple). On weekends the place tends to get like a sardine can, and the band becomes just a loud rumor in the corner, hidden from half the crowd. This may be when the Distillery is at its best. Two drawbacks: Bernie's food does not make it a destination place, and jazz or blues take over the stage on Sunday and Monday.

Best national acts: Since the days when the Replacements were playing only to the opening band and whining for their next beer,

Stache's was ground zero for the alterna-indie rock scene. Numerous now-famous or near-famous bands used the ramshackle, 250-capacity, north-campus bar as a launching pad for wild-eyed glory. The club's status rose with the music, too: Daily the mail brought a tubful of demos from touring bands hoping for a gig. All this despite (or because of) a gruff but colorful owner (Dan Dougan) whose first love is roots music and who professes a profound hatred of all things "trendy." For any local band wishing to make a living, this club was essential. The Distillery has a steadier bar crowd, but people willing to pay for music went to Stache's. In April of '97, Stache's vacated its old premises and became **Little Brother's** (1100 N. High St., 614/263–5318). The location has changed, but its importance in the Columbus scene hasn't.

Best sound system: The owner of **Skankland** *(1151 N. High St., 614/299–6896)* took the shell of an old Quonset hut and fashioned what has to be the most physically impressive bar in the city. The place just exudes the atmosphere of a job done right (and expensively), from the immaculate block-shaped tiled restrooms to the monstrous speakers that hover over the spacious dance floor. Those speakers pound Caribbean rhythms seven nights a week. Songs that would sound snoozy at home sound like they're straight from the Jah head here. Live bands mix with DJs in Columbus' most integrated nightspot. It's located on a stretch of High Street still untamed by gentrifiers. The wide-windowed front room houses a Jamaican restaurant that gets mixed reviews but provides a good hangout for the dreadlocks. Early in the evening the DJs blast reggae and its variations from a balcony above the bar in the center of the room. They take the stage beyond the dance floor when the place fills up after 11 on weekends. Toots and the Maytals and War are two major acts to recently play this smallish (350-capacity) club.

Best big-dance scene: The adventure starts in just finding the mammoth warehouse enclosing **Mekka** *(382 Dublin Ave., 614/621–2582)*. Long deserted by daytime people, downtown's mazelike streets by the old Penitentiary wind through a burnt-out landscape that makes a perfect prelude to Columbus' trendiest dance club. Once there, parking is plentiful and supervised. A huge hit when it opened in 1995, Mekka has suffered from the fickleness of its hard-core patronage and the dabbling of the suburban crowd. Lounge lizards dressed in black have remained a constant in the club's small, dimly lit barroom. The ornately industrial dance floor in the big room doesn't usually get going until the A.M.. Special occasions feature dancers in cages and oil-drum fires. The music currently ranges from super high-energy house music to jungle varieties, techno, and more commercial flavors. Admission is $5.

Runner-up: The gay club **Garage** *(40 E. Long St., 614/461–0076)* is nearby, providing the discerning dancer with all sorts of bar and bed-hopping possibilities.

Best teenscene: Drive by this sprawling former Dental College house and the scene might resemble a frat party from its recent past. Look closer, however, and you'll see that none of the crowd lounging out front has the requisite beer in hand. In fact, a good portion of the kids are not yet of college age. The **Neil House** *(1473 Neil Ave., 614/299–1160)* provides a valuable function both for locals and nationwide hardcore bands taking a quarter off school to see the country and play in basements. The grrls and boys who hang out in this alcohol-free but smoke-filled environment are surprisingly sympathetic to the mostly anonymous performers. The music is not exclusively hardcore, nor always obscure. Calvin Johnston's Dub Narcotic System and Dischord's frantic Make-Up are two outfits that have graced the House's living-room "stage."

Best punk-rock ghosts: In 1979, the glittery disco rock club Crazy Mama's invented nightlife for the local punk-rock scene. In the pre-AIDS era it was the place to go; then years of decline and disintegration set in. Now the original owner has opened up the **Kool Kat Klub** *(1536 N. High St., 614/299–5287)* at the same upstairs spot. A hit with Goths, the black walls, shag carpet, and mirrored dance floor remain the same. Additions include a modest platform for go-go dancing and a DJ (Nick Creature) hip to the '90s garage scene. Bands make for an awkward fit in this three-roomed, L-shaped watering hole. They usually perform on slow nights like Tuesday, although recently national rockabilly acts like Wanda Jackson and Ronnie Dawson have been packing the joint. There are drink specials early, but the lounge lizards don't come out from under their rocks until late. The neighborhood has deteriorated, but the place can still get going on a good night. Old-timers see dead friends out of the corner of their eyes.

Best gay cruise scene: Outlands *(1034 Perry Ave., no phone)* has grabbed the club scene by the *cojones* with special parties and a cock-out attitude. Propositions fly fast and furious to even the most buttoned-down observers at the split-level, converted country bar. Midnight Masses (for Goths with a Catholic fetish), dunking booths, and other wet sports keep the mayhem level high. The alcohol gets locked up at 2:30 A.M., but sometimes the fun continues till dawn. The bar's flirtation with punk has faded, and the music has reverted to its gay techno dance roots.

Best special occasion club: The **Alrosa Villa** *(5055 Sinclair Rd., 614/885–9125)* is an 800-capacity nightclub located in the suburban north near a strip *USA TODAY* named "Fried Food Row." The music at Alrosa is usually the fried-food type, too; Kiss and Ozzy tribute bands go over big here. When the stage is taken by good groups (like Guided by Voices, Nick Cave, and Pavement—all recent guests), the alien environment gives the gigs a once-in-a-mating-season aura. The freestanding, brick roadhouse boasts perfect sound, a great panoramic view of the stage, and an owner who likes to play god over the P.A. system.

bars

Best hangout: **Larry's** *(2040 N. High St., 614/299–6010)* is the place where many of the city's scenesters hang out when Bernie's and Stache's are clogged with bands playing happy funk or scary hardcore. This windowless tavern with a long bar, mini–pool table, and whirring ceiling fans, has been a longtime haven for the disaffected and arts-inclined. Its battered wooden booths boast graffiti carved back in the Beat days. Legend has it that '60s folk singer Phil Ochs performed his first public show here before he quit OSU. Music has since been reduced to a barely audible antique jukebox in the corner. Paintings that look like rejects from a Yes album dot the walls. The bar's relationship with the behemoth school across the street is problematic. Grad and foreign-exchange students comprise the largest percentage of its non-slacker clientele. Larry's is the perfect place for life-and-death arguments that will seem pointless in the next day's hangover haze. A good sign: It's by far the most popular bar for returning ex-residents who have spurned Columbus for bigger cities.

Best jukebox that never plays your song: At **Dick's Den**, *(2417 N. High St., no phone)*, if you press Billie Holliday's number, it plays the Isleys. Press the Isleys, it plays the Troggs. Press the Troggs, and it doesn't play at all—until the bartender comes over and gives it a swift kick. Thank God, the entire selection is tasteful. The most popular table in the split-level bar's three rooms provides an excellent view of High Street and its malcontents, especially neighboring Stache's and the ever-loitering crowd out front. The clientele is culled primarily from the half of the '60s generation that didn't die or get rich. On the walls are photos of the Norwich Marathon, held each March, when most of these folks (who shouldn't) run two miles to the liquor store and back. There's too much smoke and too many tasteless T-shirts, but the pool table and pinball are fine and the beer is cheap. The bar itself may be considered a dive by young innocents who have never dived before.

Best cigar bars: Whatever your opinion on cigars, Columbus is severely lacking in smoke lounges for the stylish but impoverished. Only upscale Downtown bars like **Barrister's** *(338 S. High St., 614/222–0501)* and **Flatiron** *(129 E. Nationwide Blvd., 614/461–0033)* have picked up on the trend. The sand-blasted Barrister's is more committed to the cigar (a chalkboard lists 16 varieties), but Flatiron is the better bar. A former tiny warehouse once squeezed between two now-demolished buildings, it's a miniature replica of its skinny NYC namesake, thoroughly and expensively remodeled, with high-end whiskey and a jukebox that caters to adult-alternative faves like G. Love & Special Sauce. The place also has great eats like catfish po'boy sandwiches.

Best hotel bar: The padded, perfectly round bar at the **Claremont** *(650 S. High St., 614/228–6511)* achieved its fame when Jodie Foster filmed a scene from her movie *Little Man Tate* here. The bar has arguably garnered more publicity from the movie than Jodie did. The room seems a bizarre afterthought to the main hotel building, with large windows offering a great view of the usually unused pool. This tiny spot has a peculiarly '60s, space-age look to it. It's shiny yet comfortable too, especially if you don't mind large TVs blaring sports. The clientele mixes barflies with nearby German Village upscalers and black-attired nightlifers looking to keep their love affairs secret. Too bad beer is only served in cans. The hotel itself gets mixed reviews ($44 for a double)—Jodie Foster didn't stay there. The restaurant next door is a good steak-and-chops joint.

Best bar window: Over a decade ago, the **Short North Tavern** *(674 N. High St., 614/221–2432)* was the first bar to brave the ungentrified waters of its namesake neighborhood, until the early '80s a seedy, white-trash blemish on Columbus' big-city aspirations. Many of the darters and drinkers there today were the original pioneer artists of this now-booming neighborhood. The table by the front corner window provides a great view of High Street in its glory. A fresh wooden bar and high-stooled tables provide a good view of the downtown workers unloosening ties and letting off steam. Service is especially good during the day; draw a portrait of the barmaid on your napkin and you may get a free draft.

Best gay bar: The new owners of **Blazers** *(1205 N. High St., 614/299–1800)* are lesbian bar vets who've done a great job of turning this redneck dive into a place your mom would love. The new carpet, paneling, and attitude go a long way in making wayward juiceheads (endemic to the area) behave themselves. If you're a straight juicehead who doesn't sleep on the street, the place is welcoming. The service is attentive beyond the call: Put your beer on a table, go to the head, come back, and there's a napkin beneath the brew. The girls gather around the pool table, and if you ever find same-sex dancing in one of this town's country bars, it will be here. The jukebox has Madonna and Village People, but also plenty of George Jones.

Runner-up: **Downtown Connection** *(1126 N. High St., 614/ 299–4880)* just down the street is a very clean and new gay sports bar. During the Atlanta games, Olympic swimming was very big here.

Best microbrews: Barley's *(467 N. High St., 614/228–2537)* sells the ales it brews in its basement to both hard-core hops fans and nearby downtown suit types, including Columbus' nominally most powerful man, Mayor Greg Lashutka. The cavernlike room makes for a raucous beer-hall atmosphere when filled with upscale drunks. The wide vintage mirrored mantel behind the bar contrasts nicely with the new wood-and-brass surroundings. Favorite pints include Barley's own Scottish Ale, for three and change. Darker, more exotic brews are also popular; seasonal favorites like the Russian Imperial Stout come and go. One topic for drinkers is architect Peter Eisenman's decidely non-Midwestern Greater Columbus Convention Center, in full view across High Street. "What the hell is that?" (Trivia: Eisenman also designed OSU's Wexner Center.) Barley's serves good food and hosts so-so bands in its basement.

Best two-dollar 23-ouncer: For $1.75 before 9 P.M., you get a huge quaff of cold Bud draft at the two jock-and-trivia franchises called **BW3** *(1608 N. High St., 614/291–2500; and 7 E. Woodruff St., 614/291–2362)* on campus. Service is fine, but don't drink too much or you may be tempted by the dangerously hot chicken wings that are the BW3 specialty. Wide-screen sports and tinted windows dominate the Woodruff space. The North High Street basement has more serious wing eaters and, through its window, a view of campus' most riotous block.

food/coffee

Best cheap food: Former alternative-country singer Ricky Barnes decorates his two **Galaxy Restaurant**s *(in nearby Grandview at 1099 W. First, 299–5140; and in rural Powell at 2470 State Route 750, 614/ 846–7776)* with folk art and circus arcana, creating an atmosphere that recalls a bygone America of small-town eccentrics. His food does the same, usually for under $10. Cuban sandwiches, seafood burritos, and fried plantains make the Galaxies reasons to see the parts of Columbus that don't center on campus. The Powell site, adjunct to a shooting range, relies on the art to overcome its storage-space origins. The two-room Grandview spin-off is located across from a little-league ball field in an old-style strip mall (much of its folk art focuses on the Cincinnati Reds). Both spaces have open kitchens and are immaculate. Grandview is closer to the city and serves alcohol; Powell doesn't. Many a Columbus hipster has spent time serving at either spot.

Best family diner: Nancy's *(3133 N. High St., 614/265–9012)* is the ultimate in family dining to many Columbus diner afficionados. To a stranger, it may seem like somebody else's family. Everybody seems to know each other in this 30-capacity shoe box. There's no menu. If you like bacon and eggs, you won't be disappointed. Each day has its own lunch special. Sometimes the best policy is to order whatever the person next to you is having. Be warned: If you think about things twice, your friendly but businesslike server may not be back for a while. On weekends there's a long line of people waiting to grab a stool at one of two yolk-colored counters or a chair at the few flanking tables. Prices are rounded down for the cashier's convenience but rarely top four bucks for a meal.

Best no-frills diner: Tommy's Diner *(914 W. Broad St., 614/ 224–2422)* lacks the eccentricities of Nancy's but is more reliable. The spacious, clean West Side joint does a Denver omelette or a meat loaf dinner well and promptly. Coca-Cola machines and "Happy Days" decor make it a little too self-conscious in its retro-diner identity. The regulars range from hipsters taking a day off from the Galaxy to the West High School wrestling team. This is a popular place for smokers. Broad Street is the main thoroughfare of the working-class West Side, only a few miles from OSU via route 315.

Best expensive meal: Tapatio *(491 N. Park St., 614/221–1085)* is one of a cluster of upscale restaurants that's fueled the Short North's resurgence. This postmodern pueblo houses two large cafeterialike dining rooms and a more intimate, bizarrely painted bar area that many regulars prefer to eat in. There's outdoor dining when it's warm. The customers include theatergoers, off-work restaurant workers, and poorer folk intent on blowing their last 20 bucks creatively. South-of-the-border influences are everywhere on the menu, but the chefs are not afraid to try anything. A recent hit appetizer was poached calamari, scallops, and shrimp on a bean-thread-noodle bed. Fresh baked bread, great margaritas, and micro-brews make it a place to go even if you can't afford the $12-dollar quinoa cakes or even pricier striped bass.

Best vegetarian without vegetables: Southwest of campus, across the street from the seriously vegetarian **King Avenue Coffee-house** *(247 King Ave., 614/294–8287)*, is **Estrada's** *(240 King Ave., 614/294–0808)*, a place to go if you like beans and have very little cash. There are better Mexican joints (LaBamba, El Vaquero), but this indoor/outdoor, rambling brick place has been adopted by scenesters as their own. The nearby Neil House makes it a convenient before-gig spot for the veggie-but-broke, all-ages crowd, who scarf up $2 burritos. They've got beer and meat, too. Bands have started playing in the base-ment recently. The entirely anonymous but well-named I Have Mass was a recent accompaniment to the nachos.

Best slice: Right in the middle of the action at 15th and High is a cubby-hole with the best pizza in town: **Flying Pizza** *(1812 N. High St., 614/294–1011)*. The slices are chewy, cheesy, and wider than your face. The New York style goes further than the food: The employees resemble the hot-headed, dough-slinging brothers in *Do the Right Thing*. Order a slice cold and not heated and the owner goes "Easy customer! I love easy customers!" It's a perfect, cheap, portable meal for a High Street cruise.

Runner-up: **Lost Planet Pizza** *(680 N. High St., 614/228–6191)* is a stylish new addition to the Barnes family restaurant empire in the Short North (see "Best cheap food" above).

Best spicey meal: Indian Oven *(2346 N. High St., 614/784–0635)* is located in a walk-up row-house apartment no larger than the average undergrad's. The powers that be are itching to call this area of North Campus the "International Village." If you can convince the server you're serious about spice, the vindaloo or curry can be heated to the point that it makes your vital organs want to explode. You have to try the pakoras too: fried veggies with a great nihilistic green sauce. Carryouts are available, but the table in the picture window makes for great people watching. It's expensive by Columbus standards, like all Indian food here—over $10 for a good meal.

Best barbecue from an oil drum: Crooks *(1049 College Ave., 614/239–1881)* recently made the big move from a mobile wagon to a more permanent stand on the east side near Capital University. Owner Pat Crook and family have retained the smoked North Carolina–style flavor that's made his outdoor picnic table a top destination for diners all over central Ohio. The favorite on the limited menu is the Linwood, a tasty pulled-pork-shoulder sandwich. Vegetarians have been known to brave the traffic for Crook's greens. Speakers in the trees pump Miles Davis and Jimmy Smith to the picnickers in the parking lot of this reclaimed inner-city storefront. Hours are irregular, so call first.

Best 24-hour coffeehouse: Insomnia *(1728 N. High St., 614/421–1234)* is Columbus' number one loitering spot. Located in the no-man's-land between the wild turf of South Campus and the relatively sedate North Campus, it's open all night, seven days a week. During the day both the barely enclosed patio and the lower-level storefront are easygoing places, perfect for a cup of house blend and a leisurely read. At night feral, tattooed punks and their dogs roll out of the bushes and have the run of the place, sharing the $3 plastic lawn chairs with slumming suburban teens and artist types willing to pay the psychic price. Drive by three times after five o'clock and you're likely to see the same pierced faces. Crowds are especially intense when the Newport (see Clubs) hosts a concert next door.

Best gay coffeehouse: Coffee Table *(731 N. High St., 614/297–1177)* is home base for the Short North's gay culture. Its pickup potential compares favorably with the bars. If you crave caffeine instead of sex, you can round up the usual suspects like their excellent lattes, mochas, and cappuccinos. Don't bother trying to understand the AIA-award-winning sculpture strewn throughout the place—just go with it.

shopping

records

Best rare records cheap: No record salesclerk, however knowledgeable, is immune from the "gotcha" that goes with mispricing valuable vinyl. But when one lucky shopper recently copped the first three so-rare-they-don't-exist Pere Ubu singles for five bucks total at **Goldmine Records** *(2446 N. High St., no phone)*, the entire collector-scum world shook. Goldmine is a hit-or-miss, cluttered but comfy place, where overpriced Paul McCartney 12-inchers jockey for space with Scott Walker imports. Sometimes it's not the easiest place to patronize. Every so often the eccentric owner locks the door and hangs the sign, BACK IN 15 MINUTES, DOG HAS TO PEE, in the window.

Best $3 CDs: Ten years' worth of students have passed through Ohio State without ever paying full price for a compact disc. If you don't mind bumping elbows with bargain hunters in a basement, **Used Kids** *(1992 N. High St., 614/294–3883)* is the place to find this year's hits for seven or nine bucks and last year's hits (Green Day) for a paltry three. Used Kids is also a contrarian indie-rock retail center: Built to Spill outsells Pearl Jam. The Annex next door is devoted to vinyl and CDs. Q-Tip of Tribe Called Quest and Fred Schneider of B-52's are two celebs who walked away with bagfuls. All sorts of wiseass scenesters (like the author) work there.

Best dance tracks: The stairwell at 1980 N. High St. turns upward to the spacious, well-lit, and high-ceilinged **World Record** *(614/297–7900)*. The most design-oriented CD store on campus (yellow and black are ubiquitous) has always been the quickest to pick up on national trends like listening booths and midnight sales. Manager Pappa Hopp helps make this independent a leader in the rave-trance-techno-gabba dance scene. Like most campus stores, World Record lowballs new releases—most are $10.99.

Best roots music: Two blocks south, Johnny Go's **House O' Music** *(1900 N. High St., 614/291–6133)* specializes in garage and roots music and is also competitive with used CDs. Owner John Petric is one of Columbus' most notorious rock critics.

clothes

Best thrift clothes: Columbus is known for its excellent thrifting. Stores have not yet been completely plundered, and you're likely to find classic American labels like Macgregor at good prices. The four **Thrift Stores of Ohio** outlets, formerly known as the Kidney Foundation stores, can provide the discerning but scraping-by scenester with the kind of shirt or blouse that will make friends go "Oooh" at the next big concert. The stores have tons of stuff but are remarkably well organized—shirts are grouped according to color. Shirts and pants go for as low as 39 cents while two dollars is the average. The new store in an abandoned grocery store off S. High St. *(67 Great Southern Blvd., 614/491–5305)* may be the best.

Runner-up: The **Village Thrift** at the Amos Center *(3400 Cleveland Ave., no phone)* is worth doing too, if you've got the browsing bug. A good place to find corduroy jeans for $3.

Best club clothes: Avalon *(1434 N. High St., 614/294–9722)* is a national new-and-used clothes chain that caters to club kids looking for oil-based apparel like vinyl skirts and plastic shirts. Jumbo and tiny are the favorite sizes at this south-of-South Campus freestanding store that employs some of Columbus' most visible trendsters. **Avalon Shoe Salon** *(1443 N. High St., 614/291–4101)* fits the hipsters across the street.

Best vintage: Atlantis *(1359 N. High St., 614/294–7080)* was a vintage store before new clothes were made to look retro. Now it sells both new and used to a loyal clientele.

Runner-up: **Relapse** *(1990 N. High St., 614/297–1244)* is the only store in the neighborhood that's now completely vintage, a favorite for campus kids throwing '70s parties.

books

Best used books: It's no coincidence that **Penguin** *(2500 N. High St., 614/267–6711)* opened in an abandoned plasma center only a block away from **Karen Wickliff** *(2579 N. High St., 614/263–2903)*—the two bookstores dovetail as a one-stop for discriminating book lovers. Karen Wickliffe is more stately and hardbacked, but a lot of sci-fi paperbacks gather like moss around the towering stacks of collectibles. Penguin is a good spot to pick up a $4 Cormac McCarthy paperback. But both places could waste your valuable drinking time if you decide to browse.

Runner-up: **Roy Willis**, farther up the street *(3150 N. High St.)*, is smaller but cheaper.

Best punk zines: The hippie owners of **Monkey's Retreat** *(1190 N. High St., 614/294–9511)* help organize the annual alternative festival, the Comfest, and peddle everything from material on Tai Chi and tattoos to Phillip K. Dick books and *Maximum Rock N Roll*. Monkey's is a good spot for radical and gay literature, yet you can also find *Penthouse* trading cards on the counter. There are also plenty of corners to poke around in.

et cetera

Best junking: On Wednesday, Saturday, and Sunday, hillbillies drive up and empty their trunks out at **South High Drive-In** *(S. High St. by I-270).* Occasional bargains include original Air Jordans for three bucks. **King-man Drive-In** on Route 23 north of town gives you similar opportunities on Sundays, weather permitting. All the thrift stores purvey junk, too. The best central Ohio flea markets are held monthly in Springfield, 30 miles away.

Best vintage toy store: Big Fun *(1782 N. High St., 614/294–4386)* is a spin-off from its mothership store in Cleveland. A walk-up, refashioned brick duplex just around the corner from Insomnia (see Food/coffee), it's actually just off High Street. Cute reminders of Gen-Xers' childhoods (like Mr. T puppets) make a visit there potentially expensive if you're feeling sentimental. The hypodermic ballpoint pens have been banned by public schools everywhere, but here they go for two bucks. Rebellion comes cheap.

body alterations

Best tattoos: When the tattoo convention makes its annual pit stop in Columbus, all the young disciples gather around the booth of Marty Holcomb from **Marty's Artistic Tattooing** *(3160 W. Broad St., 614/272–8821).* It's easy to tell his nontrendy roots: His salon is in a Harley shop. Members of Econothugs have given their bodies to him. Specialties include biker (duh) and flower tattoos.

Best buzz cuts: At **Teck's** *(17 E. 13th Ave. 614/299–1759),* family values of yesteryear intersect with prevailing punk aesthetics. Get a buzz for ten bucks. It's around the corner from Insomnia (see food/coffee).

hotel/motel

Best local hotel chain: Red Roof Inn is headquartered in suburban Dublin, so if you stay at the one near campus, at Route 315 and Ackerman Road *(614/267–9941),* you're experiencing a real homegrown corporation. The closest cheap motel to the campus hotspots is a five-minute drive over the Olentangy River from High Street. Bands making more than gas fare at Little Brother's find this a very convenient place to crash. Double rooms start at $45.99. The early settlement cemetery across the road is one of the few things to distinguish this Red Roof from the 233 others across the country.

Best downtown hotel: The mammoth red-brick **Southern Hotel** *(310 S. High St., 614/228–3800)* was a toney destination 70 years ago. It's recently been refurbished, but be ready to fork over your savings. Affiliated with the Westin chain, rates can vary from $99 to $145 for a double. The theater hidden within the bowels of this behemoth promises to soon be a civic jewel. The restaurant is highly rated.

local wonders

Best mound: Shrum Mound *(on McKinley Ave. north of Fifth Ave.)* is a 30-foot-tall earthwork sculpted by Native American hands over a millennium ago. If you cruise out there at three in the morning and perform bizarre rituals, what civil authority would have the nerve to quibble? What did the Indians build it for, anyways? From the top, you can look out over the black-and-silvery river (the Scioto) that brought the builders.

Best $25-million skateboard ramp: The Wexner Center is a pricey showcase at the 15th Avenue entrance to the OSU campus. It's a postmodern mishmash of grids and turrets, financed by Columbus' very own billionaire, Les Wexner of the Limited clothing chain. The museum hosts cool movies and neat exhibits, but its slanting cement exterior has found its real value as a sidewalk spot for the city's more daring boarders to show off. Lest we forget, art is something you can use.

Best shadow of Jesus: Columbus isn't as religiously entrenched as nearby Cincinnati, but don't blame Jesus. Thanks to a spotlight, during most of the year his shadow shoots up 40 feet or so onto the **Livingston United Methodist Church** *(614/224–2006)* known here as the "Church with the Shadow," where 70 and 71 merge near S. Fourth Street and Livingston. Look for three crosses during Lent and Mary and Joseph during Advent.

transmissions

Best radio (by default): Browse through the *CMJ*, and it seems that every little cosmetology school has a radio station. Every school, that is, except the one with the largest single campus in the country. OSU has no student-run radio. This dismal state of affairs has eaten up the insides of many an idealistic punk. Others bless the fact that the scene is not plagued by bands who honed their chops by repeatedly listening to Veruca Salt or Jon Spencer. **WCBE (90.5 FM)** is the pretender to the public-radio throne. Owned by the Columbus Board of Education, the station flirts with the adult-alternative format. It calls itself "the true alternative," even though a number of their favorite artists (e.g., Sheryl Crow) move seamlessly into the mainstream. But recently a set concluding with Scrawl and Stereolab recaptured the childhood magic everyone wants to feel when they turn on the radio.

detroit
by David Merline

"A giant heart made of flesh and bone, bricks and steel,
fueled by the electricity of its past, present, and future."
— Vinnie Dombroski, *Sponge*

Detroit has a public-image problem. During the 1967 race riots, paratroopers and tanks swarmed the downtown streets and dozens of people were killed. Then there was the Detroit Tigers' 1984 division title victory. Remember the picture of drunken revelers holding pennants aloft while an overturned cop car burned in the background? There's never a shortage of artful photographs of the urban decay that has plagued the city since the riots. Yet in that same 25-year time span, Detroit has made more seminal contributions to American music than just about anywhere else.

You can thank Detroit for the soul stylings of Stevie Wonder, Marvin Gaye, and the Jacksons (all of whom sprang from the modest Motown Records studio in the '60s); the legendary protopunk of bands like the Stooges, MC5, and Alice Cooper; the infinitely influential funkateering of George Clinton's Parliament/Funkadelic; the ultra-aggro angst of hardcore legends like Negative Approach, the Necros, and the Meatmen; and the groundbreaking dance-floor revolutions of techno pioneers Derrick May and Juan Atkins.

Still, ask the average Detroiter what's the best thing about the town Kiss crowned "Rock City," and they're likely to say, "Easy access to freeways and airports." Self-deprecation is de rigueur for Detroiters—you could say it's our version of civic pride.

With its crumbling urban core (resembling some of the less affluent parts of war-torn Bosnia), its failing industrial infrastructure (which has left the downtown streets virtually devoid of non-boarded-up storefronts), and its extremely high poverty level (evident in the general decay of all but a few neighborhoods), Detroit deserves much of the disrespect it gets. But what strikes most Motor City visitors is the fact that, shockingly, Detroit is nowhere near as bad as it's reported to be.

Aside from adding a healthy dose of "bad-ass" credibility to anything and anyone coming from here, Detroit's multifold problems have actually aided the growth of the city's diverse and ever-growing underground. The cost of living is about as low as it gets, and the city is nowhere near as dangerous as it is purported to be. Add to that the fact that there are few legitimate forms of culture left in the city, and you can easily see why Detroit is a virtual paradise for artists, musicians, and poets.

Since its drastic decline in the late '60s, the "Renaissance City" has itself become an underground phenomenon. At any given coffeehouse, hipster boutique, or club, you're likely to see grunge kids, ravers, and rude boys mixing with skinheads, metalheads, and greasers. The only unifying aspect of Detroit's alternadenizens seems to be their lack of one.

Likewise the local music scene. There's the bubblegum indie pop of Outrageous Cherry, the ambient soundscapes of Fuxa, the Helmetesque metal of Speedball, the retrograde rockabilly of about a hundred different Link Wray wanna-bes, and the bizarre but hugely popular harlequin-faced gangsta rap of the Insane Clown Posse. And though it may be known and loved throughout the rest of the world, techno is all but ignored in the city that spawned it. Except for a handful of underground parties (far, far less than you'll find in cities like New York or Chicago), there's really no sign of the musical revolution that originated here: Most club jocks spin either Top 40 alternative or early '80s retro.

lay of the land

When most people refer to Detroit they are actually speaking of the Greater Detroit area, which extends about 30 miles in each direction from downtown, encompasses about a dozen townships and suburbs, and only incidentally includes the city itself. So when people talk about Detroit, what they really mean is anything east of Ann Arbor, south of Pontiac, and west of Lake St. Claire—an area also known simply as Southeast Lower Michigan.

In these parts, **Ann Arbor**, home to the University of Michigan, has always been considered the epicenter of cutting-edge activities. Never mind that it's nearly an hour from Motor Town, Ann Arbor (or A-squared as some like to call it) has always been the yardstick by which all trends, past and future, can be measured. In the '70s there were head shops, which in the '80s begat frozen yogurt stores, which in turn begat coffeehouses, which at last count numbered nearly a dozen in a mere two-mile radius.

Currently, **Royal Oak**, located 11 miles up Woodward Avenue from Detroit's downtown, is the best area for shoppers who like cool record stores, vintage cloth shops, and coffeehouses. However, the gentrification that has recently swept through the town like a plague has driven many of the city's diehards to **Ferndale**, which borders the northern edge of Detroit. Other suburban burghs like **Pontiac** and **Rochester** (full 30- to 40-minute drives from downtown via freeways) are also sprouting record stores, secondhand shops, salons, and galleries where once only hardware stores, feed shops, and country buffets stood.

getting from a to b

It's no big surprise that the city that Ford built is also the city you can't survive in without an automobile. There are no subways; city buses run almost as infrequently as taxicabs, and Detroit's only form of modern public transportation—a largely unused monorail referred to ironically as the "Detroit People Mover"—only covers an eight-block radius. Metro Detroit is a suburban sprawl; so while there are plenty of places to check out, it's a safe bet that there's at least a 20-minute drive between any one cool thing and another. If you get stuck call Yellow Cab *(313/961–3333)* or Checker Cab *(313/963–7000)*.

sources

The best way to find out what's going on in Detroit is to ask around and look for fliers. Most of the best parties and even some of the better shows are underground and move frequently, so the local media is usually one step behind when it comes to things that are actually worth doing. As in any city, the true underground events, whether they are concerts by the Nirvanas of tomorrow or parties thrown by any of the city's many world-class DJs, are seldom at any fixed location, so asking a clerk at Off the Record (see Shopping) what's going on will undoubtedly prove much more fruitful than looking in any local publication. The *Metro Times* is Detroit's free weekly paper (available just about everywhere) and while its far-left-leaning, *Village Voice*–aping editorial content leaves everything to be desired, it has the best up-to-date listings for all things cultural. *Orbit Magazine* (also free, but only published monthly) offers a wittier, sharper slant on the town. Much more stylish and infinitely more readable than the *Metro Times*, *Orbit* offers a humorous (and ultimately more on-target) take on the Detroit scene, but it is far less useful as a guide for what to do.

Local bands get press attention from the *Jam Rag* (free at record or music stores, published monthly), the area's only paper dedicated solely to the local music scene and the best way to find out where to see any local band, whether they're heavy metal, punk rock, or a Doors tribute band.

Hour Detroit, the new city mag on the block, attempts to offer a cooler alternative to the bland predictability of the mainstream glossies that cover the town, and achieves mixed results. It's undoubtedly the best-looking of the three, and is arguably somewhat more hip, but like its main competitors, *Hour Detroit* skews to a decidedly suburban audience. For an underground city magazine that actually writes about things going on in the city, the sporadically published *Left Banke* is the best place to turn. It's sometimes hard to find; look at the commie bookstore on Wayne State campus.

For online tips, there is metroguide.com, which lists all of the city's major attractions; but to find out about the best shows in the area, www.rust.net/r-net features the complete listings for most of the area's clubs and includes links to all of Detroit's coolest techno/rave sites.

clubs

Best martini lounge: Although the number of retro martini 'n' cigar bars now equals the number of gin blossoms on W. C. Fields' nose, **Clutch Cargo's**, at the three-story club called **Mill Street Entry** *(65 E. Huron, Pontiac, 810/333–2362)*, is really the only one worth attending. This groovy, high-ceilinged, newly remodeled room is replete with comfy, overstuffed Dean Martin–era sofas and lounge chairs and a fine selection of single malts and stogies. The music is a pleasing mix of rockabilly, big-band, salsa, and lounge music, and the crowd is diverse, unpretentious, and, when decked out in what sometimes passes for suitable lounge attire (cheap vintage tweed sports coats, turtlenecks, and greased-back hair), extremely entertaining.

Best hip-hop night: Without question the most consistently popular club night in Detroit is **Three Floors of Fun** at **St. Andrew's Hall** *(431 E. Congress St., 313/961–6358)* on Friday nights. On the top floor (a small ballroom usually used as a dressing room for bands appearing at St. Andrew's) is techno; on the bottom floor (a smaller, fully equipped club called the Shelter) is "alternative" (all those obscure underground bands like Pearl Jam, Nirvana, and Nine Inch Nails); but the real action is on the main floor. DJs Tony "Slimfast" Olivera and Mike Buchanan provide a boomin' mix of gangsta-free hip-hop, featuring everything from old-school staples like the Sugar Hill Gang and Schooly D to perennial crowd-pleasers like A Tribe Called Quest and the Fugees.

Runner-up: For a mellower groove, check out Monday nights at the **Gold Dollar** *(3129 Cass Ave., 313/833–6873)*. The cozy atmosphere of this legendary neighborhood bar (during the disco era it was the place for the wildest drag shows in the city) is further enhanced by the soulful sounds of Cal Tjader and Roy Ayers as well a surprisingly deep selection of obscure old-school hip-hop. (Anybody remember Choclaire?)

Best club night: Despite the fact that it happens only one night a week (and on Wednesdays, no less), Family Funktion at **Alvin's** *(5756 Cass Ave., 313/832–2355)* is without question the most fashionable night in town. With its *Giant Step*–inspired mix of acid jazz, hip-hop, trip-hop, jungle, techno, and soul, the Funktion attracts a refreshingly eclectic crowd of shiny-shirted ravers, look-of-the-month-club club kids, and jaded old-school scenesters. Its daunting location in the heart of Detroit's Cass Corridor (notorious haven for junkies, crackheads, and prostitutes) keeps it unsullied by timid suburban voyeurs, and its weekly offering of guest DJs, merchandise giveaways, and complimentary comestibles has made attendance at the Funktion mandatory for the area's über-hipsters—not to mention visiting luminaries like Moby, Groove Collective, and Tricky. Alvin's capacity is around 500, which the Funktion usually outdraws, leaving many a frustrated fashion plate to loiter on the sidewalk.

Best small rock club: In the heart of the newly upscale New Pontiac (as opposed to the pre-gentrified "old" Pontiac, a place few people ever visited on purpose) the **7th House** *(7 North Saginaw, Pontiac, 810/335–8100)* is unquestionably the best small venue in the area. Intimate without being obnoxious, this cozy 450-seat room utilizes its limited space well, with tables and risers perfectly arranged so that whether you choose to sit or stand by the bar (which serves coffee and juice, as well as hooch), you are guaranteed an excellent vantage point. The booking leans heavily toward minor-league alternative acts who can't get booked into larger venues (Me'Shell Ndege Ocello, Scud Mountain Boys, Joe Henry, etc.), so the patrons are generally older, half-cap-sipping neofolkies who want to be alternative without having to change out of J. Crew.

Best meat market: Teenage Sodom! **Club X** at the State Theater *(2115 Woodward Ave., 313/961–5450)* is the perfect place to wonder where it all went wrong. This Saturday-night affair (broadcast live on local alternative station 89X) attracts a shocking number of hormonally imbalanced teens who don't seem to mind getting hit on by 40-year-old men whose wives think they're working late. The music is an oppressive mix of bad techno and mid-'80s industrial; parking is expensive; and the drinks are watered down. It is, in every way imaginable, the very antithesis of cool. Which is exactly what makes dropping by such a bizarrely worthwhile experience.

Best blues joint: While Royal Oak has been the true rags-to-riches suburban success story, going from boho backwater to yuppified alternatown in under ten years, its neighbor to the south, Ferndale, has been quietly doing some gentrifying of its own. Case in point: the **Magic Bag** *(22920 Woodward Ave., Ferndale, 810/544–3030)*. Once a rundown porn house just up the street from a "Swedish" massage parlor, the Bag is now a hip, upscale blues joint just up the street from a coffeehouse. While many people argue about whether or not this is an improvement, few disagree that this newly gentrified burgh should stop referring to itself as SoRo.

Best after-hours jazz: Located in the heart of Eastern Market, **Bert's Market Place** *(2727 Russell, 313/567–2030)* is the type of joint jazz greats like Marcus Belgrave or James Carter are likely to drop in post-gig to let off steam. There's a classy air to the club's decor, but the atmosphere (particularly on Friday and Saturdays when the jams flow till 5) is anything but uptight. The crowd is generally a pleasing mix of old-school pork-pied jazzbos, neobopheads, and assorted barcrawlers just looking for somewhere to hang out till they're sober enough to go home and pass out. Food and drinks are offered, but the service is slower than Chuck Mangione's comeback; so be prepared to sit through a couple of sets before you catch sight of your order.

Best gay nights: Ann Arbor has a long-standing reputation for its open-mindedness and diversity, so it's not too surprising that it's home to one of the best gay clubs in the area. Although only officially designated "gay" on two nights, the **Nectarine Ballroom** *(510 E. Liberty, Ann Arbor, 313/994–5436)* seethes with the postpubescent undulations of sexually adventurous college students every night of the week. Featuring different music styles every night (ranging from techno to disco to Eurobeat) and the occasional over-the-top drag show, this spacious, high-tech, bilevel club (with plenty of side rooms and dark corners for privacy) is every young queer's wet dream come true.

bars

Best bar for frugal alcoholics: At any ordinary watering hole, $5 will probably get you either a couple cheap beers or a single watered-down cocktail, but at the **Norwalk Bar** in Hamtramck, a town northeast of downtown Detroit *(9607 Conant, Hamtramck, 313/872–8923)*, a five-spot will set you well on your way toward a blackout. With 90-cent drafts and dollar shots, it's no wonder this joint is a favorite of retired factory workers and budget-minded slackers. Check out the truly vintage deco-style bar and the less-than-modern jukebox (which sounds remarkably like someone frying eggs while a radio plays in a distant room), and you'll realize why true ambience is definitely a dish that's best served old. The Norwalk's working-class neighborhood-bar charm is legendary, as is Eddy, the teetering septuagenarian owner/bartender who greets wayward suit-and-tie types ordering Long Island Ice Teas with a distrustful grimace and asks, "What kinda place you think this is?"

Best crowded hole-in-the-wall: Considered by some to be the single hippest place on the planet (or at least the block), **Gusoline Alley** *(309 S. Center St., Royal Oak, 810/545–2235)* is loud, obnoxious, and ridiculously crowded. In short, it's everything a good bar should be. What passes as decor is car parts, Texaco signs, and old gas pumps nailed to the wall. The service may be surly and slow, but the beer selection is first-rate (Gusoline's ads claim 90 beers and 60 seats), and the jukebox is trés hip (everything from Tom Jones to Tom Waits). For those who drink to get unashamedly drunk, there is no better place on earth. (Apparently, it was formerly called Gasoline Alley until some guy named Gus bought it.)

Best draft selection: Most bars simply *serve* beer, but **The Berkley Front, Ltd.** *(3087 W. 12 Mile Rd., Berkley, 810/547–3331)* damn near worships beer. Offering more than 100 beers, with no fewer than 15 of them on tap, the Front is a hops-head's paradise. The crowd tends to be large and foreboding (not too mention a bit too suburban-preppie for some folks' taste), and the no-smoking policy (smoke dirties the taps and spoils the taste, says the owner) puts may people off, but patrons have no choice but to be friendly. Aside from the barstools, the only seats are at the long picnic-benchlike tables where you're gonna socialize with strangers whether you like it or not. You may or may not feel too comfortable with this arrangement, but after a few pints of Guinness and a Woodpecker or two, such trifles will cease to matter.

Best local celebrity sightings: If you want to find the crème de la crème of Detroit's artists, musicians, merchants, professional types, and assorted ubiquitous scenemakers, **Union Street** *(4145 Woodward Ave., 313/831–3965)* is where you need to go. Located minutes from downtown and seconds from the campuses of both Wayne State University and the Center for Creative Studies, Union Street is forever abuzz with the comings and goings of the city's chic coterie. Full menu and an even fuller beer and wine list.

Best queer bar: If you've grown tired of cybersex and find that looking for love in online chat rooms is not all it's cracked up to be, **Doug's Body Shop** *(22061 Woodward Ave., Ferndale, 810/398–1940)* is where you should go to meet your man. This unassuming, run-of-the-mill pub has become the official off-line rendezvous for those searching for sincere romance or special friendships. Doug's typical pub ambience (leather booths, dartboards, etc.) is as straight-appearing as is much of its clientele—which makes this the preferred place for those who value discretion.

Best old-school punk bar: Although it's been a real long time since the Motor City Mutants made their ill-fated lunge toward punk stardom, and even longer since the Detroit punk scene (which, in the post-Stooges, pre-hardcore late '70s produced exactly no bands of note), you'd never know it from the looks of **Lili's 21** *(2930 Jacob, Hamtramck, 313/875–6555)*. Iggy posters and memorabilia, as well as fliers from clubs defunct for over a decade, cover nearly every surface in this legendary Detroit punk hangout. But what gives this place its peculiar charm is not so much the decor but the patrons: genuine old-school glam/punk/greaser types whose passion for alcohol consumption is rivaled only by their penchant for spinning sorrowful soliloquies about how much more punk punk was when they were punk.

food/coffee

Best Pad Thai: Although Thai restaurants in metro Detroit are now as common as hash bars in Amsterdam, **Siam Spicy** *(2438 N. Woodward Ave., Royal Oak, 810/545–4305)* was the first, and remains the best. The cramped, cozy, dimly lit dining room can pack in only 100 or so, but it's well worth the inevitable wait. A bit more pricey than many other area Thai joints (dishes typically go for $8 or $9), Siam Spicy is nonetheless worth the extra pence. The curry dishes are especially scrumptious, but there's little on the menu that isn't worth trying. The Pad Thai is a big fave. One word of caution: Although there are seven levels of spiciness, most of them are extraordinarily hot. Medium is very hot; mild is sometimes quite hot; and hot is for masochists.

Best cheap Chinese: The owners of **China Ruby** *(157 W. 9 Mile Rd., Ferndale, 810/546–8876)* are actually Vietnamese but, thinking that their native cuisine was a bit too exotic for the locals, they opted to fill their menu with typical Chinese fare. It's too bad, in a way, because judging by the quality of their Cantonese-style dishes, they could have provided Detroit with some much-needed Vietnamese flair. You can't get too upset though, since this is just about the best Chinese food in the area, not to mention the cheapest. Located on Ferndale's soon-to-be-too-trendy-for-its-own-good 9 Mile strip, China Ruby's cuisine is as basic as its diner decor (white walls, white counter, half-a-dozen tables, and copious press clippings on the wall), but the cashew chicken, the moo-shoo, and the immodestly named "chicken amazing" will be among the best you've had. If you get the $5.95 lunch special, you'll even have enough green left over to go across the street to Old Navy.

Best breakfast: Located just off the lobby of the Park Shelton Apartments, **Cappy's Fine Food** *(5408 Woodward Ave., 313/871–9820)* is one of the best breakfast spots around. Within walking distance from both Wayne State and Harper Hospital, Cappy's usual crowd of art students, medical residents, and Park Shelton tenants gives it a friendly, laid-back feel. It's perfect for both breakfasting businessmen and up-all-night partyers. With a dining area spacious enough for the large breakfast crowds it usually attracts, Cappy's rarely makes you wait long before you gorge yourself on any of its two- or three-egg breakfasts or its many heart-stopping omelettes.

Best soup 'n' sandwich: If you go to **Russell Street Deli** *(2465 Russell St., 313/567–2900)* any time between noon and two o'clock, be ready to wait. This tiny, unpretentious deli located in the heart of Eastern Market is one of the most popular lunch spots in the city and deservedly so. Its robust, perfectly flavored soups (try the black bean, the gazpacho, or the mulligatawny if they're among the daily specials) are the best around, and its deli fare has a distinctly gourmet feel to it. Saturday is the only day to go for breakfast, which, like the lunches, is second-to-none (try the corned beef hash or the French toast topped with the fresh fruit of your choice), and, thankfully, is served well into the afternoon.

Best cheap veggie food: You're going to want to get your food to go from Ann Arbor's **Jerusalem Garden** *(307 S. 5th St., Ann Arbor, 313/995–5060)*, since the place is about the size of a typical Manhattan apartment and has approximately five seats. This old-school Ann Arbor veggie joint has been serving the area's best falafel since about 1971, and in all that time has never raised its prices. So, for just over a dollar you can have one of the best-tasting meals of your life and bask in the glow of Ann Arbor hippiedom.

Best health food: Avoid the standard vegetarian fare like the veggie burgers or Greek salads and go straight for the daily specials at **Inn Season** *(500 E. 4th St., Royal Oak, 810/547–7916)*. Winners like Mediterranean vegetable pie, Southwestern lasagna, and the fresh-baked whole grain breads are what make this Detroit's best-loved health food spot. Of course, there's nothing wrong with their veggie burritos or their spaghetti marinara, but why go to a restaurant to eat what you can easily make at home? The rustic, artsy, New Age decor is as eclectic as the patrons, who usually range from upscale suburbanites dressed in their finest business casual wear to tie-dyed-in-the wool hippies.

Best late-night hot dogs: There is no single spot in the entire city of Detroit more beloved by clubgoers and barhoppers than **Lafayette Coney Island** *(118 W. Lafayette, 313/964–8198)*, one of the few remnants of Detroit's once-thriving downtown. Its coneys are among the best anywhere, according to people who actually bother to rank the quality of chili dogs, and the activity level in this loud, bustling, always busy spot provides a suitable foreshadowing of what happens to your insides after you eat here. The vintage '50s decor (counter in the front, a bunch of round tables everywhere else, glass storefront windows on either side of the dining area) and the delectable greasiness of the food are so genuine you might even get the vague sensation that you're in a real city, but don't worry, that too shall pass.

Best burgers: Although its somewhat quaint practice of relying on the "honor system" makes **Miller's** *(23700 Michigan Ave., Dearborn, 313/565–2577)* the perfect spot to scarf 'n' scurry, the considerable downscale charm of this neighborhood eatery's paneled walls and matronly staff (the kind who call you "hon"), not to mention what many call the best burgers in the free world, will make you more inclined to leave a generous tip. That is, unless you're unfortunate enough to break one of the long list of taboos (asking for your burger well done, requesting mayo or fried onions, ordering a cheeseburger with no cheese, etc.) that will send the fry cook into a furious rage.

Best clubby coffeehouse: There's no DJ, no cover charge, and the only thing you can get from the bar is fancy coffees and desserts. Nonetheless, once you set foot inside the posh, ultrahip coffeehouse **Brazil** *(305 S. Main St., Royal Oak, 810/399–7200)* you'll think you're in the hottest club in town. After dinner and before club time, club kids lounge around in the overstuffed couches, sipping lattes and discussing where to end up later that night.

shopping

records

Best vinyl: Perhaps one of the last music stores in the Western Hemisphere to dedicate most of its floor space to LPs, **Car City Records** *(21918 Harper St., St. Clair Shores, 810/775–4770)* is a Valhalla for serious record collectors. Whether it's a Blue Note original or a rare Grecian Beatles import, if you've been looking for it forever, Car City is likely to have it. Its massive, overstuffed shelves offer a huge selection of classical, international, folk, electronic, R&B, indie rock, blues, big band, and that's just for starters. All this, and an impressive selection of new and used CDs means that if you aren't prepared to make a serious commitment of money and time, you might be better off at a chain store.

Best imports: At **Off the Record** *(401 S. Washington, Royal Oak, 810/398–4436)*, rarities by everyone from Springsteen to Sabbath have "Made in Germany" written on their Xeroxed covers. Including live recordings and studio outtakes, these are just one of the many things that have made OTR one of the best-loved alternastores in the area. It's been selling imports and indies since Eddie Vedder was wearing Osh Kosh flannels, and store cat Wendell has been visited by rock celebrities from Soundgarden to Paul Shaffer (check out the gallery of Polaroids).

Best (and only) techno: Techno who? Although Detroit is the city that spawned techno, it has since cold-shouldered its own club music revolution. **Record Time** *(27360 Gratiot Ave., Roseville, 810/775–1550)* is still the *only* store in the city to devote a significant amount of space to this homegrown bionic revolution. Record Time sports the area's first "dance room," where discriminating DJs can sample the latest grooves (oftentimes to the annoyance of other patrons) before laying down their ducats. In addition, Record Time boasts the lowest CD prices in town, the best used selection, and it even features live bands and DJs every Friday night, so you can check out some of Detroit's homegrown talent without paying a cover.

books

Best hard-to-find books: When you consider that most independent booksellers in the area have succumbed to the seemingly endless proliferation of mega-chain stores and closed, the continued success of **Book Beat** *(26010 Greenfield Blvd., Oak Park, 810/968–1190)* is all the more amazing. But not surprising, considering that art-rocker-turned-tome-peddler Carey Loren (a founding member of the recently reunited Destroy All Monsters) literally stuffs his store's shelves (you'll have to get used to stepping over huge stacks of books throughout the store) with endlessly impressive selections of new underground, hard-to-find, and out-of-print titles (both John Waters and Thurston Moore regularly call on Carey for special orders). Whether it's an out-of-print book of Joel-Peter Witkin photos or a self-published book of verse by Lee Renaldo, Book Beat either has it or has just sold the last copy in existence.

Best haunted book warehouse: You'll want to set aside at least a couple of days to properly shop at **John King** *(901 W. Lafayette Blvd., 313/961–0622)*. This four-story warehouse in an old glove factory (the side of the building still bears the image of a huge mauve mitt) is a thrifty reader's paradise. Rare titles, paperbacks, old photographs, maps, and other assorted readables are literally falling off shelves, sticking out of randomly strewn boxes, and tumbling off carts. The store does its best to keep organized, but with thousands of new titles coming in every day (and with a legendary poltergeist said to be haunting the third floor), it's a safe bet that there are as many books on carts as there are on the shelves. Persistence and patience will be rewarded: Bargains abound, and rarities can occasionally be whisked away for next to nothing.

Best gay bookstore: Back before Royal Oak had become the alternative mecca of Michigan, **Chosen Books** *(120 W. 4th St., Royal Oak, 810/543–5758)* had to fend off militantly homophobic protesters and repair brick-damaged windows almost every other week. But now even local old-school residents seen to have finally tired of getting offended by Chosen's eclectic selection of queer, bi, and pansexual literature and erotica. That probably has more to do with the constant stream of alternative-minded shoppers the store has brought to the area than to any sort of newfound open-mindedness, but no matter—progress is still progress.

clothes

Best vintage racks: The Detroit area has long been a rich source for quality secondhand attire, but while many of the trendier shops seem to have traded in their vintage racks to make room for more ringer rock T-shirts and best-worn-backward baseball caps, Ferndale's **House of Chants** (210 W. 9 Mile Rd., Ferndale, 810/414–9170) is the one store that gets back to the resale basics. From mod gear to ravewear, from punk styles to silk ties, there's no fashion statement you can't make here. And though you can certainly find cheaper threads at the nearest Salvation Army, you won't find such a nice selection of vintage '50s sports coats or suits (expect to pay around $50 to $75), retro '70s disco gear, incense, and assorted jewelry and accessories.

Best urban depot: Offering everything from oxblood Dr Martens to spray-on hair dye, **Showtime** (5708 Woodward Ave., 313/875–9280) is the alterna–Value Village. Location is surely the secret to this hipster megastore's mega success. Its warehouselike storefront and red-and-black sign loom large on Woodward Avenue right off the campus of Wayne State. Pouty-faced punkettes will sigh, put down their copy of *Geek Love*, and saunter up to offer assistance, which you might in fact need to navigate the store's seemingly endless selection of new and used leather jackets, punk rock and rave logo T-shirts, vintage and new slacks, shoes, and boots, not to mention incense, beads, and jewelry.

Best kitschy clothes: One look at the leopard-print paint job on the storefront of Royal Oak's **Cinderella's Attic** (322 S. Main St., Royal Oak, 810/546–7209) should prepare you for what's inside. An air of Hanna-Barbera faux elegance permeates this shop. With more short-sleeved shirts that used to belong to some guy named Gus than you've ever seen in your life, and a wide selection of '50s and '70s clothing, jewelry, jackets, and jeans, Cinderella's has everything today's cocktail nation citizen needs for a fully customized lifestyle.

Best skater/raver boutique: Want Goofball Gear, ravewear by SoulKist, or a way-punk T-shirt with a slogan like I NEVER LIKED KURT COBAIN AND I'M GLAD HE'S DEAD? **Changes** (369 E. Maple, Birmingham, 810/644–4320) has got it and more. Located in Birmingham, Detroit's oldest old-money suburb, Changes is a beacon of hipness in an other-wise stuffy designer-shop town. Here's where to find the disembodied, bean-shaped Goofball head (the trademark of local artist/designer Gary Arnett that can be seen on T-shirts, jackets, caps, key fobs, cloisonné pins, and stickers all around town), and the gritty street-smart urban ravewear created by Family Funktion.

et cetera

Best comix and lunch boxes: Hardly a day goes by at **Dave's Comics** (*407 S. Washington, Royal Oak, 810/548–1230*) without some slack-jawed mutha coming in and waxing regretful about the demise of his cher-ished Kiss doll collection or the loss of his beloved Archies comics. Dave's is the place to restock: lunch boxes, trading cards, dolls, models, and, most importantly, comix galore. It's a veritable shrine to adolescent obsessions. Whether you want to relive your misinvested youth, or just pick up the lat-est issue of *Eightball* or *Hate*, Dave's has got what you need.

Runner-up: Out-of-the-way, but well worth seeking out is **Funhouse Noise and Toys** (*621 S. Main St., Plymouth, 313/416–0099*), which offers a modest but impressive selection of used vinyl, CDs, and cool collectibles.

Best fetish gear: One of the handful of businesses responsible for turn-ing Royal Oak from a redneck backwater (it was once home to notorious anti-Semitic radio preacher Father Coughlin) to an upscale-alternative hipster haven, **Noir Leather** (*415 S. Main St., Royal Oak, 810/541–3979*) began selling used leather jackets to thrifty Goths and punk-rock wannabes back in the early '80s but quickly turned into a hugely success-ful sex empire. Noir not only stocks a full supply of every imaginable sex-cessory, from cock rings to S&M workout gyms, it also sponsors regular fetish fashion shows throughout the area (many of which require proper fetish attire and at least a $30 fee for entrance).

body alterations

Best shave and a haircut: Though the old Ann Arbor, that bastion of hippiedom where Iggy Pop and John Sinclair walked the streets and pot was plentiful and cheap, has long been subsumed by a more strip-mall, Bob Dole feel, you can still stroll into **Dascola Barber Shop** (*615 E. Liberty, Ann Arbor, 313/668–9329*) and get a taste of the town's former charm. Most of the employees are old enough to remember when they hated hippies the first time around, and with haircuts as cheap as $8, Dascola is the best time-warp clip joint around.

Best piercing parlor: Far and away the most successful at all the latest neotribal trends (from inkwork to frenums, and every other conceivable manner of fashionable festoonery), **Ink Slingers** *(29323 Gratiot Ave., Roseville, 810/777–6390)* has practically cornered the market on flesh mutilation. With nine locations throughout the Detroit area, Ink Slingers is quickly turning into the Wal-Mart of tattoo and piercing parlors. Although its reputation for tattoos is not exactly stellar, its well-maintained autoclaves ensure piercings that are sterile, safe, and guaranteed to alienate you from police officers, school principals, and senior citizens.

Best tattoos: Jo-D Bonz's **Ink For Life** *(50 N. Huron, Ypsilanti, 313/485–8288)* is one of the area's premier parlors. Jo-D's specialty is blackwork and her Celtic symbols and intricate detail adorn the derma of many a local hipster. Her prices are reasonable, and her joint is fully outfitted to help meet all your needs, whether it's a tattoo of Gallagher or of a steel rod in your spleen.

hotel/motel

Best revolving restaurant: For the best vantage point in the entire city, nothing beats the **Westin Hotel** in the Renaissance Center *(Jefferson Avenue at Woodward Avenue, 313/568–8000)*. Although accommodationswise the Westin is indistinguishable from any other premium hotel anywhere in the world (rooms at about $100 per night, swimming pool, health and fitness center, etc.), the Ren Cen Westin does offer the unique opportunity to dine in a revolving restaurant located on the building's 71st floor. Like the six-towered glass structure in which it sits, the Westin is generally underutilized (the available office and retail space in the Ren Cen never even neared capacity), but all that is bound to change now that the building is becoming the new General Motors World Headquarters.

Best (and only) bed and breakfast: The idea of a bed and breakfast in Downtown Detroit may seem anachronistic, but that's only because it is. Located only blocks from Tiger Stadium (which means only blocks from some of the worst neighborhoods in Motor City) is the **Corktown Inn** *(1705 Sixth St., 313/963–6688)*. This historic, all-brick building has only four suites, each one available for $125 a night. Or you can have the run of the whole place for a mere $500 a night. Without question the best place to stay in the city, assuming you can manage to get a reservation.

Best cheap lodgings: Looking for a decent, affordable place to stay in the Motor City? Good luck. Since the vast majority of people who travel to Detroit do so for business reasons, your only real option is to stay at a large chain hotel and pay between $80 and $125 a night. But if you're feeling adventurous and are looking for a cheap thrill, feel free to flop at any of the city's better dumps. Check out fab '50s-era motels like the **Dunes** *(2324 N. Woodward Ave., Royal Oak, 810/545–8303)* or the **Palms** *(2428 N. Woodward Ave., Royal Oak, 810/548–2345)*. A personal fave is the **Eight-Wood Motel** *(330 W. 8 Mile Rd., Royal Oak, 810/548–6767)*, where a person can have a room for a mere $25 a night and enjoy some of the city's greasiest pizza in the adjoining Eight-Wood Inn.

local wonders

Best junk art: The brainchild of controversial Detroit artist Tyree Guyton, the **Heidelberg Project** *(3600 block of Heidelberg, just west of Mt. Elliot, 313/884–8882 for info)* has inspired both awe and outrage among city residents since its construction in 1986. Collecting assorted pieces of scrap and urban detritus such as old dolls, bicycles, shoes, and street signs, Guyton began attaching them to several of the dilapidated houses on his block, nailing them to trees, and using them to erect sculptures in the empty lots across from his family home. Two of Guyton's junk-covered homes were demolished in 1991, but the artist continues to expand his creations, and hopes to include all the homes on his block (all of the neighborhood homeowners strongly support Guyton's project) in the next several years.

transmissions

Best alternative music (for real): Way back when they had no idea what to call this crazy new music the kids were listening to, people were turning to Detroit's public radio station, **WDET (101.9 FM)** to hear it. It has an eclectic-yet-solid string of programs, including world music, jazz, and all varieties of alternative sounds (it's the only station in town that plays acid jazz and trip-hop—thanks to Ralph Valdez's nightly 10 to midnight program). And then of course there's *All Things Considered.*

Best community station: Where do you hear techno, speedcore, industrial, spacerock, indie, and just about everything else? If you aren't sitting outside Henry Ford Community College's student-run station, **WHFR (89.3 FM)**, with a portable radio, you probably won't hear it on the radio. But if by chance you manage to tune into the weak signal, you'll be damn glad you did. With a spectacular mix of music that never gets played on commercial radio, HFR is the kind of station that made people care about college radio in the first place.

Best jazz: Eastern Michigan University's **WEMU (89.1 FM)** is not for fusion and TV themes. EMU has one of the deepest jazz libraries anywhere, and some of the most knowledgeable jocks (a few of whom teach courses at Eastern). From *Morning Jazz* to *Evening Jazz* WEMU kicks out a full 13 hours of commercial-free, quality jazz. So whether you prefer the big band swing of Ellington, Armstrong, or Shaw, or the out fusion of Pharaoh Sanders, Miles, or Cecil Taylor, you won't find better sounds anywhere on the dial.

los angeles

by Kerry Murphy and Daniel Weizmann

"L.A. stings like a hundred bees per hour, but when you
find the honey it's somehow sweeter than in a town that's
easy to love." — **Carla Bozulich, *The Geraldine Fibbers***

"I couldn't live anywhere else. Here I am in a T-shirt and it's
75 degrees; anywhere else I'd be in a jacket and crying."
— **Rob Zabrecky, *Possum Dixon***

Los Angeles embraces the present with mad confounding glee. Yesterday's Superstar Poster Emporium is today's Mel's Mongolian Bar-B-Q; tomorrow, it's all getting plowed down to make way for Liquor-a-Go-Go. So, don't hold on too tight. Don't believe in anything you see. Sure, like any city, L.A. has its sacred sites, from the simply weird to the wholly macabre. Hollywood Boulevard's Mann's Chinese Theater bears witness to the excesses of the early studio era—you can almost see scenes from Nathanael West playing out in the courtyard. Meanwhile, the Tate and LaBianca homes have become tourist sites for a generation of L.A. artists and rock stars manqués who are enthralled by Charles Manson's savage chic.

And other only-in-L.A. sites, from its snazzy cocktail and Tiki lounges (both the *real* thing and equally swinging fake '90s versions) to its behemoth rock clubs like the Troubador, may or may not have been plowed to make way for a parking lot by the time you visit. Corner-mall development is an all-too-familiar shame that unnerves two or three Angelenos while the rest hardly blink…but it won't get in the way of the true L.A. experience: driving.

Because of its lack of a center, both figuratively and literally, Los Angeles is where you go to get lost. It's easy to be invisible—to be truly underground—in this town because no one is watching. And that's the beauty of driving. In a state of passive/aggressive, almost childlike spying, you cruise, look, never engage. If you're looking for a *place* to *get to*, you won't get what you want. What's magical about L.A. is the drive between here and there. You have to "go with" as the gangstas say.

Joyride. In the movie *Sunset Boulevard*, the out-of-work screenwriter played by William Holden holes up in the Alto Nido Apartments on Ivar above Hollywood Boulevard. On the lam from repo men, he is sweating out the darkest L.A. nightmare: No wheels means no life.

Angelenos are beautiful because they don't know what in the hell they're doing. Charles Bukowski's tombstone reads: DON'T TRY. As local writer Steve Abee put it, "New York is Port Authority—the place where you go to get your membership—but in Los Angeles *we don't need no stinking badges.*"

The same goes doubly for its hit-or-miss music scene. Los Angeles alternately suffers and thrives in the shadow of the music industry. To understand indie rock in L.A., it helps to remember its perceived enemy. In a '70s haze of high-res hippie superstardom, Jackson Browne, the Eagles, Linda Ronstadt, and Fleetwood Mac checked into the Hotel California and are still waiting to get out. Youthful discontent simmered then: glitter, glamour, Flipper's Roller Disco, the Sugar Shack, Rodney's English Disco, and a teenage nightclub called Osco's that was shaped like a whale: "EVERYBODY here tonight must boogie: Let me tell ya, you are no exception to the rule."

From this shimmering hurricane came the best punk-rock explosion on the globe: the Germs, the Weirdos, X, the Go-Go's, Fear, the Screamers. While 49.5 states were sleeping in an AOR daydream, Angeleno teenyboppers creepy-crawled the Fleetwood with Black Flag, the Circle Jerks, Red Cross, the Adolescents, the Minutemen, Mad Society, Vicious Circle, China White, the Stains, the Chiefs, and a whole battalion of beachside bands who cut the new American style when it was brand-spanking-new: supershort hair, super-gnarly skateboarding, super high-speed rock 'n' roll, and superalert mod values 15 years before Green Day learned to fake a British accent!

Black Flag's Greg Ginn and Chuck Dukowski helped lay the tracks for today's indie-rock scene with their label SST, recording everybody from the Meat Puppets to Sonic Youth. In the same way that bands found their own venues, putting on shows everywhere from old bowling alleys to barges in the San Pedro Harbor, SST just went out and *did* it. Though the rock scene nosedived into one of its familiar sloughs sometime after D. Boon of the Minutemen died, South Central was ready to hit with its own music. When Eazy-E said "Fuck Tha Police" it was a familiar sentiment, and the gangsta rappers smartly set up their own means of production and distribution (Ruthless) to back it up.

Beck and the Dust Brothers production team are defining a new, grasshopper-pastiche of rock and rap; Silver Lake bands like the bratty, post-punk glam Touchcandy and the new-wave-meets-'60s-spy-rock Possum Dixon are playing kitschy, loungey variations of indie rock. The raucous, militant P.C. band Extra Fancy also draws big crowds. And while the gangsta rap scene has peaked, new-school hip-hop acts like Pharcyde are playing a freewheelin', open, funky style that takes off from Fishbone and A Tribe Called Quest. But the patron saint of L.A. is still the Germs' Darby Crash, who, when he wasn't passing out on stage or writing apocalyptic poetry, invented the crazy-as-possible aesthetic and, along with it, hardcore singing.

In the brilliant original *Gidget* movie, a schlepped-out beach-bum beatnik named Kahuna teaches a pack of surfurbian teenyboppers the Zen art of surfing. The ultimate Angeleno, Kahuna has come to the Pacific shore after a disillusioning stint in World War II. Ukulele in hand, he turns his back on the roaring city, faces the mighty ocean, and *let's go*. Los Angeles, like Kahuna, is here to teach us mortal citizens the Zen art of surfing. Catch a wave, catch a moment, catch serendipity, and you're here, you've made it.

Los Angeles defies all the traditional urban relationships—between underground and mainstream, between city and nature, between journey and destination, between concrete and dreams. Darby called it "progress to the point of no distinction, dementia on higher order." One of the folk myths surrounding Darby is that he liked to drop acid, jump off the Santa Monica Pier, and then swim to shore. Kahuna's star pupil. Gotta let go. A go-go.

lay of the land

Los Angeles is spatially the largest city in the world. With more than 350 named communities and only very imaginary borders, L.A. is often described as a basin or a city of suburbs, but what it actually looks like from on high is a honeycomb. (Gliding into LAX over the miles of lights is proper preparation for the exhilarating physical culture of L.A.) The Santa Monica Mountains, a beautiful coastal range filled with trails for hikers, gear-heads, and BMX night riders, wrap around L.A. on the north, dividing it from the San Fernando Valley (home of *Fast Times at Ridgemont High*), bleeding into the Hollywood Hills, and finally petering out near Chavez Ravine, where Dodger Stadium overlooks Downtown.

To get a handle on the city, remember that it started at Downtown, at a Spanish pueblo you can still visit on touristy Olvera Street, and grew out from there. Many major boulevards and freeways extend outward from Downtown. Take **Sunset Boulevard**. Sunset snakes from Downtown to the north and west through many of L.A.'s most hopping communities. First is crime-ridden **Echo Park**, where *cholo* gang-bangers patrol the streets after dark. Then comes mondo **Silver Lake**, equal parts Latino, queer, modern primitive, and lowlife scenester, which gives way to an amorphous area known as **East Hollywood**. Just to the north here, off **Vermont Avenue**, is **Los Feliz**, a quieter, mixed white and Latino neighborhood, where groovy stores have taken root alongside the old-school lounge the **Dresden Restaurant** (see Bars). Next, Sunset Boulevard enters the trashy, sleazy, glam wilds of **Hollywood** (the Strip runs roughly from Fairfax Boulevard to Doheny Boulevard), and then through some of the priciest real estate in the world in Beverly Hills, Bel Air, Brentwood, and Pacific Palisades before finally draining out on the **Pacific Coast Highway**, or Route 1, just south of Malibu. You also have a southern option, Venice Boulevard, taking the low road through Normandie and ending at a dingy concrete fishing pier in **Venice Beach**. X's John Doe once said this drive was the best way to introduce somebody to L.A.

When people refer to West L.A., or the Westside, they mean the generally wealthy communities that run from Hollywood to the beach, like Beverly Hills; Westwood, where the UCLA campus and the Village are a youth zone; and Santa Monica, home to a great outdoor mall (the Third Street Promenade) and a lot of British pubs. Hollywood includes **Boy's Town** on Santa Monica Boulevard, and the **Fairfax** and **Melrose** districts in West Hollywood. Fairfax is an old Jewish neighborhood where a lot of punks settled next to Hasidic Jews in the '80s. And before it became a chic hotbed of pricey eyewear and window-shopping, Melrose was briefly a center of a freaky British hand-me-down punk culture, complete with vintage stores, vinyl, and punk accessory shops. To the east of Downtown, **East Los Angeles** is largely Latino, and it has some amazing fish taco stands as well as cheap rehearsal spaces. To the south is **South Central**, including **Watts** and **Compton**, where the West Coast gangsta rap scene went down. Los Angeles has always been a segregated city and is even more so after the Rodney King riots. Distrust rules, and racial tensions run high throughout. So, the fact remains that if you are white, going into South Central after dark is not recommended. Likewise, black youths who venture into the Westside after dark will likely be shaken down by the LAPD or private security forces.

getting from a to b

The Beach Boys didn't sing about buses or trains very much. To experience the City of Angels, you need wheels. A car is to Los Angeles is like an egg is to meat loaf. The whole world knows about L.A. traffic jams, but what few realize before getting here is that L.A. traffic actually flows pretty consistently. Before you try to get anywhere, buy the latest *Thomas Brothers Guide*, a thick tome of detailed block-by-block maps that is absolutely indispensable to L.A. veterans and first-timers alike. Study the arteries before you launch into Tomorrowland. To the north, Pasadena and the Valley—that's the San Fernando Valley—are connected by the 134 freeway. Centrally, I-10, called the Santa Monica Freeway, stretches all the way west from downtown Los Angeles to the beaches. On the east side, I-110, called the Harbor Freeway, will get you north and south from Downtown to San Pedro; while on the west side, I-405 (a.k.a. the San Diego Freeway) will get you north and south. Of course, Los Angeles does have a terrific bus system, referred to by locals as the Shame Train. The blue buses cost 50 cents and mostly cover the westside; yellow buses go farther, but they cost more—$1.35 or more depending on how far you're going, plus 35 cents for a transfer.

There is also a growing train system, including the Blue Line, which runs from Downtown to Long Beach, and the Red Line, which has several stops within Downtown; but these lines do more for laboring commuters than sightseers. A train is currently being developed that will run from Hollywood Boulevard to MacArthur Park. Locals are affectionately referring to the train-to-be as the Crack Express.

Sources

The free *L.A. Weekly* provides a reliably party-line p.c. take on the world; and even if the paranoid, left-of-center muckraking isn't your cup of tea, it has the best club and music listings in town—everybody advertises in it. Its main competitor, the *New Times*, has thorough listings and sharp, funny critics. The monthly music rag *BAM* has recently been spruced up, and does a good job keeping up with the scene: Look for Jennifer Schwartz's music gossip column, "Hearsay." For the gay scene, check out listings in *4-Front*. Even though zines may not be as helpful in terms of getting you to a specific event, they are always a sure barometer of that ever-important, ever-elusive thing we call style. All the down tribes have their own. To wit: *Giant Robot*, a totally cool, futuristic zine with a jones for Pacific Rim culture, including *Speed Racer*, Japanoise, and Hello Kitty. Also worth looking at is *Dragazine*, where you can catch up on the complicated ins-and-outs of Hollywood's transvestite scene. *Ben Is Dead* has reported on music and kitsch since the '80s, while *Flipside* offers a more fun-loving alternative to No Cals's *Maximum Rock N Roll*.

Los Angeles is very wired. Some of the thousands of Web sites include @LA, http://emporium.turnpike.net/A/atLA/index.html, for a general overview and Musi-Cal, http://calendar.com/cgi-bin/music-search?state=CA, for concert listings.

clubs

Best old-school punk club: Tucked away in a loft neighborhood downtown, blocks from both Little Tokyo and streets where homeless live in cardboard refrigerator boxes, **Al's Bar** *(305 S. Hewitt St., 213/626–7213)* has been a home-away-from-home for artists, punks, and other nightcrawlers since the days of Sue Tissue. The walls are covered with decades of feverish, chemical-induced scatological and anti-everything doodlings. The club's motto: "Tip or Die." Over the years, its bare-bones music room (which can be seen from certain well-positioned stools at the bar) has seen sweaty, crowded performances by never-got-their-dues L.A. acts from Savage Republic and the Nip Drivers to the Creamers, as well as by mainstays of the alt.canon like the Minutemen and Black Flag. Al's continues to be a mainstay of the L.A. music scene, even though exciting bookings have dropped off in the past few years. An exception is Thursday nights, booked by a woman named Toast who was recently named best booker by *Flipside*. Prepare to sweat like a stuck pig.

Best indie-rock club (all ages): Despite its Pico Boulevard waste-land location and the astounding lack of oxygen inside, all-ages **Jabberjaw** *(3711 W. Pico Blvd., 213/732–3463)* is one of the top, albeit smallest, rock clubs on the West Coast. Thanks to forward-thinking booking and a raw, pared-down P.A. system that's perfect for rock, Jabberjaw is the little coffeehouse that could, offering bands who have nothing to show for themselves but their music and a seven-inch or two. Expect tiny-backpack attitude in spades, but it's worth stomaching because this place is for real. Pre-major-label Nirvana, Jon Spencer Blues Explosion, Jesus Lizard, and Helmet have all played here. It's cheap, with covers topping at $7. No alcohol is served, but natural mind expansion can occur by playing vintage videogames (like Space Invaders, Tempest, and 'Stroids) or checking out the Keane doe-eyed velvet paintings on the walls. If the heat gets to be too much, just take your latte outside to the patio and play with the club's cats. Word to the wise: The neighborhood is filled with bad-intentioned people lurking in shadows. Park on Pico if you value your car windows, and don't stray too far from the club if you value your pocketbook.

Best neighborhood rock club (with liquor): On the opposite end of town in Silver Lake is **Spaceland** *(1717 Silver Lake Blvd., 213/413–4442)*, where you can drink beer while you bang your head. Formerly a Latino disco called Dreams of L.A., it has a '70s porn movie vibe, with enough tables and chairs and two pool tables. Spaceland booking is consistently inconsistent, so on any given night a decent local or touring band plays along with five or six unsigned bands destined to remain that way. The stage has become a second home to happening Silver Lake bands like the drunken party-rockers Lutefisk. With covers ranging between zero and $10, the place is friendly, low-key, and racially mixed—with a crowd that ranges from Beck to locals popping around the corner for a drink.

Runner-up: An up-and-coming club is **Hollywood Mogul's** *(1650 Schrader Blvd., 213/871–1424)* just below Hollywood Boulevard, where Flaming Lips and Helmet have played.

Best punk-rock beer bust: It's Sunday afternoon, you're dreading Monday, you're probably hungover, but you're antsy and have a few crumpled bills in your pocket. Where do you go? To **Sucker**, held at the **Garage** (4519 Santa Monica Blvd., 213/683–3447). L.A.'s only afternoon punk-rock beer bust starts at 5 P.M. and goes until that last straggler stumbles away. Hosted by the eight-foot-tall beauty queen and former UCLA student Ms. Vaginal Creme Davis, the ab-fab dahling of the cross-dressing set, Sucker offers fun for gays and straights alike. (It's one of few clubs in L.A. that caters to a mixed crowd.) Each Sunday, it's three bands for five bucks (past performers have included the Geraldine Fibbers and Imperial Teen), with entr'acte DJs spinning indie-rock hits from Make-Up to Team Dresch. If you're lucky, Ms. Davis will try to dance with you or suck your toes. With beers at $1.50 and well drinks a low, low $2, you may find yourself meeting equally soused people with the quintessential query: "Are you gay?"

Best Sunset Strip legend: Ah, the wonder that is Los Angeles. Within a four-block stretch on high-rent Sunset Boulevard, there's Billboard Live, the Roxy, the Whisky A-Go-Go, and the Viper Room. If you can visit only one, make it the **Whisky A-Go-Go** *(8901 Sunset Blvd., 310/535–0579)*. Where else can you touch one stage where the Germs, Jim Morrison, the Cramps, and X all rawked out? The Whisky brings out the best in everybody: This is where Darby Crash started a food fight while screaming the words to an Archies song, and where Jim Morrison jumped off the stage and ran out into traffic on Sunset

Boulevard. The Strip is no longer the heady mecca of ironed-haired, good-to-go-go blondes it once was; and the Whisky runs hot and cold booking-wise, occasionally shutting down altogether, but always seems to rise from the dead. What other club has nurtured every band from Love to the Go-Go's to the Gun Club *and* is the subject of a tremendously inspired *Beverly Hillbillies* episode?

Runner-up: Just down the Strip from the Whisky lurks its evil brother, the **Roxy** *(9009 Sunset Blvd., 310/276–2222)*. About twice a month good bands play the Roxy, but even then it's hard to recommend. Enter at your own risk: A can of beer is $4; it's $1 for tap water, and bouncers are likely to shout at you to stand behind the white line painted on the floor by the fire marshal. Getting tired of standing? Gee, those tables and chairs on the side look mighty inviting. Well, they're reserved for Members of the Industry; the plebes who actually pay to see the show don't deserve seats.

Best nouveau Strip legend: Also near the Whisky and the Roxy is Johnny Depp's infamous club, the **Viper Room** *(8852 Sunset Blvd., West Hollywood, 310/358–1880)*, which has begun to recover from the Babylonian PR attending River Phoenix's 1993 OD out front. The Viper Room has a familiar art-deco-in-the-'90s look, complemented by pretty consistent booking—most of the bands are okay, if not good. Cover charge and drinks can be expensive, but you're paying for the atmosphere, babe. After two or three drinks you'll feel like you blacked out and woke up on the "Fashion Don'ts" page of *Glamour*. And yes, Johnny Depp has been known to hang out there.

Best old-school/industry club: Hampered in the '80s by a ridiculous pay-to-play booking policy, the **Troubadour** *(9081 Santa Monica Blvd., 310/276–6168)* is on the rebound, drawing acts like Stereolab, Soul Coughing, and Steel Pole Bath Tub—though it still feels like an industry showcase. There's less big hair and leather than in its glammetal heyday, but many bands see the tavern-style West Hollywood stalwart as the next stop to fame. The sound system is good from the middle or back of the club, but don't get wedged on the side of the stage if you want to hear everything well. When the club gets too crowded and sweaty, head upstairs to the bleachered balcony. Industry weasels or those with the band get passes to the Loft, an upstairs schmooze pen with windows overlooking the club and a full bar for expense-account drinking.

Best unplugged: On an otherwise anonymous stretch of Pico near the Santa Monica Freeway overpass, **McCabe's Guitar Shop** *(3101 Pico Blvd., 310/828–4497, 310/828–4403)* has been selling stringed wares since 1958. More than just a store, though, McCabe's has an intimate back room for music. The Spartan fold-out chairs help you get into McCabe's purist, back-to-basics frame of mind. Keeping the torch burning for Southern Cali's great experimental-folk reputation, McCabe's has put on acoustic shows by Allen Ginsberg, Linda Ronstadt, Elvis Costello, Ry Cooder, John Doe, and the Spinanes. As might be expected of a serious music store, the sound system is impeccable. There's no smoking or alcohol, so come prepared to get a West Coast natural high from the music. Heck, you can even buy a decently priced ukulele.

Best rock club west of I-405: On most nights in sleepy Santa Monica, driving to a British pub for a game of darts passes for excitement. That's why you've got to love the **Alligator Lounge** *(3321 Pico Blvd., 310/449–1844)*. A New Orleans–themed bar with red walls, pints of Sierra Nevada for $3, and kitchen treats like gumbo and Cajun burgers, it's not only the West Side's best alt.rock club—it's the only one. The friendly staff helps foster a mellow, music-first vibe. Bookings vary from experimental sonic noise on Monday nights to rockabilly and surf bands. On the first Tuesday of every month, the Alligator hosts the local college station's (KXLU) demo-listening night, featuring raw beginners. Because it has the corner on the live-music market in the 310 area code and has recently upgraded its sound system, the Alligator also books of-the-moment touring bands like Silkworm, the Grifters, and old reliables like Yo La Tengo.

Best coffeehouse hangout: For decades there was nothing to do in Culver City, a burb east of Venice, except shoot pool and trim your mustache. Then **Petterson's Frisch Roast** *(10019 Venice Blvd., 310/839-3359)* took on the task of shaking things up. Fridays and Saturdays at Petterson's have become a mecca to those seeking good live music from experimental jazz to hardcore hip-hop, comedy, and poetry (it's free!), and strong coffee and good conversation. If you find yourself needing a smoke or some fresh air, check out the outdoor newsstand, which stocks some of the best, hardest-to-find magazines and papers. On a Friday night, while the Westside sleeps and the traffic hums, Petterson's is an uncharacteristic oasis of social interaction, packed with backgammon, domino, and chess players, tall-tale tellers, and major cultural and racial cross-sections of L.A. actually speaking to each other.

Best swing dancing: The drinks are classy, the bar is brassy, the velvet-curtained dining booths are elegant and discreet. Everything is BIG at the **Derby** *(4500 Los Feliz Blvd., 213/663–8979)* in Los Feliz, and the best retro club in town. Women turn out with pin curls and vintage dresses, their escorts in picture-perfect zoot suits and spats. Some nights feature live R&B, jazz, or rockabilly—but when the swing bands cut loose two nights a week, watch out. These boppers can jitterbug. (There are free lessons before the shows.) Actually, it draws a wide age range, including everyone from nostalgic old-timers to movie people, boomers, slackers, and fringies. An adjoining Cali-Italian restaurant— Louise's Trattoria—serves solid Italian dishes in the club (feel free to smoke between courses!). The cover ranges from $5 to $10; once you set foot inside, you're destined to dip, baby. Note this bit of local folklore: The Derby's lot served as the exterior for Arnold's Drive-In in "Happy Days." You'll recognize it if you stand on Los Feliz Boulevard to the east.

Best strip club: Tucked away on an unusually desolate stretch of Hollywood Boulevard, surrounded by strip malls and transient hotels, **Jumbo's Clown Room** *(5153 Hollywood Blvd., 213/666–1187)* is a seedy must-visit for curious slummers. It's got its share of lonely old schnooks, but the Clown Room also draws a younger crowd as inter- ested in their drinks as the tawdry action on stage. Despite the fact that it's women-owned, Jumbo's can be depressing, because the dancers would obviously rather be doing something else and the lucky ones leave the stage with only a few bills stuffed in their tattered g-strings. Nine Inch Nails and Nirvana are big hits with the strippers—er, artists— here, most of whom will brag that they are dancing on the stage where Courtney Love got her start.

bars

Best tropical drinks: Credited with inventing the rum drinks Trader Vic's made famous, **Tiki Ti** *(4427 W. Sunset Blvd., 213/669–9381)* in Sil- ver Lake has been serving mysterious concoctions like the Shark's Tooth since 1961. The Hawaiian-shirt-wearing father and son owners will whip up any of the 72 drinks on the menu. Drinks are listed only by name and primary liquor, so pick the one that sounds most interesting and pray (fa- vorites are the tart Blood and Sand and the coconutty Bayanihan). The shack walls are covered by what son Mike calls "35 years' worth of Tiki junk given to us by patrons who've returned from vacations to the tropics." Look for the hundreds of little placards with people's names on them. Explains Mike: "Those cards are the people who have paid their drinking dues here." The Cramps' Lux and Ivy claimed that they moved to Los Angeles because of the Tiki Ti. Drink prices may seem high at $6 each, but with about three shots per beverage, it's a big bang for your buck. Don't be surprised if you can't stand up when you try to leave. Warning: It's closed Sundays through Tuesdays and November and July.

Best place to drink alone: Little has changed about **Hank's All-American Bar** *(Hotel Stillwell, 840 S. Grand Ave., 213/623–7718)* since it opened in 1963. Walk through the Western-style swinging doors and back past the bar to the cocktail lounge. The walls are covered in red-velvet bordello-ready wallpaper and there's a buffet that never has anything to offer except prepackaged popcorn. Whimsical touches that keep the locals coming back include the blond mannequin in the sequined dress propped up in a chair, having a drink, and the Make-Believe Ballroom, a small, mirrored room. Unless you forget the point of being here, the drinks are strong and cheap. People come here to black out on a tight budget, so be prepared to reassure the guy next to you that his wife didn't leave him for a schnook.

Runner-up: **H.M.S. Bounty** *(3357 Wilshire Blvd., 213/385–7275)* serves strong cocktails to non-sissies and landlubbers with style. The walls are decorated with ships and nautical shtick. Strange, considering that the Bounty is a solid half-hour from the sea. But don't ye complain, matey. Just drink your grog and you'll feel a bit o' the tide.

Best karaoke dive: The name alone sets Los Feliz's **Smog Cutter** *(864 N. Virgil Ave., 213/660–4626, 213/667–9832)* apart from the rest of L.A.'s watering holes, but that's not all there is to the story. With fake wood paneling, neon beer ads, dust-covered signs like MY OTHER CAR IS A BEER, and pickled, hard-core barflies at the tables, the Cutter is a genuine Los Angeles dive. Every night, the pool table gets tripped over several times, while comatose drinkers stare at the scantily clad Thai babes on the Miller Lite posters. Lately, it has also drawn 20-ish locals who gossip over cheap drinks. Weekends get especially crazy at the Smog Cutter, as the karaoke machine is dusted off for an evening of self-humiliation. The one drawback about karaoke nights here (aside from actually having to listen to the girl with the nose ring do "Summer Lovin' ") is that when groovy youngsters pack the joint, the lifers go elsewhere.

Best beach-town watering hole: The **Circle Bar**'s *(2926 Main St., 310/392–4898)* bar is more like an oval than a circle, but, hey, after a few of the drinks these bartenders pour, it can assume any shape necessary. In contrast to Main Street's chichi shopping environs, the Circle offers a more friendly, down-home atmosphere, with cheap drinks and pool tables. The stools at this exceptional watering hole harbor a mix of surfers, students, and professional drinkers—a mixture that tends to breed interesting, albeit slurred, conversations.

Best German beer and potato pancakes: Don't be a sauerkraut! For the proper weltanschauung, walk through the unassuming doors of the **Red Lion Tavern** *(2366 Glendale Blvd., 213/662–5337)* and enter a world of all things German. Order a drink from a lederhosen-clad fraulein who will *wilkommen* you and answer any question you might have about the eight beers on tap. Feeling like a mad Viking? Ask for The Boot: a 42-ounce boot-shaped glass filled with any beer—it'll run about $30. The Red Lion also serves liquor, but the bulk of the drinkers come for suds. Downstairs, a live accordionist plays Beatles favorites and Keno is an option. For a slower-paced vibe, try the quiet upstairs bar or the beer garden in back, complete with resident cat. The Red Lion serves decent German grub (the potato pancakes are greasy and great), so during dinner hours, transplanted German families and old couples fill tables alongside the younger drinking set. You'll be joining the sing-alongs before the night's through!

Best real cocktail-nation lounge: The **Dresden Restaurant** *(1760 N. Vermont Ave., 213/665–4294)* first opened its doors to feed and water Hollywood in 1954. And on many nights it feels like not a day has passed since then. The dining room is beautiful, in a deco-mobster kind of way, with plush pink booths and real (!) silverware. Among the nocturnal masses, the Dresden is known more for its bar than its food. Complete with cork wall coverings and an elaborate grand piano in the bar perfect for making on-the-spot requests, the lounge packs in local crowds of old-timers and spooky youngsters—it's near the Amok bookstore and X-Large (see Shopping). Marty and Elaine, the married lounge act who play the piano, have a vast repertoire of originals and covers, and will take pretty much any request given to them. (Tip: Request "Staying Alive" and check out Elaine's vocal accents—a guaranteed crowd-pleaser.) The bartenders make great, moderately priced cocktails. The Dresden was David Lynch's favorite bar during the years between *Blue Velvet* and *Twin Peaks* and was featured in *Swingers*, which has challenged its capacity every night since.

Best faded Hollywood glamour: The **Formosa Cafe** *(7516 Santa Monica Blvd., 213/850–9050)* isn't just a bar. It's a night in itself—among the best L.A. has to offer for anybody who wants a stiff drink, a darkly lit room, deep booths, and the glory of has-been Hollywood. This Tiki room/Chinese lounge has been an A-list watering hole for generations of Hollyweird hipsters—including, recently, leather-bound BMW aficionados and cocktail nation sharpies. Hundreds of autographed head shots from Jack Palance to Gary Coleman testify to its staying power. It also has an impressive Elvis decanter collection given to the bar by Colonel Tom Parker (Elvis's business manager), who would while away the hours here while his client was at the studio across the street making movies like *Jailhouse Rock*. Skip the scary Chinese grub.

Best new Hollywood bar: If **Jones** *(7205 Santa Monica Blvd., 213/850–1727)* had been around in their day, Rat Packers would have made it a second home. Special touches like individual table lamps, shiny black tiles with sea-foam-green accents, and gingham tablecloths make the Jones drinker feel like Hollywood sharkskin royalty—except, guess what, it's surprisingly inclusive and attitude-free. In contrast to other Hollywood hot spots, there is no velvet-rope hassle over who you are. So, the Jones bar tends to be packed on weekends, drawing a varied group of entertainment execs from the Hills (Rick Rubin is a regular) and down-at-the-heels youth who drink and hobnob glamorously before going home to eat ramen. If you can afford it, the food at the restaurant is delicious, with highlights such as the rotisserie chicken salad. Weeknight happy hours that feature specials on drinks like the Lemon Drop.

Best meet market: Los Feliz's **Good Luck Bar** *(1514 Hillhurst Ave., in the Davidian Building, 213/666–3524)* has come to be known as the "Get Lucky Bar." And that about says it all. With paper lanterns everywhere, this dark Chinese bar is where youngish actors and scenesters in X-Large threads have come to drink potent tropical punches and hit on each other since it opened in 1994. Come with lots o' cash, though, as none of the drinks are cheap. The jukebox offers Motown and '60s faves, and there's a plush art deco couch room. No cover charge, but on the weekend, be prepared to stand in a line of coolios.

Best Hollywood hideaway: The **Burgundy Room** *(1621 1/2 Cahuenga Blvd., 213/465–7530)* was opened in the late 1980s by two British expats who saw a need for a dark, dank bar with a great jukebox. Regulars came for nights of Snakebites and rowdy conversation. Known as the BR, it has since come under new management and is still dark and still beer-only but has become rather subdued. Which means it's a great private clubhouse for you and your pals.

Runner-up: As the Burgundy Room grew in popularity, its original owners opened the **Room** *(1626 Cahuenga Blvd., 213/462–7196)* across the street. A hideaway in every respect, you have to enter through the alley—look for the doorman by the Dumpster—and the narrow room, lined with booths, is so dark you have to squint. It's a huge scene on weekends, with standing room only and beautiful people on the make. For a cozy, more quiet environment, come early on a weeknight—it tends to get crowded around 11. Factoid: This is the bar where Drew Barrymore married the British guy.

food/coffee

Best Hollywood Boulevard surf 'n' turf: Laying claim to the title of "Oldest Restaurant in Hollywood," **Musso & Frank Grill** *(6667 Hollywood Blvd., 213/467–5123)* opened in 1919 and has hosted everyone from a bourbon-sipping William Faulkner to a Caesar-salad-munching Madonna. The menu is haute American, featuring classics like lobster thermidor, macaroni au gratin, and chicken à la king. For a real treat, order the Caesar salad, which is prepared at the table. The formal dining room's cream-colored walls are lined with tall oak partitions, where Hollywood types can talk business. A second dining room has a counter with stools for loners. The bar is one of L.A.'s grandest, with oak and mirrored panels. Try a martini—and marvel at the size of the olive, surely the biggest, most tasty in town. Be prepared to spend a lot of money, though, starting with valet parking—if you value your rig, park it securely. Rumor has it that Nathanael West and Raymond Chandler chatted plots over gin and steaks here weekly. Closed Sundays and Mondays.

Best see-and-be-scene: Finding a good restaurant to take schmoozees to is a favorite pastime in Los Angeles, and **Vida** *(1930 Hillhurst Ave., 213/660–4446)* is a current front-runner. Beastie Boy Mike D and restaurateur Fred Eric opened Vida in 1994, offering dishes with names like No Okra Winfrey gumbo and Love Me Tender chicken. Of the hodgepodge of cuisines served, the common denominator is that all the dishes are stacked, e.g., potatoes on bottom, steak on top. The bar, with corrugated metal siding and sunken pillowy booths, is a good spot for a drink; and in the glass-and-bamboo-accented dining room, you'll find a family in Armani next to a table of music-biz comers showing off their green dreads and piercings. On a recent visit, Bob DeNiro was finishing off a hot date with a big fat stogie.

Best 24-hour Jewish deli: The *only* place to eat matzo-ball soup at 4 A.M., **Canter's** *(419 N. Fairfax Ave., 213/651–2030)* is the oldest, truest Jewish deli in L.A. The veritable center of nocturnal Hollywood, Canter's is a rock 'n' roll institution. Charles Manson used to wait outside with his guitar and audition for passersby. The full-blast fluorescent lighting is covered with plastic panels, lending Canter's an early-'70s, trailer-park psychedelic feel. A second dining room is another throwback, with colored plastic disks suspended from the wall panels. And then there's the bar: the Kibitz Room, where Tuesday night jams draw self-indulgent scenesters for rambling, nepotistic blues sessions.

Runner-up: For years Canter's had no competition, but then **Jerry's Famous Deli** *(8701 Beverly Blvd., 310 /289–1811)* opened a restaurant not far away, creating a pricier, high-gloss alternative. If Canter's is the Lenin of L.A. pastrami, Jerry's is the Stalin. Lunch draws a stunning list of stars on the cusp of fame or just past it, like Ike Turner, Rob Lowe, and Elizabeth Berkley, while late at night, the post-drinking crowd is youngish and rich. Leave the cell phone in the car? Don't worry, each table has its own calling-card-operated telephones.

Best 24-hour diner: With its California '60s architecture à la "The Brady Bunch" and its vast menu, **Astro Family Restaurant** *(2300 Fletcher Dr., 213/663–9241)* is the favorite round-the-clock hang for Silver Lake and East Hollywood. Astro is packed with clubbers after midnight thanks to its proximity to a handful of newly hip bars like Spaceland (see Clubs). The menu offers diner food with an international twist: Feta-filled omelettes and the french burger are hits here. Astro was one of the first L.A. diners to acknowledge vegetarians by adding veggie burgers and good salads to its menu. The prices are higher than the typical diner, with burgers and breakfasts (served all night!) in the $6 range. There's an outdoor patio to satisfy the smoker's needs and, because of thoughtful planning, the parking lot is huge.

Best late-night, low-budget Thai food: In the wee hours odd cravings can emerge, and if it's Thai food you want, go to **Sanamluang** *(5176 Hollywood Blvd., 213/660–8006)*, the favorite of critics and locals alike. With fluorescent lighting and Nagel-inspired wall hangings, this isn't the place for a romantic meal, but the chefs here dish up the best Thai noodles in L.A. Open until 5 A.M., Sanamluang is constantly packed with police officers and young, Thai-speaking transplants. Almost every dish on the menu is under $5, and the portions are big enough to take home tomorrow's lunch. Order by number, but be sure to clarify the order, as it can be a bit disconcerting to get the curdled blood soup instead of the noodles with broccoli.

Best $1 tacos at 2 A.M.: El Gran Burrito *(4716 Santa Monica Blvd., 213/665–8720)* is a family-owned taco stand and restaurant that stays open until the last drunk leaves with a full stomach. If you have a hankering for burritos and quesadillas, go inside the restaurant, which serves made-to-order Mexican food over the din of the salsa jukebox. But the real treat at El Gran Burrito is the outdoor taco stand, packed every night of the week with drinkers postponing bed spin and cops, all in pursuit of the delicious $1 tacos. The *carne asada* and *carnitas* tacos are favorites here—with tender meat piled so high that rolling the tortilla around it becomes a challenge. Don't overlook the salsa bar for large spoonfuls of onions and cilantro, hot sauce or jalapeño-pickled carrots.

Best lunchtime taco stand: Yuca's *(2056 Hillhurst Ave., 213/662–1214)* is one of Los Feliz's best-kept secrets. The tacos, burritos, and chili burgers(!) have been attracting neighborhood lunchers for ten years, and for good reason. The food at Yuca's is reasonably priced ($1.50 tacos, $3 burritos) and always delicious. All of the meat is perfectly tender and flaky, the tortillas are deliciously fresh, and the beans are smooth and creamy. (If adding cheese sounds good, beware, because Yuca's will throw a piece of American cheese on any *con queso* order.)

Best rotisserie chicken with addictive condiment: A Middle Eastern pit stop near Highland on Sunset, **Zankou Chicken** *(5065 Sunset Blvd., 213/665–7842)* is an institution that demands one visit. Thing is, though, having gone once, the Zankou craving pops up again and again, making this unassuming restaurant one of the busiest eateries in L.A. Delicious and cheap, the rotisserie chicken is king here, with the spits turning about 50 whole chickens simultaneously at any given moment. A whole chicken meal (with pita bread) costs $6.95 and can feed a family of four well. The sandwiches ($3.50) are good, too, with either meat or falafel (called best in the city by veggies and omnivores alike) wrapped in pita bread. The meats and falafel are great, but they're really just an excuse to smear Zankou's mysterious garlic paste—the restaurant's crowning glory—on everything.

Best reason to eat meat: A burger is a burger, right? Well, in L.A. there's a burger, and then there's a Jayburger. Don't confuse the two. Right across the street from the Garage, **Jay's Jayburgers** *(4481 Santa Monica Blvd., 213/666–5204)* is the perfect burger shack. The Jayburger is a cheeseburger with a dollop of the best, most greasy chili served in the 213 area code—where there's lots of competition. This joint has charm even though it's in a part of East Hollywood known for car break-ins. It draws a perfect cross-section of Silver Lake: Mexican families bring their kids, hipsters indulge their once-a-month meat cravings, and crusty old men sit at the counter all day. Drug dealers (and their customers) used to cite Jay's as their favorite beef and as their territory, but then Jay (yes, there is a Jay) added the Jay-A-Dog—a hot dog with cheese, chili, pickles, and peppers—to the menu, and the pushers moved elsewhere. Who can conduct business with such competition?!

Best original drive-thru burgers: In-N-Out Burger *(locations citywide, 800/786–1000)* opened in 1948 in a quiet suburb of Los Angeles. Even then Angelenos were car-crazy, and the wise owner of In-N-Out gave local Kustom Kar Kommandoes their first-ever drive-thru. In-N-Out serves some of the best burgers and fries in the city, and serves 'em fast. All the ingredients are superfresh—none of the stands have freezers. The fries and burgers are prepared to order, but the wait is never more than a few minutes. The shakes are damn fine as well, made with real ice cream instead of soft-serve. Finally, In-N-Out's meals are cheap, with a burger and fries clocking in at three bucks.

Best French dip: A lot of L.A. restaurants claim to be culinary pioneers or institutions, but few are. Downtown's **Philippe the Original** *(1001 N. Alameda St., 213/628–3781)* is both, having invented the french dip sandwich in 1918 and been serving it ever since. A big stucco warehouselike building, with sawdust on the concrete floor, Phillipe has a stark, cavernous two-room interior. Long community-style high tables with stools and private booths are crowded with people from all walks of L.A., from suits to cops to Latino construction workers and the odd bag lady nursing her nine-cent coffee. Phillipe is also the central feeding station for City Hall employees who swap hot Russian mustard and tales from the urban jungle. The prices are hard to beat at about $4 per sandwich (beef, pork, lamb, or turkey) and 70 cents for potato salad. An excellent stop for lunch or dinner after a day at Olvera Street, Chinatown, Dodger Stadium, or the Temporary Contemporary.

Best Hollywood pizza: Right across the street from Canter's on Fairfax, **Damiano's Mr. Pizza** *(412 N. Fairfax Ave., 213/658–7611)* draws patrons in droves for tasty, cheap pizza and huge house salads. It's as dark as a bar inside, and maybe that's why it has more than its share of leather-clad barflies after last call. It's a staple of young Hollywood (everyone here is in a band, waiting to get the Screen Actors Guild card, or working as a studio page). The bottled-beer list is stellar; the pizza toppings, in high Cali fashion, range from sausage to avocado, and each table gets free celery and carrot sticks to munch on.

Best late-night espresso: Insomnia *(7286 Beverly Blvd., 213/931–4943)* opened during the late '80s coffeehouse craze in L.A. and is one of the few remaining originals. Comfortable couches and chairs make it a nice place to flop, and the gold-painted walls are lined with consistently interesting art installations. Quiet jazz or blues adds a nice soundtrack, and because the environment is lax and friendly, people feel at home coming here to read a book or cram for finals. It's in a neighborhood where hip clothing stores and eateries sit next to Hasidic synagogues. What's more, the coffee is good.

Runner-up: Vermont Boulevard in Los Feliz is home to a slew of interesting stores like Amok, X-Large, and MOA (see Shopping). Another stalwart on the L.A. coffee scene is Hollywood's **Bourgeois Pig** *(5931 Franklin Ave., 213/962–6366)*, where it's so dark your eyes have to adjust.

Best breakfast: Every morning hungover-looking waiters and customers descend on **Millie's** *(3524 W. Sunset Blvd., 213/664–0404)* to (respectively) serve and eat delicious, cheap breakfast fare. Full meals run from $3.95 to $5.95. Egg dishes include the Jackie G. Scramble, named after a lesbian city councilwoman whose office is across from the diner; the Eleanor R. Scramble; the Millie's Special (eggs, fresh spinach, and cream cheese, scrambled). Those and the muffin-shaped fresh buttermilk biscuits keep the Silver Lake locals coming back again and again. Millie's seems to employ only starving-artist types, many of whom have made names for themselves in the Silver Lake music scene.

Best chicken and waffles: Can you say cardiac arrest? If you have even the slightest interest in fried chicken, you'll love **Roscoe's House of Chicken and Waffles** *(1518 Gower St., 213/466–7453 and 5006 W. Pico Blvd., 213/936–3730)*, known as home to some of the best soul food outside of South Central. While the combo of chicken and waffles may strike some as odd, it works fantastically: golden-fried pieces of juicy chicken with fresh, spongy small-grid waffles and a large dollop of melting butter. The walls of the crowded dining room are covered in fake wood paneling and 8x10s of famous African-Americans from Cosby to Sinbad. Long lines form out front.

Best vegetarian deli: Hollywood's **Erewhon** *(7660 Beverly Blvd., 213/937–0777)* is a full-scale whole foods supermarket, but when you're hungry for a healthy meal in a hurry, the huge soup and salad bar and deli here are reliable. The closest the copiously stocked deli comes to deli meat is chicken, fish, and, on occasion, turkey. Prepackaged sandwiches and burritos are also available, and there are picnic tables out front. Vegans should be forewarned that many of the delicious sandwiches rely on cheese.

Runners-up: A popular standby for Angeleno vegetarians and vegans is **A Votre Santé**, which serves vegetable curries, stir fries, and fat-free dishes; there are branches in three hip locations—Venice *(1025 Abbot Kinney Blvd., 310/314–1187)*, Brentwood *(13016 San Vincente Blvd., 310/451–1813)*, and on La Brea *(345 N. La Brea Ave., 213/857–0412)*. A slighter pricier option is **Inaka Natural Foods** *(131 S. La Brea Ave., 213/936–9353)*, which has drawn music-industry honchos like Rick Rubin down from the Hollywood Hills with its vegetarian Japanese dishes.

shopping

records

Best music emporium: Specializing in every type of music, and employing the most hyperalert music sharpies in town, **Aron's Records** *(1150 N. Highland Ave., 213/469–4700)* has been satisfying L.A.'s musical needs for 30 years, and will continue to after the term "alternative" fades to black. If the ReSearch title *Incredibly Strange Music* inspires cravings for the hard-to-find, check out Aron's Strange Music section. It stocks everything from Archie Shepp to Schleprock, and if they don't have it new or used, the staffers will order it for you.

Runner-up: On the Westside, **Rhino Records** *(1720 Westwood Blvd., 310/474–8685)* was one of the best all-types-of-music stores during its heyday in the late '80s but has since fallen a few rungs and has stock shortages.

Best indie-record shop: Near Formosa Cafe and Jones (see bars), **No Life Record Shop** *(7209 Santa Monica Blvd., 213/845–1200)* often feels more like a kids' clubhouse than a bona fide business, and that's how the owners want to keep it. With the comfy chairs and couches, Atari, pinball, and free coffee, it's easy to forget why you came here in the first place—except that buyer Peter Taylor has stocked No Life's shelves with arguably the best indie-rock selection in town: rare Stereolab 10-inches, out-of-print 7-inch Japanoise, the latest from small labels like K or Merge. Saturday afternoons, L.A.'s music scenesters crowd into this tiny space for free rock shows by touring indie bands like the Folk Implosion and Sleater-Kinney. The sound system is remarkably good for a store, but it gets hot and crowded quickly, so come early to mark your territory.

Best DJ stores: The best options for house 12-inches are both on Melrose: **Beat Non-Stop** *(213/930–2121)* and **DMC** *(213/651–3520)*. On the straight-hip-hop front, remixes and small label tracks can be found in **Fat Beats** *(213/663–3717)*, a small boutique inside the X-Large clothing store (see clothes).

books

Best lefty books (Westside): Just blocks from bluffs that look over the vast Santa Monica beaches, the Third Street Promenade is a winning choice for an afternoon or evening of loitering, movie watching, french fry eating, shopping. One great stop is a bookstore that dates back to the mall's days as a place to buy discount beach sandals and watch Mexican movies. A snappy makeover hasn't totally obscured the **Midnight Special**'s *(Third Street Promenade, Santa Monica, 310/393–2923)* old-school lefty roots: Not only do you come here for Chomsky and conspiracy theory, but also for the great California history section. What really set Midnight Special apart are events like an Internet for Progressives talk series and a homelessness discussion group led by a local homeless man. Every Friday night at 8, open mike poetry readings pack the place for pro and am readers.

Best New Age books: An anomaly in the Melrose area, the **Bodhi Tree** *(8585 Melrose Ave., 310/659–1733)* is at once flaky and beautiful. An only-in-California (or maybe Sedona, Arizona) experience, it specializes in matters of the spirit: Buddhism, European philosophy, ESP, chakra points, and all types of meditation (with accompanying wind chimes) are specialties here. You can sip herbal tea, sniff incense, and recline on cushions while catching up on past-life awareness. Higher-awareness seekers come from all corners of the city to this mecca—for good reason: The selection is vast, with a good used room. You might walk in feeling like Jack Webb, but by the time you leave, you're gonna be higher than the Baba Ram Dass.

Best anti-everything bookstore: If you visit only one bookstore in Los Angeles, make it **Amok** *(1764 N. Vermont Ave., 213/665–0956)*. Located a few doors from the Dresden Room (see Bars) in Los Feliz, Amok is the nation's foremost outlet for the literature of apocalypse. Run by Stuart Swezey, an ahead-of-his-day entrepreneur who once put on a Sonic Youth concert in the California desert, Amok manages to offend all sensibilities at once with its desire to make public what Swezey calls the "extremes of information in print"; the store offers survivalist tracts, serial killer bios, alien abduction tales, drug lore, and conspiracy theories, just to get you started. An example of the dark side of L.A. at its best, it's a scary bookstore for scary times—but contrary to appearances, given the shop's fixation on bodily mutilation, Swezey and his staff are the nicest hepcats this side of China. Drop by and say hi.

Best comics and comix: Right on the trendiest stretch of Melrose, **Golden Apple** *(7711 Melrose Ave., 213/658–6047; 24-hour info line: 213/651–0455)* is not just a store but a complete archive of all things comics, with a vast selection of *Superman*, *Mad*, *True Adventures*, *Hate*, *Eightball*, you name it. It also stocks models, masks, and goodies like a scaled-down reproduction of *Alien*'s alien, and Clive Barker's *Hellraiser* puzzle, Hellbox. Angelenos know it for hosting events like an Indie Zine Festival and a party for the premiere of the TV show "The New Adventures of Superman."

clothes

Best place to buy your Mom's old prom dress: Looking for something to wear on a hot date but living on food stamps? Or maybe you're looking for a "Mork and Mindy" T-shirt to wear with those bell-bottom cords? Well, stop scouring the malls and head over to **Jet Rag** *(834 N. La Brea Ave., 213/465–0128)*. With old suits and cocktail dresses, this store caters to sensible shoppers with thrift-store tastes and pocketbooks to match. Thanks to Jet Rag's eye for quality vintage stuff, movie-studio costumers also make weekly Jet Rag pit stops to fill their stars' wardrobes. Every thorough Jet Rag shopper works up a sweat fishing through rack upon endless rack of clothes that the Partridge

Family would have died for. Be sure to examine each item, as the store's no-return policy is law. The prices are reasonable: $5 for a June Cleaver–esque sundress to $20 for vintage 501s.

Best pricey vintage store: If you want the thrift-store look at designer prices, try **American Rag Cie** *(150 S. La Brea Ave., 213/953–3154)*. A warehouse of vintage clothing, American Rag specializes in beautifully refurbished clothing. The sections are divided by gender and era, with the '40s, '50s, and '60s figuring most prominently. Adjoining storefronts feature American Rag Cie Youth (for the real kids), American Rag Shoes, and American Rag Cie Maison Et Cafe, a kitchenware store.

Best place to check your thread: Want to look like a *cholo* who wishes he was Bobby Brady? Beastie Boy Mike D and partners Eli Bonere and Adam Silverman have got your number. Their **X-Large** *(1766 N. Vermont Ave., 213/666–3483)* store offers durable—albeit pricey—unisex garb, most of which is designed specifically for X-Large. Corduroy and heavy denim are the favored materials, and tiny, '70s-inspired striped T-shirts were repopularized here. When Kim Gordon of Sonic Youth fell for the X-Large look, she joined with Mike D to open the equally expensive X-Girl (same address, same number) for really girly items like mini-T-shirts and microskirts. Like its sibling, X-Girl's clothes take cues from skateboarding and hip-hop, but the threads are less durable and come in sizes that make woman with average bodies consider anorexia. Warning: The racks tend to be thin, with multiples of few items. And you might just find yourself a fashion victim of the '90s when you realize the whole city is wearing your "cutting-edge" trousers.

Best clothes to wear to your alien abduction: The retro-futuristic clothing sold at **MOA** *(1756 N. Vermont Ave., 213/665–1735)* has been a big hit with L.A.'s rave, trance, and indie-rock sets in recent years. Like a wardrobe from *Logan's Run*, these day-and-night-glo jumpsuits and miniskirts put the shock in future shock. Must-haves like polyester pants are durable, making them good buys even though the prices aren't cheap. One of the owners of MOA started his own line called Mondorama, which has become a staple at hip clothing outlets nationwide.

et cetera

Best odds and ends: Silver Lake's **Uncle Jer's** *(4459 W. Sunset Blvd., 213/662–6710)* is where Angelenos who have everything go to find something. A family-run business since it opened in 1978, Uncle Jer's specializes in knickknacks: exotic art and jewelry, candles and incense, soaps and essential oils, clothes, and great odd toys. The store is always busy, filled with those who've been there hundreds of times before and those who heard about it through the grapevine. Bonus: nifty wrapping.

Runner-up: At Exene Cervenka's **You've Got Bad Taste** *(3816 Sunset Blvd., 213/669–1718)*, you can find both dirt from the Tate House and Mr. T coloring books.

Best big-hair music store: Musicians shop at **Guitar Center** *(7425 W. Sunset Blvd., 213/874–1060)* but are embarrassed to admit it. The Guitar Center is the temple of Big Rock, a.k.a. Big-Hair Rock. Metal-mavens and other noodlers will have a field day. But you also might catch Thurston Moore on a shopping spree! The walkway is paved with foot- and handprints of rock stars past and present like B. B. King, Les Paul, and Eddie Van Halen. Guitar Center always has some kind of sale in progress, during which the prices are hard to beat. Otherwise, though, the cost of music gear is way high, dude, but can be haggled down. The sales staff is mostly male egotists working to pay for demo tapes or hair extensions, but don't let the decidedly macho vibe deter you: This place is a music-industry mecca.

Best vintage guitars: After an excursion to the Guitar Center, **Black Market Music** *(841 N. La Cienega Blvd., 310/659–6795)* seems like heaven. Consistently cited by local musicians as the best vintage music store L.A. has to offer, Black Market Music sells good guitars, effects, and amps at reasonable prices. The people here actually care about the products (rather than the commission they'd make through a sale). There's no macho posturing at BMM, so guitar grrls tend to feel less alienated.

Best swap meet: On the second Sunday of each month all walks of life converge on the **Rose Bowl Swap Meet** *(Rose Bowl Stadium, Pasadena)* to haggle with dealers who peddle new junk, vintage threads, furniture, collectibles, as well as stereo equipment, antiques, art, disco balls. Admission costs $5, and the early bird rate is double that. The asking prices aren't cheap, but haggle—that's the point. Professional dealers come to unload their stuff at boutique prices. The massive meet requires a full day's walking, and the free parking can be a major pain. As the day progresses, the lot fills and the hike from car to meet gets longer and longer.

Best adult toys: A pierced lesbian couple discuss their dildo options alongside the suited businessman and his wife getting advice about cock rings. Oh, the wonder that is L.A.'s **Pleasure Chest** *(7733 Santa Monica Blvd., 213/650–1022)!* There is something for everyone at this huge West Hollywood store—from high-end bondage gear (and lots of it) to condoms, dildos, and lube. The staff is extremely friendly, forthcoming, and have heard it *all* before, so it's hard to make them blush. The Pleasure Chest offers a relaxed, secure vibe—even women feel safe shopping alone.

body alterations

Best tribal tattoos: Way back in the old-school hardcore days of the early '80s, Leo Zulueta of **Black Wave** *(118 S. La Brea Ave., 213/932–1900)* was one of the founding fathers of the tribal tattoo movement. Leo's Filipino descent and Hawaiian upbringing inspired the South Pacific islander designs that have become de rigueur for punks and poseurs alike. Black Wave's walls are covered with original stark, black designs by Leo and the three other artists who work there, and you can choose from any of those designs, or commission a revision or an original. Because of his stature in the tattoo community and his immeasurable talent, it can be tough to get an appointment with Leo. There's usually a multiweek wait, so call ahead.

Best piercings: The Gauntlet *(8720 Santa Monica Blvd., 310/657–6677, call for appointment)* has been a staple of left-of-center L.A. before the term "modern primitive" was coined. The Gauntlet's clients include yuppie couples waiting for matching genital piercings and true believers waiting to graduate to the next gauge. You're in the hands of pros here; before work begins, the piercer explains every aspect of the job, the cleaning process, and aftercare methods, which tends to put your mind at ease. Pretty much any part of the body can be pierced, and the Gauntlet has trained its staff to do delicate work.

hotel/motel

Best clean, cheap hotel: Who can argue with below-ground parking and a pool in the courtyard? Hollywood's **Regency Plaza Suites** *(7940 Hollywood Blvd., 213/656–4555)* may be in an anonymous '60s apartment building, but at $70 a night it's cheap and honest. A sweet tabby named Timmy patrols the halls, perhaps a reincarnation of John Waters's favorite freak, Divine, who died in his sleep in one of the second-story front rooms. Each of the 45 bland but comfortable rooms at the Regency has a kitchen and a bedroom separate from the living room (a few rooms have dens and two suites have two bedrooms). The Regency tends to be popular with touring and recording bands who can't afford to wreck a suite at Le Mondrian.

Best grand old Hollywood hotel: Directly across the street from Mann's Chinese Theater sits the **Hollywood Roosevelt Hotel** *(7000 Hollywood Blvd., 213/466–7000)*. The roster of this classy Spanish revival hotel was once a who's who of stars: Shirley Temple learned to dance on the hotel's spiral staircase, David Niven slept in the servants' quarters before he hit stardom, and Clark Gable and Carole Lombard had many trysts in the building's hideaways. The Roosevelt hosted the first Academy Awards ceremony in 1929, and Montgomery Clift's ghost is said to haunt Room 926. After a two-year renovation, the Roosevelt reopened in 1984 with, among other touches, the bottom of the Olympic-size pool painted by L.A.'s own (by way of London) David Hockney. With cred like this, it's no wonder that the Roosevelt has become a favorite among bands and label execs. A double costs $109 plus taxes, nightly; and the two-story Gable-Lombard suite goes for $1,500.

Best Sunset Strip hideaway: Tucked away behind a Marlboro Man billboard at the armpit of Sunset Boulevard, the **Chateau Marmont** *(8221 Sunset Blvd., 213/656–1010)* is *the* place to stay in L.A.—if you've got money. Famous as John Belushi's death site, the French Gothic Chateau Marmont is known among paparazzi flee-ers as being the most private, exclusive hotel L.A. has to offer. Back when movie studios cared about stars' personal lives, Columbia mogul Harry Cohn told his charges, "If you must get into trouble, go to the Marmont." The reclusive Howard Hughes called the hotel home for months on end; James Dean and Natalie Wood were cast for *Rebel Without a Cause* here; and Evan Dando holed up at the Marmont for several months while mucking about in L.A. The standard rooms (bedroom and bathroom) run for about $150; junior suites ($200 a night); and one- and two-bedroom suites ($230 to $300) all come with fully equipped kitchens. The spacious private cottages and bungalows ($200 to $500) are what set the Chateau apart from other L.A. hotels.

local wonders

Best cave: Untouched by human progress, the **Bronson Caves** *(just a few blocks north of central Franklin Avenue, near where Victor's Deli meets the Bourgeois Pig Coffee Shop)* have long been a refuge for knowing tai chi trainees and four-year-olds' birthday parties. Here's the best place to have cuckoo visions of massive insects attacking Los Angeles (wishful thinking?). If you sit in the dank, cool caves on a weekday afternoon, you can hear the sound of the city buzzing, yet you are completely surrounded by nature. Maybe it's the city that's the massive insect after all!

Best roller boogies: The **Venice Beach Boardwalk** has changed greatly since it was the roller-skating capital of the universe in 1977. But it remains a major crossroads for weirdniks, groovers, droolers, muscle builders, aromatherapy addicts, rastas from Mars, disenfranchised yuppies, ballsy tourists, and semiprofessional roller disco experts. Venice has a rich history as an underground city, and you can find traces of all its freak scenes, past and present, on a crowded weekend day. Conceived by renaissance man Abbot Kinney as an actual Venice on the Pacific, the small canals from 1905 remain *(just blocks from the main drag, south of Venice Boulevard)*. By the 1950s, the slum by the sea had evolved into Venice West, Southern Cali's homegrown attempt at a beatnik poetry and art movement. Stragglers gathered at joints like the Gas House to recite free verse and grok the vibrations. It was into this semicivilized maelstrom that young UCLA film scholar Jimmy Morrison slouched, looking for oceanic satori. By the late '70s, the boardwalk was *the* center for the burgeoning clams-on-the-half-shell and roller-skate culture immortalized in Chic's epic "Good Times." And many breakdancers, lockers, and poppers cut their teeth robotically on the Boardwalk's promenade. Perhaps the most drastic changes came to the Venice Boardwalk in the early Reagan Age, before the Olympic summer of 1984, when developers bought up the whole place, scrubbed it down, and raised the rents. For a while, you couldn't recognize it! FREE HOMEOPATHIC MASSAGE gave way to SUNGLASSES $7 TWO PAIRS. Still, the hippies and fringies who make Venice the hot property it is today could not be squeezed out, and the Boardwalk remains a groovy circus. There are thrift, record, and health-food stores on Winward Avenue; and just south of Winward on the Boardwalk, you'll find both **Muscle Beach**, where bodybuilders do obscene presses in an open lifting pen, and, nearby, the famous basketball courts where self-styled playground legends show their monkeys and get in ridiculous arguments over fouls.

Best courtyard marketplace: The Fairfax District's immortal **Farmer's Market** on the corner of Fairfax and Third started as a dirt parking lot where farmers hawked their produce. Today, it's a massive outdoor sprawl of eateries, tchotchke boutiques, and fresh veggie stands, packed to the gills with the local elderly, the local tattooed hipoisie, and the local hungry. Farmer's Market has got every flavor from gumbo to gummy bears, and on a Sunday morning, brunchtime, you can't find a cooler place to hang out, people-watch, and kill time.

transmissions

Best community station: Big with Westside culture vultures, **KCRW (89.9 FM)** broadcasts NPR news by day and eclectic music by night. One of KCRW's musical highlights is soft-spoken music director Chris Douridas' weekday show, *Morning Becomes Eclectic*, which is big with young and old music fans who want their world music (Nusrat Fateh Ali Kahn) mixed in with their mellow pop (Stereolab). When he's not moonlighting at the powerhouse KROQ, Jason Bentley hosts a great ambient show called *Metropolis* weeknights 8 to 10 P.M. And, Mondays through Thursdays (10 P.M. to midnight) KCRW great Tricia Halloran spins an educated, innovative mix of truly alternative indie and major-label music on her show, *Brave New World*. Saturdays from midnight to 3 A.M. is a trip-hop and ambient show.

Best college station: Broadcasting from the Jesuit Loyola Marymount University near LAX, commercial-free **KXLU (88.9 FM)** plays great punk and indie rock from early morning to 6 P.M. (when the classical programming takes over) and then continues with rock programming at 10 P.M. Fridays from 6 to 8 P.M. is a raw, unrefined demotape show.

louisville

by Chris Iovenko

"Lots of bands from Louisville have songs that call out
local landmarks. The music I like from Louisville doesn't
sound like it came from anywhere else. It doesn't sound
like it necessarily came from Louisville either, until you
start getting those lists of streets and neighborhoods."
— **David Grubbs**, *Gastr del Sol*

Louisville sits on the cusp of the North and South. It has qualities of both, belongs to neither, and consequently strikes some
visitors as backward, remote, and strangely isolated. But to
look at Louisville in terms of its lacks—no big-league team
sports, no big museum, no fashion mavens—is to miss the point.
Louisville is not just an outsider to the American scene, it is a *content*
outsider, a city so oblivious to progress that it ends up reinventing the
wheel every so often—and doing a fine job of it. Mark Twain said he
wanted to be in Louisville when the world ended because everything
gets to Louisville 20 years late.

Celebrity native sons like prettiest man alive Muhammad Ali and
gonzo journalist Hunter S. Thompson were known for talking big games
and taking no prisoners. In the '80s, the town's bumper crop of great,
hard-rocking bands showed the same what's-there-to-lose free spirit.
The underground music scene—if it can be called that, since there's no
music establishment to affront—started at a transvestite bar known as
the Beat Exchange in the late '70s. Then came the dark, smelly biker
bar named Tewligan's, where groups from Louisville's art scene, like the
Babylon Dance Band and Antietam, played a distinctive brand of guitar-
wave that attracted big local crowds as well as scattered national
acclaim. Younger bands began to follow on their heels, while more (and
weirder) venues opened up.

In 1985, one of Louisville's finest sluggers, Squirrel Bait, cut an
eponymous album with the then-small label Homestead and rocked living rooms across the nation. The music scene shifted and grew even

more vital—no one sound predominated, and experimentation was the rule of the day. Squirrel Bait descendants like guitarist David Grubbs's Bastro and later Gastr Del Sol and Brian McMahan's Slint began to record under the tutelage of Steve Albini, the Rapeman-cum-producer who dubbed the scene Planet Louisville.

Nobody in Louisville can give you a break or a record deal, and so the pressure to perform, or to conform, is off. Music (or art or filmmaking, for that matter) functions as an end in itself, and so musicians have a great deal of freedom. Since bands aren't competing for money and opportunity, you won't find big-city internecine bitterness and bitchiness. Experimentation and diversity are—and have always been—the name of the game. Art-wave bands like Folks on Fire played and recorded contemporaneously with grunge-metal bands like Kinghorse and indie sensations like Squirrel Bait and Slint. Currently, there's plenty of room in Louisville for the faux traditional country of Palace, the guitar blues and bop of King Kong, the loungey funk of Love Jones, the hardcore of By the Grace of God, and the avant-garde ensemble the Rachel's Band. In fact, so much good music is coming out of Louisville, it's hard to imagine that both Louisville and its music scene will go off the map. Who knows if Louisville will hit the big time; when or if it happens, no doubt it will be 20 years late.

lay of the land

Louisville, originally a thriving river town (the Ohio river forms the Northern border) and then a railroad hub (the L&N, or Louisville and Nashville railway, was headquartered here), was built up around its downtown port and rail stations and banded by feeder rural communities and farms. Much of the downtown has now been thinned of its old buildings (parking lots and high-rise office buildings predominate) and sapped of vitality by the aggregate long-term effects of white flight and urban renewal, while the suburbs have sprawled and become bloated with strip malls, subdivisions, and traffic. Louisville's most vital and unique areas are the historic neighborhoods of **Old Louisville** (immediately south of Downtown), the **Highlands** (southeast of Downtown), and **Clifton** (east of Downtown). These are all turn-of-the-century (and older) neighborhoods that, after having gone through separate periods of neglect and decline, have been rediscovered and restored. Old Louisville has one of the nation's most impressive concentrations of Victorian houses and mansions (take a sightseeing drive down Third and Fourth Streets as well as St. James Court). For dining and entertainment the Highlands' **Bardstown Road** and **Baxter Avenue**, or

Clifton's **Frankfort Avenue**, are the best bets. As for nightlife, Louisville is generally a hard-partying town, with the Highlands having the largest and best concentration of bars. Last call is 4 A.M., except during Derby, when the whole town stays open 24 hours.

getting from a to b

Louisville is a medium-sized city that's fairly spread out, so most likely you'll need wheels of some sort, though if you are located in the Highlands walking is certainly feasible. Downtown is pretty compact and rationally organized, with building numbers aligning with their cross streets (1035 W. Broadway is between Tenth and Eleventh Streets, 150 W. Main Street is between First and Second Streets, and so on). The Highlands are likewise easy to navigate, and only when you get into the suburbs do things get complicated. There is a good bus system called TARC; schedules are available at local libraries as well as at TARC's main building at Tenth and Broadway (or call 502/585–1234). The fare is 75 cents, and during the day the wait for a bus shouldn't exceed 15 minutes.

sources

Louisville's newspaper *The Courier-Journal* was once considered a first-rate newspaper, a feeder for the *New York Times* and regular winner of Pulitzers. But since the once-proud Bingham family sold the paper to the owners of *USA TODAY* it's become strictly average. In Friday's Weekend section, it does a fairly complete summary of upcoming events, including a long listing of clubs and bars, and Saturday's entertainment insert, "The Scene," covers local events and trends. Louisville has a number of free weeklies (available at most restaurants and stores) that all compete to cover the area's news and entertainment front. The *Leo* is the largest of these and offers the broadest spectrum of regional news, as well as the most extensive listing of local shows, readings, events, and personal ads. Both *Hard Times* and *Burt* focus on the local youth and music culture, with lots of features on local bands and personalities—good insider resources for current local trends and hot bands.

If you're surfing the net, check out *Planet Louisville* (www.iglou.com/planet/) for a listing of a couple dozen active local bands and their upcoming gigs, both regionally and nationally, as well as e-mail addresses, and downloadable video and audio clips. In addition to the "Active Band" section there is an interactive section called "Rock Archives" that has constantly growing and changing libraries and information about the town's known and lesser-known (and sometimes) defunct acts. Text from *Hard Times* and *Burt,* as well as *Slamdeck A-Z* (a book documenting the history of one Louisville's important independent labels) is also available.

clubs

Best nightclub (or just weirdest): Since Tewligan's closed in 1996, there hasn't been a home field for alt.rock in Louisville. So, bands like Jesus Lizard end up playing places you wouldn't expect, like the South End's blue-collar, hard-partying **Toy Tiger** *(3300 Bardstown Rd., 502/456–1137)*. Once Louisville's premier after-midnight-rocking-through-the-dawn heavy metal meat market, the Tiger continues to lure rowdies with raunchy Spring Break in Daytona Beach scenes, its main barroom often packed with jarheads ogling Wet Nightgown or Banana-Eating contestants. Through swinging doors on the left-hand side, you'll find the concert room, a circular space with comfortable red vinyl booths and a plastic chandelier, sort of a low-end supper club. This 400-plus capacity room is home to Louisville's best sound system and most inscrutable booking policy, where tried-and-true local crowd-pleasers like Crazy Train (an excellent Ozzy cover band) dominate but local alternative acts and occasional touring bands (from Fu Manchu to Great White) also play. In a way, the Tiger epitomizes Louisville the way Times Square epitomizes New York; you'll see extremes of fashion and taste (airbrushed jeans, sprayed extra-large hair, exposed midriffs, Tasmanian Devil muscle shirts, and groomed mustaches) which, while not telling the whole story, do give you a unique sense of the place.

The Homemade Bikini Contest draws the year's biggest crowd, packing the large show room. Former winning bikinis have included three marshmallows and a piece of clear plastic wrap, a tissue-paper sari that accidentally dissolved under a shower of hurled beer, and several clear-plastic bags filled with a goldfish each. (Don't blame us.) Look for the winking neon tiger with the martini glass and wagging tail.

Runner-up: A handy place to go for locals who are too wasted to drive all the way out to the Tiger, the **Phoenix Hill** *(644 Baxter Ave., at Broadway and Baxter, 502/589–4630)* is a 25,000-square-foot monster complete with three stages, a roof garden, a deck, a solarium, and an arcade. The decor is Spirit of '74 cracker-barrel bordello: an expansive clutter of dusty horse-collar mirrors, huge brass chandeliers, old tubas, old movie posters, and big stained-glass kites and butterflies. Phoenix Hill's bread and butter is cover bands that play current radio hits on the main stage, though it frequently books has-been extended-run acts like Kansas, America, and Meat Loaf. The lineup has generally been improving, though, with recent visits from such luminaries as Stereolab and Jonathan Richman. Also, the roof-garden stage regularly programs local alternative bands. Mega Beer Friday Happy Hour (from 5–8 P.M.) draws a crowd with its 22-ounce Coors bottles for a buck, plus free tacos.

Best drag shows: Home of Louisville's most crowded dance floor, the **Connection** *(130 S. Floyd St., 502/585–5752)* is the inverse of the Toy Tiger. Both are multifaceted entertainment compounds with a penchant for the unusual, and both cater primarily to men, but the similarities end there. A massive 20,000-square-foot complex downtown, the Connection draws an omnisexual crowd, has several bars, a piano lounge, a cabaret showroom, DJs, and nationally known drag shows. Though it's primarily gay, you'll find mixed crowds on the weekends, lured by the throbbing dance scene. Don't expect much action before midnight, except on Wednesdays when dollar well drinks (until 1 A.M.) pull folks in early. The show room has terraced cocktail tables surrounding a stage with a red velvet curtain; pools of light come from table lamps and jazz hums, creating the mood of a classic Vegas dinner theater...until the curtain parts on a sequined Marilyn Monroe or red-robed Diana Ross facsimile, shimmying, emoting, and lip-synching to "My Heart Belongs to Daddy" or "It's Raining Men." On Friday nights an impressive display of line-dancing is conducted on the dance floor, with free dance lessons.

Best honky-tonk: The **Do Drop Inn** *(1032 Story Ave., 502/582–9327)* is located between the stockyards and the meat-packing plant and marked by a sign that reads NICE PEOPLE DANCING TO GOOD COUNTRY MUSIC. Open the outer door and you'll see a wall filled with autographed photos from country Hall of Famers and fathers of country music Charlie Louvin and Roy Acuff, and plaques proclaiming winners of past waltz contests. Open the inner door and you don't see anything at all; it's as dark and dank as the inside of a car's closed ashtray. Despite—or maybe because of— the darkness, this feels like a private club, and, as advertised, draws a large, friendly crowd of older dancing couples. Weekends are the liveliest, with the house band playing contemporary country, but Sunday's traditional country night is the best; the band's beat slows, the mood darkens, and the keen of the slide guitar draws you back to the days of Hank Williams. There's no better bar in which to sit alone with your boilermaker and your thoughts, listening to "Ramblin' Man."

Best dance club: Just around the corner from the Connection, **Sparks** *(104–108 W. Main St., 502/587–8566)* has a reputation as one of the top clubs in the country. Nothing fancy, Sparks is a rambling space with several bars and a dance floor. The decor is industrial tubing on the walls, Plexiglas and aluminum sci-fi tables, and hypnotic pink lighting. Call it an unconvincing futuristic milk bar. So, what's the fuss? Sparks has something hard to find these days—a genuinely decadent pickup scene. With house and techno DJs drawing Louisville's younger, hipper nightcrawlers, cruising here is conducted by four or more sexes with a pre-AIDS fervor. Hired strippers dance on platforms above the fog-shrouded dance floor and sometimes between cocktails on the bars; frequent saucy theme nights draw huge crowds. If Slave Auction Night isn't your cup of tea, there's always Foam Party Night (when the front bar is filled with bubbly warm foam), Wet Night (when the bar is sheathed in plastic from top to bottom and hoses spray continually), or Blonde Night (blondes drink free). Sparks also hosts meetings of the local bondage club: Latex.

Best late-night blues jam: Portland, located just west of Downtown, is one of Louisville's oldest neighborhoods, home to not only to the world's largest statue of a bourbon bottle (a water tower sculpted into a giant Old Forrester bottle at 18th Street and Broadway) but also a remarkable cafeteria called the **Coffee Cup** *(2530 W. Market St., 502/774–8166)*. It's got good cheap food, but the real reason to come here are the late-night (11 P.M. to 4 A.M.) weekend backroom blues jams. Past the cafeteria counter and booths is a small space with a fan and tables seating a dozen or so. There's no stage, a minimal sound system, just a drummer and a couple of guitar players. The house band takes its time, drinking and talking about numbers before playing them, and members of the blue-collar neighborhood audience frequently get out of their chairs to sing.

bars

Best jukebox: Rumor has it that the face of Jesus was once spotted in the giant and corroded trough urinal at **Dedden's Highland Fling** *(1359 Bardstown Rd., 502/451–0005)*. But DT-inspired delusions are rarer (or at least less religious) these days since the whiskeyed Catholic crowd has been largely replaced by a hipper scene. Dedden's is the current refuge of Louisville's alternative set, offering cheap drinks (a can of Falls City runs $1.15), a pool table, pinball machines, and best of all, a great jukebox flavored with favorites by the Stanley Brothers, Big Star, Al Green, and the Nuge.

Best microbrews: One of two microbreweries in town, the **Silo Micro Brewery** *(630 Barret Ave., 502/589–2739)* is located in an old brick warehouse lying in the shadows of abandoned cement grain silos. There is fierce competition between the Silo and the Bluegrass Brewing Company *(3929 Shelbyville Rd., 502/899–7070)*, and though it's close the Silo's Red Rock Ale distinguishes itself both with mellowness and body. In addition, the bar itself is a nice brick-and-beams affair, with a great deck and a small, laid-back clientele. The Silo also has the best happy hour, with $4 pitchers, $1 pints, and often cheap wings or shrimp. In addition to happy hour, Monday is $4 pitchers till midnight, and Tuesday is $1 pints of a select beer. Come here if you're planning a party: They sell kegs.

Best Old Louisville watering hole: The **Magnolia Bar & Grill** *(1398 S. 2nd St., 502/637–9052)* is in Old Louisville, a district named for its large turn-of-the-century Victorian houses. Even with the University of Louisville nearby, this stately area has stayed largely residential, keeping its gaslight-era charm intact. One of few Old Louisville bars, the Mag Bar, as it's known, has block-glass windows and largemouth bass gaping down from the walls; it's a top choice for relaxing in a booth with a vodka tonic and listening to good tunes on the jukebox. You'll find stool-roosting neighborhood regulars along with a young, nose-ringed gay or straight upwardly hip crowd tanking up before a night at nearby Sparks (see Clubs). The Sunday beer blast (all the draft beer you can drink for $6) attracts a good crowd, as do a variety of weekly special events like Karaoke and Talent nights.

Best bender-ender: If you haven't been to bed for a few days, are recently missing a tooth or two, and have only four bucks left, going to the **Tavern** *(1532 S. 4th. St., 502/637–4200)* will have the exhilarating effect of validating what you've always known to be true: You don't have a drinking problem. Or at least not like the people in this bar do. Everybody in the place, from the one-armed drunk guy shouting into the pay phone to the one-eyed drunk guy staring into the jar of prewar pickled eggs sitting on the counter to the withered barmaid who's had a bad day, is here for a reason. They're not here because they want to be, they're here out of a sense of duty; drinking isn't an easy profession but somebody's got to do it. To lift the financial and scheduling burden a little bit, the Tavern serves the cheapest drinks in town 22 hours a day (legally, they have to close between 4 and 6 A.M.) seven days a week. In case you're tempted to confuse this workplace with somewhere convivial or fun, signs behind the bar will bring you back to reality: NO DANC-ING admonishes one, while another confirms the obvious, PEOPLE ARE NO DAMN GOOD. Last stop—everybody off.

Best gay country bar: Rundown and grungy on the outside, opulent as a *Rawhide* set on the inside, **Tryangles** *(209 S. Preston St., 502/583–6395)* sets the local standard (a standard of one) for gay honky-tonks. If it's Wednesday, sidle on up to the bar in your underwear, receive a free shot, and get happy hour prices all night long. Not recommended for breeders or the uninitiated.

Best Downtown dive: Jake's Club Reno *(226 W. Jefferson at 2nd St., 502/584–9475)* is a smoky cinder-block dive just about big enough to park a vintage Chevy in. Formerly one of dozens of old bars on a Downtown drinking strip, Jake's is now, thanks to urban renewal, the only one left, a little drinking oasis surrounded by parking lots. While it draws its share of raincoat-wearing flotsam who've roamed over from the nearby adult theaters, Jake's is also a favorite haven for the local alt.music crowd. Proprietor Jake, in his pressed plaid shirt, belt, suspenders, and slouch hat, looks like a man from another era—and is. A handwritten sign behind the bar proclaims, SERVING THE BEST DRINKS IN TOWN FOR FIFTY YEARS (SINCE FDR). It's no lie—the drinks are good (Jake often uses Maker's Mark as a shelf bourbon) and inexpensive. But don't try tipping Jake; he'll just smile, shake his head, and push it back to you, saying, "Your business is enough."

Best place to go to after you've broken up (again) with your girlfriend: The **Silver Slipper** *(3608 S. 7th St., 502/363–2811)*, on the seedy, rough 'n' tumble Seventh Street strip, is a dark hellhole filled with skittish bake-your-own-crank scarecrows and seen-better-days topless dancers. Close your eyes, do a shot of whatever they're calling tequila and pretend you're far, far away (like in Tijuana), and then go pick up that pay phone, mister.

Best foosball table: One side of **Wick's Pizza** *(971 Baxter Ave., 502/458–1828)* in the Highlands is a pizza joint; the other side is a frat basement game room, where barroom Olympians battle it out with dart, cue, and (sometimes) beer bottle. At 1 A.M. drinks go down to happy hour prices and the joint starts jumping. The crowd is somewhat jockish, the pizza good.

Best gay sports bar: Score *(252 E. Market St., 502/561–1043)* is low-key, with brass railings, green carpeting, good pool tables, and drink specials during ball games…just like any hetero sports bar. Except that the sports murals on the walls show two guys working out on with weights while a third looks on with his pants down; on weekends you'll find baby-oiled weight lifters flexing on the stage before collecting tips in their thongs.

food

Best catfish sandwich: Indy's *(1033 W. Broadway, 502/589–7985)* is a pop-topped Downtown fast-food joint painted in bright bubble-gum-colored stripes. Since the employees are sealed in with the deep fryers by a bulletproof shield, you order through a P.A. The spicy chicken is hot enough to singe your nose hairs, but a slab of catfish in its thick gamy glory is the way to go. Indy's stocks a full line of malt liquor, so you can quench the fire in your gut with a 40-ounce Colt 45. For your further drinking convenience, on weekends Indy's is open until five in the morning. Daytime crowds include suits, while at night it's a little out of the way.

Best cheap cafeteria food: Just ten minutes from Downtown, the **South Side Inn** *(114 E. Main St., New Albany, 812/945–9645)* is one of few good reasons to cross the I-64 bridge into Indiana. Old-school cafeteria dining at its finest, the South Side serves up home-cooked victuals that will fill out the butt in your Lee jeans. From the famous fried chicken at $1.30 a plate to whitefish and roast beef, the food is always tasty and plentiful. Even with a slice of pecan pie for dessert, you can get out of here for a song.

Best bear claw: Krispy-Kreme Doughnut Co. *(3000 Bardstown Rd., 502/451–4880)* is a Louisville institution. Open 24 hours, this roadside '50s joint marked with a huge neon double-K is sometimes frequented by ragged men, with eyes as black and round as Mickey Mouse's, who stare into their own reflection in the huge plate-glass windows. It's very safe, though, thanks to Louisville's finest, a number of whom can usually be found drowsing over their free paper cups of joe and crullers.

Best bowl of burgoo: Kentucky's answer to goulash is made with beef, corn, okra, and corn starch. For an exemplary bowl, try **Mark's Feed Store** *(main branch, 1514 Bardstown Rd., 502/458–1570; 11422 Shelbyville Rd., 502/244–0140)*, a big barn of a barbecue stop in the

Highlands. In addition to the burgoo, the ribs are top-notch and the honey-wings (chicken wings fried in a honey sauce) are guaranteed to boost your serotonin levels. Also, the way the waitresses slip a freezer-bag of ice in your pitcher of beer to keep it chilly defines good service, Southern style. Prices range from $4 to $13.

Best vegetarian: Eating green things that don't come boiled or in a sticky sauce is something of a novelty in this part of the country, but the **Veggie Vault** *(2113 Frankfort Ave., 502/897–3612)* with its No Moo Burger and Tofu-4-U Reuben is bringing the meat-is-murder revolution one sandaled step closer. Close to the Highlands in the Clifton neighborhood, the Vault has the vegan market cornered, and is one of a string of good eateries (including Thai) on the recently revitalized strip. Prices range from $1 to $10.

Best pickle on a stick: Everything tastes better on a stick, and the humbly skewered gherkin has long been the staple dish of such regional standbys as the drive-in and the demolition derby. Though judging differences in pickles is a subtle art, the **Georgetown Twin Drive-In** *(8200 Indiana Rte. 64, IN, 812/951–2616)* wins by virtue of its unparalleled pickle-eating environment. The Georgetown is upscale for a drive-in: no horn-honking, beer-guzzling renegades here, it's more of a blue-collar family hangout and benefits from a superb country location nestled in the hills of Floyd's Knobs in southern Indiana. Bring a lawn chair, a boom box (the sound is broadcast over an AM band), a cooler of beverage, and relax on a grassy knoll. You have the pick of two screens and two films; during intermission be sure not to miss the vintage dancing–hot dog concession trailers. From Downtown allow 25 minutes: Follow I-64 west, take the Georgetown exit, go right, and after a brief jaunt look for the big neon Georgetown sign.

Best 24-hour diner: Even though it's in the middle of Louisville's biggest black urban neighborhood, the West End's **Irma's Cafeteria** *(2531 W. Broadway at 26th St., 502/776–9576)* has a rural, small-town feel to it. Pictures of family members decorate the walls, and the food is real country cooking, from the mashed potatoes to the fried chicken that's a guaranteed late-night cure for a hangover. The house specialty, chess pie, a silky yellow pie made of egg yolks and brown sugar, is an experience in itself. There are a number of good blues bars nearby, and for those interested in great live jazz, **Syl's Lounge** *(2403 W. Broadway, 502/776–9105)* is just a block away.

Best all-you-can-eat tandoori: The **India Palace** *(3315 Bardstown Rd., 502/473–1779)*, located in the bottom of a Quality Inn across the street from the Toy Tiger (see Clubs), has the only game in town as far as Indian food goes. Everything on the menu is fine, but at $5.95 the lunch buffet's spread of steam dishes filled with tandoori, chicken vindaloo, and the like (with scrumptious tiger balls in honey sauce for dessert) is where it's at.

Best scoop of caramel ice cream: When old-timers mourn the passing of yesterday's America, it's probably ice cream parlors like **Ehrmin's** *(1250 Bardstown Rd. in the Mid-City Mall, 502/451–6720)* that they miss most. Even though it's moved from its original location to an indoor mall, Ehrmin's retains all the trappings of an old-time fountain atmosphere, like marble tabletops and stained glass behind the counter. The ice cream is still made on the premises in a really big pot in the back room. People from all over town know and love this place.

Best coddle: An authentic Irish pub in front, a smoked-salmon-and-potato-gratin-serving restaurant in back, the **Irish Rover** *(2319 Frankfort Ave., 502/899–3544)* in Clifton caters to Louisville's resident Irish, as well as those interested in an unparalleled black and tan, a glass of Murphy's Irish Whiskey, or an excellent dish of Dublin coddle (a potato and cheese casserole). This place gets crowded and lively on the weekends, and often, just like in the old country, an impromptu Irish band will get to playing and folks will start to sing along.

shopping

records

Best bluegrass: Blue Moon Records *(1382 Bardstown, 502/485–9300)* was started by Louisville punk-rock scene veteran Mike Bucayu (Solution Unknown and Caroline recording artists Kinghorse), who traded in his Fender for a mandolin after listening to the Stanley Brothers (the Beatles of bluegrass). In testament to his punk past, Bucayu still carries alternative labels like Drag City and Victory, but his heart and most of his stock is in traditional bluegrass and country. Whether you're looking for an informed opinion on where to start with bluegrass, or you're a collector looking for rarities, Blue Moon is the place to go.

Best independent superstore: An 1,800-square-foot emporium, **Ear X-Tacy** *(1534 Bardstown Rd., 502/452–1799)* was started years ago by John Timmons as a tiny alternative record shop and today has listening posts, clothing, and magazines—as well as a huge stock of alternative, jazz, rock, bluegrass, folk, country, classical, and blues. Arguably the best used-CD bins in town.

Best indie labels: Ground Zero Records *(1765 Bardstown Rd., 502/485–9717)* is run by Ed Lutz, a former Ear X-Tacy clerk who started his own shop to cater to Louisville teens' more obscure tastes, especially on the hardcore front. A regular mom 'n' pop owner, Lutz stocks the music he likes, does special orders, and has an index of hard-to-find indie and punk-rock CDs ranging from Burnt Hair and Karate to the Queers and the Delta 72. He keeps a board listing his latest arrivals, and he's a reliable and honest source for what's worth your dollar and what's not.

Best reggae: Underground Sounds *(2003 Highland Ave., 502/485–0174)* is a tiny store, but owner Craig Rich, a goateed young entrepreneur, retails in a quantity of CDs under murals of Bob Marley and Robert Johnson. The store has a decent alternative selection, good jazz and blues, but reggae and dub—with over 600 titles—is the main focus; everything from roots to dancehall is here. Also, though the selection of used CDs is limited by space, it boasts the city's cheapest prices ($4.99).

Best vinyl: The city made owner and local eccentric Lew White take down an enormous Easter Island head perched on his store's roof, but even in the face of civic oppression **Electric Ladyland** *(2325 Bardstown Rd., 502/458–4259)* soldiers on as a proud bastion of mystical hippiedom. It's filled with dusty bins of cheap records, black-light posters of nudes in Eden, purple-plastic four-chambered super hitters, and other celebrations of the past (remembered or imagined).

books

Best comics and stuff: The **Pop Culture Emporium** *(1365 Bardstown Rd., 502/456–5553)* is like visiting your cool friend in seventh grade, the one who had all the Deep Purple records and lived in his dad's basement. This store, run by twentysomething Kevin Town, is a one-man operation and labor of love that boasts a plethora of '70s tchotchkes, *Star Wars* action figures, and "Dukes of Hazzard" bedsheets. On the comics front, in addition to Fantagraphic favorites like *Acme* by Chris Ware, there are also rarer finds like *Hothead Paisan—Homicidal Lesbian Terrorist* and original comic book art like Charles Burns serigraphs.

Best first editions: A dusty maze of used hardcovers and paperbacks, **Twice-Told Used Books and Jazz Records** *(1578 Bardstown Rd., 502/458–7420)* is the best bet in town for choice first editions, as well as the place to go for jazz vinyl. Owner Harold Maier keeps the front of the store filled with inexpensive paperbacks and jazz records, and the back with reasonably priced hardcovers. If you're a book collector, or just curious, check out Harold's side room, which is stacked to the ceiling with first editions. Whether you're looking for a first edition of John Dos Passos' *U.S.A.*, or a dollar copy of *Fear and Loathing in Las Vegas* for road reading, this is the place. Maier is the best at cool recommendations, especially when it comes to offbeat detective novels by writers like James Crumley, and literary pulp material.

Runner-up: Right across the street from Twice Told, **All Booked Up & More** *(1555 Bardstown Rd., 502/459–634)* has oddball regional and historical books, as well as an upstairs filled with discount fiction.

clothes

Best pair of used Levi's: Stone Fish *(1602 Bardstown Rd., 502/451–5545)* started out as a handmade jewelry and pottery gallery and has grown into an important local fashion stop. Though it retains a smattering of jewelry and decorative crockery it's known for having the highest quality selection around for used jeans and cords ($10–$22), as well as other carefully used and new duds.

Best thrift store: Want to pay $100 for a moth-eaten parachute or a moldy wet suit? Need a pair of used Jockey shorts big enough to act as a bug bra on a Toyota? Then the **Unique Thrift Store** *(1617 Carter St. at 22nd St., 502/772–9304)*, with its 36,000-square-foot display of the bizarre and the bizarrely overpriced, is the place for you. In addition to the Believe It or Not Museum appeal of its specialty items, this place is worth it for its more reasonably priced acres of blue jeans, winter jackets, and work shirts—you're sure to find something. While you're visiting be sure to look up (literally). Suspended from the rafters like the bounty of a successful faith healing revival meeting is an array of prosthetic legs and arms, walkers, crutches, children's wheelchairs, and other dusty, discarded emblems of physical misfortune. It's a mystery.

Best hip hideaway: If you're lusting after a Sweat Hogs T-shirt, a pair of red-velvet hip-huggers, or a stylin' Shaft-style leather jacket, go to **Sasquatch** *(1019 Barret Ave., 502/561–8485)*. A little frame house in the Highlands, its front room is filled to the ceiling with furniture and collectibles ranging from '70s Raymor op-art, '60s end tables, infinity lights, and artwork running the gamut from folk-pop sickle lamps and patchwork stars to contemporary sculpture. The two back rooms are crammed with an extensive retro-chic collection of clothing and shoes.

et cetera

Best guitars: Though the **Guitar Emporium** *(1610 Bardstown Rd., 502/459–4153)* sells guitars to Bob Dylan, Sonic Youth, and ZZ Top when they come through town, it isn't a high-priced, big-city guitar shop—the workers are local musicians, as are the majority of the clients. Guitar Emporium just happens to a have a first-rate stock of hard-to-find axes, from $200 '60s Kay True Tones to museum-quality pieces like a $20,000 Harmony pearl-bound acoustic guitar. Also, if you need a guitar or amp repaired, these are the guys: They have a huge parts warehouse in the basement.

body alterations

Best old-school biker tattoos: If you've been hankering for a foot-long chest tattoo of the Grim Reaper brandishing an AK-47, or perhaps just Betty Boop poised on the rim of a martini glass, **Tattoo Charlie's** *(1845 Berry Blvd. 502/366–9635)*, located near Seventh Street, is your kind of place. Charlie Wheeler wields the most trusted needle in town; and while he is best known for traditional designs (more than 60,000 paper the walls of his small studio), he also displays photo books that show past work like impressive skin transcriptions of art by William Blake and M.C. Escher. Charlie charges per tattoo, with the smallest designs starting at $30.

Best modern body shop: A full-service custom shop for the modern primitive, **Eternal Images Tattoo** *(2235 Bardstown Rd., 502/452–9231)* serves up all styles from custom tattoos, primitive and traditional, to a full line of body piercing. Tattooing costs $100 an hour; nipple rings go for $45, Prince Alberts for $70.

hotel/motel

Best concrete teepee: The **Wigwam Village** *(601 Dixie Hwy., Cave City, 502/773–3381)* is 80 minutes south of Louisville off I-65, but it's well worth the drive for the opportunity to live like the Indians never did—in air-conditioned cement cones, watching reruns of *F-Troop* on the color TV. Weekday prices start at $25 for a single ($30 on the weekend) and $35 for a double ($40 on the weekend).

Best country motor court: The **Melrose Inn Motel** *(13306 U.S. Hwy. 42, Prospect, 502/228–1136)*, located half an hour east of Downtown in the suburban town of Prospect, consists of a restful series of little white row buildings. It's got clean beds, and the adjacent restaurant serves a great biscuit and gravy breakfast. Prices range from $35 for a single to $49 for a double.

Best fancy hotel: Built by two Swiss brothers at the turn of the century, the **Seelbach** *(500 S. Fourth Ave., 502/585–3200)* is an old world gem and favorite resting place of the well-heeled. The rooms, which come with antique furnishings and marble bathrooms, start at around a $100 and go up. One of Louisville's best kept architectural secrets is in the hotel's basement: The Rathskeller, formerly a restaurant and now a banquet room, is the world's only existing intact Rookwood Pottery room. Call it Bavarian Rococo, call it simply nuts, it's a must-see for fans of decorative excess.

Weirdest hotel: The **Galt House** *(Fourth Ave. and the River, 502/589–5200)* is a garish 25-story 1972 period piece composed of a hodgepodge of materials and ordered with the aesthetic of a Tom Brady on Angel Dust. It's a building that Louisvillians love to hate, but it's popular with conventioneers and does command one of the best views of the Ohio. Its revolving roof-top restaurant, the Flagship, a creepy nautical affair decorated with household cast-offs poorly disguised as naval antiquities (the ceiling is mysteriously studded with doorknobs), is a good place for a sunset cocktail. The whole joint is about as subtle, as Elvis would have said, as a turd in a punchbowl. Rooms start at about $100.

local wonders

Best quarry: You stop digging for limestone when you hit the water table, at which point the quarry fills up like a bathtub draining in reverse. The result is a quickly abandoned mining operation, but often a huge and most excellent swimming area, dude. The **Hanover Quarry** *(Hwy. 62, Hanover, IN, 502/897–64810)* is a pretty good example: low cliffs, deep cool water, and throngs of sunburned youths guzzling Sterling and flailing around on inner tubes. From Downtown, take the Second Street

Bridge to Jeffersonville, follow 62 east toward Hanover, and look for the sign. Allow 45 minutes.

Best sunrises: The **McAlpine Locks** *(802 N. 27th at Canal streets, 502/774–3514)* give ships passage around the Falls of the Ohio River and also provide an amazing downriver view of the city. The locks are ten minutes west of Downtown off Main Street and are a great way to wind down from a hard-driving all-nighter at the Tiger. Toward dawn you can watch coal barges push closer to the locks, their searchlights picking out the banks, and the city's skyscrapers further upstream gradually turning silver in the sunlight.

Runner up: Known primarily for a particular horse race (starts with *D*, ends with *y*) **Churchill Downs** *(700 Central Ave., 502/636–4400)*, whose regular season runs from late April to December, offers **Dawn at the Downs** in the summer, admitting early rising visitors in to watch the racehorses warm up and run through their exercises. Watch millions of dollars of Derby Winner hopefuls prance and pace around the mist-shrouded track before the average pony fan has even brushed his teeth.

Best place to catch a 15-pound sucker fish: Grab a pole and a six-pack and head to the **Falls of the Ohio River** *(201 W. Riverside Dr., Clarksville, IN, 812/280–9970)*, the natural barrier that caused the first settler to hang up his paddle and call Louisville home. The Falls are dammed now and fishing for huge channel catfish and paddlefish below the dam is good sport. As for eating the often-contaminated catch, call the Fish and Wildlife Bureau (502/595–4039) for an advisory on blacklisted fish. When the floodgate's up, the river recedes and you can climb out for about half a mile over the exposed Devonian fossil beds formed when Kentucky was under sea. Marvel all ye at the frozen face of time, but when you hear the blast of the dam's siren, get back to shore or you'll be washed down to Owensboro.

Best figure-eight racing: "Let us have moment of silence for Jimmy Austin in critical condition still at Baptist East," squawks the P.A. at the **Louisville Motor Speedway** *(1900 Outer Loop, 502/966–2277)*. The moment passes, and then several thousand bowed heads rise as the engines of 25 stockers roar. The checkered flag waves, and the cars speed off in packs around the banked asphalt. As the cars separate, crossing the intersection in the center of the track becomes a dangerous, often hair-raising spectacle. Figure-eight racing is the closest thing we have to public dueling or gladiatorial bouts and should be cherished as an important relic of less-sophisticated times. The track is located 20 minutes south of Downtown, off I-65 at the Outer Loop exit. The season runs from May to October, with prices varying per event but averaging about ten bucks.

Best bong collection: People smoke a lot of weed in Kentucky (it's the state's largest cash crop), and if you want to see evidence of this visit the **Metro Narcotics Unit** *(810 Barret Ave., 502/574–2057)*. Displayed in glass cases are seized paraphernalia, including some works of considerable craft and ingenuity. A favorite is the homemade bong made of copper pipe, a doll's porcelain bathtub, and a miniature toilet. The bathtub is your stash, and the toilet is your "bowl." Smoke that shit, man.

Best free smokes: Tobacco is the Kentucky state leaf, and you can light up for free. **Philip Morris USA** *(1930 Maple St., 502/566–1293)* offers visitors a feel-good-about-our-time-honored-tobacco-tradition video followed by a tour of the plant. Reward? Free fresh packs of Marlboros.

Best junk-art house: **Gus Ballard**'s house *(1018 Mulberry St., Germantown)* is a sight: the backyard and shed are covered with a faded plastic compote of headless dolls, decomposing stuffed animals, blue plastic whales, bowling pins, and everything old and toylike under the sun. Mr. Ballard likes circles, and many of the toys are curiously reduced to their round elements (wheels, gears, spinners) before they are allowed to grace his residence. Though Mr. Ballard doesn't mind the attention, this is a private residence, so be discreet and courteous when visiting.

transmissions

Best public radio: Relief from Louisville's roster of oldies and pop stations can be found on public radio's **WFPK (91.9 FM)**. Though it plays mostly jazz, WFPK does have some alternative programming, as well as having a great bluegrass show from 8 P.M. to midnight on Sundays. Another FM option is the 24-hour supply of news and entertainment programming on National Public Radio's **WFPL (89.3 FM)**.

memphis

by Robert Gordon, Andria Lisle, and Tara McAdams

"Must be something in the water, cause 'that thing' inhabits every fluffy boll of cotton, every greasy piece of fried chicken, and every human being within a hundred miles. Those that feel it can never leave it, those that don't can't wait to get away. Many make the pilgrimage to find out just what that thing is."

— Scott Taylor, *The Grifters*

Even though this city is the missing link between Delta blues and rock 'n' roll, Memphis is easily mistaken for a town of nothing but doughnut shops and churches. You might wonder what in this podunk could have inspired the rebellion that is rock 'n' roll; and the answer is not readily apparent: When you stand in front of the one-room Sun Studio—where Elvis Presley recorded his first single, "That's All Right (Mama)"—even the neon radiator shop sign next door seems cosmopolitan by comparison. Nevertheless, this capital of the Mississippi Delta is the bright lights, the Manhattan of the region, for everybody within 200 miles.

Memphis is a cultural meeting point: country and urban, rich and poor, black and white. It is a place where people have traditionally come in contact with people unlike themselves and ideas unlike their own. Dr. Martin Luther King's assassination took place within a few blocks of Stax Studio, where blacks and whites were working together to create soul music. Wildness and independence roil in the doughnut hole and beneath the church pews, but finding the hole ain't always easy.

In Memphis, the spirit of blues greats like Bukka White and Memphis Minnie thrives in the same hearts that thrill to the Rolling Stones or post-Cramps garage blues. Many Memphis bands have direct ties to the original masters. The four members of the willfully-obscure Mud Boy and the Neutrons were instrumental in the '60s blues revival and polished their style at the feet of Bukka White and Fred McDowell, among others: Jim Dickinson (who also played piano on the Rolling Stones's "Wild Horses") and Sid Selvidge have solo careers, Jimmy Crosthwait is a puppeteer (call the Pink Palace Museum at 901/320–6320 to find out his show times), and Lee Baker (who was taught by bottleneck blues great Furry Lewis) has passed away. Look for the surviving members individually or together—they gig rarely—and it's worth missing your plane if you have a chance to catch 'em.

The quintessential underground band, Mud Boy is the father—literally and figuratively—of today's Memphis music scene. Children of Selvidge and Dickinson play in two prominent local bands, Big Ass Truck and DDT Big Band. Big Ass Truck bring a hip-hop sensibility to their Memphis funk, and DDT blend bebop and country blues into a Delaney and Bonnie-ish, family rambling thing.

Meanwhile, indie-rock favorites the Grifters are making the most compelling music to come out of Memphis since the '70s and Alex Chilton's Big Star. The pride of Memphis's Shangri-La Records, the Grifters have also recorded for several other labels, including Sub Pop. What separates the Grifters from their so-called low-fi cohorts—Pavement, Sebadoh—is their Memphis inheritance: They can apply slow soul and pop to the high-octane thrash aesthetic they learned while rehearsing for years in a flower shop. While in Memphis, look for the Grifters or side projects Champ, Those Bastard Souls, or the Hot Monkey, often at **Barristers** (see Clubs). The Simple Ones, friends of the Grifters both sonically and socially, also play frequently.

Memphis's burgeoning garage-rock scene is anchored by three acts. For instrumental hijinks, check out Impala, who add scorching sax and thumping bass drums to surfy, chicken drag-strip guitar. The Oblivians are a furious punk-rock-meets-R&B-styled three-man tempest à la Jon Spencer; and a former Gibson Brother, Jeffrey Evans, leads '68 Comeback, a powerhouse of garage-styled rockabilly and blues.

Also vital are some of the local roots acts. Like a one-stop Southern music shop, the music of Lorette Velvette snakes through country, blues, rock 'n' roll and the various mutations thereof, all of it real and not for tourists. A former member of the Panther Burns and the Hellcats, Lorette's reedy, breathy vocals front superior originals and interpretations, drenched in all the Southern sweat and sex you can fan yourself to. Also great fun is a girl band known variously as the Chiselers and the Alluring Strange; they also feature former Hellcats, and they rock like a rickety garage.

lay of the land

Memphis sits in the southwest corner of Tennessee, right across the Mississippi River from Arkansas. Located near the river and south of

I-40, the city's small downtown is most active during business hours, but there are night haunts, including touristy **Beale Street**, and some fine dining. Memphis spreads eastward, away from the Mississippi River, and it's about four miles to **Midtown**, where a sense of the city's '20s charm lingers, and where, day and night, you'll find people looking to get tight. Driving through Midtown's tree-lined neighborhoods can make for a lovely afternoon and a good way to orient yourself. There are plenty of large homes to gawk at, and a plethora of different bars to drink at. Some neighborhoods of note include **Cooper-Young** (named for the intersection of those two streets) where you'll find many offbeat restaurants and stores; there's a relatively nice and diverse commercial strip on **Madison Avenue** between Cooper and McNeil Streets. The city begins to lose its character east of East Parkway, and by the time you hit Highland Street, you could be in your own suburbs. For an interesting cross-section of the city, drive the three Parkways (North, East, and South) that were once the city's borders; it'll take about an hour, and you'll see mansions, ghettos, and everything in between.

Memphis has never really developed its riverfront but you can picnic in **Tom Lee Park** at sunset. The finest view of the river is from the **National Ornamental Metal Museum** *(374 Metal Museum Drive, 901/774–6380)*, which is built on the bluffs that attracted the earliest settlers; the museum warrants a visit.

Drinkers should note that while beer is sold in stores and bars and is widely available until 3 A.M., hard liquor and wine are sold only in liquor stores until 11 P.M. On Sundays, beer sales start at noon; no liquor. Many bars are beer-only but most will happily provide setups (glass, ice, and mixer) for your own brown bag.

getting from a to b

You'll need a car to figure this town out. The public transportation is sparse and inconvenient and there are few taxis—Yellow/Checker Cab *(901/577–7777)*. The bus system is slow and complicated; call 274–6282 for schedule information. The coolest car ride you'll ever hire is Tad Pierson's American Dream Safari *(901/274–1997)*. He and his restored 1955 Cadillac (like the one Elvis bought his mama) will tool you in style around Memphis or on extended rides to the delta.

sources

Memphis's only daily paper, *The Commercial Appeal*, has a decent entertainment guide on Fridays. The alternative weekly *The Memphis Flyer* reads like a high school yearbook, but has good club ads. The unofficial tourist center at **Shangri-La Records** (see Shopping) is the best tip for hip, and their official *Lowlife Guide to Memphis* will be the best three bucks (including postage) you spend on the Mississippi. (Write: Shangri-La, 1916 Madison Ave., Memphis, TN 38104.)

For those who give a dot com, access Memphis Mojo's informative Web site (http://www.membership.com) for a monthly calendar and various features about local goings-on. There are also links to other Memphis sites.

clubs

Best cheap, loud rock club: Hidden in a downtown alleyway, the inconspicuous **Barristers** *(147 Jefferson Ave., 901/523–9421)* remains Memphis's premier indie-rock club. National acts such as Guided by Voices, the Jesus Lizard, and Make-Up, and local bands, from the Grifters to Big Ass Truck and Cornfed, have paid their dues in this tiny sweatbox of a bar once owned by Jerry Lee Lewis. The attitude at Barristers is strictly no-frills—admission is cheap, the bands are loud, the bar serves cold beer (no liquor), and there are no other amenities to speak of. What you see is what you get, and if the music is good, you'll have a night to remember. Keep your ear to the ground—bands recording at Memphis's top alt.rock studio, Easley Recording, often play impromptu gigs at Barristers. (Seeing Sonic Youth try out "The Diamond Sea" in front of an intimate crowd of 200 was an unforgettable rock moment.)

Best Beale Street rock hall: Many Memphis music greats spent their childhoods Saturdays watching westerns at the **New Daisy** *(350 Beale Street, 901/525–8979)*, a Beale Street gem that retains its neighborhood movie house feel today, its walls reverberating with a soulful history. Now a music hall, it hosts touring bands as well as more popular local acts. The booking is totally eclectic, with GWAR swapping nights with nonrock crowds. There's seating in the balcony and, when appropriate, chairs and tables are set on the dance/mosh floor.

Best gay dance club: Amnesia *(2866 Poplar Ave., rear parking lot, 901/454–1366)* has everything a dance club could wish for: outdoor swimming pool, volleyball court, two bars, and a large dance floor with pulsating, gyrating, sweaty…uh…music. One of the bars is enclosed in glass so the dancers can be seen but not heard. Very in among the younger preppy collegiate crowd and locals who like to hang out with them.

Runner-up: Stationed in a warehouse under an overpass on the edge of downtown, the **Apartment Club**'s *(343 Madison Ave., 901/525–9491)* covert location may be what makes it the best drag bar in Memphis. The large dance floor accommodates RuPaul lookalikes and low-rent LaToyas, as well as the occasional ebullient Nell Carter.

Best teenscene: Robert "Mongo" Hodges' **Teen Atonement Center** *(56 S. Front St., 901/526–3333)*, formerly known as Prince (and later Saint) Mongo's Planet, has been a center of Memphis teenage nightlife for over 15 years. Mongo, who claims to be a native of the planet Zambodia, runs for city mayor each election on platforms like "We are surrounded by 'funky skunks'… Save us, Mongo!" He promises to "open city buildings from 5:33 P.M. to 7:33 A.M. for the homeless, serving supper and breakfast, including bedside wine" and to force Memphis city councilmen to "feed criminals from canoes during hurricanes." The scourge of most Memphians, Mongo is a luminary among the under-21 set. His club looks like a cross between "Pee Wee's Playhouse" and junked sets from an Ed Wood movie. Call before you atone—Mongo's is open odd hours, features live bands sporadically, and serves pizza only occasionally.

Best place to dance the Electric Slide: In the mood to get down? Put on your high-heeled sneakers and head downtown to **Raiford's Lounge** *(115 Vance Ave., 901/528–9313)*, where neighborhood soul-sters and suburbanite hipsters meet late every Saturday to dance the night away. There's a wall-length mirror so you can check out all the other dancers as you glide across the floor (if, that is, you can see through the fog-choked room—the smoke machine operator is quick on the draw). The resident DJ is a Prince fanatic, so be prepared to do the Hustle to "1999." Beer and setups for your own hard booze are provided.

Best free Sunday gigs: Huey's *(1927 Madison Ave., 901/726–4372)* is a long-running Midtown haunt with great bar food. On Sundays, tables in this restaurant/bar are moved to make a bandstand for free afternoon jazz, and free blues and R&B in the evening. The gamut runs from the Hi Records Rhythm Section to post-frat blues bands (most with a national recording contract). The jazz is always local and right for the day, bop not feared. The West Coast Burger, onion rings, and french fries are all recommended. It's owned by a former replacement member of Alex Chilton's first band, the Box Tops.

Best live bluegrass: Much is made of the African-American soul of Memphis but if you want a window onto the town's funky Appalachian side, check out the decades-old Friday night gig at the **Lucy Opry** *(2984 Harvester Lane, 901/358–3486)* on the northern outskirts of town. Running from 8 to 10, it usually costs $6. This is bluegrass's answer to **Junior Kimbrough's** jook joint (see below). No drinking—it's a family event, drawing farmers, and blue-collar country folk—only coffee and soft drinks are served. It's held in a Union Hall (and sometimes spills out into the parking lot); so, you'll be up close to fine local bands as well national bluegrass acts. If you're feeling bold, bring your own instrument. Directions: Take Interstate 40/240 north to exit 2A for Highway 51. Stay on 51 north (toward Millington) until the first traffic light, Whitney Street, where there's a Church's Fried Chicken on the left. Go left on Whitney and after about four blocks the road will split; veer right and the Union Hall will be immediately on your right.

Best live jook in Memphis: Wild Bill's *(1580 Vollentine Ave., 901/726–5473)* is the place to see live blues in Memphis. The players are better and less showy than in the Beale Street tourists traps. It's inconspicuously located on the north side of Midtown in a strip shopping center, and the first clue that you're in the right place is the legion of '70s Cadillacs parked out front. This is a local party scene, drawing a mixed crowd. Be warned that the neighborhood might seem rough to some tastes. Friday, Saturday, and Sunday, Sun and Hi Records alumnus Big Lucky Carter fronts the Hollywood All Stars, a rhythm and blues Memphis-based band. Host Wild Bill provides the quarts of beer and setups, but if you're drinking liquor you have to bring your own.

Runner-up: In an industrial area right across from a fenced-in auto smashing yard, **Green's Lounge** *(2090 E. Person Ave., 901/276–4970)* used to be the Saturday-night haven for authentic blues, and after changing hands several times, may be regaining some of its former vitality under the proven hand of Wilroy Sanders, the uncredited writer of the blues standard "Crosscut Saw."

Best country jook joint: Junior Kimbrough's is the kind of rural place you thought no longer existed. About an hour from Memphis by car, this country party feels like a step back in time. There's no sign out front, parking is in the field next door, and there's no phone to find out if they're open. Inside, it's always brighter than you think a club should be, but the exposed bulbs never hinder late-night partying. On the walls are colorful folk paintings by a local artist. Proprietor Junior Kimbrough plays a hypnotic north Mississippi blues drone, and when he's not holding court, R.L. Burnside often is. The band sets up in a corner and makes do with whatever equipment is available—we've seen cardboard boxes used for drums—but it never fails to get folks dancing. With its irregular hours, sometimes this place is gloriously empty, sometimes there's a film crew from Japan. Beer is sold; many patrons share their white lightning; and a bit further up the road is a barbecue joint if you have to eat before you ride back to town. From Memphis, take Lamar/U.S. 78 south about half an hour to Mississippi Highway 7; take a right on 7 (south) about one mile to Mississippi 4; take a right (west) on 4 and go about 10 miles. It's on the right after the second "school" sign; if you hit the crossroads at Chulahoma, you've gone too far.

bars

Best public rec room: When your eyes adjust to the smoky dimness of **Printer's Alley Lounge**, the first thing you will see is red—guaranteed! The walls, carpeting, tablecloths, bar, and even the lightbulbs are all colored the same sanguine red. The bloodbath theme continues with taxidermied specimens of every wild animal unfortunate enough to encounter the owner. Once you can see, approach the bartender for beers, quarters, and a cue ball. Then, unless you really want to do time with the redneck front-room habitués, cut past the pool table and take a right into the back room. It's the ideal place for having a party when you don't want guests messing up your house—there's another pool table and a jukebox. The carpet (yes, it's red) is of the indoor-outdoor variety that's perfectly okay to spill a beer onto. The juke, which is stocked with '70s and '80s classics ranging from Led Zeppelin to Willie Nelson to the Fat Boys acts up occasionally, so don't feed it more than $1 at a time.

Best anonymous beer bar: In Midtown, not far from Cooper-Young mall, dark and cozy **Charlotte's** *(244 S. Cooper St., 901/274–9913)* will absorb you into its slightly mildewed, shag-carpeted warmth. With the Mills Brothers on the jukebox and Charlotte's Bavarian accent, you can daydream yourself anywhere. Beer only.

Best neighborhood bar: The **P&H Cafe** *(1532 Madison Ave. 901/726–0906)* has everything good you could want from a neighborhood bar. Run by Wanda Wilson, a former trucker who changes wigs daily but keeps friends for years, the P&H has a good beer bar, a spacious back room with several pool tables, and a restaurant serving good burgers, pizza, and its famous cheese fries. The front room is decorated with caricatures of famous Memphians, all of whom have patronized the P&H. Several years back a couple of folks were in the P&H and were almost dead out of money. Wanda came over with cheeseburgers, fries, and drinks and took their three quarters and five dimes as payment—"Didn't you know that 'P&H' stands for 'poor and hungry'?"

Best downtown neighborhood holdout: A leftover neighborhood relic in a regentrified downtown area that keeps the corner of South Main and Calhoun exciting, **Wolf's Corner** *(530 S. Main St., 901/525–4538)* has great blues on the jukebox, bottled beer, one pool table, and some soul food. The weekend DJ plays 45s that were new when his Board of Ed turntables were designed. The regulars are an older black crowd, salted by visiting white scenesters. Sometimes the place breaks into wild dancing, and the club can get transcendent.

Runner-up: Across the street, **Earnestine and Hazel's** *(84 E. Calhoun Ave., 901/523–9754)* has survived a facelift and can be fun; it sometimes has live bands. Imported beers and brass accents have replaced malt liquor; out of towners think this is as deep as it gets.

Best gay bar: Practically a Memphis institution in the gay community, **The Pipeline** *(1382 Poplar Ave., 901/726–5263)* has a friendly, laid-back atmosphere and a backyard tree house that evokes the French Quarter. It has a CD jukebox for the dance floor. Check out its Sunday afternoon Tea Dance/Beer Bust. Four dollars buys all the Michelob you can drink ($3 for Old Milwaukee) plus a free buffet meal. Other highlights include Underwear/Flashlight Nights, Full Moon Nights, and the Halloween and New Year's Eve extravaganzas. Beer only.

Runner-up: For late-night trolling, hit **Backstreet** *(2018 Court Ave., 901/276–5522)*, an out-of-the-way hole in the heart of Midtown behind an old dairy and next to a flea market.

Best redneck dance floor: Visit the redneck way o' life at **Sweet's 4-Wheel Drive Lounge** *(3117 Summer Ave., 901/452–9358)*. Sandwiched between fast food neon signs off a once grand '50s U.S. highway, it's right down the road from a trailer park and looks like what it is—a low-rent roadside dance club with a disco ball. Get a trailer hitch put on your car while dancing to the DJ's tracks or shooting pool at one of the many tables. Check out the glossy photos of muddy trucks and fast boats on the wall.

Best late-night beer bar: Alex's Tavern *(1445 Jackson Ave., 901/278-9086)* has been a hangout for Rhodes (formerly Southwestern) college students for decades. It's got a concrete floor and plenty of room in which to get drunk and fall down—aforementioned drinkers have been doing just that since the '50s. Famous for its extensive jukebox selections (now on CD—RIP vinyl) and for its juicy hamburgers, Alex's has also become the late-night hangout spot for those not ready to call it quits at 3 A.M.—it seems to stay open well past last call in the rest of town. Bartender Rocky (son of Alex) is a favorite with customers.

food/coffee

Best hangover cure: Wash down a Goody's headache powder with a swig of Coke, get dressed, get into your car, then head across the bridge to West Memphis, Arkansas, to **Earl's Hot Biscuits** *(2005 Interstate 55, 501/735-5380)*. The drive is worth it. Breakfast food here is *so* reassuring—no matter what time of day it is, especially when it's served by a gum-chewing, beehived waitress who calls you "honey." The biscuits with gravy are the best item on the menu, but everything is delicious and nothing takes longer than five minutes to reach your table. By the time your meal is over, you'll be ready to stop at a grocery in West Memphis to stock up on imported beer (for some reason West Memphis stores carry a much better selection than Memphis) for your next go-round.

Best greasy omelettes: Though tastefully rehabbed, the **Arcade** diner *(540 S. Main 901/526-5757)* feels comfortably lived-in and still makes classic greasy omelette and hash browns-type fare for breakfast. Lunch and dinner, however, have options for the more health conscious. Treats include the best beignets north of New Orleans and great milkshakes. The Arcade's time-stood-still air, with its plastic and Formica decor and big booths, inspired Jim Jarmusch to film much of *Mystery Train* here. This corner of Main and Calhoun (Wolf's Corner and Earnestine and Hazel's are also here, see Bars) is a great launching point for Memphis exploring. The river is a couple of blocks west, and you can drive slowly through this warehouse section, discover great views, take in the vibe, or ask for directions to Cybill Shepherd's nearby Memphis digs.

Best bargain lunch: Payne's BBQ *(1762 Lamar Ave., 901/272-1523)* serves up the best lunch bargain in town—a savory chopped-shoulder barbecue sandwich with slaw for just under $3 six days a week. Their south Midtown location (formerly a garage) has become a favorite for indie rockers recording at nearby Easley Recording. The ladies at Payne's merited a "thank you" in the liner notes of Sonic Youth's *Washing Machine* LP. As local rocker Eric Oblivian put it in his magazine, *Memphis Garage Noose*, "eating a Payne's sandwich is religious in a way that unreligious people like me don't want to believe exists." If you're brave, order yours extra-hot.

Best deep-fried hamburger: Welcome to the deep-fried South. When **Dyer's** *(288 N. Cleveland St., 901/725–9903)* recently moved from its wooden shack to this strip shopping center with indoor plumbing, they hired an armored vehicle to transport their vat of 50-year-old grease. Order your burger "dipped" and watch them dunk the whole sandwich before serving it. Truly a taste treat, but as one regular warns, "Eat 'em quick before they clabber up!"

Best cornbread, rolls, and cobbler: Offering soul food white Baptist style, the **Buntyn** *(3070 Southern Ave., 901/458–8776)* sets the Memphis standard for both yeast rolls and cornbread, serving them Southern soft. Waitresses with blue eyeliner and tall hair serve crisp, sweet fried chicken, homemade meat loaf, mounds of veggies (some simmered with meat). Dessert will be unthinkable after a Buntyn meal, but the texture and the spices and the buttery crust of its cobbler à la mode is not to be missed. Get a small portion and share it with the table.

Runner-up: **The Barksdale**'s *(237 S. Cooper St., 901/722–2193)* chocolate chess pie is a silken ending to their good, quick "meat and three" plate lunches.

Best Sunday afternoon soul food: There are many soul food restaurants in Memphis, but **Miss Ellen's** *(601 S. Parkway East, 901/942–4888)*, in an unassuming yellow building in south Memphis, has no real competition. Both her fried chicken and meat loaf are absolutely heavenly, and each plate comes loaded with more vegetables than you can eat. Every meal is accompanied by a plate of Ellen's mouthwatering cornbread pancakes that taste sweeter than chocolate cake. (She has that too, but most folks don't have room after the main course.) Even her sweet tea is exceptional—each sip makes you feel like a diabetic hooked up to a glucose IV—you can't stand it, but you've got to have more! Don't arrive too late, because the food begins to run out around 6 P.M.

Best vegetable plate lunch: A preferred lunch spot for Memphis's senior citizens (chiefly because most menu items can be imbibed through a straw), the **Cupboard** *(1495 Union Ave., 901/276–8015)* is famous among all ages for its comforting "just like grandma used to make" vegetable plates. Outstanding selections at the Cupboard include the tart but sweet fried green tomatoes and the nourishing, mushy eggplant casserole. Baskets of cornbread and rolls accompany every meal, and drink refills are free. Best of all, meals here are inexpensive, and the waitresses don't waste time getting your food to the table. A second location, the **Cupboard Too** *(149 Madison Ave., 901/527–9111)*, serves up home cookin' to downtown business-types in too big a hurry to make it to Midtown. Strict vegetarians should inquire before ordering.

Best chocolate shake: Wiles-Smith Drug Store *(1635 Union Ave., 901/278–6416)* houses one of the last surviving members of an endangered species—the drugstore lunch counter. Pick up a prescription, buy a package of bobby pins, or just browse the aisles before heading to the back of the store for an authentic chocolate shake. Their Joe's Special is extra thick and chocolatey, and if you need extra protein, try the tuna fish sandwich.

Best wet ribs: Forget sex—for a few minutes, anyway. You will never feel more sated than at the exact moment you push yourself away from a plate of gnawed-on Cozy Corner ribs. Modestly located in a strip shopping center on the north side of downtown, nothing about the exterior of the **Cozy Corner Restaurant** *(745 N. Parkway, 901/527–9158)* will prepare you for the delights inside. Cozy Corner ribs are the juiciest, their sauce the most tantalizing, their slaw the tangiest. After a plate of this ambrosia, you'll understand why humans were created to eat meat. If you're tired of pork (heaven forbid!), try the Cozy Corner barbecued Cornish hen. When you're through feasting, splurge and buy a beautiful orange Cozy Corner T-shirt (sauce optional) to remind yourself of the joy that is Memphis's finest barbecue.

Best dry ribs: Don't act surprised when the rack of ribs that you just ordered at **Nick Charlie Vergos' Rendezvous Restaurant** *(52 S. Second St., 901/523–2746)* arrives without sauce. Don't make an ass out of yourself by asking for any, either. The Rendezvous, which has been one of the city's least kept secrets since its opening in a downtown alley in 1948, has built a reputation by doing what everyone in Memphis does well—pork barbecue—in its own unique way. Some barbecue aficionados swear by wet (that is, with sauce) ribs, others claim that the sauce merely masks the flavor of the meat. If you're not dogmatic and can take barbecue wet or dry, there is no other choice but the Rendezvous for the dry mood. Not much in the restaurant has changed in the last 45 years. The servers wear starched white dress shirts, and the decor has remained '50s-era Memphis, with political and entertainment relics added throughout the years.

Best vegetarian barbecue: Memphis' best Vietnamese restaurant, **Saigon Le** *(51 N. Cleveland St., 901/276–5326)*, has a variety of vegetarian fare, but their most delicious (and admittedly, the most dubious sounding) dish is the barbecue wheat gluten, a TVP-based recreation of the real deal, served over rice. Their spring rolls with plum sauce make a perfect appetizer and, to quench your thirst, the coffee with sweetened condensed milk over ice can't be beat! Other recommendations include the very spicy tofu with pineapple and the catfish "hot-pot" (soup).

Best coffee bar: In Cooper-Young, **Otherlands** *(641 S. Cooper St., 901/278–4994)* has an earthy atmosphere, a flowering wooden deck, imported Central American clothing for sale, and exotic cards and gifts. Owner Karen Lebowitz supports local craftspeople and exhibits local artists. Monthly Psychic Teas are an established tradition: A half-dozen psychics gather to offer tarot card readings for curious customers. Otherlands opens early in the morning, closes in the evening, and serves bagels, scones, and other light food.

Runner-up: If you prefer gritty to earthy, follow the cigarette butts across the street from Otherlands to **The Edge** *(532 S. Cooper St., 901/272–3036)*. It's got a good jukebox and minimal atmosphere. You'll find everybody from recovering alcoholics to Deadheads to grungy youths here. The Edge opens at 5 P.M., but doesn't really start rocking until Otherlands goes to sleep. Both places have smoking and nonsmoking areas.

Best Elvis coffee bar and wedding chapel: **Java Cabana** *(2170 Young Ave., 901/272–7210)* serves up Southern irony at its sweetest and coffee at its bitter best. The front window features a must-see homemade dancing Elvis impersonator shrine, just drop a quarter in the slot. The gallerylike room is packed with local art, neofolk art, and especially good Elvis humor. There's even an Elvis Wedding Chapel where Colonel Tommy, proprietor, will marry people. Walking distance from the other bars and restaurants in Cooper-Young.

shopping

records

Best record store, period: Whether you're seeking the latest alternative disc or vintage vinyl from Memphis jug bands, **Shangri-La Records** *(1916 Madison Ave., 901/274–1916)* is your Memphis one-stop. A store, a record label (home of the Grifters), and a distributor, it's also the only place on earth where you can purchase an authentic brick from the legendary Stax recording studio. The staffers know music and Memphis. They will give directions for both ear food and stomach food, as well as hip you to the latest news about gigs and everything else.

Best vintage jazz: The stock at **Audiomania** *(1698 Madison Ave., 901/278–1166)* is determined by the owner's appreciation for Sun Ra, Bobby Dylan, Bobby Lee Trammell, and Jimmy Durante. The store's emphasis is on vinyl, especially jazz, blues, and local music. Many buried treasures make for good browsing. CDs, cassettes, and singles available too.

Best vinyl archeological dig: Got a few years to spare? Determined to find a vinyl copy of *Black Monk Time* or some other rare out-of-print LP? Head over to **Nostalgia World** *(2492 Summer Ave., 901/327–6522)*, roll up your sleeves, and start diggin'. An optimistic record lover's heaven, it's a huge room randomly stacked four feet deep in LPs and 45s. You'll have to wade through at least 35 copies of Cheap Trick's *Live at Budokan* to find that $1 Modern Lovers *Beserkeley* LP. But what a sense of accomplishment! When the dust becomes too much, take a deep breath, stagger to the Coke machine out by the baseball cards, take a breather, and if you're tough you'll come back. At some point in the '60s, someone in Memphis bought a Monks LP on Polydor, and you just know it's gonna be somewhere in this room.

Runner-up: **River Records** *(822 S. Highland, 901/324-1757)* is a store for serious LP collectors. Their pricey but breathtaking selection leans heavily toward rockabilly and Memphis music, especially Elvis Presley. Located near some excellent book stores on Highland (see below).

books

Best Memphis bookstore: Burke's Books *(1719 Poplar Ave., 901/278–7484)*, a decades-old bookstore, offers some of everything, new and used. They have a solid literature section, a noteworthy first-edition section, and carry a superlative offering of works on Memphis and by Memphis artists like Shelby Foote, Margaret Skinner, and Steve Stern. Burke's was the first to support then-unknown author John Grisham with a book signing. It continues to make consistent and exceptional contributions to the Memphis literary scene. The staff is roundly well-read. Memphis loves its Burke's.

Best old books street: In the '60s and '70s, the Highland Strip was Memphis' Melrose Avenue and Sunset Strip all rolled up into three blocks. Now there's interest enough to sustain only a handful of hep stores in this University of Memphis neighborhood. Of course, they all deal in nostalgia. **Mid America Books** (571 S. Highland Ave., 901/452–0766) carries a variety of both common used books and rarities, and is a great place to get lost in for a few hours. Walking into **Memphis Comics and Records** (665 S. Highland Ave., 901/452–1304) a few blocks south is a trip through time. You'll find pulp fiction paperbacks, comic books (superhero and underground), Kojak dolls, Darth Vader masks, original art, rock 'n' roll posters, jazz LPs, and more.

clothes

Best mariachi suit rentals: Rent to own, or for just one night. **Vintage Mania** (2151 Young Ave., 901/274–2879) has a vast array of clothing from the '30s on up. The fashion tends toward *Pretty in Pink*–era Molly Ringwald, though there are also outfits for the cocktail set and the garage mechanic. Their prices are moderate and their turnover is high, so a return visit is usually in order.

Best club threads: In this fashion Sahara, **Puss 'N' Boots** (2149 Young Ave., 901/276–9970) is a welcome oasis for fans of Betsey Johnson's rubber dresses. Their selection of forbidding attire is countered with remarkably friendly service.

Runner-up: If you can't afford the real thing but want to remain a teenage trendsetter, try **Betty's Resale** (2027 Madison Ave., 901/274–5333), where you can dress like a menace to society (Dr. Martens included) for under 30 bucks.

et cetera

Best vintage junk shop: Even if you don't have the cash, browsing through **Midtown's Flashback**'s (2304 Central Ave., 901/272–2304) collection of art deco and '50s pieces makes for a great afternoon. From bedroom suites to Bakelite jewelry, Flashback has it all—admittedly pricey, but beautifully preserved and presented.

Runner-up: Ten minutes east of Midtown, **Bo-Jo's Antique Mall** *(3400 Summer Ave., 901/323–2050)* has a much broader range of objects—both in price and period—in a flea-market setting. No clothing, but if you had $8 left from your visit and you were yearning for a giftie like '60s daisy rings, lighters, or a piece of furniture, Bo-Jo's would do ya right.

Best thrift store: Near Bo-Jo's, the **Disabled American Veterans Thrift Store**, or DAV, *(3440 Summer Ave., 901/327–4601)* is the classic model: slightly musty inside, fluorescent lights, clothes, records, and kitchen sinks. Prices begin at a dime.

Best voodoo counter: A. Schwab's *(163 Beale St., 901/523–9782)* dry goods store carries a little bit of everything. Overalls (in every size), underwear, boots, ladies' hats, pots and pans, steel traps, tacky Memphis souvenirs, Freemasonry books, and voodoo candles and potions. Their array of "lucky" soaps will set your mind racing with possibilities—gain power over a friend or enemy, become prosperous, win your court case, or just "confuse" someone (the soap wrapper art is a spiderweb with an all-seeing eye in the center). The sky is the limit! While at Schwab's, be sure to meet the proprietor Abe Schwab and check out his Memphis museum on the landing between the first and second floor.

hotel/motel

Best hostel: The **Lowenstein-Long House** *(217 N. Waldran Blvd., 901/527–7174)* is the bargain of Memphis. Ten bucks a night is a great deal for a bed in this beautiful old mansion. You get a bunk bed in a room with up to seven people. There's a common room with cable TV, a microwave, and refrigerator. A full deposit is required to guarantee rooms, and summer months are prime time, so send your money in advance.

Best motel for a Colt .45 party: Although both the decor and clientele have declined in recent years, the **Admiral Benbow Motel** *(1220 Union Ave., 901/725–0630)* still features the cheapest rooms in Midtown Memphis ($29.95 for a single). In high school, this was the place to rent a room, fill the bathtub with malt liquor and ice, and invite 20 of your closest friends over for a marathon TV party. Today, the Benbow is a little older and their Escape Hatch Lounge stays more closed than open, but then how tight a ship do you expect the Admiral to run for $30 a night these days?

Best Holiday Inn: In 1952, the Holiday Inn chain was started in Memphis. (One of the original investors was Elvis's record producer, Sam Phillips.) The chain has since been absorbed into another corporation, and the original site is a vacant field. But Memphis has made hotel rooms as dependable as candy bars. If you stay at the **Holiday Inn Midtown** *(1837 Union Ave., 901/278–4100)* branch, check out the weird sunken bar. You'll feel like Gulliver with a vodka and tonic. Double rooms start at $65.

Best place to stay on an expense account: The rooms are smaller than you would expect from its grand lobby, but **The Peabody** *(149 Union Ave., 901/529–4000)* is beautifully furnished in a grandiose Southern belle style. The lost-in-time cotton-baron era atmosphere is the best reason to stay here, but the downtown location, the Sunday brunch, and the roof parties don't hurt. Memphis's finest. Double rooms start at $160.

local wonders

Best church service: For a complete rejuvenation of the soul, attend a Sunday morning service at Rev. Al Green's **Full Gospel Tabernacle** *(787 Hale Rd., 901/396–9192)*. Memphis's foremost soul singer ("Let's Stay Together," "I Can't Get Next to You," and "Take Me to the River," among others), Green found the Lord at the height of his career in the mid '70s after an unfortunate accident involving two women, a bed, and a pan of hot grits. Today, Rev. Al preaches with music, dance, and the spirit of the Holy Ghost. Services begin at 11 A.M. Sunday and last until about 2:30 P.M. Visitors are welcome (no cameras), dress as you choose, but please show the congregation proper reverence. After the service, head over to Miss Ellen's (see Dining) for a delicious lunch.

Best police art: Although you may think that the police station would be the last place any sane person would choose to visit during a Memphis trip, we urge you to put aside all prejudices and check out the free **Memphis Police Museum** *(159 Beale St., 901/528–2370)* in the downtown precinct next to Schwab's (see Shopping). Without risking your life in a crack house, where else could you see handmade syringes and crudely fashioned zip guns? Their display of confiscated home-made dice rivals any craps table in Tunica—nearby site of many casinos. Open 24 hours a day, seven days a week.

Best place to see Isaac Hayes's head razor: A very funky survey of Memphis music history, the **Memphis Music Hall of Fame** *(97 S. Second St., 901/525–4007)* is a great multimedia (but not hi-fi) exhibit, much more like an attic than a corporate Hall of Fame. See Isaac Hayes's Head Razor! Hear obscure jug band jams! See Johnny Woods and Van Zula Hunt on video! The history begins at the Civil War, emphasizes blues, Sun Studio, rockabilly, Stax Studios, Hi Records Rhythm, and soul. Puts Cleveland to shame.

Best Elvis day trip: Before touring **Sun Studio** *(706 Union Ave., 901/526–0664)*, the infamous one-room studio where Elvis, Howlin' Wolf, B.B. King, and Jerry Lee Lewis cut their hits, dine on biscuits and fried banana pie at the adjacent cafe. When you're leaving downtown, drive north of Poplar on Third Street and see Lauderdale Courts, the government housing projects where the King was raised. Pick up the interstate and drive south out to the **Graceland Plaza** *(3734 Elvis Presley Blvd., 901/332–3322)*, where you can take a tour of rock and roll's most fabled mansion—Graceland itself. Lunch on peanut-butter-and-banana sandwiches or a bacon cheeseburger at **Rockabilly's**, a diner nested among the gift shops. Now that you've seen the straight stuff, visit **Graceland Too** *(200 East Gholson St., Holly Springs, MS, 601/ 252–1918)* in Holly Springs, Mississippi, (see "Best snake drive"), residence of the world's number one Elvis fan, Paul MacLeod, and his son Elvis Aron Presley MacLeod. Paul and Elvis, who have dedicated their lives to tracking Elvis in the media, tape every mention of Elvis they can find (using their six televisions and VCRs), log each mention in a journal, then file the reference away for further use, repeating the process for books and magazines. Tourists are invited to observe these happenings as well as tour their house, which may be the most amazing Elvis tribute in the world today. There is a record room, filled with rare Elvis recordings, and a bed with an Elvis quilt on it, a stairway to Elvis heaven, and hallway after hallway overflowing with newspapers and magazines chronicling the King in life and after death. A snapshot of you with Paul and Elvis is included in the $5 tour (three visits qualify you for a lifetime-membership photo ID). The exhibit is open 24 hours. Back in Memphis, pull a cholesterol hat trick and have dinner at the **Western Steakhouse Lounge** *(1298 Madison Ave., 901/725–9896)*, where Elvis liked to eat huge steaks and the Cimmerian atmosphere makes an inviting setting for riding out narcotics. Elvis International Week climaxes on August 16, the anniversary of his death, and is an annual gathering of Elvis fans from around the universe. Their candlelight vigil is an awe-filling sight, especially in contrast to the week's impersonator contest.

Best Highway 61 day trip: If you have a day to spend driving outside Memphis, one of the best routes you could take would be south down U.S. Highway 61. You'll first encounter the **Mhoon Lake casinos** in Tunica county. Tunica, once the poorest county in the state of Mississippi (itself the poorest state in the United States), wagered on the profits of casino gambling in the early 1990s and passed new laws inviting the big guns from Vegas. The ten-plus casinos, each built with a particular theme in mind (ski chalet, Mardi Gras, pirate ship, Irish castle), look surreal in the Delta landscape. If you're feeling extra lucky, pull over—but our advice is to ignore the billboards and klieg lights beckoning from across the cotton fields and hit the accelerator. Wait until the city of Tunica to stop, where you'll have breakfast or lunch at the **Blue & White Restaurant** *(Highway 61, 601/363–1371)*. Its sandwiches and entrees are standard Southern truck-driving food, good hearty fare, but its fried dill pickles are what make the Blue & White great. After your meal, head further south to Clarksdale, birthplace of Ike Turner, Sam Cooke, Little Junior Parker, and Son House. Spend a few hours in Clarksdale's newly renovated **Delta Blues Museum** *(114 Delta Ave., Clarksdale, MS, 601/624–4461)*, located in its library, just off the town square. Be sure to buy a blues map and inquire about the annual Sunflower Blues Festival, held in mid-August. After exploring Clarksdale, turn your car back north toward Memphis. When you reach the intersection of Highways 61 and 49, turn west on 49 to Helena. After a few miles, you will cross the Mississippi River and then dead end. Turn right into Helena, home of Sonny Boy Williamson and the King Biscuit Flour Hour. Head downtown to Cherry Street and park the car. Bubba Sullivan's **Blues Corner Record Shop** *(105 Cherry Street, 501/338–3501)* is located here, and Sonny Boy Williamson's house is just up the street. Harmonica player Frank Frost, who recorded for Sam Phillips in the 1950s and '60s, has a fish restaurant in Helena where he and drummer Sam Carr play on occasion. Every October the city of Helena puts on a first rate three-day blues and gospel celebration, the King Biscuit Festival. Past performers have included Dr. John, Pinetop Perkins, Buddy Guy, and Levon Helm. Best of all, the festival is free, and if you're not afraid of a little nature, camping is great in West Helena's St. Francis National Forest.

Best snake drive: The North Mississippi Hill country is an impoverished region of the state farmed by sharecroppers and bootleggers who make corn whiskey. Recognizable from the timeless lyrics of bluesman R.L. Burnside (author of the tune "Snake Drive") and cohort/neighbor Junior Kimbrough (see Clubs) as well as from the inhabitants of Faulkner's fictional Yoknatapawapha County, this scrap of Mississippi can easily fill a day's exploration. Begin the snake drive on U.S. 78 (Lamar Avenue in Memphis), heading southeast toward Birmingham, Alabama. Your first stop will be the antiquated hamlet of **Holly Springs, Mississippi** (approximately 28 miles down 78). Drop by **Phillip's Grocery Store** *(500 E. Van Doren, 601/252-4671; 2406 S. Lamar Blvd, Oxford, 601/236–5951)* for lunch, downtown next to the old train station. When on a search for the country's best hamburgers, *USA TODAY* tried Phillip's cooking and named its burgers among the best in the nation. Try the Phillip Burger—a hamburger wrapped in bacon and ham, covered in cheese, and fried. If that ain't enough cholesterol for you, get a side of fried okra or onion rings and listen to your heart falter. After lunch, browse Holly Springs' beautifully preserved town square (complete with picturesque Gothic courthouse) and make a stop at Mr. Caldwell's **Aikei Record Shop** (no phone; look for the sign half a block off the town square). (If you're in town during September, ask about Rust College's annual gospel festival.) Next, drive to the end of Gholson Street, stop at the last antebellum home on the left, and get ready for a tour of Graceland Too (see Best homage to the King, above). Stagger back to your car and head west down Highway 7 to **Oxford** (70 miles from Memphis), home of William Faulkner and Mississippi's largest public college, Ole Miss. Oxford is an idyllic (although fast-growing) village that has become a Southern mecca for scholars and artists. The town boasts one superb bookstore/coffee shop **Square Books**, *(1126 Von Buren Ave., 800/648–4001)*, an excellent record store, **Uncle Buck's** *(135 Courthouse Square, 601/234–7744)*, some decent live venues including **Proud Larry's** *(211 S. Lamar Blvd., 601/236–0050)* and the larger Lyric Hall, and a myriad of notable restaurants, from the funky **Taylor Grocery and Restaurant** (it's the only store in Taylor, on Old Taylor Road, about 15 miles from Oxford, 601/236-1716) to the inviting and somewhat refined **City Grocery** *(1118 Von Buren Ave., 601/232–8080)* to the Lebanese ethnic eccentricity of **Mare's Cafe and Shoppe** *(1006 Jackson Ave., E., 601/236–7502)*. While in Oxford, be sure to drive out to Faulkner's farm, Rowan Oak—the woods are majestic—and the pastoral setting, complete with hiking trails, will mellow the most high-strung city dwellers. When you tire of rural life, head back east on 7, then retrace U.S. 78 north to Memphis. If your stomach starts growling on the trip back, try the **Chatterbox** *(3443 Redbands Rd., 601/838–3300)* in Ingram's Mill for delicious fresh fried catfish and hushpuppies. Their Mississippi Mud Pie is also out of this world.

Best wrestling: Local rock 'n' roll entrepreneur Sherman Willmott of Shangri-La noted that "one of the few 'sports' Memphis fans can claim a birthright to is professional wrestling." Memphis has given the wrestling world Jackie Fargo, Jerry "the King" Lawler, and, one of wrestling's greatest managers of all time, former Gentry Jimmy Hart. Even Jerry Phillips, Sam Phillips's youngest son, began a short-lived wrestling career at the age of 12 as a midget wrestler under the tutelage of the legendary Memphis wrestler Sputnik Monroe. Memphis was the place where comic genius Andy Kaufman of *Taxi* and *Saturday Night Live* began appearing in the ring during the early '80s, first wrestling women, then incurring the wrath of the city by threatening to buy Graceland, and finally succumbing to Jerry "the King" Lawler on David Letterman (after the King accosted Kaufman with a literal slap in the face). Alas, Kaufman is no longer with us, but it's still possible to see local heroes Lawler, Coco B. Ware, Brian "Too Sexy" Christopher and tag teams like PG-13 and the Moondogs grapple every Friday night at an indoor flea market, **The Big One** *(2585 N. Hollywood St., 901/276–3532)*. Each Saturday morning, local channel **WMC-TV 5** sponsors a commercial promoting the Friday night card. Tickets for the Saturday show are free, but must be ordered at least six weeks in advance. (Write to: WMC-TV 5, 1960 Union Avenue, Memphis, TN 38104. Include a SASE for tickets.)

transmissions

Best indigenous music: WEVL (89.9 FM) is a community radio station. While probably the best place to hear great programs of Delta blues from the '20s to today, soul, rockabilly, and gospel, it also mixes in alternative rock, Latino music, a gay-pride show, and anything else you can hum. If the station is sponsoring a spaghetti supper, a blues concert or any other event during your stay, go: You can bet you'll hear good music and meet interesting people.

Best Memphis DJ: As the inventor of dance crazes like the Funky Chicken, the Dog, and the Breakdown, and the artist responsible for the first hits on both Sun and Stax, Rufus Thomas proudly declares himself the funkiest man alive. He's been a disc jockey as long as he's been a performer, and on Saturday mornings from 6 to 10, you can hear him play blues on **WDIA (1070 AM)**, where he and B.B. King and Johnny Ace got their starts.

miami

by Todd Anthony

"My favorite part of Miami is Little Havana. You can get
great, cheap coffee on any corner."
— **Raul Malo**, *The Mavericks*

More than a decade has passed since the Armani-clad super-
cops Crockett and Tubbs chased aspiring mobsters down
the pastel art deco canyons of South Beach to the sounds
of Jan Hammer's quintessentially '80s synth-rock score.
Much has changed: Cocaine cowboys have become quaint anachro-
nisms—far more powder blows across the U.S.-Mexico border nowa-
days than through Miami's ports of entry. Fifteen years have elapsed
since the one-two punch of race riots and the Mariel boat lift crippled
the area's tourism industry. A few highly publicized attacks on German
tourists notwithstanding, the city's murder rate has fallen precipitously
from its mid-'80s high. And Jimmy Johnson has replaced living legend
Don Shula as the coach of the Miami Dolphins.

One era ends, another begins. Whatever happened to 2 Live Crew?
Vanilla Ice? Washed away from our memories like sand from the eroding
shores of South Beach, an area that has emerged as an international
modeling hot spot and dance-club mecca. While Miami has a lot more to
offer visitors than glitz and glamour, the Deco District's mix of sun, sand,
sex, and surly waiters still attracts tourists by the tens of thousands.

It all starts with music. It's important to remember that Miami is the
town where disco never died. Spending your last dime on gaudy clothes
and dancing the night away at a crowded club that treats you like dirt
are time-honored local traditions, so the mob scenes that invariably
erupt at the entrances to the hottest spots offer the most entertaining—
and pathetic—street theater south of Manhattan. Models, muscle boys,
Eurotrash scenesters, New York trendoids, and drag queens flock to

South Beach's ever-changing clubs-of-the-moment—Liquid, Bash, Groove Jet, Salvation, Ready Bar, Lua, and Lost Weekend—spreading money and attitude as liberally the Army Corps of Engineers does sand.

Most dance clubs play the same tired house and techno, though old-fashioned garden-variety '70s disco—the BeeGees, Gloria Gaynor, Donna Summer—has infected a whole new generation of boogie men and women. Rap, dancehall, salsa, and R&B all have their niches and one-nighters, but Latin pop rules South Florida airwaves. MTV Latino calls the area home, as do Jon Secada and Gloria Estefan, the pop-music equivalents of homecoming king and queen.

Of course, not all Miamians choose to dance the macarena: Country superstars the Mavericks, shock-rock poster child Marilyn Manson, and noise gods Harry Pussy all grew out of the Miami–Fort Lauderdale rock club scene and testify to the area's surprising musical diversity. From the introspective balladry of Brian Franklin to the obscenity-laced spew of pasty punks like Load, from the earsplitting, unstructured squawk of the Laundry Room Squelchers to the retro rockabilly of the Underbellies, from the angst-rock of sex symbol Rene Alvarez and his crack band Sixo to the husky acoustic folk blues of Magda Hiller, you can get it if you really want. Bad news for misogynist cock rockers, though: Miami is an equal-opportunity rock scene. Goldilocked vocal powerhouse Diane Ward beats Melissa Etheridge at her own game; former country rocker and Atlantic Records recording artist Mary Karlzen has retooled her band and her repertoire to work more of an alt.rock vein; and enigmatic songstress Amanda Green adds her own playful spin to Liz Phair–like femme-rock.

Besides the music, a surprisingly active boho-hippie scene awaits the artistically inclined and you don't need to do coke or heroin to fit in.

lay of the land

To understand Miami, it may help to view Miami International Airport as its center. From the airport it's a straight shot east to **South Beach's Ocean Drive**, where in-line skaters, clubbers, surfers, and gawkers pack back lit glass-and-brick bars, drink machines churn out concoctions with obscene names, and neon flashes on art deco buildings. Take 836 east across the MacArthur Causeway and go until you hit sand. Remember that **Miami Beach** and Miami are two separate cities and that the two are connected by several causeways. On the island, Collins, Ocean, and Washington avenues are the major north-south thoroughfares, and the east-west streets are numbered; the higher the number, the farther north you are.

To the southeast of the airport is Downtown Miami; to the west is an industrial wasteland. The major neighborhoods of interest curl from the far south along the immediate west side of the airport. Starting furthest away, **Kendall** is a suburb far to the southwest. **Coral Gables** is an older residential area where luxurious houses sport coral entrance ways. I-95 ends at a stoplight in Miami, near the north end of Coral Gables and the south end of **Little Havana**, and thereafter it becomes the South Dixie Highway. To the west of this is **Coconut Grove**, a hippie mecca back in the days when Bob Marley was known to hang out here. Today it's a big weekend party zone for teenagers. North of Little Havana and five miles north of the City of Miami is **Little Haiti**, where on a crack-plagued corner you'll find the landmark English dive, Churchill's (see Clubs). The further north you go the more dangerous it gets. A final note of interest is the **Upper Keys**, directly off shore; the Rickenbacker Causeway leads out to Key Biscayne, on the way passing through Virginia Key.

getting from a to b

Public transportation in Miami is lousy, with a few exceptions. You can take the Metrorail from Kendall to Downtown Miami in 20 minutes for a bargain $1.25, and a branch of the rail circles Downtown. However, it doesn't provide easy access to much else; and both buses and the Metrorail close too early to be of any use to nightcrawlers. Taking a cab out to Miami Beach can be prohibitively expensive ($15 to $25, from the airport); however, once you're in South Beach, cabs will get you anywhere in the area cheaply—often for $2. To see greater Miami, you need a car; and if you have one, be forewarned that traffic and parking in SoBe after dark—especially on weekends—can be nightmarish.

sources

Tracking the vicissitudes of Miami's capricious hot-today, gone-tomorrow nightclub landscape daunts even experts such as the writers for Miami's free alternative weekly paper, *New Times* (available at most record stores and newsstands, and at hundreds of bright-red street corner boxes throughout the city). Yet despite its creeping corporatizing, *New Times* still offers the best-written and most comprehensive guide to Miami's ever changing roster of diversions. *Miami Herald* columnist Tara Solomon has been chronicling the comings and goings of club kids since before the beach became fabulous; her piquant musings appear every Friday in the daily rag's "Weekend" section. Several free publications, notably *TWN* (*The Weekly News*) and *Wire* (which offers trenchant local political commentary to augment the usual gossip and club advertising but limits

its scope to South Beach), serve the area's gay population. Glossy monthly mags *Ocean Drive* and *Fashion Spectrum* aren't as timely, but mix profiles of notable locals with lush fashion spreads and plenty of celebrity interviews. If Crockett and Tubbs were around today, you could count on the latter two publications to keep everyone apprised of the duo's wardrobes.

clubs

Best rock club: Miami Beach may have become the nightclub capital of the Western Hemisphere, but it hasn't exactly welcomed live music venues with open arms. Only two—**Rose's Bar & Music Lounge** *(754 Washington Ave., Miami Beach, 305/532–0228)* and its neighbor across the street, the **South Beach Pub** *(717 Washington Ave., Miami Beach, 305/532–7821)*—regularly showcase local bands. Rose's, owned and operated by jazz saxophonist Arthur Barron and his restaurateur wife, Charlotte, has the better room and the longer track record. Local alt.rock acts commandeer the club's velvet-curtained stage Thursdays through Sundays (expect a $3 to $5 cover Fridays and Saturdays), but the place really blooms on two traditionally slow weeknights: Hippies and models flock here Wednesday nights for Hendrix-esque power trio Manchild. And on Mondays, musicians congregate for an open-mike night and jam session hosted by singer, model, and resident bartender Kayce Armstrong.

Best English pub-cum-rock dive: Talk about big fish outta water—members of U2 somehow broke from South Beach's celebrity feeding ground one vodka-saturated morning not long ago to soak up Brit soccer via satellite at **Churchill's** *(5501 NE 2nd Ave., 305/757–1807)*, an odd compound in Little Haiti where locals swill cheap pints, rockers stage eclectic concerts every night, and lunchers choose from Scotch eggs, shepherd's pie, and other Anglo delicacies. Hard-core graffiti graces the bathrooms, parachutes billow from the ceiling, a big-screen TV and several smaller sets beam broadcasts from around the world, and a giant mural by avant artist Antonia livens up the patio. It's all very British, quite rocking, and not nearly as dangerous as neophytes might think. Even if it is in a pretty seedy section of Little Haiti.

Best Cuban roadhouse: Forget the mirrored disco ball, the red vinyl banquettes, the polyester suits (not to mention the polyester hair) and the cramped parquet dance floor. **La Covacha** *(10730 NW 25th St., 305/594–3717)* in the west Dade hinterlands is as far removed as it gets—both aesthetically and geographically—from the cheesiness of generic Little Havana and Hialeah salsa clubs. On Friday and Saturday nights this converted truck stop roughly four miles west of Miami International Airport offers a boisterous, wide-open atmosphere where patrons merengue, salsa, rumba, and cumbia the night away under the stars on a spacious outdoor patio. Out-of-breath revelers can relax at a patio table between songs and snack on succulent barbecued pork, then rise from their repast as the fevered hip-shaking spills out into the parking lot.

Best DJ: Flip a coin to decide between Luis Diaz and Carlos Menendez, resident turntable gods at the phenomenally durable dance club **Groove Jet** *(323 23rd St., Miami Beach, 305/532–2002)*. The duo spins house, trance, salsa, disco, and anything else that'll motivate your feet. Diaz and Menendez tweak the beat with a fluid ease born of decades in the sound booths at such hallowed South Beach hot spots such as Club Nu, Boomerang, the Island Club, and Velvet. Their current home is a low-ceilinged place where hormone-driven causeway kids (Groove Jet draws a predominantly young Latin crowd) escape on weekends to party away their suburban mainland angst. The going gets really weird—and crowded—on Sundays, when Menendez helms a spooky-funky Goth night called the Church.

Best dancehall DJ: You'd have to travel to Kingston, Jamaica, to find a better dancehall selecter than Waggy Tee, the irrepressible DJ whose encyclopedic knowledge of every reggae, ska, rock-steady, and dance-hall tune ever recorded packs up to 1,500 sweating music lovers into the cavernous **Cameo Theater** *(1445 Washington Ave., Miami Beach, 305/532–0922)* every Saturday. Waggy Tee moves the masses with a steady stream of island-accented funk, blending Shabba Ranks, the Skatalites, and the freshest house and hip-hop into one smooth riddim cocktail.

Best amateur male strip contest: Warsaw Ballroom *(1450 Collins Ave., Miami Beach, 305/531–4555)* is where the boys are. The pretty boys and the party boys, a virtual village peopled by men who love men, all of them dancing gaily and having relatively good clean fun. Women are welcome, natch, and there's nothing here to make you uncomfortable (or, if there is, the problem is you). On Wednesdays the party gets especially, um, joyful as local studs bare their flesh and shake their thangs for cash and prizes.

Best party: The longest-running "one-nighter" on the Beach, Monday night's **Fat Black Pussycat** has long since outgrown its humble origins as a dark, smoky, ultrahip speakeasy in the rear room of a small Italian restaurant. In the old days, you needed a secret password to get in, you entered from a garbage-and-glass-strewn alley, and you mingled with a crowd of shady, glamorous insiders. More recently the Pussycat has moved to trendy New York–style, dance-club-of-the-moment **Liquid** *(1439 Washington Ave., Miami Beach, 305/532–9154)* and taken on a decidedly hip-hop flavor, attracting a chicly dressed, predominantly non-Beach African-American crowd including plenty of Miami Heat and Dolphin players.

Best tea dance: In South Beach, the Sunday tea dance is a gay community institution. The fun begins at 6 P.M., allowing guests to kick up their heels and knock back their drinks—and still make it home early enough to recover in time for the start of the workweek. Historically an open-air event, the megapopular party has bounced around from location to location, most recently finding a home at the cavernous South Beach disco mall **Amnesia** *(136 Collins Ave., Miami Beach, 305/531–5535)*.

Best disco: Miami is the hometown of K.C. (of Sunshine Band fame). Enough said. Boogie fever grips polyester-and-platform partyers on Sunday nights at the **Cameo Theatre** *(1445 Washington Ave., Miami Beach, 305/532–0922)*, where DJs George Jett and Jack DeMatas warm over Donna Summer, K.C., and other great oldies.

Runners-up: **Bar None** *(411 Washington Ave., Miami Beach, 305/672–9252)* draws a hipper, upscale crowd to its Funkadelica disco-funk party on Thursdays, and Tuesday nights at **821** *(821 Lincoln Rd., Miami Beach, 305/532–7912)* appeal to fun-seeking, nostalgia-minded locals willing to return to seventh grade.

Best Latin dance club: True fans of Afro-Cuban music have found a home at Little Havana's **Cafe Nostalgia** *(2212 SW 8th St., 305/541–2631)*, open Thursdays through Sundays. The unassuming decor and subdued lighting lend the club a romantic, surreptitious aura. The house band, an otherworldly combo comprised of top-notch exiled musicians, blows away the competition from more tourist-oriented nightclubs. Owner Pepe Horta feeds the fever with reels of classic performance footage culled from pre-Castro Cuban TV shows. The call of the dance floor is irresistible. There's no cover on Thursdays and Sundays; Fridays and Saturdays, it's a manageable $10.

Best all-ages raves and ska/punk shows: The vintage animal rhythms of ska and the fury of punk haven't exactly captured the hearts and minds of adolescent South Florida males as they have elsewhere. But those intrepid kids with a taste for winging, slinging, and flinging have found a home at **Cheers** *(2490 SW 17th Ave., 305/857–0041)*, Miami's only all-ages live music venue. The one-time lesbian bar now caters to snot-nosed brats in oversized clothing who converge on the place to rock out to local faves like Less Than Jake and Against All Authority or trip to biweekly Saturday raves.

Best mosh pit: Maybe slam dancing just isn't violent enough for this gun-totin' town, but for some reason South Florida is the pits when it comes to moshing orders. The younger crowds try their best to rough it up at Cheers. But for full-blown body slopping, better head north 45 or so minutes to Fort Lauderdale and the oversize, under-friendly **Edge** *(200 W. Broward Blvd., Fort Lauderdale, 954/525–9333)*, which brings in both national acts (like Social Distortion) and regional instigators (Ruder Than You, Against All Authority, Skankin' Pickle).

bars

Best blues bar: The downstairs walls of **Tobacco Road** *(626 S. Miami Ave., 305/374–1198)* read like an encyclopedia of blues greats: Framed mug shots are everywhere, autographed by a thousand sad-string artists who've played the club over the years. Miami's oldest boozing establishment (it opened in 1912 and holds liquor license 001) stages its inspirationally booked live music up a flight of creaky stairs in the eerie, red-walled Diamond Teeth Mary Cabaret, where believers of speakeasy lore can still smell Al Capone's cologne hanging in the air. Visiting blues legends like Buddy Guy and John Lee Hooker are right at home here, but so are a range of now popular local bands who were welcome at Tobacco Road before they were booked anywhere else. Excellent munchies include the best burgers in town and killer salads.

Best dockside drinking shack: Just minutes from downtown Miami, **Jimbo's** *(no address, 305/361–7026)* is the perfect antidote to modern America. Hidden off a sandy path on a secluded Virginia Key inlet, Jimbo Luznar's dock is a lost-in-time refuge, where, during the day, you can drink beer at picnic tables, play bocce, or watch manatees loll in the lagoon. Trawlers use Jimbo's docks to wholesale bait shrimp, while Jimbo himself drinks RCs, chomps cigars, and holds court between the games of bocce he plays like a Genoan (that is, very well). Jimbo's operation is protected both by unofficial squatter's rights and local power brokers' reverence for ol' Jimbo. (One mayor, since deceased, could be found here most afternoons during his retirement.) Model and movie shoots have become a regular occurrence, thanks to Jimbo's tropical lagoon ambience, complete with prop shacks. There are also real junked cars, a psychedelic bus, and a few RVs. Beer is sold by the can from barrels filled with ice; grizzled sea dogs share seating space with real canines, while fires burn in metal trash cans (keeps the bugs away). To get there, take the Rickenbacker Causeway toward Key Biscayne; on Virginia Key, follow signs to the sewage plant, and look for the last turnoff before the sewage plant. There is no sign; if you get to the plant, go back.

Best neighborhood bar on South Beach: Leave the skates at home. While the **Irish House** *(1431 Alton Rd., Miami Beach, 305/534–5667)* doesn't exactly frown on bladers (or sunburned tourists or lissome models or overdressed poseurs), unpretentious locals make up the majority of the beer-and-burger joint's clientele. Look elsewhere for hard liquor; the Irish House only holds a beer and wine license, which is all you need for a well-drawn pint of Guinness. Jeans and T-shirts are the attire of choice; and the two pool tables, four TV sets, foosball table, classic-rock jukebox, and three dartboards all see plenty of action. Septuagenarian pool room monitor Jack—as much a House fixture as the neon four leaf clover—looks tough, but he's really a softy who keeps the eight-ball action clean and the fellas in line around attractive women who just want to unwind with their friends.

Best gay bar: If all the guys from the TV show *Cheers* came out of the closet and moved to Miami Beach, they'd feel right at home at **Twist** *(1057 Washington Ave., Miami Beach, 305/538–9478)*. True, Twist's cramped dance floor occasionally overflows with writhing, bare-chested men, but it usually sees less activity than the long, inviting bar where you would most likely find outed Norms, Cliffs, Sams, and Frasiers. For a change of scenery, there's also an upstairs terrace ideal for conversation or low-stress hobnobbing. Plus, Twist is flanked by a pair of outstanding budget eateries, the '50s-throwback **11th Street Diner** *(765 Washington Ave., Miami Beach, 305/534–6763)* to the north and the kitschy-funky Elvis shrine-cum-southern hash house **Lulu's** *(1053 Washington Ave., Miami Beach, 305/532–6147)* to the south.

Best place to meet models: For day-in, day-out gawkability, no other eating or drinking establishment rivals **Bar None** *(411 Washington Ave., Miami Beach, 305/672–9242)*. Exotic cars disgorge a phalanx of impossibly glamorous gazelles who glide through the velvet ropes to mingle and couple off according to some tacitly understood hierarchy of beauty and money. Dim triangular lights illuminate portraits of pop icons past maintaining a vigil from the walls while their contemporary flesh-and-blood counterparts—Madonna, Cindy Crawford, Melanie and Antonio—pile into the two VIP bunkers and do whatever it is that beautiful people do.

Best martini: Smoldering dames. Muted lights. Polished mahogany bar. A bartender—John DeLuca—who takes the art of mixing seriously and would fight James Bond to the death before substituting vodka for top-shelf gin. The **Raleigh Hotel** *(1775 Collins Ave., Miami Beach, 305/534–1775)* annihilates the competition (not to mention patrons) with nine perfectly chilled ounces of elixir served in a setting that leaves regular Joes feeling stirred, not shaken.

food

Best stone crabs: There's no point visiting Miami without visiting **Joe's Stone Crab** *(227 Biscayne St., Miami Beach, 305/673–0365)*. Your friends back home are going to ask if you did, and if not, why. Just remember, everything you've heard about the famed crab house is true: Be prepared to cash in your 401K to pay the tab, be prepared to wait hours for a table, be prepared to hobnob with poseurs and politicians (pardon the redundancy). In other words, be prepared to have the time of your life. Stone crabs, by the way, are remarkable creatures that regenerate the claws that are removed by harvesters and served here with a dandy mustard sauce. Oh, and remember to schedule your vacation during stone crab season (October to May). Joe's closes for the summer.

Best seafood: Fresh and well-prepared seafood is as easy to cop in Miami as crack. But the **Fishbone Grille** *(650 S. Miami Ave., 305/530–1915)* breaks from the norm via exotic preparations involving imaginative spices, sauces, and side dishes (the jalapeño cornbread rules). Further, the 'Bone is located in what will soon be SoFlo's latest boom 'hood, near Brickell, just south of downtown and the Miami River. A rebirth is what the biz journals call it, and many of the deals are being made over lunch at the 'Bone. By dinnertime, the bankers thin out and the crowd that files in is more likely to be filling up before a show at Tobacco Road next door.

Best sidewalk cafe for people-watching: A few rumpled locals still pick up copies of Euromags and out-of-town newspapers at the **News Cafe** *(800 Ocean Dr., Miami Beach, 305/538–6397)*. But the newsstand-cum-coffee shop's golden location at the busiest pedestrian intersection on tourist mecca Ocean Drive has transformed the News Cafe into more of a haven for hipsters and gawkers than for readers. Umbrella-shaded sidewalk tables offer the best view of the flesh parade—but good luck finding one during peak hours. Despite the occasionally slow service, you can always count on a healthy crowd of people-watchers, even when there aren't many people to watch. Inside booths and tables are usually available no matter how crowded it gets outside, and the food holds its own (although the menu bears careful scrutiny; some items like the toma-to-basil pasta are bargains while others—especially some of the pas-tries—are overpriced). And don't overtip; like most Ocean Drive bistros, the News Cafe automatically includes a gratuity on the check.

Best South Beach meal (if someone else is paying): Pacific Time *(915 Lincoln Rd., Miami Beach, 305/534–5979)* is a favorite of gourmets with deep pockets. Chef and co-owner Jonathan Eismann won the Robert Mondavi Rising Star award for his Asian-accented health-conscious haute cuisine. No thick, heavy sauces for this kitchen mas-ter—Eismann specializes in seafood dishes infused with all manner of exotic herbs and spices. Cases in point: Florida Keys grouper with shal-lots, sake, and ginger; big-eye tuna with mango, tomato, and vinaigrette.

Best guava-barbecued ribs: You don't have to be a Young Upscale Cuban-American to appreciate either the delectable (and pricey) *nuevo cubano* cuisine or the traditional music served at **YUCA** *(501 Lincoln Rd., Miami Beach, 305/532–9822)*. You won't find tastier black-bean soup anywhere in the world, and the plantain-smothered dolphin and chocolate *tres leches* can be addictive. And of course, there's plenty of yucca; the restaurant prepares the Latin staple in dozens of exotic vari-ations. On Thursdays YUCA travels back in time to stage Havana Nights, a nostalgic evening of traditional music and *mojitos*; resident diva (and Crescent Moon recording artist) Albita Rodriguez revitalizes Cuban standards on Fridays and Saturdays.

Best Haitian cuisine: At the charming and spacious restaurant **Tap Tap** *(819 5th St., Miami Beach, 305/672–2898)*, the vivaciousness of Haiti is well-represented with murals that capture the natural beauty of the tropics and pay homage to the religious traditions of voodoo. But not only are the walls covered with original art—so are the chairs, tables, and anything else that sits still long enough to get painted. Various sculptures and objets are on display downstairs. And, yes, the food is art too, from the pumpkin soup to the *charbon bwa* (hardwood carbon-grilled snapper) to the sweetly succulent shrimp with coconut sauce.

Best South Beach après-club dining: Say you got ten bucks in your pocket, the munchies have hit you, it's the middle of the night, and you want something you could never find back in Frozen Sneakers, Iowa. No problem. A handful of SoBe eateries have prospered by serving bounteous and damn good meals priced right. Authentic Cuban without pretension? Hit **Puerto Sagua** *(700 Collins Ave., Miami Beach, 305/673–1115)* for rice, black beans, plantains, maybe a sizzling onion-swathed steak. The menu is vast, and the service as tuxed and slick as at the pretentious joints. How about Beach Italian by way of New York? **Pucci's Pizza** *(651 Washington Ave., Miami Beach, 305/673–8133)* is cheesy in the best sense of the word: The menu features real-deal thin-crust slices along with other ways to carbo-load, New York style. Deli for your belly? The legendary **Wolfie's** *(2038 Collins Ave., Miami Beach, 305/538–6626)*, with its unmissable green-and-orange neon signage, offers overstuffed sandwiches with the slaw and the pickles served by no nonsense—c'mon, hon, eat up, enjoy—waitstaff. Something relatively healthy in the wee hours? **La Sandwicherie** *(229 14th St., Miami Beach, 305/532–8934)* serves up fat sandwiches on crusty French bread or puffy croissants topped with all the usual suspects—but the lettuce is greener, the tomatoes sweeter, the olives blacker than at a Subway. And if you really want to push it, this outdoor walkup will set you up at its long lunch counter with a variety of veg and fruit juices and will even sell you hits of bee pollen and ginseng. Right across the street from the Deuce (see Bars) is the budget taco shop **San Loco** *(235 14th St., Miami Beach, 305/538–3009)*, home of the budget-friendly *guaco loco*, an exquisite double-decker taco with an overstuffed hard corn shell slathered in guacamole and encased in a soft flour tortilla, with which drinkers can satisfy alcohol-amplified appetites for less than five bucks.

Best flan: Miami is not so much a part of North America as it is an annex of Cuba, which translates into a cornucopia of cultural and culinary treasures not found in most other American cities. Take flan, that silky, milky, creamy, sugary, caramel-drenched Cuban custard that melts in your mouth and sends your blood-sugar level soaring off the chart. Give in to the temptation and start with two at **Victor's Cafe** *(2340 SW 32nd Ave., 305/445–1313)*, where the decor evokes the elegance of Old Havana and the menu offers half a dozen flan flavors, from exotic mamey to ever-popular coconut, each of them smothered in Victor's sublime guava-based sauce.

shopping

records

Best record store: Simple. Bob Perry, owner-manager of **Blue Note Records** *(16401 NE 15th Ave., North Miami Beach, 305/940–3394)* knows, loves, and stocks good music. Yeah, he's got blues and jazz. Punks—choose your obscurity level and Perry will meet you there. Rock, African, Latin, Caribbean, and—let's put it this way, it takes three rooms to hold the endless array of recorded stuff kept in stock by the most knowledgeable sales staff you're likely to find anywhere. If this was your record collection, you'd never need to acquire another title.

Best record store-cum-indie label: For years Rich Ulloa has offered the underground, the independent, the import, and the just plain hip at **Yesterday and Today Records** *(8336 Bird Rd., 305/552–1011; 4008 SW 57th Ave., 305/665–3305)*. Always evolving, Y&T's two outlets (one overseen by '60s-rockologist and DJ Evan Chern) offer up bounties of vinyl and those newfangled CD things, plus sundry zines and accoutrements. Y&T employees possess a contagious passion for music and a breadth of knowledge they're willing to share. A genuinely nice guy whose involvement with the music biz began as and remains a labor of love, Ulloa has extended beyond retail, becoming a Midas of local music by starting up an independent record label (Y&T Records) that launched major label acts such as the Mavericks, Mary Karlzen, and For Squirrels, and that hopes to do the same for Ulloa's latest find, Amanda Green.

Best used CDs: Giant Florida-based retail music chain **Spec's** *(501 Collins Ave., Miami Beach, 305/534–3667)* recently opened a megastore on South Beach, but savvy locals—particularly club kids and music consumers whose budgets dictate CDs but who hate sifting through all the outdated, secondhand trash clogging the racks at most used CD shops—prefer **Uncle Sam's Music** *(1141 Washington Ave., Miami Beach, 305/532–0973)*. A smallish boutique fronting busy Washington Avenue, Uncle Sam's offers better odds than any other Miami record store of locating Cake, the Chemical Brothers, Red House Painters, or Beck in the secondhand bins.

Best Haitian: From Creole rap to compas, reggae to rasin, **St. Andre Records and Video** *(5912 NE 2nd Ave., 305/757–2112)* carries nearly all the sounds the island has to offer. Music blares constantly from this colorful shop in the heart of Miami's Little Haiti district; don't be surprised to hear tapes of last year's Carnival celebration in Port-au-Prince. Whether your taste runs to Haitian heroes like King Posse and Boukman Eksperyans or to wider Caribbean fare, St. Andre's has tunes for every voodoo child.

books

Best bookstore: Mitch Kaplan's two well-stocked **Books & Books** stores *(296 Aragon Ave., Coral Gables, 305/442–4408; 933 Lincoln Rd., Miami Beach, 305/532–3222)* have defied the odds by emphasizing service, employing knowledgeable, book-loving staff, and by playing host to dozens upon dozens of prominent authors who read from their own works. The chains appeal to your wallet; Books and Books appeals to your soul.

Best gay bookstore: The books aren't gay at **Lambda Passages** *(7545 Biscayne Blvd., 305/754–6900)*, and for that matter much of the clientele isn't either. Though it does have a big section of queer tomes, Lambda also offers some 50,000 titles, ranging from religion and New Age to fiction to women's studies to poetry. New releases and avant-garde clips are well-represented in the video collection, as are the hot-and-heavy skin flicks.

Best newsstands: Worldwide News *(1629 NE 163rd St., North Miami Beach, 305/940–4090)* and its funky little sister shack, **Plaza News** *(7900 Biscayne Blvd., 305/751–6397)*, stock thousands of print publications from all over the globe, as well as nearly every major daily, weekly, or monthly in the U.S.

clothing

Best clubwear: Hey ladies! For designer looks without designer prices, **Bisou Bisou** *(9700 Collins Ave., Bal Harbor, 305/865–5597)* offers styles under its own label that compare to the latest couture of Versace or Prada, but at a fraction of the cost. Of course, value is all relative; $100 stretch pants or micro-minis might send a thrift-store habitué into sticker shock. Bisou Bisou can dress you for a night of clubhopping on South Beach and leave you with enough money for drinks (on the outside chance that the hot threads don't persuade an admirer to order drinks for you).

Best secondhand clothes: Travel back with us now, to a time when shoes had platforms. Back farther to when shirts had paisleys. Velvet and vinyl. Leather and lace. And if you don't want to dress in authentic duds from the '20s to the '70s, you still might want to browse away an afternoon in west Miami's retro repository **Miami Twice** *(6562 Bird Rd., 305/666–0127)*. There's jewelry and accessories and furniture and antiques, too.

et cetera

Best hand-rolled cigars: Master Cuban cigar makers with hooded eyes, creased faces, and deft fingers sit hour upon hour at weathered wooden workbenches and roll stogies the old-fashioned way at the Little Havana factory of **El Credito** *(1106 SW 8th St., 305/858–4162)*. *Cigar Aficionado* magazine, the cigar smoker's bible, ranks El Credito's La Gloria Cubana brand among the world's finest smokes, comparing it favorably with the best puffs Fidel has to offer. While demand for El Credito's wares from cigar stores around the world often exceeds available supply, visitors to the warehouse can purchase dozens at wholesale prices.

Best botanica: What the hex is a botanica? Voodoo, Santeria, and black magic practitioners alike gather at these spooky little joints to purchase oils and beads and icons. Then they alter reality at their altars. In some parts of town it seems like there's a botanica on every corner selling everything from live (but not for long) sacrificial chickens to shrines to Chango. Not for nothing do they call Miami the Magic City. **Nena Botanica** *(902 NW 27th Ave., 305/649–8078)* has the widest assortment of mysterious gewgaws to help you get your spirits up.

body alterations

Best hair salon: You don't have to be a star to feel like one at **Some Like It Hot** *(630 Lincoln Rd., Miami Beach, 305/538–7544)*. Refreshingly free of the pretension and attitude that seem to plague upscale South Beach beauty parlors, this busy but attentive salon located on fashionable Lincoln Road offers outstanding haircuts at prices ranging from $30 for men to $45 for women. And if knowing your hair looks its best doesn't bring you peace of mind then maybe a facial, manicure, pedicure, or massage will. (Leg and body waxing are another story.) Appointments are recommended; Tuesdays offer your best shot at getting one on short notice.

Best tattoos: Though the colorful (literally and figuratively) owner-manager Lou Sciberras of **Tattoos by Lou** *(231 14th St., Miami Beach, 305/532–7300)* died in 1996, his long-running ink parlor on South Beach continues to needle the flesh. Lou's stays open later than some bars and welcomes gawkers as well as paying clientele. After dark, it becomes one corner (with Mac's Club Deuce, see Bars, and San Loco, see Dining) of a popular lowlife triangle located at the epicenter of the Beach's nightlife swirl (near Washington Avenue and 14th Street).

hotel/motel

Best swimming pool: No greater monument to old Miami Beach exists than the **Fontainebleau Hotel** *(4441 Collins Ave., Miami Beach, 305/538–2000)*. Now part of the Hilton chain, the sprawling complex screams Vegas-style excess; you feel like a high-roller just entering the vast marble-floored lobby. Filmmakers have repeatedly featured the hotel's legendary ameba-shaped pool with its trademark waterfall and tree-covered island on screen. Tony "Scarface" Montana reclined in one of the Fontainebleau's chaise lounges while his partner-in-crime Manolo wiggled his tongue at bikini-clad beauties. Nearly two decades earlier, Agent 007 disrupted a rigged card game organized in one of the hotel's poolside cabanas by arch-villain Goldfinger. Singles start at $220.

Best guest house: Nestled behind an incongruous thicket of trees and bushes just off Collins Avenue in the heart of Miami Beach's glitzy Deco District, the **Mermaid** *(909 Collins Ave., Miami Beach, 305/538–5324)* attracts a bohemian crowd of writers, artists, and world travelers. The Mermaid is more Key West mellow than Miami manic; you won't find a TV in any of the ten bright, handpainted rooms. A dozen of South Beach's loudest, most frenzied clubs lie within a five-minute walk and the beach is just two blocks away. Rates are reasonable by Beach standards ($75 and up, depending on size of room and time of year).

local wonders

Best beach scene: Though the sands of South Beach attract a fair share of bold, all-but-nude sun worshippers, the real freaks head further north to the clothing-optional scene at **Haulover** (rhymes with all over) **Beach** *(just south of Sunny Isles at Collins Avenue and 140th St.)*. Pierced genitalia and tattooed buttocks are commonplace. Gay men constitute a majority of the au naturel crowd, and women can generally enjoy hassle-free sunbathing. Nude volleyball aficionados take note: On weekends buff boys square off for games ranging in competitiveness from friendly to heated.

Best swimming hole: Ah, Coral Gables. The dream city of developer George Merrick remains an anachronism eight decades down the road, a place with so many regulations (no pickup trucks allowed, houses must be painted certain colors, hedges can be only so high, etc.) you wonder why people are so eager to buy into the shady, quaint town. Perhaps because the city is so strict, there are many excellent reasons to risk violating some code or another and entering the Gables—a primo library, fine youth center, a couple of nice parks, and, best of all, the **Venetian Pool** *(2701 DeSoto Blvd., Coral Gables, 305/460–5356)*, the ultimate faux tropical island man-made paradise. Filled by the clear cool waters of a natural spring, Merrick's one-time excavation site sports caves, grottoes, diving cliffs, and other cool features that make it seem like anything but a public swimming pool. And from September through May, while the kids are in school, a handful of weekday swimmers and sunbathers have the water all to themselves.

Best diving/snorkeling spot: Still haven't found Jesus? Try looking underwater. There aren't too many places in South Florida where submerged browsing isn't thrilling and fun—artificial and actual reefs dot the underwater-scape from Miami to Homestead and throughout the Florida Keys. But **John Pennekamp Coral Reef State Park** *(Key Largo, 305/451–1202)* makes it simple and safe, just right for novices and tourists and novice tourists. Plenty of colorful fish and plants and coral lurk in the warm benevolent waters. And then there's the giant subsurface statue of the Son of God. If that doesn't send your spirituality soaring, the rainbow-hued parrot fish, red-silver snapper, and crimson coral will.

transmissions

Best rock radio: After Home Shopping Network mogul Buddy Bud Paxson bought WSHE-FM in 1996, WSHE changed musical formats. It used to be South Florida's premier rock station. This leaves the University of Miami's campus station, **WVUM (90.5 FM)**, as the only choice worthy of recommendation. You won't hear college-chart stuff like Cake and the Jon Spencer Blues Explosion anywhere else in Dade, and VUM does an admirable job of mixing local, unsigned bands into the mix.

Best late-night reggae DJ: For 18 years sleepless South Floridians have tuned in Clint O'Neil's *Sounds of the Caribbean*—Mon. thru Sat., 2 A.M. to 6 A.M.—**WLRN (91.3 FM)**. Known locally as the Godfather of Reggae, O'Neil's raspy, low baritone, unflagging effervescence in the wee hours, and close friendship with the late Bob Marley (who frequently dropped in on O'Neil in the studio) have made Clint O. as much of a fixture as Red Stripe beer in the Miami reggae firmament.

Best Latin show: In Miami when you want to direct someone to, say, WAXY (790 AM), you tell him, "Third English-language station from the left." The dial is so full of chatter in different tongues and dialects that it feels like a regular Radio Babel. Español dominates the AM airwaves, where listeners apparently never tire of anti-Castro vitriol. Those with a taste for a little sanity and humor seek out **WQBA (1040 AM)**—La Cubanisima—and Julio Estorino, the station's news director and cohost of *Primera Plana*. His short segments titled "Candeleria" are the tip, a rare case of Latin radio having some good clean fun. In these surreal snippets, Estorino creates scenarios for Candelaria, a middle-aged Cuban woman who is one of the few members of *el exilio* who has regular telephone contact with Fidel—on the air, no less.

minneapolis/ st. paul

by Terri Sutton

"First Avenue is one of the top ten clubs in America. But I like some other joints too, so it's definitely worth the trip."
— **Slim Dunlap**

Although both parties have tried to forget it, Courtney Love lived for a short time in the Twin Cities of Minneapolis–St. Paul. After a few dramatic months, she fled back to California, complaining that Minnesotans in general were hopelessly unpretentious. Minnesotans—especially the shaggy, dreaded ones—took it as a compliment.

Truth is, however, that Twin City bands like the Replacements, HüskerDü, and Soul Asylum were extremely self-conscious about their scruffy, self-deprecating pose. As we know now, their ragged flannel shirts and guitar squalls were a prescient rock fashion—just as much as that other Minneapolitan's purple brocade suits and flagrant sexuality were. In fact, more than one famous Twin Citian rock guy has an eyeliner-wearin' Goth skeleton in his closet.

A gloomier, more decadent impulse underlies Minneapolis' ardent rock 'n' roll classicism, with a definitive thread running from Prince through the cabaret punk of underground heroes the Cows, to the moody constructions of today's emerging techno DJs and dream-pop bands. Dark artifice plays with (and off) that patented Minneapolis punky sincerity—in the same way bedroom rockers, Minneapolis College of Art and Design (MCAD) videomakers, style-mongering hairdressers, and University of Minnesota dropouts all intermingle in the Twin Cities' crowded enclaves of cool. It's a small town....

Or rather, two small towns. Both Minneapolis and St. Paul started out with (and still harbor) more than their fair share of Scandinavian and German residents; consequently, the white natives (bohos not excepted) have an irritating blend of open generosity and northern reserve. Meaning they *talk* a good line in racial politics but keep their neighborhoods well segregated. The habitats of white alternative youth generally nestle between lily-white enclaves and hard-core black zones; unfortunately, no fiery cultural miscegenation has yet erupted. And Minneapolis' rap scene has so far remained perpetually nascent (for an update, check out the specialty rap radio shows on KMOJ 89.9 FM and KFAI 90.3 FM).

Credit should also be given to the weather for that special Minnesota friendly/distant schizophrenia. While all windows, doors, and skin are open to the steaming, endless days of summer, nothing whatsoever is exposed in winter, when the thermometer drops below zero. To be anything less than miserable during a January visit to Minnesota, you need a heavy coat, wool socks, a full-spectrum light, and a plan. Carpe the frigid diem, either by: 1) keeping warm on skates (or, less elegantly, with boots, brooms, friends, and a soccer ball) at one of the area's ubiquitous ice rinks; 2) driving around wildly in the glare of iced parking lots; or 3) settling down with a stack of blueberry pancakes at **Rick's Ol' Time Cafe** *(3756 Grand Ave. S., Mpls., 612/827–8948)* to read newspaper accounts of fingers chopped off in snowblowers, snowmobilers clotheslined by barbed wire fences, and cars drowned in "frozen" lakes. Choice No. 3, especially, will make your cold visit way sweeter.

lay of the land

The downtowns of Minneapolis and St. Paul are separated by a big body of water, but it's not an epic bay-crossing like San Francisco to Oakland. St. Paul is a 15-minute freeway jaunt east and down the Mississippi from Minneapolis. If you can't exactly see the river's mighty cleaver chop through the Twin Towns, you sure can feel it. With its weathered buildings, narrow streets, and established ethnic enclaves, St. Paul looks like an East Coast city; Minneapolis, meanwhile, embraces the Western imperative to destroy, rebuild, and keep moving. The same applies culture-wise: St. Paul has long been the bastion of heavy metal clubs, while Minneapolis is either setting or following national music trends.

Neither downtown has much to offer visitors: St. Paul because there's nothing going on; Minneapolis because it's become so corporate and allergic to loitering. With the exception of downtown's granddaddy rock club First Avenue (featured in Prince's *Purple Rain*!!) most of the action goes on in other neighborhoods. South of downtown Minneapolis, **Uptown** *(Hennepin Avenue at Lake Street)* began alt.culture life as a funky hangout for upper-middle-class white kids living slightly west around the city's lakes. It still serves that purpose, though the bowling alley, greasy spoon, and cozy music bar have been replaced by Borders, Urban Outfitters, and the Gap. Much of the old Uptown edge has moved east on **Lake Street** to **Lyndale Avenue**, where alternapreneurs have opened hair and tattoo salons, coffee shops, vintage and rave clothing stores, and a retro bowling alley.

North from Lake Street about 12 blocks, **Hennepin** diagonals into Lyndale; the area between the avenues and Lake Street is known as the Wedge. Rich with rental duplexes and apartments, the **Wedge** and neighboring **Whittier** (east to Nicollet Avenue) have served as the traditional nesting ground for musicians, students from nearby MCAD, and other post-college temp workers. As rents rise, however, these sundry types are increasingly moving across the Mississippi to **Northeast Minneapolis**, a traditionally Polish working-class neighborhood, and to St. Paul, especially around Grand Avenue and the liberal arts college Macalester.

getting from a to b
Since the destruction of the streetcar system in the '50s, the Twin Cities have had no trains. You can get around on Metropolitan Transit Commission buses, although it may take some time (bad news when the temperature's stuck at minus 15 degrees). A 20-minute drive that actually takes an hour by bus, the #7 runs regularly to downtown Minneapolis from the Minneapolis-St. Paul International Airport in the southeast suburbs. From downtown, buses go south on Hennepin and Nicollet Avenues, north on 7th Street, and northeast on Hennepin. Greyhound stations are situated within blocks of each city center. To reach St. Paul from the airport, take the #54D. From the St. Paul Amtrak station, the #16 bus line extends east and west on University Avenue; it'll bring you to downtown Minneapolis by way of the main University of Minnesota campus and environs (Dinkytown and the West Bank). The last city buses generally leave around 1 A.M.; after that, call a cab. Yellow Cab is 612/824–4444 and 612/222–4433 in St. Paul. For MTC information, phone 612/373–3333.

sources
Even before *City Pages* was purchased in 1997 by the owners of New York's *Village Voice*, the largest free Minneapolis-St.Paul newsweekly focused as much on national arts and politics as on local versions thereof. *City Pages*'s saucy and well-traveled tone assumes its audience's sophistication, which is a nice way to say that it can occasionally strike

people as impenetrable or trendy Still, you'd be hard-pressed to find another weekly with such extensive and urbane arts coverage anywhere between the coasts. Another free local magazine, *Cake*, mixes club listings with relentlessly superficial music coverage. Gay-oriented reviews and entertainment info can be found in the weekly *focusPOINT,* biweekly *Lavender* and the monthly *Q.*

clubs

Best Twin City rock club: Most Twin Citians have resigned themselves to spending way too many nights at **First Avenue** *(701 1st Ave. N, Mpls., 612/332–1775).* Any rock act with more edge than Bonham will inevitably end up playing either the cavernous 1,200-capacity main room or the adjoining sweaty shoe box known as the **7th Street Entry**. With the demise of the Uptown Bar's (See Dining) schedule of major alternative local bands and get-'em-before-they're-huge touring acts, First Avenue has no real competition—on any front. This former bus station regularly books rap and reggae showcases, African pop marathons, and, under its Half-Note series, avant jazz grooves. On all-ages friendly Sundays, kids in baggy pants and barrettes mob the dance floor, while their more serious (read: music dweeby) peers scrutinize local talent in the Entry. Hard beats and Wonderbras rule the Friday and Saturday night danceterias, drawing crowds of hairdressers and salesclerks. Otherwise, the headliners set the tone: brutish suburbanites for Blur; bespectacled nerds at Tortoise.

Runner-up: **The 400 Bar** *(400 Cedar Ave., Mpls., 612/332–2903)* has languished for years as a stagnant local band venue frequented by boorish students from the nearby University of Minnesota campus. In 1996, the building was purchased by Bill Sullivan, infamous former tour manager of both the Replacements and Soul Asylum. Sullivan immediately hired Maggie Macpherson, the longtime booker of the Uptown Bar, who was the first to bring Uncle Tupelo, G Love, and Nirvana, among others, to town. It's worth a look-see, and has already put on great shows by Alex Chilton, R.L. Burnside, Vic Chestnut, and Semisonic.

Best local bands and cheap pints: On any given Saturday night at the **Turf Club** *(1601 University Ave. W, St. Paul, 612/647–0486),* a middle-aged country quartet plays syrupy requests for an enthusiastic cluster of fifty- to eighty-something hoofers. Scarred paneling covers the walls, along with a large mural of racing quarter horses. Speckled linoleum covers the dance floor. Although the bar's mixed schedule of local alternative and trad dance music is still tentative and sometimes strange, the Turf Club has already endeared itself to area musicians and fans with its cheap pints and a comfortably frayed *mise-en-scène*. If only it weren't in St. Paul.

Best Wednesday night hoedowns: Country pickup gang Trailer Trash has owned Wednesday nights in Minneapolis since they first took the stage more than two years ago at an unpretentious, rec-room-style downtown drinker's bar named **Lee's Liquor Lounge** *(101 Glenwood Ave. N, Mpls., 612/338–9491)*. Arrive early (ten o'clock, say) and the regulars' watery eyes look bemused by the well-groomed rockabillys and betties, two-steppin' dykes, shaggy thrifters, and college kids. But by closing time, both old and young are lost in a honkytonk haze of George Jones, Ray Price, Doug Sahm, and Herb Alpert (!), swingingly provided by a loose group of ex and current alt.rockers. Son Volt's Jay Farrar, the Jayhawks' Gary Louris, and Soul Asylum's Dave Pirner have all sat in with Trailer Trash. The how of this hoedown, though, has less to do with famous talent than with Leinenkugel in cold cans, secondhand smoke, and the felicitous moment when the band leans into "Amarillo by Morning."

Best gay club packed with straight people: It probably started with het girls stopping in for hassle-free techno. Then the La Femme drag review pulled in the curious. And now seventy-something ladies from the suburbs celebrate their birthdays at ringside tables, cheering for vampy impersonations of Madonna. **The Gay Nineties** *(408 Hennepin Ave., Mpls., 612/333–7755)* may not be completely gay any more, but it's very '90s, with a couple of pulsating dance rooms, a strip show, a piano bar, an alcohol-free coffee area, a full-service restaurant, and bodies, bodies, bodies (eccentric shapes, all ages and colors, and at least six sexual persuasions).

Best new jack lounge scene: For all its liberal cache, Minneapolis maintains an amazingly segregated nightlife. With the exception of world music shows at the Cedar Cultural Center and rap events at First Avenue, very few clubs bring black and white together. Which is why the low-key hip-hop DJ and band jams at the **Front** *(15 N.E. 4th St., Mpls., 612/378–5115)* feel so fresh and promising. Adjoined to the Ground Zero disco, notorious for its S&M nights, the Front wears a mellow, boho-sophisticated face. Art prints line the walls of the high-ceilinged room, vintage couches and chairs group conversationally on oriental rugs, and a handsome polished bar stretches along the back wall. The midweek improvs—ranging in vibe from Jack Kerouac meets trip-hop to energetic funk—attract the multiracial friends of the artists, white Gen Xers in thrift dresses and work pants, sharp black couples in '70s threads, and baggy-jeaned singles. The Front also features a "Cocktail Nation" theme Saturdays. Sit back, sip draft microbrew, and thank god guitars don't rule every club in town.

Best polka lounge: Although the predominantly working class and German/Polish Northeast (or "Nordeest") supports a bar on nearly every corner, most of the joints tend to be clannish and downright frosty to strangers. **Nye's Bar and Polonaise Room**, *(112 Hennepin Ave. E, Mpls., 612/379–2021)* perched on the area's southern border, just parties—with or without the bohos. Two generations of patronizing rock hipsters and a swarm of suburban Johnny-come-latelies have not destroyed the gold-sparkle-booth ambience of Nye's. Gracious crooner Lou Snider continues her soulful reign in the Polonaise Room, egging on would-be Sinatras with bolstering piano chords, the lyrics to "My Way," and her own thin soprano. Old regulars still claim a spot at the piano bar, craving their turn at the mike. Thursdays through Saturdays, romping polka music leaks through the swinging doors that lead to a smaller, darker bar; here, frail white-haired musicians stare death down with raging accordion and a hopping beat, spurring the couples on the postage-stamp-size dance floor into demolition derbies.

bars

Best rock dive: Back in the mid-'80s, rock 'n' roll tourists used to stop by the legendary **CC Club** *(2600 Lyndale Ave. S, Mpls., 612/874–7226)* hoping to get a glimpse of Paul Westerberg and Bob Stinson (Tommy was still underage). Often enough, they were there, along with the rest of the local rock cognoscenti—most of whom lived in the area squared by Franklin and Lake streets, and Hennepin and Nicollet avenues. Those folks eventually vacated the roomy duplexes and apartment buildings of the Wedge and Whittier, only to be replaced by the next lot of aimless college grads and Minneapolis College of Art and Design dropouts. Like the area, the CC is useful, so it never goes out of fashion. Featuring deep black Naugahyde booths, pool tables, a jukebox stuffed with local music (CDs now, not singles), the smallest women's bathroom in the city, frigid summer and hell-hot winter temps, and almost always packed crowds at closing, the CC will not die. The next generation of ragged swillers waits in the wings.

Best bar and bowl: There are probably people who miss Lake Street's old bowling alley, with its dusty windows, cracked linoleum, and video games, but they certainly can't be heard above the crash of the pins and the babble of the crowd at the funkily renovated and wholly reinvigorated **Bryant Lake Bowl** (*810 W. Lake St., Mpls., 612/825–3737*). Owned by the same folks who opened gay-friendly coffeehouse Cafe Wyrd, the BLB draws a comfortably eclectic crowd of after-work parties, groups of butch women, het couples, post-theatergoers (the Jungle Theater performs well-regarded dramatics across the street), and bowling fans who prefer microbrews to Bud. Bowling is not, by the way, essential; the airy front room is jammed with rickety tables and chairs, and enhanced by a colorful art deco-ish mural. The BLB gets noisy, but never manic, perhaps because only beer and wine are served. An ambitious menu of pasta, salads, and sandwiches is hit or miss. The bar's intimate theater space next door regularly presents plays, comedians, and quieter touring rock bands in the K Records style.

Best expense-account bar: With its polished wood, imposing bar, and tony menu, the **St. Paul Grill** (*350 Market St., St. Paul, 612/224–7455*) is about as alternative as Wall Street. Then again, who thought martinis would get hip? Or (thank you, Soundgarden) single malt scotch, which the St. Paul Grill happens to have quite a lot of. Like, 55 flavors. Including, claims bartender Tod, a Japanese single malt, "which is not all that great." To dig in, you can order a one ounce pour of three different scotches for $9.95 to $11.95, depending on the age. Or better yet, go with friends, double the fun with six samples, and really scope out the range of peat, brine, and malt. Cigars may be purchased at the bar. People-watching is usually at a premium, as gussied-up wedding guests from the adjoining St. Paul Hotel weave in and torch up. At the end of the night, pass the check to the stooge with the corporate credit card.

Best Irish entertainment emporium: Okay that's a bit of an exaggeration, but the **Half Time Rec** (*1013 Front Ave., St. Paul, 612/488–8245*) does provide live Irish and Cajun music for dancing, pool tables, underground bocce ball, and plenty of friendly and comfortably inebriated regulars. St. Paul was settled with much help from Irish immigrants, and, with its wobbly barstools and battle-scarred walls and floors, the Half Time is absolutely a traditional neighborhood tavern. It just happens to also attract long-haired and gauzy-skirted folk dance devotees. And college kids, who come to drink black-and-tans and toss bocce balls down the clay courts in the bar's crumbling basement. The wooden dance floor lies directly above the bocce courts; when those heels are really hoofing, you can fear for your hearing, and your life. Have another Guinness. It can only help your aim.

food

Best bohemian diner: A chef at various posh Minneapolis restaurants goes AWOL, jumps the river, and brushes up a faded Northeast grill with his wife's help: the result is the **Modern Cafe** (*337 13th Ave. NE, Mpls., 612/331–9557*), a casually deco diner with a beer and wine license and a shabby, arty clientele drawn from both sides of the Mississippi. Although the menu changes, the Modern emphasizes belly-busting American food made with confidence and some imagination. Favorites include apple French toast and *huevos* at breakfast, spicy chili cheese fries at lunch, and meat loaf for dinner (yeah, you heard right). Musicians and artists have been expatriating to the Northeast from their usual Wedge/Whittier/downtown haunts in droves, and the Modern is the first place they stop for weekend breakfasts. Ask for one of the intimate wooden booths and eavesdrop on your neighbors' self-congratulations for finding such a cool spot. Then join in.

Best after-club chow: Hungry bar closers have few late-night restaurant choices in Minneapolis—and one of them is **Ember's** (*2516 University Ave. SE, 612/379–1982*), a local Denny's equivalent. If you're not inebriated enough to deal with cold toast and rubbery pancakes, check out **Little Tijuana Restaurant** (*17 E. 26th St., Mpls., 612/872–0578*), affectionately known as Little T's. Not the most flavorful Mexican food, sure, but a friendly, scuffed-up feeling, lounge-able booths, and dim lighting make it a welcome after-hours haven. Magenta-haired waitresses will take your order until 2:30 A.M., 365 days a year.

Best breakfast with Bloody Marys: Back when the **Uptown Bar** (*3018 Hennepin Ave., Mpls., 612/823–4719*) booked bands, a semi-alcoholic music aficionado (the most common Minneapolis type) could find herself there three times a day: watching a show till close, returning ten hours later for a huge plate of greasy vegetarian hash and a Bloody, then stopping by that night for more music. It got ugly. These days, the only reason to frequent the Uptown is breakfast—the selling point being the drink. Liquor licenses are as rare in southwest Minneapolis as coffeehouses are ubiquitous (zoning laws from the dark ages).

Runner-up: If you're after a quality brunch and Bloody experience, go downtown to **Nikki's** *(1007 Third Ave. N, Mpls., 612/340–9098)*, where you'll spend more, sit next to a yuppie artist, and enjoy your meal.

Best dramatic monologues: God knows why you'd be lurking in downtown St. Paul in the middle of the night (talk about a ghost town) but given that accidents happen, **Mickey's Diner** *(1950 W. 7th St., St. Paul, 612/698–8387)* may be your refuge. A dolled-up railway car tucked away at the foot of glassy skyscrapers, Mickey's has been around forever and has the imposing waitresses to prove it. Proximity to the downtown bus station keeps the joint jumping and the conversations (with the dead, God, even other people) lively.

Best cheap eats: With a couple of notable exceptions, Twin Cities restaurants can't seem to get a handle on that magic combo of congenially hip ambience, good food, and cheap prices. Here's a short list of those that manage the latter two. The **Phuong Cafe** *(2424 Nicollet Ave., Mpls., 612/874–7560)* may be only one in a parade of Vietnamese and Laotian restaurants and grocery stories up and down Nicollet, but it offers more than 150 noodle dishes, mostly in hot and homey soups, but also appetizers and salads. At **Baja Tortilla Grill** *(2300 Hennepin Ave., Mpls., 612/374–9900)* the *nuevo burritos*—packed with grilled zucchini, squash, peppers, onions, and black beans—only vaguely resemble Mexican food. So what. They're juicy, toothsome, and monstrous. **Taco Morelos** *(14 W. 26th St., Mpls., 612/870–0053)* trades in plainspoken tacos and burritos, a kissing cousin to the row of *taquerias* on St. Paul's Concord Street where you used to find the only "authentico" Mexican available. Finally, **Ruam Mit** *(475 St. Peter St., St. Paul, 612/290–0067)* puts the higher-priced Minneapolis Thai restaurants to shame with thick savory curries and peppery stir-fries.

shopping

records

Best drum 'n' bass: Even before it expanded next door and downstairs, **Let It Be Records** *(1001 Nicollet Mall, Mpls., 612/339–7439)* outshone any local store for rave, ambient, techno, jungle, house, and dub tracks. Now the basement Dance Room presents racks of import and domestic 12 inches with two turntables, a mixer and a clerk/DJ, while the rock, jazz, reggae, dub, and, uh, *nuevo* progressive rock sections upstairs grow wider and deeper in the extra room. Let It Be is the first and sometimes only place to get aboveground imports such as Spring Hill Jack or Mad Professor, along with bunches of obscure remixes—like the Tortoise 12-inch series—and club hit knockoffs. The unpretentious staff (this is Minnesota, remember) knows its stock; and a listening station allows you to check out any new or used recording in the place. Frequent in-store performances spotlight artists from bent country rockers Wilco to freaky French disco DJs Daft Punk. A vast collection of videos—from Frank Zappa's *200 Motels* to live Oasis—takes up one long wall; and various books, rock bios, and magazines fill up a corner. Can there be too much of a good thing?

Best promo discs: Welcome to the Twin Cities Rock Crit and Music Bizzer 5K: Whoever races their promotional rejects into **Cheapos** *(seven TC locations; not to be missed, the store at 404 W. Lake St., Mpls., 612/827–0646)* quickest gets the highest payoff. Which is all to the good of Jack and Jill consumer, happily scooping up new Metallica and Dwight Yoakam CDs for $9 and under. (Those "promo only" stickers? Don't even try to peel 'em off.) Other stores hawk used product, but not in the sheer volume and dimension of the Cheapos outlets.

Best punk HQ: Tucked into a run-down strip mall east of Uptown, **Extreme Noise** *(124 W. Lake St., Mpls., 612/821-0119)* serves as a community center, yellow pages, and supply store for the Twin Cities' dusty p-rock youth. Cassettes and singles of local bands the Strike, Dillinger 4, and Empty Set can be hunted down here; information about all-ages shows in basements and VFW halls is tacked up on the bulletin board outside. Studs, belts, and other necessary accessories call from the display case next to the cash register. Scene stalwarts, the staffers know their customers and their stuff. Gathered in these friendly bins is a history of punk rock that includes not only the latest Los Crudos but old Dag Nasty singles, Public Image Ltd. records, and a surprising array of current Matador, Drag City, and Thrill Jockey releases. (Never mind the bollocks, here's Gastr Del Sol?) Extreme Noise also carries a dandy selection of books from Research and other oddball publishers. A homey, appealingly openminded venture.

Best alternarama: Keep to the left as you stroll into **Roadrunner Record Exchange** *(4304 Nicollet Ave., Mpls., 612/822–0613)*, and you'll be confronted with the staff's polarized picks: Each Tom, Dick, and Shari has six or seven discs under his or her name, complete with scrawled annotations. Let's see, somebody's into Bloodshot Records punkabilly, someone else buys Japanoise imports. There's an African pop hound, a die-hard punk rocker, and one poor soul heavily into 20th-century avant-garde composers. In other words, Roadrunner stocks a number of odd things very well, and not because they're trendy. Probably the only neighborhood record store in America where the noise-damage fanzine *Bananafish* sits spitting distance from Guy Klucevsek CDs and Slobberbone 7-inches.

books

Best bargain one-stop for Philip K. Dick and James M. Cain: In the deep shadow of the deserted Lake Street Sears Tower sit two little hermetic shops with two of the most voluptuous used books selections around. Purveyor of fantasy, sci-fi, and horror, **Uncle Hugo's Science Fiction Bookstore** *(2864 Chicago Ave., Mpls., 612/824–6347)* has developed an avid clientele who buy new books and then sell the books back so poorer (but no less avid) folk can snag 'em off the used shelves. Accustomed as they are to dreary nerds with armfuls of space operas, the avuncular clerks warm to nonobsessional chat and will likely ask what you're reading; they're also quick with the "what next?" recommendation. Ditto **Uncle Edgar's Mystery Bookstore** *(same address, 612/824–9984)*, with its bulging rows of bestsellers and obscurities.

Best comix: The three branches of **Dreamhaven Books** *(1309 S.E. 4th St., Mpls., 612/379–8924; 912 W. Lake St., Mpls., 612/823–6161; 1403 W. Lake St., 612/825–4720)* don't just sell comics, they sell everything comic-book lovers might possibly be into (and they should know). So you can get not just *Love & Rockets,* but magic realism and horror novels, not just *Sandman* but serious film bios and Goth music-related surveys, not just Magic Comics but Magic Cards and other sword-and-sorcery games. Dreamhaven still does the comic thang pretty darn well, furnishing the usual indies and majors, along with plenty from the new waves of female-drawn books and self-published mini-comics.

Best full-service literary bookstore: Since the Cities were invaded by superstores, two well-loved independent general bookstores have gone belly up. Across the street from lefty Macalester College, the **Hungry Mind** *(1648 Grand Ave., St. Paul, 612/699–0587)* may be the last of the breed, but it's definitely still kicking. And screaming. Owner David Unowsky is an unrepentant advocate of the benefits of independent bookselling; his cheerfully frayed Hungry Mind harbors way deep fiction, poetry, and literary criticism sections, with odd volumes from Serpent's Tail, Dalkey Archive, and Copper Canyon Press. They've also built up a busy author reading series that's among the best in the nation, with visits from the likes of music crit Greil Marcus, vampire chronicler Anne Rice, and poet/biographer Quincy Troupe. An adjoining cafe, Table of Contents, serves espresso drinks and moderate-to-pricey, admirably adventurous food.

clothes

Best place to find a hot-pink polyester sundress: Rock girls in the Twin Cities have a serious jones for vintage dresses, maybe because they can be hunted down with relative ease around these parts. **Lula** *(1587 Selby Ave., St. Paul, 612/644–4110)* stocks to fix these girls, with racks of sequined, sleeveless cocktail costumes, neon minis, cotton print housedresses, droll quilted '70s jumpers, flowery halters, and silky slim maxis. The men's section gets only a tiny corner in the front of the store. Tough luck, sucker. (If you would show your legs...) Lula also has a Minneapolis outlet at 710 W. 22nd St., 612/872–9877 and shares space at St. Paul's **At the Hop** (see below).

Best vintage warehouse: If you want dresses for somewhere between $2 and $20 and don't like getting your hands dirty, try **Ragstock**, a Minnesota-based vintage chain (even an outlet in Duluth!) that's de rigueur for thrifters. The biggest Ragstock *(830 N. 7th St., Mpls., 612/333–8520)*, seems to fill a city block (well, maybe half of one); sifting through the suit coats alone can take an hour (men are particularly well-served here). Besides the usual well-aged gear, the warehouse displays some vintage goofs: yucky fabrics and strange styles that tend to get snapped up around Halloween. New underwear, stockings, and tights round out the merch.

Best overall thrift: For a sophisticated thrifter, walking into the **Disabled American Veterans Thrift Store** (or DAV) a decade ago was like stumbling into heaven: $2 Red Wing work boots, fluffy fake fur coats for under three bucks, $10 couches, 25-cent long underwear (don't laugh—you'll need it). These days, of course, the Cities are hipper, so the produce tends to get cleaned out more quickly, and is pricier. The two DAVs *(1808 Emerson N, Mpls., 612/522–0047; 572 University Ave., St. Paul, 612/292–1707)* still beat major coastal-city thrifts with their one-two punch of low cost and varied selection. Quilted hunting vests? Snowmobile suits? All that. Minnesotans are driven to make fashion of the functional. And the true bargains—$2 Levis, fine-condition $5 Pumas, vintage wool sweaters for a couple bucks—can still be found with a little persistence and nothing better to do.

Best thrift, specials: The lowest common denominator in used rags is a bit higher at **Savers** *(2124 E. Lake St., Mpls., 612/729-9271; 245 Maryland Ave. E, St. Paul, 488-6293)*, with a corresponding rise in cost. But that's not counting their everyday sales, which put certain items at half-price (it's the old colored-tag trick). With the discounts, Savers' better-quality clothing can become agreeably cheap. Don't leave without finding the "vintage" rack, a random collection from sundry synthetic eras usually concealing an offbeat treasure or two.

et cetera

Best found art: Parts of obsolete toys, machines, and stereo equipment lay over at **Ax Man Surplus** *(1639 University Ave., St. Paul, 612/646–8653)* on the way to the landfill, making this jumble-strewn store an essential stop for pomo artists and curious collectors. Bins of circuit boards, capacitors, nuts and bolts, ceramic tiles, and doll parts ("Extra didjits for only a quarter") weigh down the shelves; speakers, spools of wire, and unidentifiable stuff clutter the aisles. Marbles go for $2.50 a pound. Don't miss the Rambo erasers.

Best color-coordinated merchandise: At the Hop *(1752 Grand Ave., St. Paul, 612/699–0405)* has the corner on kitschy antiques that make you drool: a lamp-cum-bulletin board made out of cork; a shiny black Zenith transistor radio as big as a Kleenex box; one of those *Dazed and Confused* wicker basket chairs dangling from a chrome support. Cooler still, though, the proprietors of At the Hop display their wares in wacky groupings according to color. Big red lunch boxes sit next to frosty orange glasses and fiery candle holders. All the black and chrome things crouch along one wall. Shades of turquoise clash and coo. Who knows why this is so absurdly pleasing.

body alterations

Best club-kid skin preparation: St. Sabrina's Parlor in Purgatory *(2751 Hennepin Ave., Mpls., 612/874–7360)* may not knock the leather boots off a hard-core New York or San Franciscan fetishist, but, hey, it's all we've got. The kindly be-ringed and be-dyed folks at St. Sabrina's will pierce anything from a septum to a scrotum for up to $38. Vinyl corsets and wigs of various neon colors may be had. The selection of metallic/shiny/hot pink/black/white/polka-dotted platform footwear takes up most of one wall. Perhaps most importantly, St. Sabrina's serves as a conduit for info on the Twin Cities' underground, roving raves: Check your maps and go.

Best haircut, guinea-pig division: The Horst Education Center *(400 Central Ave. SE, Mpls., 612/331–1400)* has been chopping the locks of both sexes since the '70s, albeit at varying locations. This airy, glass-walled space has the feel of an ultramodern laboratory, what with the white-coated students, rows of gleaming workstations, and shiny rows of tubes, bottles, and vials. You get a head massage with your haircut, and a big hit of the house's renowned aromatherapy (otherwise known as Aveda hair and body-care products), all for $9. By the way, students at all levels of the eight-month program cut hair. Under supervision, of course.

Best extensive dyes and dyed extensions: Safe above the crash-prone intersection of Lake and Lyndale, stylists in a darkly painted, second-floor warehouse space braid ropes of hair onto willing heads and change naturally colored strands to the hues of birds. This is **Hair Police** *(611 W. Lake St., Mpls., 612/824–1641)*, the established stop for coiffure-conscious Twin Citians seeking more than just a different haircut. A couple of thick books on the waiting room table disclose the evidence: Hundreds of snapshots brimming with long-maned, beaded, dyed, and joyous neoprimitives—young, less young, even suburban. At the same address, **Tatus by Kore** *(612/824–2295)* delivers some of the richest color tattooing around, according to no less an expert than Babes in Toyland drummer and tattoo enthusiast Lori Barbero.

hotel/motel

Best alternative to somebody's couch: Located in a slightly run-down turn-of-the-century brick mansion across the street from the Minneapolis College of Art and Design, the **City of Lakes International House** *(2400 Stevens Ave., Mpls., 612/871–3210)* offers the cheapest—and most engaging—commercial lodgings in Minneapolis. The user-friendly independent hostel ignores the notion of curfews and proffers private rooms for couples. Guests from America and abroad congregate in the roomy kitchen and outside on a smoking porch. Proprietors Pete

Schmit and Lori Klein, thirty-somethings and big travelers themselves, provide city maps and bicycles (with a small deposit). Last a boarding-house, the place combines the awesome (sinfully luxurious bathtubs) and the eccentric (bargain renovations have turned the once spacious design into warrens of little rooms). Best of all, a bed (no bunks!) in the dormitory goes for $14. Reservations required only for private rooms.

Runner-up: An AYH-affiliated hostel operates June 1 through August 15 at St. Catherine's College, called **Caecilian Hall** *(2004 Randolph, St. Paul, 612/690–6617)*. You must have an AYH card. Bunk beds go for $14; pricier private rooms are available. The St. Kate's hostel has no curfew. Reservations may be made after March 1.

Best downtown hotel bargain: The owners of two Hennepin Avenue gay bars were bound to raise some eyebrows when they opened the 30-bed **Hotel Amsterdam** *(828 Hennepin Ave., Mpls., 612/288–0459)* above the **Saloon**. Ah, yes, one of the Twin Cities' most popular pickup joints—with rooms to let directly overhead? After two years, though, the joke is on anybody who lets their prurient suspicions keep them from a $24.95 single right on Minneapolis' nightlife mainline and a couple floors above some of the hardest disco in town. Its flowering window boxes and comfortably worn furniture and carpets are reminiscent of a funky European *pensione*. The Hotel Amsterdam advertises itself as "the inn that's out"; queerness is encouraged, but not required.

Best rock hotels: Imagine an up-and-coming indie band, say from Seattle. The first couple times they van-tour into Minneapolis, the humble musicians sleep on the floor of a friend of the club booker. The next time through, with a bit of buzz on their second album, they open for Mike Watt and put up $92 for a double at the **Regency Plaza** *(41 N. 10th St., Mpls., 612/339–9311)*, the usual anonymous motel just a few blocks from First Avenue. The band then signs to a major and—flash—goes halfway to platinum; they're headlining now and staying for $110 a double at the **Hotel Luxeford Suites** *(1101 La Salle Ave., Mpls., 612/332–6800)*; the decor looks just as bland, but the rooms have refrigerators, and the band runs into Freedy Johnston in the hall. The next album hits the jackpot. Strippers are showing up backstage, and the guys are booked into that lushly appointed ex–flour mill, the **Whitney Hotel** *(150 Portland Ave., Mpls., 612/339–9300)* at $175 for a suite with spiral staircase and river view. If they're very lucky, they'll make it to the penthouse ($1,600 a night), where Keith Richards jams on the grand piano when he's in town.

local wonders

Best inner-city skinny-dipping: Punk kids use the waters at Cedar Lake's Hidden Beach, on the lake's east shore directly across from a public beach. But the muddy green water, the kids' mangy dogs, and regular visits by Minneapolis' finest make stripping down here a dubious pleasure. The payoffs are much higher at **Twin Lake**, which boasts cool depths, clear spring-fed water, and no canal connection to the increasingly murky string of southwest city lakes. Technically located in the suburb of Golden Valley and surrounded by parkland, this isolated spot lies only a couple of miles north of Cedar Lake (walk west from the Wirth Park 9-hole golf course). Nudists have cavorted at the beach since the '40s at least; a man drowned here in the '50s when, drunk and feverish, he followed a well-endowed lady into the drink. Maybe that's why Twin Lake now has a gay vibe. Also frequented by young straights, children, and bathing suit wearers.

Best inner-city fishing: Forget the lakes—there's a river running through it, remember? Go downtown to **Lock and Dam No. 2**, use chicken livers for catfish or corn for carp, toss a line in and hold on. Just remember not to eat the poor fish—it's the Mississippi, stupid. (Fish from the city lakes can be eaten, but don't make a habit of it.)

Best place to escort an under-16-year-old: Since its opening, the Taj Mahal of conspicuous consumption otherwise known as the **Mall of America** *(60 E Broadway, Bloomington, 612/883-8800)* has attracted a slew of teenagers on weekend nights. Also since its opening, said teens have been browbeaten and bedeviled by mall security, chiefly, it seems, for the crime of being young, black and noisy. After 6 P.M. on weekends, mall officials now deny entrance to any person under 16 not accompanied by an adult. The only reasonable response to such a restriction is for right-thinking adults to gather packs of teens and deliver them to Mammon; while your charges gambol and giggle, you can catch a movie, wander through the indoor amusement park (Camp Snoopy), take an overpriced tour through a massive underground aquarium, or simply watch overstimulated, overweight, and overextended Americans do what they do best: shop.

Best butter sculpture: One of the largest cow shows in the country, the **Minnesota State Fair** takes place not in some boondocks but right along a busy St. Paul thoroughfare (North Snelling Avenue). Consequently, these 12 days at the end of August make for some weird sights: Pale heavy-metal kids watching the butter sculptors make busts of Dairy Queens and Princesses; punk rockers immersed in spin art; thick lines of already chubby folk at the fried-cheese-curd stand; rave teens walking the carnival midway to the strains of bandstanding Willie Nelson; black-clad sophisticates cooing over seed-art portraits of Ronald Reagan. If you're lucky enough to be in town, count on spending at least three hours and *mucho dinero*—time and money enough to catch the wiggy chickens, farm machinery (you'd be surprised), and a gigantic sow, grub a bellyful of mini-doughnuts, curds, corn dogs, beer, and walleye-on-a-stick, and turn upside down on the rides until you're pale. Beer is available, but you have to remain at the bars. Better to sneak in a flask and spike a lemonade; there's too much to see for lingering. The rest of the year, the empty fairgrounds lend themselves to nicely eerie strolls.

transmissions

Best pop tarts: Radio K, the University of Minnesota's laboratory at **KUOM (770 AM)**, cannot broadcast after sundown (5 P.M. in the winter), shorts out under bridges, suffers the usual fumbling college DJs, and *still* owns the car radio. Mostly because every time you turn on the ignition, a bright, cool, mesmerizing, and vaguely familiar shambling pop song reaches out to pull lightly at your ear. Music with more muscle—rap, punk, techno—does live at K; it just doesn't set the tone the way Stereolab, Air Miami, or the 6ths have, in their respective days. The DJs also play local bands, as a matter of fact (don't be expecting Hüsker Dü, Soul Asylum, or any remote facsimile). Catch local critic Simon Peter Groebner's definitive show Fridays from 4 to 6 P.M. (3 to 5 P.M. in winter).

new orleans

by Michael Tisserand

"Don't think of it as the least-safe city in America, think of it as the fourth-safest city in the Carribean." — **James Hall**

P eter Fonda and Dennis Hopper weren't the first. When they rolled into New Orleans on chopped hogs in *Easy Rider*, dropping acid in the French Quarter and gamboling in great Gothic graveyards, they were joining the spirits of countless other fictitious and real dropouts, hippies, and vagabonds who have made a mecca out of this swampy city. William Burroughs lived here; Charles Bukowski wrote here. Tennessee Williams defined this town's flamboyant gay life. And Bobby McGee thumbed a diesel just to get here.

Located below sea level next to the Gulf of Mexico, New Orleans remains a haven for the odd and offbeat. Its hard-core drinking culture and generally hedonistic temperament make it an island of laid-back insouciance in the South. Credit the port, which historically has brought to the city a constant supply of customers for the bars, music joints, and whorehouses of the Quarter and the legendary, turn-of-the-century red-light district called Storyville. Today New Orleans is a major drug port, with big shipments taken along the interstate's "Cocaine Corridor," going west toward Houston and points beyond. (Although most drugs are available here, alcohol remains the party favorite. Consider yourself forewarned against open drug use or drunk driving: A night in the scary Central Lockup will remind you that, after all, you are still in the South.)

With zero indie labels to claim as its own, New Orleans doesn't have the infrastructure to support an alternative music scene, but the '90s brought a much-ballyhooed influx of music celebs to town. For the record, here are some of the latest comings and goings: Daniel Lanois has a studio here; Trent Reznor lives here and has a studio here;

Marilyn Manson doesn't live here but works at Reznor's studio a lot; Eddie Vedder does not live here but has gotten into scuffles here (in a French Quarter bar and he was exonerated of any responsibility); Pantera's Phil Anselmo was born, raised, and still lives, here; Lenny Kravitz has a house in the French Quarter; nobody ever knows about Dylan; Keb' Mo' and Michelle Shocked moved here; Dr. John, Harry Connick Jr., and Wynton Marsalis moved to New York a long time ago. But Aaron Neville's still here.

Also in town is a pack of clubs that opened in the '90s to showcase new local talent. In the Mermaid Lounge and the Dragon's Den, bands such as the jazz-thrashers Lump, the surfabilly Royal Pendletons, and Royal Fingerbowl have built their followings. In hot jazz clubs such as Donna's, the New Showcase Lounge, and the Funky Butt, local horn players follow the paths of Wynton Marsalis and Nicholas Payton. Hopping local music scenes include brass bands, Mardi Gras Indian groups such as the Wild Magnolias, and zydeco.

The city's favorite rock band is Cowboy Mouth, who made their major label debut in 1996. The Mouth's live shows are a theatrical blend of muscle-rock energy and hard-core country, tempered with some plaintive angst. Burly drummer Fred LeBlanc is a cross between a Southern preacher and a Flying Karamazov Brother, and often performs stunt aerials on club scaffolding and rafters while exhorting the crowd to jump in the air and scream. Other local favorites include glam rocker James Hall and alternative pop songsters Better Than Ezra. For belly-rubbing dancing, locals pack the room for the rootsy Tex-Mex/R&B outfit the Iguanas. And as for the next band likely to sign to the majors: Look for the Southern rock band the Continental Drifters, a superfriends group with former members of the dBs, the Bangles, and even the Cowsills.

lay of the land

Throw out your compass when you come to New Orleans. On the north is **Lake Pontchartrain**—easy enough. But the south is bordered by the winding **Mississippi River**, which cuts a huge S through town, and many streets slant rather than run on grid. Think in terms of upriver and downriver, with the **French Quarter** sitting on a huge bend in the river. Downriver, across Esplanade, is the **Faubourg Marigny**; upriver is the **Warehouse District**, across Canal Street, which ends on the river. Heading further uptown (that is, Upriver), you hit the **Garden District** and beyond that the university area, home to Loyola and Tulane Universities. Much of New Orleans is composed of the inland **Mid-City**, mostly residential and largely below sea level.

When looking for clubs, there are only a few neighborhoods to keep in mind: the French Quarter, the Faubourg Marigny, the Warehouse District (occasionally called downtown), Uptown, and Mid-City. Of these, the French Quarter sees the most tourists, ranging from down-and-out drifters to groups of conventioneers in name tags. Some tourists begin and end on Bourbon Street, while others head to a new entertainment district that features the Hard Rock Cafe and the House of Blues. As you take Bourbon Street toward Esplanade Avenue, the strip becomes a gay district. Go across Esplanade, and you're in the Faubourg Marigny, home to various clubs and bars with a local, boho clientele.

The Warehouse District has a few main clubs spread out over several blocks, many in old river-industry warehouses. It's not really a strip, since you'd need a car to get to them all. Same too with the Uptown area, which is especially popular with local college students. The residential Mid-City is really known for just one club—the Mid-City Bowling Lanes. It's not wise to stray far from known, well-lit areas after hours. Seedy areas hem the Garden District and the Quarter.

getting from a to b

Because New Orleans is patterned around a crescent-shaped Mississippi River bend, driving can get surreal, as you'll notice when you pass the intersection of South Carrollton and South Claiborne. Most directions lead you "away from the river" or "toward the river," or "to the lake" or "away from the lake" (Pontchartrain). Keep a map with you to make sense of these aquatic landmarks. If you know where you're going, it'll take less than 15 minutes to get from any one part of town to another.

As far as public transportation goes, it goes feebly. Buses run infrequently at night. So does the St. Charles streetcar, but it's still a romantic way to get from downtown to Uptown. Board at the intersection of Canal and Carondelet streets; it runs to the Audubon Park near Tulane. Fare is a buck. For more info, call Regional Transit Authority (RTA) at 504/248–3900. Parking in the French Quarter is difficult and confusing; read the signs carefully. If your car isn't there when you return from your revels, try calling the auto pound at 504/565–7450. A good cab company is United *(504/522–9771)*.

sources

Unlike many cities, the daily *Times-Picayune* provides the best guide for shows and club action. The paper runs club listings every day, and Friday brings a comprehensive tabloid section called "Lagniappe." The alternative paper is *Gambit Weekly*, where the writing is a bit more hip than the daily, although it's certainly not radical by weekly standards. Check out Rich Collins's "Swell" column and the picks in the "24/7" section. *Gambit* can be found free in most area restaurants and clubs. The most comprehensive music coverage is in *OffBeat* magazine, a free monthly distributed in clubs and record shops. Check this out for local music gossip and feature articles; Mark Miester's "Feedback" column is the best available guide to the local rock scene. Both *Gambit* and *OffBeat* run good web sites; *Gambit* (http://www.gambit-no.com/) has the best Mardi Gras coverage, but *OffBeat* (http://www.neosoft.com/~offbeat) is the place to go for the earliest Jazz Fest listings. Both provide links to other New Orleans sites.

clubs

Best rock club: The Howlin' Wolf *(828 S. Peters St., 504/523–2551)* has snagged on-the-way-up performers such as Alanis Morissette just months before they return to town to sell out the local arena. Located in a dark, sturdy building that used to be a cotton warehouse, the Wolf has emerged as the best progressive rock club in town. With massive wooden beams and supports, concrete floors, and a new balcony, this two-story hall attracts anyone from yuppies to hippies to punkers, depending on who's playing. Though generally a local-heavy lineup, out-of-towners such as Sonic Youth, Wilco, John Cale, and Victoria Williams have played here. Keep an eye out for Alex Chilton, who comes by every few months. While it's not a big slam scene, there's more testosterone dancing here than in most local clubs. Before the new balcony was even completed, a couple of meatheads used it as a launch pad for crowd surfing one night. A rare occurrence, though; most here, including the bar dog, are pretty mellow.

Best sound and light systems: When the **House of Blues** *(225 Decatur St., 504/529–2624)* blew into town in 1994, reactions ranged from cheers to grumbles. With a price tag of $7 million, an old French Quarter shoe factory was transformed into a space-age blues franchise, similar to branches in Los Angeles and other cities. It features walls lined with folk art, a fairly small dance floor, second-floor seating, a pulsating sound system, an array of movable vari-lights, and a separate restaurant with monitors of the stage action. Some nights it can fill with tourists who don't care what's on stage, but as in all clubs in this town, the crowd changes with the bands. After the live band ends, the curtain falls, and the dance tracks begin. By one, there's usually a line of club kids and drag queens on Decatur Street waiting to get in; compared to the live shows, this is a strictly local scene.

Best local party: The comfort and superior sound of the House of Blues notwithstanding, hearing a local favorite like the Neville Brothers or the funky Meters at **Tipitina's** *(501 Napoleon Ave., 504/895–8477)* is still one of those only-in-New Orleans experiences. You dance around to "Iko-Iko" in a giant, un-air-conditioned hall. Overhead hangs a banner depicting the legendary pianist Professor Longhair, who wrote the song "Tipitina." During set breaks, you cool out on a patch of land in the center of Napoleon Avenue, called the neutral ground, with a young crowd of Tulane students—the club is not far from campus—and some older local music fans. When the first beats of "Cissy Strut" start thumping, you go back in for some more.

Best zydeco: On Thursday nights at **Mid-City Lanes** *(4133 S. Carrollton Ave., 504/482–3133)*, bands such as Boozoo Chavis and Beau Jocque drive into New Orleans from their homes in rural south Louisiana. The bowling alley gets the best, most serious zydeco bands—stay away from the collection of tourist-oriented restaurants downtown and in the French Quarter. Other nights, the Mid-City Lanes books classic New Orleans R&B and other upbeat party sounds, but it's still a bowling alley: between songs, you may hear announcements like "Tami, your lane is ready." One of the many celebs to stop by has been Tom Cruise, whose bowling shoes are mounted on the wall, near a picture of the Virgin Mary. Mick Jagger also came in one night to see Beau Jocque; his entourage was chased down by the woman at the door because they neglected to pay the $5 cover. Hot tip: the kitchen here serves a mean turkey and *andouille* gumbo.

Best new jazz clubs: Thanks to the local army of squeaky trumpeters who are willing to toot "When the Saints Go Marchin' In" wherever and whenever a tourist will pay for it, the birthplace of jazz has some of the worst in the world—as well as some of the best. Luckily, 1996 was a good year for the music. First, the **Funky Butt** *(714 N. Rampart St., 504/558–0872)* opened its doors on Rampart Street. This renovated restaurant is reminiscent of an old, high-rent Storyville bordello. It's a lavish, two-floor hall, with blood-red walls and carpet, a rickety elevator, art deco etched glass, and a giant painting of a reclining nude that pays tribute to the local brass band tune "I Got a Big Fat Woman." Trumpeters Michael Ray (formerly with Kool and the Gang and Sun Ra) and Wess Anderson perform here frequently.

Runner-up: Also in 1996, a great neighborhood jazz joint called the **New Showcase Lounge** *(1915 N. Broad St., 504/945–5612)* expanded its music schedule. A mix of neighborhood regulars and local musicians comes to hear names like Mark Whitfield, Wess Anderson, Nicholas Payton, and Henry Butler while digging into plates of butter beans and ham hocks. In both clubs, attire ranges from suits to T-shirts, and the cover is usually an outrageously low $5 or so.

Best only-in–New Awlins dance: Without doubt, the liveliest scene in town is the one surrounding the brass bands. On Sundays, bands march through the streets—especially in the Uptown and Treme (across Rampart Street from the Quarter)—surrounded by crowds of dancers waving white handkerchiefs and umbrellas overhead. It's called second-lining, and it's a loose-limbed, acrobatic dance—sort of like break dancing on the run. At night, the brass bands bring their tubas, trombones, and trumpets indoors, to a number of clubs throughout town. Located on the edge of the French Quarter, **Donna's Bar & Grill** *(800 N. Rampart St., 504/596–6914)* has the busiest schedule, with music nightly from the best groups, including local favorites Re-Birth, the Soul Rebels, and the Treme brass bands. Donna's is a small, table-filled restaurant with walls papered with snapshots of musicians. Dancing is in front of the band, by the bar, or between the tables. (You have to walk right through the band to get to the bathroom.)

Best musical Laundromat: In the back of **Check Point Charlie** *(501 Esplanade Ave., 504/947–0979)* sits a row of coin-operated machines popular with bikers trying to "Shout" out those stubborn oil stains. This joint is also a popular no-cover venue for local bands; sounds range from blues to roadhouse to acoustic rock, all played at high decibels—even the acoustic. Small and dark, this multipurpose institution also has a paperback lending library, and big burgers served up 24 hours. Located on a street corner between the French Quarter and the Faubourg Marigny, Charlie attracts a mix of Decatur Street's punks, Goths, and hippies. The bands are often local rockers making their first club appearances.

Runner-up: In case you're curious, the other great Laundromat in town is the bright **Hula Mae's Tropic Wash and Beach Cafe** *(840 N. Rampart St., 504/522–1336)*, a 24-hour Laundromat and cafe that's a popular place for Quarter transvestites to wash their hosiery after their shows on Bourbon Street.

Best love den: Floor pillows, tie-dyed curtains, beaded doorways, and gilded mirrors give the **Dragon's Den** *(435 Esplanade Ave., 504/949–1750)* all the ambiance of a '60s crash pad. Up-and-coming local bands play blues, funk, and lounge music for nouveau flower children and other calm patrons. This is currently one of the hippest little scenes in town, featuring a high quality of music and a great vibe. Tea, beer, and sake are big here. Pad Thai and other noodle dishes are brought from the downstairs Siam Cafe restaurant to your floor table. If the music gets too loud, you can retreat to the balcony overlooking Esplanade Avenue and the French Quarter.

Best street scene: When the owner of laid-back **Cafe Brasil** *(100 Chartres St., 504/947–9386)* started fielding complaints about patrons sitting outside on car hoods, he simply moved his own big, blue vintage car to the space by the doors. Folks now treat it as their own outdoor sofa in the Faubourg Marigny. The Cafe Brasil is not just a musical institution, it's the anchor of a vibrant street scene. There's a little bit of everybody on the corner of Frenchmen and Chartres streets, including gutterpunks, rastas, jazzies, hippies, hipsters, tourists, and college kids; they all hang out here to drink and catch the free doorway music. The music that washes out from the doors of Brasil and other nearby clubs is as eclectic as the crowd, with an emphasis on Latin, reggae, jazz, and international sounds. This is the best place in town to hear the Iguanas and the Klezmer All-Stars. In fact, it's the best place to hear, see, buy, smell, drink, or converse with just about anything. When you don't have anywhere else to go, come here.

Best eclectic sounds: The tiny **Mermaid Lounge** *(1100 Constance St., 504/524–4747)* draws mercurial crowds—moody and meditative when Li'l Queenie is cooing a ballad, and shit-kickin' for special nights—such as a rockabilly Mardi Gras party where tattoo ink is given away as a door prize and rowdies dance on the chairs. Opened in 1994, this is a tiny, L-shaped bar where the band stands floor-level at the vertex. Most of the time, the club books local heroes like swamp rocker C.C. Adcock, with an emphasis on high-tempo dance tunes of all stripes. Mobiles hang from the ceiling and there's a small gallery in the back room, giving the place an artsy feel.

Best Bourbon Street gay discos: Located within shouting distance from each other, the **Oz** *(800 Bourbon St., 504/593–9491)* and the **Parade** *(801 Bourbon St., 504/529–2107)* are the best discos in town.

You can't choose between the two: It's the intersection that matters here. During Mardi Gras, this is a sure place to see some of the raciest activity along the parade route. Oz has nightly events such as "drag races" (people from the audience compete to see who can achieve the quickest makeover) and "dangerous disco" (lots of Village People, K.C., and Donna Summer). Music at both places is guaranteed to have a bright, thumping beat, and a few pro dancers gyrate on the bars for atmosphere. The dance floors are tight. Come here if you don't mind being touched.

Best dyke bar: By contrast, the crowd is a little younger at **Rubyfruit Jungle** *(640 Frenchmen St., 504/947–4000)*, a women's bar that appeals to all genders and orientations; music is high-energy techno and house. It's located near the jazz and world-music clubs in the Faubourg Marigny and attracts a more mellow crowd than that on Bourbon Street. Dancing is done in a narrow back room with mirrors and a concrete floor; there are also a couple of pool tables and nightly food specials.

Best raves, Goth, speed metal: It's hard to keep a good, demented youth subculture going in New Orleans. After all, it's a small town and everybody pretty much hangs out with everybody. For raves and hip-hop, check out what's happening after the live shows at the House of Blues. Look out for a local favorite, DJ Phantazm. Farther up Decatur Street, a hand-scrawled sign at the **Crystal** *(1135 Decatur St., 504/522–5011)* specifies NO HIP-HOP; the speakers issue harder industrial and Goth sounds in this narrow brick bar with a small dance floor. Suburban metal-heads go slamming at **Zeppelins** *(3712 Hessmer Ave., Metairie, 504/889–0955)*, a steel-gray club in a strip mall neighborhood known as Fat City; just follow the Camaros. Check the flyers at **Underground Sounds** (see Shopping) and other record shops and clothing stores for more Goth and hard-core shows that pop up from time to time around the city.

Best New Orleans living legend: Called "the Human Jukebox" for his bottomless bag of songs, Snooks Eaglin is an alum of the golden era of Crescent City R&B who still performs frequently around town, often with the city's best bassist, George Porter, Jr. Eaglin is an unpredictable showman, but he'll probably take his ax to the stage floor, Townshend-style, at least once a night. Look for him at the Howlin' Wolf or Mid-City Lanes. His crowd is a mix of locals and college-age Porter fans.

Runner-up: While he performs in town less frequently, Earl King is another great New Orleans guitarist, known for such songs as "Let the Good Times Roll" and "Trick Bag," and his shows are great opportunities to hear these New Orleans classics done the right way. He also has the slickest pompadour in town.

bars

Best jukebox: Deep down, every bar in the nation should strive to be the **Saturn Bar** *(3067 St. Claude Ave., 504/949–7532).* Sean Penn came here to get away from the opening party of Planet Hollywood—and if that's not recommendation enough, move to Hollywood. This cavernous tavern in the blue-collar Ninth Ward (20 blocks northeast of French Quarter) has the best neon in town, along with a psychedelic yet folky decor that comes, according to just-call-me-Neil (no last name, man) the owner, from decades of "materializing." Much of the art was donated by bygone patron Mike Frolich, whose work has a kind of visionary paint-by-numbers look, with subjects ranging from dragons descending into hell to scary clowns to mangy dogfights. Grizzled old-timers occupy the counter stools, where they nurse Dixie beers and watch George and Gracie on TV, while young hip Saturnites with names like Rain lounge in the leopard print booths. A blaring Stereo 160 jukebox in the corner has the city's best selection, from Sinatra to Ernest Tubb to Fats Domino.

Best local watering hole: Need a haircut and a shot of bourbon? On Mondays, the Faubourg Marigny's **R Bar** *(1431 Royal St., 504/948–7499)* has "hair saloons," where you can get both for $10. Decorated in retro lounge style with brightly colored vinyl couches and a real Triumph motorcycle parked on the cooler, the R is a very popular conversation bar for artists and hipsters; the jukebox has everything from lounge to punkabilly. You can even sleep here; the rooms next door are decorated in themes (the best is the bordello). Ask at the bar for more info; rooms are $60 and up, depending on the season. Historical note: Etched in the concrete outside the bar is a signature said to be poet Charles Bukowski's; look for "Hank" (the poet's nickname).

Best after-hours hangout: Once you sink into a vinyl cushion in the corner of **Snake and Jake's Christmas Club Lounge** *(7612 Oak St., 504/861–2802),* you're in for the night—the late night, that is, since Snake's starts kicking at 2 A.M. and closes around daybreak. Come here after you've been everywhere else. Trailer park furniture fills the corners of this tiny boho bar, usually occupied by goateed yappers and college couples rounding the bases. The bar looks like something the "M*A*S*H" gang might have cobbled together: a charred exterior, low-lying ceiling panels, strings of Christmas lights, fake pine trees, and a jukebox of oldies. Owner Dave Clements is a local musician, and impromptu late-night jam sessions have included Adam Duritz and members of Widespread Panic.

Best pool sharks: Once an underground casino complete with hidden trapdoors and a dynamite-proof safe, the now-legit **Racketeers** *(200 Monticello Ave., Jefferson, 504/840–7665)* is the city's most serious pool hall. The crowd, a mix of humorless sharks and college kids, goes to this austere concrete building for its 25 regulation tables and hourly rates. Be sure to read the posters on the walls to learn about the club's colorful past; ply your bartender into telling the real stories about those trapdoors, as well as the truth about the various connections the casino had with former state governors.

Best animal houses: Located near Tulane and Loyola universities, Maple Street is the weekend destination of choice for beery, hormone-driven undergrads. At **TJ Quills** *(7600 Maple St., 504/866–5205)* and **Bruno's** *(7601 Maple St., 504/861–7615)*, the preferred dress is Greek letters—across the chest for guys, across the back of the sweats for gals. Both bars are fairly identical, with generic rummage on the walls, few tables and lots of bar space. Don't ask which is better: Both are meat markets, and the sidewalks and streets stay filled all night with students going back and forth to check out the latest interpersonal offerings at each.

Runner-up: For a more relaxed scene, walk up Maple Street to **Philips Restaurant & Bar** *(733 Cherokee St., 504/865–1155)*, where the grad students shoot pool and watch big-screen sports.

Best quiet conversation bar: The flicker of candlelight and low murmur of serious discourse are all you'll find at the very romantic **Lafitte's Blacksmith Shop** *(941 Bourbon St., 504/523–0066)*, located in a crumbling wood and brick building that was once used by the pirate Jean Lafitte as a front for his smuggling operations. It's on Bourbon Street, but it seems miles away from the hubbub of the strip bars. This is a good place to order the right versions of New Orleans' classic drinks, such as the Hurricane and the Sazerac.

Runner-up: If you need a cheese board or a *muffaletta* sandwich with your conversation, try **Napoleon House Bar and Cafe** *(500 Chartres St., 504/524–9752).* The Napoleon usually has a few more tourists, but the classical music and decrepit walls inspire late-night gabbing.

Best Guinness on tap: One thing everyone in town can agree on is the Guinness at **O'Flaherty's** *(514 Toulouse St., 504/529–1317)* in the French Quarter—even other Irish bars send customers here. The bartender describes the Guinness process like it's an exact science, its success depending on the amount of nitrogen in the keg, the pouring technique, and such artistic flourishes as the shamrock design in the head. Run by a pair of musical brothers, O'Flaherty's has both a Celtic music hall and bar, along with a pretty stone courtyard that dates to the 1790s. Bar food includes Irish stew, shepherd's pie, and corned beef sandwiches.

food/coffee

Best morning-after breakfast: Do you insist on a good breakfast spot where you can nurse a headache and a cup of coffee? Of course you do. Surprisingly, given New Awlins' partytown reputation, the selection is paltry. Only the **Bluebird Cafe** in Uptown *(3625 Prytania St., 504/895–7166; 7801 Panola St., 504/866–7577)* really fits the bill: cheap, well-lit (but not too bright) atmosphere, hip waitresses who look as bleary-eyed as you do, a stack of used newspapers by the cash register. Go for the eggs with nutritional yeast, fresh squeezed orange juice, huevos rancheros with black beans and fresh salsa, or sturdy buckwheat pancakes with blueberries and bananas. The 85-cent bowl of grits is the best deal in town; the coffee is good and nobody cuts it off. Nothing on the menu is over five bucks.

Best 24-hour diner: If Edward Hopper had lived in New Orleans, he would have painted *Nighthawks at the Hummingbird.* The **Hummingbird Hotel & Grill** *(804 St. Charles Ave., 504/523–9165)* is a 24-hour place popular with transients, cabbies, and slummers. The Hummingbird sits downtown between Canal Street and a towering statue of General Lee alongside other diners, barbers, and cheap hotels in New Orleans' version of skid row. Greasy eggs, bacon, and biscuits are all good here. Until it was stolen, a sign by the pay phone warned against talking to imaginary people.

Runner-up: The **Clover Grill** *(900 Bourbon St., 504/523–9874)* is a different scene entirely, serving "Geaux Girl" waffles and bowls of Froot Loops to a clientele largely composed of gay French Quarter clubbers.

Best soul food: Most diners and even some fast-food joints here serve some version of red beans and rice. It's such a signature dish in this town that Louis Armstrong used to sign his letters, "Red beans and ricely yours…." Hands down, the best beans are at a diner with locations on two of the city's busiest streets: **Henry's Soul Food & Pie Shop** *(209 N. Broad St., 504/821–8635; 2501 S. Claiborne Ave., 504/821–7757).* Lima beans, crowder peas, mustard greens, and turkey necks are all accompanied by a giant square of cornbread. This is a strictly local scene, with couples, friends, and families coming in to fill up on this local version of comfort food. Order a whole sweet-potato pie for four bucks and keep it on the table for dessert.

Best slice: It's unusual to find a place in New Orleans that serves eggplant and spinach pizzas by the slice; **Pie in the Sky** *(1818 Magazine St., 504/522–6291)* goes one further and has big salads, hummus, and focaccia sandwiches. Small and popular, this street corner cafe is in a local gallery district and has its own artistic flourishes: bright, primary-color tables and booths painted in interplanetary themes. It's relaxed enough to keep a stack of board games by the door. The Espresso Buzzmatico ice-cream drink provides the most potent caffeine-and-sugar buzz in town.

Best Thai: The **Siam Cafe** *(435 Esplanade Ave., 504/949–1750)* is located right below the Dragon's Den music club (see Clubs) and is right in the middle of the city's busiest music district, the Faubourg Marigny. It's a small, funky place, with tiny tables in the window and along the bar, but the menu has much more than standard between-show eats. Spring-roll appetizers, heaping noodle dishes, and vegetarian entrees such as tofu curry are available, with most complete meals running about $15.

Best Big Easy bar food: **Cooter Brown's** *(509 S. Carrollton Ave., 504/866–9104)* in Uptown has an extensive international beer menu, but the real attraction here is the oyster bar. Raw oysters are shucked on the spot. Dip them in a handmade cocktail sauce and pop them in your mouth with a dry saltine to absorb that nice brine. Cooter's also sells another local delicacy: *boudin*, an intestinal casing surrounding a mixture of spicy pork, crawfish, rice, and onions.

Runner-up: Homesick East Coasters should check out **Le Bon Temps Roule** *(4801 Magazine St., 504/895–8117)* in Uptown for grinders, Philly cheese steaks, and Manhattan street-style (well, sort of) pretzels.

Best coffeehouse: Kaldi's *(941 Decatur St., 504/586–8989)* is in a gutted former bank in the French Quarter with chipped concrete floors, old Oriental rugs, and a towering papier-mâché sculpture of the joint's mythological namesake. On any given afternoon, the tables are filled with tarot-card readers taking a breather and local punks reading *A Clockwork Orange*, along with a few suits checking the stock reports in the *Times-Picayune*. Nobody is in a hurry, and on nice days, the window tables provide a good view of the Decatur Street tableaux vivant. The ice cream coffee drinks are great—especially in summer, which is half the year—the regular coffee is just okay.

Runner-up: The only other big coffeehouse scene in town is at **Rue de La Course** *(3128 Magazine St., 504/899–0242)*, which draws grad students, Sunday *New York Times* readers, and Scrabble players. Drawback: the heavy laptop-to-coffee-cup ratio.

shopping

records

Best late-night disc shopping: It's got a head-shop name and decor, but you have to settle for music at **Mushroom Records** *(1037 Broadway St., 504/866–6065)*: Paraphernalia shops are verboten in the Big Easy. Mushroom has plenty of local product; among the hottest is 7-inch vinyl from local acts like the garage surfabilly band the Royal Pendletons. Also abundant are stacks of horrible used CDs for two bucks and lots of posters and T-shirts. The Mushroom, right down the lane from Tulane University's fraternity row, is located upstairs from a coffeehouse and next door to a music bar.

Best used-CD bartering: They max out at $3 a disc, but the guys at **Magic Bus** *(527 Conti St., 504/522–0530)* will usually take most of your stack, including that Celtic rock band and the no-name blues disc you thought you'd never get rid of. Located in a big, garagelike room in the French Quarter near the Louisiana Music Factory and the House of Blues, the Bus also has the best selection of used CDs for sale, including international, folk, blues, and local discs, as well as rock. Opinionated clerks with British accents will let you play before you pay.

Best vinyl and lunch boxes: Vinylaholics know that **Record Ron's** *(1129 Decatur St., 504/524–9444)* has the best selection of those old scratchable platters, with a special emphasis on classic New Orleans

R&B. Among the many celebs who have stopped in looking for rare vinyl is Eric Clapton. Ron (who died in 1996) was best known around town as a cartoon character in his own ads. No less an authority on pop memorabilia than Paul McCartney stopped by Record Ron's and bought a Donny & Marie record tote for his daughter. He didn't, however, shell out $500 for a Yellow Submarine lunch box, one of hundreds that line the wall. Ron himself died in early 1996, and he was laid to rest in a casket surrounded by lunch boxes and lava lamps. You can find more of those lamps, along with music posters, clocks, stickers, pins, and books at another location, **Record Ron's Stuff** (239 Chartres St., 504/522–2239).

Runner-up: Also legendary is the always dusty **Jim Russell Rare Records** (1837 Magazine St., 504/522–2602), which has everything from vintage Louis Prima to someone's old, chiseled Andy Gibb and a choice selection of old jazz.

Best place to trust the clerk's opinion: For local R&B, rock, zydeco, jazz, and brass-band music, stop by **Louisiana Music Factory** (210 Decatur St., 504/586–1094). Owner Jerry Brock is usually minding the store, and his roots go deep into the local music community—he helped found the beloved community radio station WWOZ (see Transmissions). Some of the best parties in town have been the in-stores held amid these CD shelves; occasionally they have even had trumpeter Kermit Ruffins grilling turkey necks on the sidewalk. (It's especially hopping during Jazz Fest.) If you want to get some local music but you don't know what you want, ask here.

books

Best place to spend $3,000 on a signed copy of *Absalom, Absalom*: **Faulkner House Books** (624 Pirate Alley, 504/524–2940) is a small shop located in the apartment where William Faulkner wrote his first novel, *Soldier's Pay*. When he wasn't at the typewriter, Bill was writing home for money, making gin in the bathtub, and shooting BBs at the nuns across the alley in the St. Louis Cathedral—at least according to a memoir by his old roommate, William Spratling. The bookshop is select, with an emphasis on collectibles and local literature; if you don't have 3 G's for Faulkner, you can opt for signed copies of works by local authors such as Richard Ford, James Lee Burke, and Tom Piazza, available for face value.

Best zines: For national zines and the few local copy-machine-produced mags that occasionally spring up, as well as all manner of alt.rock product, check out **Underground Sounds** *(3336 Magazine St., 504/897–9030)*. This small Uptown store also carries CDs, some used vinyl, and a wise selection of punk, alternative, and industrial. The bulletin board is one of the surest ways to find out what's happening in town. This is also home to some great in-stores, which provide a rare local opportunity for an all-ages crowd to hear touring rockers such as Man or Astroman?

clothes

Best club clothes: Bongo *(415 Decatur St., 504/523–7625)* has one-stop shopping for club kids, with two floors of clothes and accessories. Typical garb includes shimmery acetate and polyester shirts and dresses, vinyl mushroom hats, red leather and lace bustiers, leather chaps, and shoes by Tredair and Grinders.

Runner-up: The perky **Heart & Sole** *(527 St. Philip St., 504/529–2280)* has techno, retro, and rock 'n' roll clothing by Dollhouse, Motor, and In Vitro. Large shoe sizes make this a popular shop for drag queens. This may also be the friendliest boutique in the Quarter—and a good place to pick up club tips.

Best Pucci purse: Mods and flappers and anyone else who wants to go reeling in the years stop at **Fred & Ethel's Jazzrags** *(1215 Decatur St., 504/523–2942)*, a small but loaded store with mint condition Puccis, Pulitzer jeans, and Schiaparelli hats. About a century of duds is covered here, from Victorian to velour.

Runners-up: Walk through Jazzrags to reach a second vintage store, **Maude Goes Mod** *(same address, 504/895–9489)* Lower Decatur Street is known for its vintage shops, and down the block from Jazzrags and Maude is **Paisley Babylon** *(1319 Decatur St., 504/529–3696)*, which is heavy in old hippie and '70s wear, including Hawaiian shirts and bell-bottom Levi's.

Best cotton print frocks: Since 1972, local hippies have been shopping **Kruz** *(432 Barracks St., 504/524–7370)* for their flowing cotton print shirts and ankle-length skirts. Located right off the French Market (see below) this happy store (expect to be greeted warmly) could outfit the global village with Indian anklets, African hats, and Chinese slippers. For make-your-own jewelry, Kruz has the town's best bead selection.

Best fake thrift-store fashion: For trendy men's and women's outerwear, **Billy Bob's Chinese Laundry** *(927 Royal St., 504/524–5578)* is the newest necessary stop. Labels include Phat Farm and Front and this is the biggest local outlet for upscale dress wear by Gene Meyer. Among the popular T-shirts available are those with hockey, drag racing, and football logos pre-stressed to give them that just-out-of-the-thrift-store-bin look.

Best real thrift-store fashion: Located in the hippest strip mall in town is **Thrift City** *(4125 S. Carrollton Ave., 504/482-0736)*, which shares the block with Mid-City Lanes. Before Mardi Gras, the store puts racks of costumes, prom dresses, and scraps out front; the place usually becomes an impromptu costume party. Luscious Jackson came by when they were recording at Daniel Lanois' Kingsway studio to buy Lanois an orange shirt.

et cetera

Best human-hand necklaces: Cheerfully called "that necrophiliac place" by its Uptown neighbors, the **Westgate** *(5219 Magazine St., 504/899-3077)* is a gallery of necromantic art and literature located in an old Magazine Street mansion that's been redone in purple and black and festooned with spiderwebs and Spanish moss. House bands such as Damien Youth play for events held throughout the year; these are the biggest Goth happenings in town. Two voodoo weddings have been performed here; one of these reportedly included Pantera lead singer Phil Anselmo as a guest. (Other visitors have included members of Faith No More and White Zombie; Courtney Love stopped in and bought a couple of paintings.) In addition to death-themed artwork (one statue is said to contain a human skeleton), this cottage industry of the netherworld publishes a newsletter and catalogue, and sells books, videos, candle holders, and jewelry, including a human hand on a chain that goes for $150. This is also a good place to get a referral for a voodoo priestess.

Runner-up: For the classic tacky voodoo experience, stop by **Marie Laveau's House of Voodoo** *(739 Bourbon St., 504/581-3751)* which hawks candles and masks and dried alligator heads, in a slightly creepy two-room shop. For the legends about various French Quarter haunted homes, check out the Magic Walking Tours (see local wonders).

Best shackles: If you don't have enough perversions when you walk into **Second Skin Leather** *(521 St. Philip St., 504/561-8167)*, you can pick up a few while you're here. Much of the regalia is male-oriented, including chrome ball-stretchers and cock rings. Accessories include chain-mail vests and various means of bondage; if you want to do away with clothes altogether, you can get a jar of spray-on liquid latex in rainbow colors. For the novice, the clerk will be happy to interpret the merchandise, including the snakebite kits, which are popularly used to enlarge one's nipples. You asked.

body alterations

Best place to go when you're drunk and you want a tattoo: Well, to bed, perhaps. But since the mid-'70s, drunk tourists have been staggering off Bourbon Street and over to the bright yellow and purple storefront of **Art Accent Tattooing** *(1041 N. Rampart St., 504/581–9812)*, for an enduring subepidermal memory of their vacation. Lots of classic white-trash designs here, including names, hearts, and roses. Among the memorable custom jobs: the guy that came in during Jazz Fest, dropped his shorts, and asked for Elmer Fudd on one buttock, and bunny ears emerging from his, ahem, rabbit hole. (All the artists refused the job, until owner Jacci bravely stepped forward, needle in hand.) Clientele has included members of Alice in Chains, and "a lot of old rockers," says Jacci.

hotel/motel

Best youth hostel: Hotels in the French Quarter can run you at least a hundred bucks a night. For exactly $12.62 (plus tax and sheet rental) you can get that Brady Bunch bedroom experience on one of 162 bunk beds at the **Marquette House** *(2253 Carondelet St., 504/523–3014)*, the local affiliate of American Youth Hostels. Single-sex dorms rooms sleep four. Rules are kept to a minimum: You get a key, there is no curfew, and you can use the hostel during the day to write letters and talk politics with visiting Australians. Private apartments and a deluxe suite are also available.

Runner-up: The **Longpre House** *(1726 Prytania St., 504/581–4540)* is a little grungier and cheaper. Bunk rooms sleep eight; coed facilities are available. For both hostels, make reservations for Mardi Gras and Jazz Fest at least six months in advance.

Best cheap hotel: A streetcar ride away from the French Quarter is a real hotel bargain, the **Prytania Inn** *(1415 Prytania St., 504/566–1518)*. In its four old Garden District buildings are pretty, somewhat lacy rooms that run $35 to $69 a night. Rooms have phones but no TVs. The newest addition to the complex is the St. Vincent Guest House, located in a 19th-century orphanage. Opt for this one if you want a pool.

local wonders

Best alligators: All the swamp tours promise that you'll see some gators, but there's something disheartening about being taken out in a boat and watching your guide coax the great beasts with marshmallows or chicken. The best unspoiled bayou vista is the free Bayou Coquille Trail in the Barataria Preserve of the **Jean Lafitte National Park** *(7400 Highway 45, Marrero, 504/589–2330)*. If you rest along the bridge and look down the bayou, you'll eventually see a gator snout slowly parting the brackish green goo and winding its way toward you. Free ranger-led walks and canoe tours are also available (with rental fees for canoes). In addition, the Jean Lafitte Park system offers free walking tours of the French Quarter and Garden District; call 504/589–2636 for more information.

Best cemetery: Called the cities of the dead, the cemeteries of New Orleans are famed for their spooky, aboveground tombs. Near the French Quarter are **St. Louis Cemetery Nos. 1 and 2**, the resting place of Marie Laveau, the famed voodoo queen. Most of the Xs marked on her tomb for good luck are, however, from tourists, not true believers. Cemeteries should only be visited in groups; this is one of those places where out-of-towners are considered easy pickings for criminals. The best regular voodoo and cemetery tours are run by **Magic Walking Tours** *(504/588–9693)*, which also runs a nighttime vampire and ghost hunt through the French Quarter. The tour is a bit campy, kind of like an on-foot haunted house, and you'll get your own garlic and stakes. It visits various sites reputed to be haunted, including one house where a woman was said to have chained her slaves; they perished in a fire and, of course, are screaming to this day.

transmissions

Best rush-hour DJ: The city's alternative station is the **WZRH (106.1 FM)**, owned by a plastic surgeon–cum–country singer named Randolph M. Howes, whose original tune "Commode Huggin' Drunk" gets airtime on his own station every Mardi Gras. But the real reason to tune into the Zephyr is for Grant Morris' wry wit on his "Afternoon Drive" show, which may be best remembered for a notorious live conversation with Nick Cave and L7, during which Cave walked out after trading insults with the host. On slow news days, the show is devoted to tracking down rumors: Morris put out a citywide net for eyewitnesses the day after Eddie Vedder was involved in a brawl at a local bar.

Best '60s radical turned DJ: At Woodstock, when Abbie Hoffman was conked off the stage by Pete Townshend, it was for making a speech about John Sinclair. In 1971, John Lennon wrote a song about him. Those were the days when Sinclair, the manager of Detroit's Motor City Five and founder of the White Panther Party, was a cannabis cause célèbre, serving two-and-a-half years in prison for possession of two joints. Now Sinclair is a New Orleans poet, bandleader of the Blues Scholars, and a gruff, mellifluous voice on the local airwaves. His shows on the city's great community radio station, **WWOZ (90.7 FM)**, feature classic New Orleans R&B and an eclectic assortment of live on-air interviews, all delivered in a congenial beat style.

new york

by Matthew DeBord with
Robert Sietsema and Chris Lawrence

"Manhattan rules: 1) Walk everywhere. 2) Talk to the homeless. 3) The water is usually fine. 4) Don't spend your money in chain stores."
— **Moby**

New York is the maximum city. It's big in height, in-yo-face postures, and health hazards. There is more fun to be had in New York per square foot than anywhere else in the world. And you don't have to be Iggy Pop to find it.

New York is also the ultimate border town. Prejudices are suspended, rules abandoned, and weird misinterpretations of "other people's" music are allowed to flower. In New York, drum machines, raps, vintage guitar pedals, and good old rock 'n' roll collide. To cite a few famous cases: With Public Enemy, a couple of Long Island rappers took old-school sounds, put them with black revolutionary politics and irritating white noise and came up with the decisive soundtrack for the hip-hop nation. With the Beastie Boys, three Jewish boys quit punk, learned how to rap, and put out a couple of really stoopid albums. With Sonic Youth, sleazy East Village garage rock met Glenn Branca's aural-accumulation orchestras, creating the Grateful Dead of the '90s. With dancehall and reggae español, island music met club music in Queens and West Side discos, and the weekend black-radio airwaves filled with Spanish and Jamaican patois toasts over funky-hard bass lines.

More legendary clubs have shut down in New York than will ever open in the rest of the U.S. combined. Let's pause a minute in honor of New York clubs, open and closed: Max's Kansas City, where the Velvet Underground refined a totemic body of rock in front of bitchy, pill-popping Factory scenesters. CBGB, where Television and Patti Smith struck the first punk poses for an intimate crowd of lowlifes, hustlers, and glue sniffers. Studio 54, where the '70s disappeared in an avalanche of powdery high jinks. The Kitchen, where Talking Heads mixed high-minded artistic pretensions with spare, pop song structures, creating new wave. Danceteria, where DJ Jellybean Benitez first played Madonna's "Everybody" tape to an unsuspecting world. The Tunnel, where DJs like Junior Vasquez worked out "bitch" tracks to crowds of drag queens at dawn ("If Madonna calls, I'm not here"). And that's not even going near jazz. Today, so many clubs crowd the East Village alone that it's hard to avoid mediocre rawk bands—let alone the occasional brilliant performance by a group like Versus. Still, there is something decisive about going out at night in New York, whether it's to a drum 'n' bass one-nighter that you find by word of mouth or to a much-anticipated Blues Explosion blowout ("It feels good to be back, New York, but I need your love!"). At the best shows, there is always an element of fear in the air, the sense that something really bad could happen any minute—or at least something gross and gratuitous, like when the Voluptuous Horror of Karen Black's Kembra Pfhaler does a handstand and her assistant gets the eggs out. And though real underground frisson has gotten rarer ever since GG Allin died, it's still what New York knows how to deliver.

Home to the country's largest gay population, New York owes much to its queer nation. While the post-Stonewall leatherman culture of the West Village is largely gone—you don't see guys in chaps on Christopher Street very often in these safe-sex days—a clubby, draggy, fabulous East Village scene has spawned one-hit wonders like Deee-Lite and the annual Wigstock party. Pro-*Shampoo* grooviness (unbuttoned print shirts, flares, feathered shaggy hair) rules the day, and the soundtrack is either Studio 54 disco or way-out techno. As the days of house and fast breakbeats fade, however, sounds continue to mutate in the club music world, with "illbient" (hip-hop meets ambient) being the latest jam. Cerebral collage artists like DJ Spooky are bringing all kinds of genres together, from mid-'70s punk to Brian Eno–style ambient to rap (look for one nighters put on by Sound Lab). While the down side of all the genre bending is that New York produces too much music that relies on schtick (whether camp or intellectual) to get by, there is always the next real ticket around the corner. Anybody remember the Ramones?

lay of the land

With a few puzzling exceptions (like the West Village, Chinatown, and Washington Heights), Manhattan is an easy-to-navigate grid: Avenues run north-south, streets east-west. Fifth Avenue usually divides east and west, with numbers beginning at Fifth. For argument's sake, let's call

14th Street the dividing point between uptown and downtown. It bisects the island of Manhattan just below Union Square. Above 14th Street, you'll find high-end shopping on Fifth Avenue, Central Park, and all the big museums. If you're looking for rock, or other forms of trouble, there are few reasons to go uptown—except some always-opening-and-closing big dance clubs on the far West Side in Chelsea and some jazz bars on the Upper West Side and in Harlem. Heading downtown, the major east-west thoroughfares below 14th are: Houston Street, above which the numbered streets begin; Canal Street, where **Chinatown**, home of excellent cheap eats, and **TriBeCa**, home of several clubs and bars, begin; and Chambers Street, below which lies the financial district.

Lots of aspiring rock stars, scarecrow conceptual artists, and silent-but-strong welders have moved into **Williamsburg**, across the East River from downtown in Brooklyn, lured by abandoned lofts, practice spaces, and cheap rents. But this funky community has not unseated the **East Village** as the center of youth culture. Since the mid-'80s, the East Village has been invaded by both really cheap heroin and coke (sold by the bag on many corners of Avenues A and B), and by increasingly upscale restaurants, coffeehouses, and bars. You'll still find homeless punk urchins begging change across from **Tompkins Square Park** on Avenue A (between Tenth and Seventh Streets), but the park's squatters have been eliminated after several cops vs. homeless riots, all reminiscent of '68 but minus the ideology. The gateway to the East Village is **Astor Place**, at Lafayette and Eighth Streets, near where Eighth becomes St. Marks Place. With several clubs in a beer-bottle's toss from each other and many excellent record stores on St. Marks between the Bowery (a.k.a. Third Avenue) and Second Avenue, this street, despite its often trollish foot traffic, is a rock mecca (of the T-shirts and memorabilia genre). The East Village has at least one bar for every mood and time of day, from computer-terminal lounges to very old-school Eastern European gay hideaways—as well as a Russian bath house.

Below the East Village, south of Houston is known as the **Lower East Side**, where several interesting bars and boutiques have roosted on Ludlow and neighboring streets, and Little Italy, where Elizabeth Street has a growing population of groovy knickknack stores and galleries that take more risks than their SoHo counterparts. As for **SoHo**, south of Hudson between Broadway and Sixth Avenue, let's just say that, since the chain stores moved in, the whole place should just be closed to traffic and made into a huge outdoor mall.

Finally, while the **West Village** is less gay and more expensive than it once was, it's still New York's primary boys' town. And the meat-packing district, a cut of land with cobblestoned streets at the west end of 14th, has lately become a nightlife destination, with several fetish clubs and some hard-partying bars.

getting from a to b

There are four main ways to move around Manhattan: subway, bus, taxi, and foot. Though the island is only 11 miles long and three miles wide, walking everywhere is definitely not an option. Just to trot from, say, St. Mark's Bookstore (see Shopping) on Ninth Street to the Knitting Factory in Tribeca (see Clubs)—an entirely Downtown jaunt—can be an exhausting hike. The subway worms its way beneath most of the city, and can get you close to almost any place you might like to go. At $1.50 a ride—with free transfers—it's hard to beat. (Those famous NYC subway tokens are becoming anachronistic; the Transit Authority is making a big push for the MetroCard, which you can buy for values of up to $80.) Buses cost the same as the subway but are often slow and, of course, enslaved to Manhattan's horrifying traffic. Taxis are relatively expensive, but since the subways and buses run less frequently late at night, it always makes sense to have an extra $20 to spirit yourself out of darkest Ludlow Street at 4 A.M.. Local wisdom suggests a tip of $1 to $10; follow the 15 to 20 percent rule.

sources

In the center of publishing, there are too many listings options, none wholly satisfactory. Despite the ongoing tarnishing of its once impeccable alternative credentials, the free-in-Manhattan *Village Voice*'s "Choices" listing remains top-drawer, if at times awfully predictable. And there's always scenester diva Michael Musto, whose dishy gossip column "La Dolce Musto" chronicles clubland and often catches the fabulous with their pants down. The *Voice* also still has the best club advertisements. Also free, *New York Press* combines a poverty-stricken slacker sensibility with a larder of gallivanting sarcasm, not to mention a fair, though not always fairly balanced, accounting of the Downtown music culture. *The New York Times* Sunday "Arts and Leisure" section contains a thorough list of the upcoming week's entertainment options, delivered in an even tone that makes few attempts to help readers figure out what's worth their trouble. A helpful source, but not much fun. *The New Yorker*'s "Goings on About Town" provides a swift, disputatious rundown of the upcoming week's events, delivered in the magazine's arch, vaguely bemused style. The cataloging of what's upcoming in underground music is often on-target, though far from exhaustive. *Time*

Out New York, which debuted in 1995, has taken the Manhattan listings world by storm. Not nearly as vindictive as its British counterpart, the rag makes up in comprehensiveness what it lacks in wit. Music and club listings are the best—and most reliable—in town. It's your best bet if an up-close and personal, up-to-the-minute verdict on the constantly mutating underground scene is what you seek. *New York* magazine covers more ground than *The New Yorker*—including bars and restaurants—but it doesn't always have much to say about the music scene. *Outweek*, *The Advocate*, and a stack of slighter weekly newsletters chronicle the city's happening queer scene. *Sound Views*, a free-in-New-York, $2-else-where fanzine has been reporting on the extremes of the subterranean music scene for more than 30 issues. If your interests run to bands with names like "Kurt Cobain Haiku," this is the zine for you.

On-line listings can be found at Total New York (www.totalny.com) and Microsoft's upcoming Sidewalk (www.sidewalk.com). SonicNet (http://www.sonicnet.com/) has its ear close to the ground and is always fun to browse. Many of the bigger clubs also have their own web sites, listed in ads in papers.

clubs

Best sidewalk punks: The stage is awkwardly angled, and a tall person often impairs the view (unless you elbow your way past the 30-foot-long cagelike bar and through the vitamin-deficient crowd to the front), but there's something about **CBGB** *(315 Bowery, 212/982–4052)* that makes for good clean fun. Just because pitiless skinheads don't slug it out during Murphy's Law sets anymore doesn't mean it's square. Despite the gallery and pizza bar/gift shop which now flank the Lourdes of New York punk, CBGB still books nearly 50 often-unknown bands or performance ranters a week. You always can tell when there's a good show because the Bowery sidewalk out front is packed with loitering grunge urchins and orange-haired *Eightball* readers, who buy cheap beer across the street at the Indian deli and drink it from paper bags. Unfortunately, the booking has lost its star power. Three years ago, CBs had Shonen Knife one month, Sonic Youth playing under a fake name the next, and the John Spencer Blues Explosion opening for Jesus Lizard the next. A recent Friday headliner: Maul Girls. Maul Girls?

Best very small club: Despite its size, **Brownies** *(169 Ave. A, 212/420–8392)* is picking up some of the slack left by CBGB, thanks to with-it booking. A block above Tompkins Square Park in the East Village, this postcollegiate alternative spot of the moment draws buzz bands who will be playing Irving Plaza in a tour or two. The space feels like one of the family-run Ukrainian bars that dot the neighborhood, and the studiedly scruffy crowds here care—giving it a touchy-feely atmosphere perfect for low-impact, moodscape bands like Spain or Idaho. Because it's a residential neighborhood, it's not that cool to loiter out front.

Best all-age matinees: If punk purity is your thing, come by **ABC No Rio** *(156 Rivington St., 212/254–3697)* for a Saturday afternoon party: five bands and lots of kids who look like they should be at home doing their algebra. On nice days the back door opens onto a tenement yard, and it becomes a giant punk playpen, complete with weenie roasts. With its rock shows, open-mike readings, and people's movement seminars, ABC No Rio resembles a youth center run by squatters in an abandoned building. The parlor room has a gauntlet of foldout tables, where vendors hawk tapes, T-shirts, zines, stickers, singles, and other can't-live-without artifacts. Downstairs lurks a fire marshal's nightmare: a bomb-shelterlike basement with exposed rotting beams, and a postage-stamp-size stage in one corner. Performers can't pogo, however, because the ceiling's too low. Bands are united by a screw-the-majors sentiment, and the true-believer crowd is generally cheery. Claustrophobics, stay away.

Best East Village club hangout: Looking to visit a place that mirrors the most desperate half-empty moods? Ready to cut the cord entirely from suburbia? If so, then a visit to **Coney Island High** *(15 St. Marks Pl., 212/674–7959)* is in order. Set in the hurly-burly squalor just east of Astor Place, CIH's primitive red-and-black exterior hints at the prevailing mood within. Downstairs, there is live music virtually every night—a parade of would-be Antichrists, both signed and unsigned, presented by CMJ. Gigs have recently included the Beastie Boys playing as a punk thrash band, and the weekly jungle-DJ night Konkrete Jungle. Upstairs, the "Detention Lounge" offers the truest window on the dark night of New York's soul. Proudly offering "vids, pinball, DJs, and sleaze," the Lounge makes good on the Coney Island premise with demented sideshow paintings and cheap Christmas-tree lights strung along the ceilings—an amusement-park goof with an exuberent sound-track of trashy '70s disco.

Best avant-krud: Blame it on the hazardous programming. The **Knitting Factory** *(74 Leonard St., 212/209–3055)* wants to transcend all performance clichés, and it often succeeds to such a degree that you can't enjoy the shows—unless you're a serious music nerd. Sure, John Zorn drops in sometimes to threaten his fans with some new, freaky, densely cerebral undertaking, but too often you'll find music dweebs fiddling around with their drum machines and effects. Still, you have to hand it to a place that gives a stage to way-out sonic-fusion jams like Ronald Shannon Jackson's recent quartets as well as high-concept punk bands. New Year's Eve often features the deconstructed funk of guitar maestro James Blood Ulmer. Much less collegiate than the old, smokey, cramped space on Houston Street, the Knitting Factory's new TriBeCa location looks like someone with a design sense did the decor, as opposed to a couple of refugees from the University of Wisconsin (the club's owners). Large front windows, banquettes, and mirrors now usher spectators into the much larger performance area. Upstairs is a merchandise shop.

Best place to wear tie-dye: If you can stop wondering why the Grateful Dead and Phish continue to have currency with today's youth, **Wetlands** *(161 Hudson St., 212/966–4225)* can be a hoot. The booking picks up where the old Knitting Factory left off. For example, there aren't too many other venues in Manhattan that would bring Rise Robots Rise—a rap-meets-Zappa outfit obsessed with the planet Mars—in for a few nights. The end of each month features ska evenings, and thanks to NYC's big scene of young mods, you won't be skanking alone. Cover is cheap and the ambience recalls the Band's *Last Waltz*, complete with dark carved-wood details and fringed hanging lamps, all of which makes this rather large Tribeca club seem downright, well, cozy. Then there's the vintage psychedelic-painted VW bus, which has been parked inside the club since it opened in 1988. Wetlands has been on-again, off-again host of DJ Frankie Inglese's Monday night Soul Kitchen, with funky remixes of '70s soul and R&B and 32 ounce bottles of Colt .45, bringing out the B-boys in full effect.

Best upstart East Village rock club: Only open since '94, the **Mercury Lounge** *(217 E. Houston St., 212/260–4700)* has unseated CBGB in the race to get prime rising bands. A narrow bar serves as an entryway to a nice music space—you don't have to pay to drink up front. The Mercury books acts like Dogwater and Scrawl, along with dozens of other cutting-edge, embryonic acts you might never hear from again—but if you do, look out! Standbys like John Lurie and the Lounge Lizards still drop by, drawing thirty-somethings in black.

Best Latin beats: At **S.O.B.'s** *(204 Varick St., 212/243–4940)* Brazil takes up where Hawaii themes of the '60s left off. What S.O.B.'s offers to the discriminating jazzbo is a headquarters for Latin worldbeat in the Big Apple, uniting bebop, jazz standards, Cubano rhythms, and that whole Mambo Kings cha-cha-cha groove in one eclectic ragout with an ever-changing cast. While some jazz purists will quibble with the legitimacy of this whole sidebar to the African swing and blues traditions, most habitués of S.O.B.'s are out less for a cerebral than a visceral experience. Behind the dark windows lurks what often turns out to be Manhattan's jumpingest nightlife alternative. Sitting down for a show will usually top the meter at around $30, with a few drinks included to fuel those subequatorial passions.

Best big club: With snooty, exclusive, Teddy-Roosevelt-era Gramercy Park down the street in one direction and Union Square in the other, **Irving Plaza** *(17 Irving Place at 15th St., 212/777–1224)* stands out in an otherwise squeaky-clean neighborhood. It's hard to argue with the booking: Nearly every great (or at least interesting) act on the cusp of the big time plays here, from the Chemical Brothers to Jesus Lizard to Tricky. A formidable cavern with multiple bars and a balcony, Irving Plaza is big enough to accommodate major-label acts but still plenty intimate. It draws a fair share of industry execs to its VIP lounge who hawkishly study the audience from above, trying to figure out which way the wind's blowing—who cares what the band sounds like? Well, the crowds sweating it out on the packed dance floor down below do. Irving draws the East Village's finest and other subterraneans who know the goods.

Best rising bands: Maxwell's *(1039 Washington St., Hoboken, NJ, 201/798–4064)* is so intimate that when a scenester once accused Henry Rollins of sounding like Mudhoney, Rollins stopped the show to debate the point ("I was doing this when Mudhoney..."). Unlike CBGB, which lets anybody who just learned their first three power chords take the stage, Maxwell's always seems to rope in destined-for-greatness bands when they're still doing their own sound checks and lugging their own amps. The club is a small room in back of a friendly cafe and bar. It's dark, cramped, and thanks to a low stage, often hard to see the band. Nonetheless, it's a prime stop for serious music aficionados, not just party animals. It's a quick ride under the Hudson River on the New Jersey Transit PATH train, then a long walk up Washington Street.

Best hip-hop mob scene: Buddah Bar *(150 Varick St., 212/255–4433)* is home to extra-large threads, Phillies Blunts, heavy-duty postfunk grooving, and the general glories of the B-boy lifestyle every Monday night, when DJ Stretch Armstrong fires up **Now and Later**. Stretch is considered one of the crown princes of NYC turntables: His record collection is so vast (hip-hop, trip-hop, deep house, and whatever else), that no one really knows what he'll mix his way into next (Donna Summer to Digable Planets). Be warned: Buddah Bar on a Monday night is not for the faint of heart, or those rendered timid by a bobbing dance floor. On Thursdays, **Giant Step** occupies the house, continuing the distinctly NYC tradition of layering hip-hop with its ancestral cousin, '50s and '60s-era hard-bop jazz. Giant Step is a lot mellower, with more sitting and grooving and less hard-assed up-and-down B-boy posturing. Wednesday nights deliver **Opium Den**, where the emphasis is on the reinvention of George Clintonesque funk.

Best queer-rock club night: Every Friday night, **Squeezebox** happens at **Don Hill's** *(511 Greenwich St., 212/334–1390)*, near the West Side Highway, hosted by the cutting, witty, rok goddess Mistress Formica. There are usually two bands and several DJs. So, what's so special? Debbie Harry and Iggy Pop have both played at Squeezebox, but the real draw are the earnest, often gay, rock acts—they're sort of glam, like T. Rex, or sort of just … strange, like Poison. The scene is so macho, it's feminine. There's nothing campy about the music, and the freaks who come out to party aren't fooling around. This is all about disenfranchised youth reclaiming their roots as adults. Go wild!

Best late-night jazz jams: Even though the Big Apple is the only serious jazz city in the world for players, there's a yawning chasm for fans. On the one hand are the expensive, "serious" Greenwich Village clubs, drenched in history and stuffed with tourists, where you can see top names for top dollars. On the other hand are little background-music gigs in mom-and-pop restaurants. The antidote to both of these not-always appealing extremes is **Smalls** *(183 W. 10th St., 212/929–7565)*, a wee room in the cabaret-and-big-hair district off Seventh Avenue in Greenwich Village. Smalls' nightly jazz marathon is home to insomniacs and all the hot young players in town: For $10, you get ten hours of music, from 10 P.M. to 8 A.M., plus free eats and drinks. Confronted with music charges at the Blue Note and Vanguard that sometimes top out at $60, this bargain-basement offering is the best way to see the town's newest chops. Heavy hitters come to unwind after their paying gigs; and the place smokes Tuesday nights after 3 A.M.

Best box of hard-core lesbians: Meow Mix *(269 E. Houston St., 212/254–1434)* is for dykes with attitude, dykes with East Village tastes, dykes who dig leather, dykes who don't want to mess around. It's also the only true Gotham venue for an anything-goes approach to lesbian culture—from DJ'd dance nights to readings to performances. On a jumping night, the small corner space can seem dark and cramped, but allowing the festivities to spill out onto the sidewalk is always a possibility.

Best meat-packing district experimental club: Accessible only through a huge stainless-steel refrigerator door, the **Cooler** *(416 W. 14th St., 212/229–0785)* manages to recall the idealistic '60s moment when intelligensia and workers were going to rise against The Man. Downstairs, low lighting, low ceilings, exposed pipes, meat scales, and chrome furniture make the place an arty, mod commentary on the notion of—what else?—"cool," specifically the blue-collar variety. The music, a nightly rotation of reggae, ska, jazz, Moroccan, and just about anything else, is perfect. For post-show sustenance, Dizzy Izzy's New York Bagels is a few doors down and open all night.

Best dance club: Clubbing in New York—at least dance clubbing—was in the 1970s synonymous with disco, which in those days meant queer. It's useful to remember that many notable Manhattan clubland experiences get jumping because gay men just gotta dance. **Twilo** *(530 W. 27th St., 212/268–1600)*, a large, extremely well-done space (not too many lights, nice big floor, no glaring visual theme) at the Northern fringes of far West Chelsea (the club is within spitting distance of the massive Chelsea Piers sports complex), used to be something of a meat market, with a rep as a place where overpumped David Barton bodies bopped with other overpumped David Barton bodies, but Friday and Saturday nights lately have seen the appearance of the rest of clubland, hot for a rich mix and a smoking dance-floor story. Straights galore—boys and girls, uptown fashion chicks, and downtown underground-music slaves—have prompted some to label Twilo the wildest experience they've had since the heyday of the '80s. If you're feeling sturdy and can keep your peepers popped until 4 A.M., the exquisite after-hours scene heats up and continues to pound until dawn, governed by an assortment of rotating DJs, most of who cleave to the club's endless appetite for deep house.

Runner-up: **Palladium** *(126 E. 14th St., 212/473–7171)*, during its expansive history, has been all things to all people: white-hot '80s club, unholy post–"American Bandstand" MTV studio, nuevo-Latino dance hall, and now, with the infusion of super-DJ Junior Vasquez, a pretty snappy joint to find yourself in the wee hours of a Sunday morning.

Best after-hours frenzy: Vinyl *(157 Hudson St., 212/343–1379)* cleaves to the idea that more is more. The scene at this way downtown venue doesn't get cooking until something like 4 A.M. on Fridays and Saturdays, and the fun ususally continues well into daylight. Lots of lights, lots of ravers, lots of bouncey kids, and plenty of room to operate on the main dance floor, along with a heavyweight sound system.

bars

Best Ludlow Street pickup scene: If you're looking for a friend and can't find him or her, go to **Max Fish** *(178 Ludlow St., no phone)*. If you've been to every Ukrainian bar in the East Village and are still standing, go to Max Fish. If you want to see ground zero of the Ludlow Street youth quake, go Fish. Vicious pool in the back, killer pinball machines in the front, shock-art installations on the walls, and very young, very pretty kids late at night showing off their plaid golf pants. On weekends, the scene usually spills out onto Ludlow Street, where you're likely to bump into 1) members of the band you just saw at the Mercury Lounge, 2) your old college roommate, or 3) the person you're going to go home with.

Best clean, spacious drinking bar: Whether you're ducking out of the summer heat for an afternoon pint or looking for a roomy bar for a read and a smoke after work, **288** *(288 Elizabeth St., 212/334–8429)* can't be beat. An airy, inviting space just off Houston and a block away from CBGB, 288 has concrete floors, large glass brick faux-windows, three metal ceiling fans, and, on shelves behind the bar, a collection of Tom & Jerry punch bowls. It's the perfect place to tune out for an hour or get soused with an old friend. An assortment of dogs snooze or shuffle around while friendly boozers tend to gather at the far end of the bar, giving 288 the feel of a German punk squat. Regulars range from publishing malcontents to guerrilla girls to a coupla regular guys talking baseball. Big tables make it good for large groups. Just don't come weekend nights, when it turns into a yuppie meat market.

Best dark bar with DJs: A mainstay in the Lower East Side party-scene world, **bOb** *(235 Eldridge St., 212/777–0588)* plays soul, reggae, hip-hop, and jazz. Candle-lit and intimate with low tables and drapes, it fosters comfort and conversation. Those points, along with a 7-to-10 P.M.

happy hour nightly, make it a favorite after-class watering hole for the area's growing student population. Be warned: Later in the evening, cozy turns to claustrophobic as the bar struggles to accommodate a wonderfully wide cross-section of downtown life.

Runners-up: Several doors away, **Sapphire** *(249 Eldridge St., 212/777–5153)* draws groovy clubbers with low-impact dance music. Several blocks away, the much-loved **205 Club** *(205 Christie St., 212/473–5816)* has recently reopened, offering a low-key, low-pressure, low-cover spot for dancing.

Best ultrahip conceptual bar: This bar is so cool it should be studied. At **Barra Mundi** *(147 Ludlow St., 212/529–6900)*, lacquered tree-trunk tables cluster beneath a ceiling fan with old skateboards for blades. None of the chairs match. Faux mosaics and cheesy Romanesque mirrors lead to the back room, which features a working fireplace. A subtle, groovy vibe is nicely complemented by the reliable mix of tunes trickling from the stereo—everything from bossa nova to opera. What to drink? The *caipirinha*, an icy Brazilian peasant concoction made with the South American equivalent of tequila, muddled lime, and sugar.

Runner-up: Yes, **Beauty Bar** *(231 E. 14th St., 212/539-1389)* is an old beauty salon, kitschily transformed into a watering hole (complete with the conehead hair-driers), and no, it's not the place to go if greasy Jim Morrison types are your bag. For those guys, you'll do better at the East Village's assorted dives, maybe **Sidewalk Cafe** *(94 Avenue A, 212/473–7373)*. However, Beauty Bar is friendly, and you can often get your nails done while you drink.

Best West Village pub with burgers: The burger is rising again, and if washing it down with a mug of Bud makes you happy, you must visit **Corner Bistro** *(331 W. 4th St., 212/242–9502)*. In front is a classic, woody pub, never too loud for conversations, but often too crowded to sit, where Dave Pirner, among others, has passed many nights. A narrow, usually congested passage leads alongside the short-order kitchen to the cramped, dark back room. Here, in one of the private, high-backed booths, you order and dine on the juicy, charbroiled burgers—called New York's best by many. Options are minimal: cheese, onions, bacon, pickles, or not. Fries on the side, or not. The Bistro's only drawback is the long wait for a table. It's never too early to get in line.

Best fashion bar: The new epicenter of high fashion has become **Pravda** *(281 Lafayette St., 212/226–4944)*, named for the defunct Soviet newspaper and done up to resemble a people's meeting hall straight out of *Ten Days that Shook the World*. Well worth checking out, if you don't miss it: The sign is dinky, typical of a nighttime hotspot that wants to avoid the overcrowding with proles that befell such predecessors as Bowery Bar and Lucky Cheng's. Inside, one drinks vodka, in all its many blessed forms.

Runners-up: In front of the nearby **Bowery Bar** *(358 Bowery, 212/475–2220)*, you are likely to find lines of desperate bridge-and-tunnelers, hoping to get past the velvet rope for a peek at a supermodel. Ironically, the models have moved on, but the converted gas station still conveys an air of haughty fabulousness. Another favorite glam haunt, with up- and downstairs bars and a separate poolroom, **Cafe Tabac** *(232 E. Ninth St., 212/674–7072)* still has moments of intrigue and drama.

food/coffee

Best bargain Mexican: Gabriela's *(685 Amsterdam Ave., 212/961–0574)* offers a pleasant "Jetsons"-esque diner setting on the Upper West Side at 93rd Street and serves regional specialties from the four corners of Mexico, including homemade tortillas, savory tripe stew, *huevos rancheros* (offered all day long), and killer rotisserie chicken with a choice of dipping sauces (pick *mancha manteles*—spicy-hot and banana-driven). There are many good vegetarian selections, including a Oaxacan potato, zucchini, and cactus stew with a pumpkin-seed sauce that is, alas, not nearly as wild as it sounds.

Runner-up: A tiny eat-in/takeout in the West Village, **Taqueria de Mexico** *(93 Greenwich Ave., 255–5212)* specializes in Mexico City–style fast food: double-tortilla tacos, enchiladas, tamales, etc. Don't miss the tortilla soup and the tiny trio of pork *taquitos*, the meat carved from a revolving cylinder on the counter.

Best late-night post-rock snacking: From a single kebab to a full-course meal, count on the strategically located **Bereket** *(187 E. Houston St., 475–7700)*, open 24 hours, to provide any volume of eats you desire. It's a stone's throw from lotsa clubs, including Mercury Lounge, CBGB, and the Ludlow Strip. Award for best dish goes to *adana* kebab, a cylinder of lamb coarsely chopped with fresh hot chiles, then charcoal-grilled to perfection.

Best street for African food: Harlem's West 116th Street between Malcolm X and Adam Clayton Powell Boulevards currently boasts seven

African restaurants—Senegalese, Guinean, and Somalian—plus an Ethiopian grocery and an Islamic meat market. The best eatery is probably **Africa Restaurant** *(247 W. 116th St., 212/666–9400)*, offering two or three Senegalese dishes per day, like *cheb*, the rice-based national dish, and *mafe*, a stew of chicken or lamb with peanut sauce. Open very late to take advantage of the taxi trade. If you dine during the day, drop in afterward at the African market catty-cornered from the mosque to shop for natty West African threads.

Best self-conscious hamburger: To be in the running, it should be made with aged Black Angus beef, cooked over charcoal, and sided with fries so good you refuse to share them with your friends. **Steak Frites** *(9 E. 16th St., 212/463–7101)* has such a burger. It's only on the lunch menu, but if you know to ask for it, they'll make it anytime. Close your eyes while you eat and you won't have to look at the stupid French-style murals, or the condescending waiters, who often act like they're not too happy you ordered the burger—but everyone does.

Best post-disco French bistro: Pick from hyper-Gallic selections, like *rillettes* (smooshed pork meatballs) and *boudin noir* (a grainy blood sausage), or you can go with the more pedestrian steak *frites* or the full line of standard breakfast offerings at **Florent** *(69 Gansevoort St., 212/989–5779)*. Founded in the meat-packing district nearly a decade ago, the restaurant has a clientele that includes transvestites, club-hoppers, dissipated roués, and other denizens of the night. For a bistro, the prices are on the low side—and it's open 24 hours on weekends.

Best cheap feed, Cuban division: The matriarchally run **National Cafe** *(210 First Ave., 212/473–9354)* is a Cuban lunch counter at 13th Street that serves entire meals, consisting of soup, yellow or white rice, red or black beans, and an entree like garlicky pork roast or the blander chicken fricassee, for only $5 or $6 (cheaper at lunch). For the more adventuresome, there's *mofongo*, made with mashed plantain and pork gravy. As is the Cuban practice, there's always spaghetti in the soup.

Runner-up: **Havana Chelsea Luncheonette** *(190 Eighth Ave., 243–9421)* would be merely more of the same, if it weren't for its knock-out Cuban sandwich and octopus salad, both of which are irresistibly displayed in a glass-walled refrigerator case that thrusts into the sidewalk.

Best totally normal food: In the heart of the East Village, the long-running **Odessa Coffee Shop** *(119 Ave. A, 212/473–8916)* has just moved into new, more spacious digs but still features standard diner food with a few Ukrainian twists, like borscht, *pierogi*, and blintzes. Heck, they've even got spaghetti and meatballs. As an added bonus, it's right across the street from Tompkins Square Park, so if a riot erupts, you can throw down your fork and join in.

Runner-up: **Leshko's** *(111 Ave. A, 212/473–9208)* has a similar menu, but a funkier interior—if you're into local color. Watch Richard Hell and Iggy Pop walk by as you down your burger and fries. Open 24 hours.

Best downscale Indian: While the famous row of Indian restaurants on East Sixth Street in the Village has suffered a gradual decline in quality, there are still excellent curry options in New York City. One unpretentious curry house moved into a former diner in Jackson Heights, Queens and didn't bother changing the name: **Jackson Diner** *(37-03 74th St., Queens, 718/672–1232)* serves a constituency that's about 50-percent vegetarian, regaling them with South Indian specialties like *masala dosa* (a lentil-and-rice crepe with a spicy potato filling) and *iddly* (spongy dumplings served with a fiery soup called *sambar*). For the carnivorous, try anything made with lamb, especially *saag gosht.* An all-you-can-eat buffet is offered at lunch. Easily accessible via the 7 train, which travels on elevated tracks out Roosevelt Avenue to Shea Stadium.

Runner-up: Okay, if you're too lazy to drag your butt out to Queens, check out **Curry in a Hurry** *(119 Lexington Ave., 212/683–0900)*, where $6 gets you two entrées, rice, flat bread, salad, and unlimited visits to the famed chutney bar.

Best authentic barbecue: New York ain't known as Barbecue Town, and if it weren't for Robert Pearson, a hairdresser from mod London turned barbecue fanatic, we wouldn't have anything worth the Tums. His **Stick to Your Ribs** *(5-16 51st Ave, Long Island City, 718/937–3030)*, located one stop into Queens on the 7 train, is doctrinaire Texas barbecue at its best. Accordingly, go for the brisket or hot links sandwiches washed down with Lone Star beer. Forget the sides.

Best Williamsburg Thai: You're probably tired of hearing that Williamsburg is the next SoHo, but the evidence is undeniable if you look in the door of **Plan-Eat Thailand** *(184 Bedford Ave., Brooklyn, 718/599–5758)* and see the tattooed and pierced masses lugging guitars and portfolios. The Siamese scarf is cheap and wonderful, especially anything made with squid or, to a lesser extent, chicken. The name used to be Planet Thailand, till the hideous Planet Hollywood chain reputedly threatened legal action.

Best place to eat if you find yourself stuck in SoHo: Crawl to the northwestern verge of Chinatown, a few blocks to the southeast, and enjoy the working-class Chinese grub at **Excellent Dumpling House** *(111 Lafayette St., 212/219–2333)*. Especially recommended is anything stir-fried with rice cakes—gooey, chewy, and white as a ghost, which makes it the perfect bland foil to other flavors. Also check out the dishes made with sour cabbage.

Runner-up: If you can't bring yourself to leave SoHo before you eat, check out **Kelley & Ping** *(127 Greene St., 212/228–1212)*, a cut-rate, pan-Asian noodle-and-dumpling joint that covers all the bases from Vietnam to Japan, with plenty of surprises in between.

Best pizza, pie division: With the rather unfriendly warning "No Slices" on the awning, **John's Pizzeria** *(278 Bleecker St., 212/243–1680, and several other locations, so look in the phone book)* in the Village specializes in thin-crust pies with minimalist toppings cooked at high temperature in a wood-burning oven, resulting in a supremely crusty crust, nicely charred on the edges, and scented with wood smoke. Pay 50 cents extra and they'll strew the pizza with fresh garlic.

Best pizza, slice division: A popular fave has long been **Stromboli's** *(83 St. Marks Pl., 212/673–3691)*, whose wide window on the corner of St. Marks and First Avenue has been feeding East Villagers for over 15 years. The sauce is on the sweet side, the crust is thin, and the cheese slice is so good, you shouldn't bother with any extras. Pies are made fresh all day long, and chances are the slice you get will be hot without having been reheated—reheating being the enemy of good pizza.

Best pizza, designer division: With ingredients like *arugula*, goat's cheese, fresh vegetables, jalapenos, chorizo, and, God help us, pineapple, the pizza at the Village's **California Pizza Oven** *(122 University Pl., 212/989–4225)* is clearly not from around here. In addition to whole pies, they'll also make slices to order, so throw your prejudices aside and use this place when your usual dinner or lunchtime slice screams for kinky variation.

Best postclub, 24-hour Greek diner: Less self-conscious than the nearby Empire Diner, the **Chelsea Square** *(368 W. 23rd St., 212/641–*

5400) is a classic New York Greek institution, with a menu that offers everything from burgers to *souvlaki* to linguini with clams, and a kitchen that prepares none of it well. Remember, you're not here for the quality of the food, and neither, it seems, are the Village irregulars (often of indeterminate age and sex) or the crowd of club kids two tables away. Convenient to many of the bigger West Side dance emporiums like Twilo, here is where you come for a plate of greasy steak fries and impeccable service from middle-aged professionals in black pants and white shirts. Floor-to-ceiling windows look out on 23rd Street.

Best East Village coffeehouses: Avenue A today supports not one, but two San Francisco–inspired coffeehouses. On the east side, near 4th Street, sits **Nation** *(50 Ave. A, 212/473–6239)*, a somber den in contrast to the west side's cheery, upbeat **Limbo** *(47 Ave. A, 212/477–5271)*. Owned by a descendent of the founder of Bergdorf-Goodman, Limbo has good coffee, off-the-street kitsch Formica furniture, and a bright Caribbean color scheme, drawing earnest young literati with notebooks and laptops. A popular Tuesday night reading series has hosted local notables like Caleb Carr, Rick Moody, and Elizabeth Wurtzel. The zine crowd prefers Nation, where a perpetual gloom is enhanced by yards of dark wood and several Gay '90s style mirrors. At night, Nation imports a DJ and turns into a lounge/dance club.

shopping

records

Best indie boutique: Forget record categories like "Alternative" and "Hip-Hop." Don't waste time at the imports section of a music megalopolis. Instead, come by **Other Music** *(15 E. 4th St., 212/477–8150)*, where sweaty-palmed record fiends browse sections with names like "Krautrock" and "The Japanese." With a clear bias toward ambient and electronic (from Eno to DJs Shadow and Spooky), this is a store with attitude: Like it or leave it. In a section called "La Decadence," Nick Cave gets lumped together with Bridgette Bardot, whereas the Birthday Party ends up with Neil Young in "Old Wave." Only vital contributors to the music of today make it into "New Wave"—where you find Harry Pussy next to Howie B and strong collections of Tortoise and Stereolab. Co-owner Jeff Gibson says he isn't quite sure where to put seminal L.A. band Savage Republic, and none other than avant-garde composer

Glenn Branca himself has complained (in person) about his placement in Old Wave. Where's Pearl Jam? "Across the street in Tower."

Runner-up: For less 909 and sample music, but more vinyl, **Adult Crash** *(66 Ave. A, 212/387–0558)* is strong on the noise and punk front. Although strictly speaking Kim's is now a chain store, the four-floor **Mondo Kim's** *(6 St. Mark's Pl., 212/598–9915, 9985)* on St. Mark's is always worth a visit, with an exhaustive selection of current indie CDs, choice old vinyl (you have to pay, though—an old Gary Numan record cost almost $20), shirts, videos, posters, and more.

Best Euro-pop: Looking for the latest Pet Shop Boys remix? Head over to the West Village's specialty boutique **Rebel, Rebel** *(319 Bleeker St., 212/989–0770)*. What's great about this store is it has a vision, and even if you don't like dandy pop, it's hard to argue with a passion that's comprehensively realized, with everything from Britain's Suede to Iceland's Bjork to Sweden's Cardigans. Befitting its location, the taste is overtly fey, complete with Madonna fixation.

Best DJ stores: Got turntables, need 12-inches? DJs in search of grooves couldn't ask for a better town than New York, where there's a boutique—or three—for every taste. Try **Throb** *(211 E. 14th St., 212/533–2328)* for a well-rounded selection of up-to-the-minute stuff—especially trip-hop, ambient, trance, techno, and jungle. A runner-up on the futurist tip is **Sonic Groove Records** *(41 Carmine St., 212/675–5284)* in the West Village, while, right across the street, **Vinyl Mania** *(60 Carmine St., 212/924–7223)* is slightly more human and danceable with good hip hop and disco. **Eightball** *(105 E. 9th St., 212/473–6343)* has its own New York–based label, specializing in acid jazz and house. The front-runner for hip-hop is **Fat Beats** *(406 6th Ave., 212/673–3883)*.

Best bargain CDs, new and used: New CDs go for way below list at **Sounds Tapes and CDs** *(16 St. Marks Pl., 212/677–2727)*, the best of St. Marks' many record boutiques. For new releases, you just can't beat Sounds' tiny store, which always has an interesting display of staff picks on the wall behind the cash register. The display racks are token; if you can't find what you want, ask the friendly clerk, and they'll usually have it behind the counter. Several doors down *(20 St. Marks Pl., 212/677–3444)*, Sounds has its main **Records and CDs** store, where you can find jazz, blues, R&B, soundtracks, as well as rock.

Runner-up: Devotees of the cheap and the cheaper than cheap will dig the Gotham CD market's answer to an OTB parlor, **Disc-O-Rama** *(40*

Union Sq., 212/260–8616). Colorless, uncarpeted, and small, the place nevertheless manages to sell the latest releases for significantly less than the chains. Eddie Vedder would approve.

books

Best zines: The largest zine collection by far in New York can be found at **See/Hear** *(31 St. Marks Pl., 212/505–9781),* a tiny shop on St. Marks Place. Whether the zine's got a readership of two or several thousand, is stapled or bound, or has a title like *Cupsize* or *Quitter Quarterly*, See/Hear has got it all. The shop also stocks great rock books, like *Hardcore California*, the best of today's underground comix (from Chris Ware to Kaz's *Underworld*), ReSearch books, and fiction from presses like Serpent's Tail. In its comprehensiveness and craziness, See/Hear affirms freedom—to print, think, and waste time.

Best used books: Maneuvering in the **Strand Bookstore** *(828 Broadway, 212/473–1452)* can be a bit like being in the subway at rush hour. Don't make eye contact with other customers. When you see an opening, take it. The Strand claims to measure books by the mile, and a visit to the crowded main store can sure feel like a marathon, especially if you're jockeying for position in front of the paperback bins. Still, one visit will convince you that the Strand is, in fact, the best bookstore in New York—for bargain used paperbacks, discounted new hardbacks, rarities, *The Futurist Cookbook*, and a first edition of Sylvia Plath's *Ariel*.

Best science fiction and geek books: Okay, so there aren't many other places in Manhattan where a guy can go and check out erotic comix and Star Trek memorabilia under the same roof. **Forbidden Planet** *(821 Broadway, 212/473–1576)* has all that an adolescent shut-in needs. This is publishing's Grand Central Station of onanism, where all the geek genres—comic books, science fiction, fantasy, baseball cards, Dungeons & Dragons—converge in a colorful parade. Godzilla action figurines? Got 'em. Back issues of *Love and Rockets*? Been there. Lloyd Llewellyn? Seen it. *Red Sonia*, *Batman*, Spidey, and the entire cyberpunk oeuvre from William Gibson to Rudy Rucker? Issues and copies to burn. Enter the Forbidden Planet at your own risk.

Best queer lit: In its lovely new space crafted by New York architect John Johnson, **A Different Light** *(151 W. 19th St., 212/243–4998)* is everything a Nancy Boy or Butch Girl could ask for in a same-sex literary emporium. Think blond wood and delicate track lighting. Think free local newspapers that supply tips to the scene. Think pleasant reading series. Think bookstore that respects its customers and shows an awareness that quality porn and erotica are necessary components of any happy modern sex life. A Different Light has what you need, everything from *Tom of Finland* to tales of bondage to fluffy romantic fare.

Best critical thinking bookstore: The **Saint Mark's Bookstore** *(31 Third Ave., 212/260–7853)* is populated by the sort of unhinged freelance intellectuals whose dissertations are written on bathroom walls, giving it just the right ax-to-grind energy. Critical and media theory are specialties of the house, with Bataille and Baudriard, Chomsky and McLuhan dominating the scene. Art and architecture are covered by a selection that's both diverse and perverse, but always engaging and provocative. And if the eclecticism (coupled with a truly literate and helpful staff) isn't enough to convince you that a smaller, better bookshop beats superstore discounts, the selection of smart erotica will.

clothes

Best Swinging London–dandy store: Look like you own the (down)town. SoHo's **New Republic** *(93 Spring St., 212/219–3005)* markets sophisticated retro men's clothing that doesn't make the wearer look like he's in period costume (Ralph Lauren, please take note). Dominated by beautiful art deco furniture and the sounds of "Swinging London," the tiny shop features its own label, as designed by Thomas Oatman. Here you'll find sleekly cut hacking jackets with double back-vents and ticket pockets, slim trousers, ascots, regimental scarves, as well as a host of distinctive accessories—cuff links, lighters and cigarette cases—guaranteed to lend authority when ordering a Pimm's Cup.

Best SoHo trashy rawk boutique: If something on the order of a woolly hot-pink cropped jacket floats your boat, you have found your muse in **Anna Sui** *(113 Greene St., 212/941-8406)*, where a strong New York edge is tempered by Haight-Ashbury. Black leather coexists with a seasonally changing palate of wild prints and textures. Popular with stylish Asian clubbers and wealthy rockers, the store has bright Kozik-style posters on the wall. In addition to '70s styles, Anna Sui has also shown appreciation for English Mod, putting out some Beatlesque designs recently. Now, what could be more music-biz than that? The mop-top haircut, however, will have to come from someplace else.

Runner-up: **Cynthia Rowley** *(108 Wooster St., 212/334–1144)* is less trendy, more whimsical, more, well ... more French. If club kids dig Anna Sui, it's post-clubbing 30ish downtowners who flock to Rowley for her attractive, clean designs with a funky edge. Recent faves: a white pique minidress bedecked with bathtub-sticker-style daisies.

Best primordial thrift store: Domsey's, *(431 Kent Ave., 718/384–6000)* in Williamsburg, Brooklyn, is a block-size warehouse, where much of the stuff that fills Manhattan's retrostyle emporia gets its start. The place is vast and musty, like a thrift shop should be. It's also dirt cheap. The stock is more carefully arranged than at Goodwill or the Salvation Army, so it's easier for a thrifting fanatic to work the racks in search of a decent suit that fits. Problem: Everyone knows about Domsey's, which means that nothing good lasts for very long before it's poached for East Village, Lower East Side, and SoHo boutiques. The trick is to catch on to trends early.

Best mock-croc vinyl miniskirts: You won't find a natural fiber in the whole store at **Kanae + Oynx** *(74 E. Seventh St., 212/254–7703)*. A cutting-room-cum-boutique just off Tompkins Square Park, Kanae makes original designs for club land, with specialties like metallic shifts in gold and silver, creamy vinyl ensembles that actually fit a girl's form rather than flare out like a stiffly-made kite, and smashing outerwear that can stand up to both a hot night at Webster Hall and an ascent of K2. Strictly women's wear.

Best playwear for boys: Bill Hallman *(357 Lafayette St., 212/673–8850)*, an Atlanta import, established a shop in NoHo in '95, offering wearable styles for men and women that move easily from beneath the disco ball to the confines of offices that aren't too fussy about dress codes. Unlike contemporaries, such as Todd Oldham, who sometimes get so lost in the past they forget that designers are supposed to deliver the future, Hallman slides from retro '60s and '70s modes to stuff that would fetch a stare from Parker Posey. Of special note are Hallman's sweaters (loose, nubby thin wool numbers with V-necks) that look great over slim leather pants, and acrylic faux boucé mock-turtles in black and gray, stippled with white, that hug the torso.

Best East Village boutique for '70s stylin': Only open since the summer of '96, **Anna** *(150 E. 3rd St., 212/358–0195)* has already hit big. Why? Cheap, shiny polester shirts for guys and girls—complete with long collars and wild patterns—that's partly why. And especially for the girls, slacks with geometric patterns. Also has vintage fashion denim from the '70s, like Gloria Vanderbilt jeans. Anna specializes in the printed-on-plastic vibe. Like Miucia Prada, she is using the '70s as a cue for the latest in street fashions; and what you can buy here at good prices today will be pret-a-porter six months later.

et cetera

Best outdoor wear: Nestled in the wilds of the East Village, **Upland Trading Company** *(236 E. 13th St., 212/673–4994)* gives New Yorkers an oddly right-on take on the outdoor experience. On a block that features derelicts, a Laundromat, and a low-grade delicatessen, Upland is a bastion of offbeat civility, where owner Armando Negron plays Davis and Coltrane records while you are initiated into classic outdoor apparel. Rather than the blinding colors and space-age fabrics of Patagonia and the North Face, you'll find canvas and bridle leather. Filson luggage and Barbour coats are the signature items, but there are plenty of alternatives, as well. And while you may not yet know that you need an oilskin coat with game pouch, a visit to Upland will convince you that the Teva crowd is out of its eco-friendly mind.

Best place to spoil your inner child: Tortured by what they did to G.I. Joe? Once upon a time, Joes were big and bearded. The mid-'70s demise of the toy serves as a poignant reminder of how damn much we lost in Vietnam. When Joe reappeared in the '80s, he was small and plastic, with high-tech weapons and no soul whatsoever: the perfect warrior for the Reagan era. A visit to **Love Saves the Day** *(119 Second Ave., 212/228–3802)* can erase some of the hurt over America's decline and your lost childhood. Yes, they do have Joes (they even have Joe's big Jeep). They also have Evel Knievel and a complete line of "Welcome Back, Kotter" dolls. *Star Wars* paraphernalia is everywhere, as is Beatles gear from *A Hard Day's Night* to *Yellow Submarine*.

Best demented giftshop: Everybody needs a place to go for rubber lobsters and voodoo dolls. **Little Rickie** *(49-1/2 First Ave., 212/505–6467)* is capably meeting these and other pressing demands. The store has blended the "cute" thing with the outright "warped" thing (and added a smattering of legitimate folk art) to create a wonderful novelty gift shop. The store's full line of Etch-a-Sketch products includes working wristwatch and key-chain versions as well as the much-loved original. The perfect place for meeting those difficult gift needs.

body alterations

Best piercing: Put it this way: The **Gauntlet** *(144 Fifth Ave., second floor, 212/229–0180)* ain't what your mom sees in her nightmares about your piercing experience. Founded in L.A. 21 years ago, the chain now includes stores in San Francisco and Paris. The New York location could be a holistic healer's office. Lavender and teal abound, as do moldings and beautiful hardwood floors. Glass cases display the store's own line of tasteful piercing jewelry, but just when one expects to hear Windham Hill on the stereo, there is Rick Rubin–era Johnny Cash to jar the New Age vibe. In back, myth debunking continues: The Gauntlet's leadership role in piercing advocacy and education is borne of its own high standards for safety and cleanliness. No piercing guns are used (they cannot be properly sterilized) and medical waste bins are ubiquitous. The store supplies a wide range of literature connecting piercing both to its ancient origins and to very contemporary notions of sexual exploration. In the '60s, they called it "hip capitalism." Whatever you call it, the Gauntlet's efficiency and professionalism deliver piercing from the realm of the scary into that of healthy exploration. It's the kind of place even a mother could love. Maybe.

Best total New York experience (with haircut): If, in Rod Stewart's words, "every picture tells a story," the window of **Astor Place Hairstylists** *(2 Astor Pl., 212/475–9854)* tells some stories that should probably be left alone. Documenting J.F.K. Jr.'s haircut may be appealing, but Sinbad's? Marky Mark's? Elliott Gould's? Hair? Even when pressed, manager "Big Mike" Saviello swears they're all "good guys." Really. Celebrity haircuts—both famous and infamous—aside, the hair factory at Astor Place should be experienced by anyone interested in American culture. Three immense floors hold warrens of battle-hardened barbers and hairdressers. On weekends, there are no fewer than 97 people taking shears to every kind of do imaginable. Cramped and chaotic, the place throbs with Latin, dance, and rap (music is supplied by a house DJ who sells tapes on the side). The haircutters alone speak 15 languages and display national flags from the four corners of the earth. Everything is basic, including the prices.

Best cosmetics store: In its airy SoHo home, **Mac** *(113 Spring St., 212/334–4641; also at 14 Christopher St., 212/243–4150)* manages to make buying cosmetics a total aesthetic experience. Every surface in the store is blond, scrubbed, and brushed. A series of sail-like white structures suspended from the ceiling evoke freshness and wind-blown purity. This Toronto-based chain has been booming since the late '80s, when Madonna's patronage became well-publicized, and yet it doesn't charge a fortune for its products. The difference between Mac and other high-end cosmetics firms? Think: Mac spokesperson RuPaul versus, say, Elizabeth Hurley.

Best rock 'n' roll haircutters: A visit to the **Mudhoney Salon** *(148 Sullivan St., 212/ 533–1160)* in SoHo offers a rare opportunity to consider the competing codes of rock 'n' roll and serious hair care. Great New York haircutters almost invariably trade in name-dropping, celebrity fawning, and delusions of grandeur. Though he may have struggled to conform, Mudhoney owner Michael Matula has resolved the contradiction thus: "Madison Avenue bitches should stay uptown because [here] they're going to get the Stooges really fucking loud." Michael isn't the least bit unfriendly—he's just not interested in catering to mindless trends or big egos. The result: Mudhoney's two faux leopard-skin chairs are perpetually filled with people who appreciate both Michael's brilliance and his refusal to take it all too seriously. The bonus? Besides doing what is widely regarded to be the best hair coloring in New York, he does play the Stooges (and the Velvets, Bowie, and the Stones) *really* loud.

hotels/motels

Best seen-better-days hotel: Burt Bacharach requests? Fond memories of the Brill Building? With a prime location on Manhattan's only private community park, the **Gramercy Park Hotel** *(2 Lexington Ave., 212/475–8000, 800/221–4083)* is misty, shabby, and downwardly chic. What you get in the dark lounge is not so much a Velvet Fog as a Velour Miasma. As such, the whole shabby thing feels like a throwback to an age before retro, to a day when Phil Spector was revolutionary and no one sung 'em like Nat King Cole. The single-room rate hovers around $80, making this one of the city's finest cheap deals. What do they serve to eat at the bar/lounge? Cocktail mix, baby.

Best boho hotel: The **Chelsea Hotel** *(222 W. 23rd St., 212/243–3700)* was the last stop for pickled Welshman Dylan Thomas, Nancy Spungen, and Beat father Herbert Hunke. It was a wild party zoo for Patti Smith and Jim Carroll. Other famous inhabitants of this actually quite scuzzy heap of red bricks and cast iron have included Bob Dylan and the painter Phillip Taaffe. As a tourist spot for the terminally hip, the Chelsea still draws crowds, if only to examine lobby art that includes an aluminum-can construct by a longtime resident. Starting at $99, the rooms are for the most part dark and creepy, though a few fortunate old-timers (and even some newcomers) possess rental apartments with coveted extras—like sunlight.

Best Parisian-style hotel rooms: The **Washington Square Hotel** *(103 Waverly Pl., 212/777–9515, 800/222–0418)* may have bad drapes, stiff sheets, depressing floral bedspreads, but it's clean as a whistle. Ideally located within a beer-bottle's toss of Washington Square Park and NYU, the hotel is a no-frills option for low-budget travelers. Rooms start at $85.

Best glam-rock hotel: Gotta hand it to hotelier Ian Schrager. The Philippe Starck–designed lobby at the **Paramount Hotel** *(235 W. 46th St., 212/764–5500, 800/225–7474)* evokes comparisons with long-departed regions of Manhattan style. At around $100 a night for a single, the Paramount is one of the city's best-kept budget secrets, featuring modest rooms, each with a Vermeer detail over the bed. Regular visitors include everyone from British philosophy editors to rock gods. And the bellhops? The mangement auditions each beefcake before oufitting him in drapey black suit and Hugo Boss haircut. The chicks who wait tables at the popular **Whiskey Bar** are a breed unto themselves as well, uniformly blank of expresion, and each looking as if her outfit was applied with a can of spray paint.

local wonders

Best boardwalk amusement park: Some people might call you crazy to head for **Coney Island** (take the D train to Brighton Beach) during the summer, when the stagnant Brooklyn beach gives off a fetid odor. Yes, the rusting hulk of the Parachute Drop once worked, and Nathan's Famous Hot Dog once was the best frank in town, and yes, times have changed (although it's still hard to quibble about Nathan's french fries). Summertime at Coney is now more about noise and Budweisers than fanciful afternoons by the urban seashore. Still, it's a fine way to kill a hot July evening. Excellent brick-oven pizza—some call it the city's best—can be had several blocks from the amusement park at **Totonno Pizzeria** *(1524 Neptune Ave., 718/372–8606)*, open Friday to Sunday only, and for $4, the creaky wood rollercoaster, the Cyclone, is a pure adrenaline rush, equal parts fear and exhilaration. Top it off with a boardwalk beer at one of the seedy open-air bars.

Best street basketball: Don't bring your sneakers to the **Cage** *(6th Avenue at West 4th St.)* unless you can play—really play, like college ball—and talk about it while you're doing it. The action in the tiny, cramped main court at West 4th Street in the Village is fast, furious, and high-intensity—the best free entertainment in New York. Its nationwide reputation as a street-ball proving ground draws many showboats to the court, but even when the games disintegrate into long conversations on etiquette, it's always fun to hang out and soak up the sidewalk atmosphere. As soon as the weather warms in spring, this is the place to go to while away free afternoons.

Best mechanical clock: A gallery inside the **Clock Tower** *(108 Leonard St., 212/233–1096)* near Chinatown has art shows, but the real lure of the building is the opportunity to stand inside New York's last remaining pendulum-operated clock. If you gather the nerve to climb the scary, steep spiral staircase, you'll see the four white clock faces from the inside; and the truly brave can even venture outdoors onto a small balcony. The clock's system of weights and gears is intricate and finely tuned—a last token of the Mechanical Age. A neat, offbeat day trip, open Thursday and Friday 4 to 10 and weekends 1 to 7.

Best cheap thrill: It's big, it's yellow, it does exactly one thing, it does it well, and it still costs only 50 cents to ride, one-way. The **Staten Island Ferry** *(departures from the Staten Island Ferry terminal every half hour between 9:30 A.M. and 4 P.M.)* offers a dazzling view of lower Manhattan, and the ride when the weather isn't cold can be romantic.

transmissions

Best dance tracks: The next best thing to actually being in a Brooklyn disco in Bay Ridge is **WKTU (103.5 FM)**. Puerto Rican drag queens, Brooklyn Trans-Am aficianados, and anybody else who likes to dance are the target audience. The playlists include disco-diva classics from the Studio 54 era, like Gloria Gaynor's "I Will Survive" and Donna Summer's "Hot Stuff." On Saturday nights, guest club DJs spin the steel wheels; and if you're up early weekday mornings and Howard Stern makes you cringe, try KTU's answer: Ru Paul (6 to 9 A.M.).

Best metal: Coming into New York faintly from across the Hudson is Seton Hall's "Pirate Radio," **WSOU (89.5 FM)**. Any time of day, any day of the week, it's metal. Death metal, speed metal, glam metal, metallic punk, just metal, you name it—they don't discriminate. The steady, pounding dirgelike onslaught that leaks from the swamps of Jersey inspires fear and pity—and in the end, it's sublime. Don't miss it.

Best tristate station: Too bad it's hard to get. New Jersey's **WFMU (91.1 FM)** offers a real alternative to mainstream modern rock stations. Sure, the DJs yak too much, and they yak about utter nonsense, but that's all just part of this upsized college radio station's charm. The DJ-customized programming has developed loyal, even obsessive, follow-ings, with jocks like the Hound spinning '60s-vintage surf-rock 45s on Saturday afternoons, and shows like Bill Kelly's Teenage Wasteland wringing arena-rock sentiments, as well as staunch opinions about Frank Sinatra, out of listeners.

Best monomaniacal jazz activist: Bud Collins, that tennis com-mentator who sends Wimbledon viewers into huffy panegyrics each spring, is irritating, but he knows everything about the sport. Phil Schaap, the bebop resource of **WKCR (89.9 FM)**, similarly knows all about Diz, Bird, Trane, Bags, and Miles, but for some reason provokes the ire of jazz junkies who prefer the slicker musings to be found on WBGO. But hey! The guy's a scholar. And don't forget, he broadcasts on the Columbia University station, so the frequent lectures shouldn't be surprising. Besides, he's the only DJ in jazz who is so devoted to Charlie Parker that he calls his 8:30 A.M. Monday-to-Friday show "Bird Flight."

portland

by William Abernathy

"Portland has the foxiest girls in the United States."
— Corin Tucker, *Sleater-Kinney*

Since it's impossible to describe Portland without addressing its Northwest rival, let's start with "The Seattle Question." In music, arts, and sports, Portland plays second fiddle to Seattle, and the folks who live here wouldn't have it any other way—it keeps out the bad element. Portland is not a suburb of Seattle, but is three hours away by car (excluding traffic jams in Seattle). Both cities have the same crummy weather, or at least the people in each complain about it as vigorously. But Seattle's coffee is a little blacker, its rents are a bit higher, and its cops are a lot meaner. Where Seattle has delusions of grandeur, Portland is just goofy. Where Seattle bands are ambitious, driven, and competitive, Portland acts are slack, fairly contented, and familial.

Getting a stage is almost too easy in Portland, and audiences are frequently more supportive than skeptical. Some have complained that the Portland scene is too insular and xenophobic. And it is, if you're out to make a quick buck. If you keep your word and return your favors, there is no more open community for the émigré. Being a small city, Portland is very much a handshake-deal town, especially in the music scene. If your word is only worth the contract it's printed on, then you won't find a colder place.

Fast-lane living just doesn't happen here. You want sushi at midnight? Suffer. You want to buy liquor in a grocery store? G'won back to Cali. You want your spiff new rock combo to get signed quick? Dream on. Portland has few amenities for would-be jet-setters. Whatever job you might get here will look crummy on paper, because you'll take home 20 percent less than you would elsewhere. So what does that pay cut buy you? *Nature.* And never you mind that it takes wheels, a tank of gas, and moxie to experience it; just having the hinterlands so close at hand makes people relax a bit. East Coasters and Californians have a hard time on the road here because Oregon drivers are maddeningly slow and polite. It's sort of like being beamed onto that "Star Trek" episode where the entire crew gets zapped by spores and turns into a bunch of space hippies.

But while the tidy orderly streets of Portland appear incapable of generating excitement for gritty modern edge-dwellers, the city can present a thrill or two. The music scene is alive and well, and has given birth to such indie successes as the Wipers (a band that one famous runty lad from Aberdeen, Washington, just couldn't get enough of when he was a kid), Poison Idea, Dead Moon (rock 'n' roll grandparents and the indie-est band known to humankind), Pond and Hazel (both survivors of Sub Pop's Portland band-buying spree of 1993), and Thirty-Ought-Six (who were just plain amazing). There's a thriving queercore scene here, with such luminaries as Team Dresch, Sleater-Kinney, Kaia, the Third Sex, and Heatmiser. And Portland has throughout the years served as a launchpad for such occasional gold and platinum projectiles as Quarterflash, Nu Shooz, Robert Cray, and (oh, yeah) Everclear.

There's a thriving blues scene here, if that's your pleasure, and without drawing too much attention to themselves, a small contingent of tremendous jazz players have made Portland their home. The city has a vital literary scene, its epicenter being Powell's (a bookstore the size of an entire city block which could distract you for a lifetime, see Shopping), and a happening poetry scene. "Legit" theater stalwarts pursue their craft here despite feeble audiences. While skateboarding remains a crime here, Portland makes up for it by having one of the world's best skate parks under the Burnside Bridge. Also home of more breweries than any other city in the world, this is microbrew mecca. And all of that beer's got to be going someplace.

lay of the land

Portland is an easy city to navigate. It's a big grid, divided into quadrants (there are five of them, okay, so it's *pretty* easy and streets are numbered out from the axes that divide the town. Burnside Boulevard divides the north and south, and the Willamette River (pronounced "wuh-LAM-met") divides the east side from the hilly west side. The "fifth quadrant," North Portland, lies between N. Williams Street and the east bank of the Willamette, which bends to the northwest until it meets the Columbia

River. Every address in Portland has a fairly obvious quadrant tag on it, which it would ill behoove you to ignore unless you like hunting for an address on the wrong side of the river. Most north-south thoroughfares are numbered avenues, while east-west streets are all named. Head far enough in any direction and you'll encounter suburbs, then farms, and, finally, stumps left over from the eruption of Mt. St. Helens.

Like Budapest, one side of the river is hilly, and the other's fairly flat. Downtown is on the west side, and as you head into the West Hills, it's money overlooking more money. Most of the nightclubs are downtown, in short Northwest (sometimes called "Old Town") and Southwest (just plain downtown)—meaning that all the clubs are within walking distance of each other. The queer bar scene is clustered along S.W. Stark Street, which has, with great originality, been dubbed (duh) "Vaseline Alley." Portland's hive of art galleries and expensive make-believe artists' lofts, the "Pearl District" or our FauxHo, is a little farther up in Northwest, from Ninth Ave. or so as far as the great trench of the Stadium Freeway (I-405). A high-dollar boutique district is a little farther northwest, on 21st and 23rd Avenues, where if you work bankers' hours, you can still get an almost-affordable studio apartment.

Grittier bohemes dwell "eastside," where honest workin' stiffs can still (just barely) buy a home, and house sharing for renters can be down-right cheap. There's a new-agey district on N.E. 28th Ave., the Lesbo-ghetto is on S.E. Hawthorne Boulevard, and new outcroppings of young-and-hip entrepreneurship are springing up on S.E. Belmont, S.E. Division, and S.E. Clinton Streets.

getting from a to b

In town, you can bicycle about fairly easily, so much so that Portland has been called the most bike-friendly city in America. Nevertheless, drivers are generally oblivious to bicycles, becoming polite only once they see you. If you have a car, parking is cheap and plentiful. If you're downtown for more than one hour but less than four during a work day, look for the Smart Park lots. The City Center Parking lots cost a lot more and their owners would probably bulldoze a church if it meant a new parking lot for this downtown monopoly. The Tri-Met bus system works great until midnight, and costs $1.05 to get you anyplace but the far burbs, which cost a little extra.

If you're jetting in on a budget, the #12 Sandy bus runs from the airport to downtown, and will save you a cab fare. Portland's Greyhound and Amtrak stations are clean, safe, and an easy walk or short bus hop from downtown. In the downtown area, called "fareless square," all buses are free. That's right! *Free!* We must be *crazy!* Don't expect to flag down a cab unless you're at the airport or in front of a hotel. The only two cab services worth a spit are **Radio Cab** *(503/227–1212)* and **Broadway Cab** *(503/227–1234)*. Your best bet is to phone, and quite a few bars have free "hotlines" direct to the cab companies.

sources

Willamette Week is the spot to go if you want to see the Baby Boom's best approximation of hip, complete with intelligible typesetting and actual proofreading. They do real news reporting and have a complete arts section. The paper has been a stepping stone for more than a few national talents, among them the late Randy Shilts and Oregon's secretary of state and gubernatorial heir apparent, Phil Keisling. This is the "establishment" alternative newspaper, along the lines of a *Village Voice* or *Bay Guardian*. The personal ads, toned town for the sake of good taste, are the established print-medium meat market for Portland. They're free and the paper's available just about everywhere.

Without a doubt, the rival *PDXS* is the most obnoxious—and, to some tastes, best—paper in town. In 1991 the Redden brothers, disgruntled *Willamette Week* employees, decided to quit and start their own rag for folks who were hacked off at what *PDXS* calls the "formerly alternative newsweekly." The newer paper is snide, catty, relishes taking the unpopular side of any issue, and is a great source to catch up on the latest way-out conspiracy theory. When an "Imperial Tombs of China" exhibit opened at the Portland Art Museum to deafening peals of praise from the mainstream media, the *PDXS* headline ran, "China Tomb Suckfest!" The *PDXS* personals section attracts the skankiest freaks in town, and the paper stays afloat on a diet of 1-976–WANK phone ads. It's biweekly and available in cool shops everywhere.

clubs

Best large hall: La Luna *(215 S.E. Ninth Ave., 503/241–LUNA)* is the longest-standing music venue in the inner east side industrial-residential zone. Formerly known as the Pine Street Theater, and before that as RCKNDY Portland, it's got a large unobstructed stage, good sound, and is a great spot for touring acts, such as the Butthole Surfers, Jon Spencer, or GWAR—acts big enough to easily draw a thousand people but not so huge as to pack a stadium. Frequently, popular local acts will play here, as well. Upstairs, there's a bar with a couple of pool tables and a video arcade complete with an air-hockey table.

Best small punk club (venerable): Founded in 1984, **Satyricon** *(125 N.W. Sixth Ave., 503/243–2380)* is the granddaddy of all Portland punk clubs, located on the north Bus Mall in beautiful Old Town. Name your favorite famous band, and if they started out small and DIY'd their way to fame, they came through here. Nirvana played one of its last small-venue shows here before being catapulted into the Rock Pantheon, New Year's Eve '90. And when Dave Grohl launched the Foo Fighters, this is where the band played its first billed gig. With live music seven nights a week, you can see anyone from obscure (and frequently bad) local bands to serious regional and national acts. Since Satyricon is a bar (and a hard-liquor bar at that), there's no all-ages activity here. The stage is small, with about a four-foot rise, and bleacher seating along the walls rings a weathered dance floor. The view is obstructed by a big pillar in the center of the floor, and if the act is likely to attract moshers, your best bet is to get in front of the pillar and to the left, because slam dancing is most likely to fire up to the front right. In 1995, Satyricon added **Fellini's**, a restaurant adjacent to the club (which enabled both to acquire a hard-to-get liquor license). Beware of the Jägermeister milk shakes.

Best small punk club (upstart): When **EJ's** *(2140 N.E. Sandy Blvd., 503/234–3535)* was younger, it was Portland's premier woman-run nude dancing establishment. But the city's glut of nudie bars cut into the profit margins enough that proprietrix Etta J. changed it into a live-music venue. A brass pole still stands in the seats as a reminder of the club's past. EJ's usually has live music seven nights a week, and has become an alternative to Satyricon for a new generation of Portland talent, bands like Iommi Stubbs, Heavy Johnson Trio, Gern Blanston, and the late, lamented Holgator. With a slightly harder musical edge and quite a bit less history than Satyricon, EJ's attracts a slightly younger crowd of drinking-age scenesters. The stage is low-slung, and the P.A. is kind of crappy, but the people are friendly, and there's a cheap beer spigot to augment the usual rack of microbrews. Hey, Etta knows how rough things can get.

Best hip-hop festival: Ugly fact—a couple of years back, an African-American bar owner was harassed into shutting down his tavern by zealous Oregon Liquor Control Commission agents, who alleged he was running a "disorderly establishment." Their proof? *There were rap tunes on the jukebox!* Given this regulatory climate and Portland's pallid demographic, it should come as no surprise that the hip-hop scene here is sorely lacking in venues. Once a year, though, the **PoHHop** festival rumbles into life for a two-night stand at La Luna. This Black Education Center fund-raiser always proves how much hip-hop talent there actually is in Portland. In '96, 26 crews, 40 MCs, and three bands got together and shook La Luna for two days straight, with (count 'em) *zero* instances of violence. Portland musicians Dave Parks and Steve Spyrit are the catalysts who bring it all together, and when these guys say "peace," they mean it. It happens one weekend out of every summer, and you'll have to keep an eye on the phone poles to learn the wherefores.

Best summer blowout: Almost every August, a bunch of bands get together under the west side of the Hawthorne Bridge and the blissfully anarchic leadership of Pond drummer Dave Triebwasser, and throw the best music festival in Portland, **AIMFest**. "AIM" stands for "Alternative Independent Music," and was first used back when "alternative" and "independent" still meant something. Oh, yeah, it's totally free—just show up. Buy a shirt if you've got the scratch. Enjoy the music. Don't talk shop. Local papers, telephone poles, and word of mouth are all good sources for more information; the Hawthorne Bridge is one of the major west side downtown bridges.

Best unplugged club: One of the more enduring spots on the Portland nightscape, the **Laurelthirst Tavern** *(2958 N.E. Glisan St., 503/232–1504)*, provides a stage for some of the most talented musicians in town, playing front-porch American country music. The funny thing is, a lot of the acoustic and folk acts that take the stage here are alt.rockers like Pete Krebs from Hazel, playing acoustic music "on the side" to get some chop time in with elder statesmen of the music scene, like Baby Gramps and Neil Gilpin. With no tubes to overdrive and no fuzz to hide behind, the quality of the musicianship has to be a lot better. Laurelthirst audiences are a lot more attentive and appreciative than rock-dive crowds; and better still, the record industry hasn't made it here yet. In other words, the musicians who play here are more interested in their *music* than getting laid and attracting labels. What a concept!

Best jazz jam: There's no shortage of seasoned jazz players in Portland, and there's also a host of young scrubs. You can catch them with their hair down and their shoes off at **Produce Row** *(204 S.E. Oak St., 503/232-8355)*. Pro Row is one of the oldest multitap taverns in town, and on Monday nights veteran drummer Ron Steen leads the Ron Steen Jam. As this occurs on the lamest of weeknights, half the audience are musicians waiting for their turn to show off their chops, and the other half are the sundry creative layabouts who don't mind waking up at 10 A.M. on a Tuesday morning. The atmosphere is totally casual and supportive. During the summer, the jam wanders out onto the large back deck, and the combination of warm outdoor seating, cool good beers, and scorching jazz serves as proof of a benevolent God.

Runner-up: At **Jazz De Opus** *(33 N.W. Second Ave., 503/222–6077)*, you'd best come to listen, because the regulars don't come to hear you yammer.

Best cocktail lounge: If you need an absurd drink while you watch a bunch of guys in matching sharkskin suits shredding their digits on heavy-gauge electric guitar strings, **The 1201** *(1201 S.W. 12th Ave., 503/225–1201)* is the spot for you. On weekend nights (which seem to include Thursdays here), you can hang out and watch live cocktail bands or surf acts. If you're a boy, wear a thin tie and chat with the pro-prietor about his days as a repo man. (When he says, "You ask a lot of questions," it's time for you to clam up.) If you're a girl, dust off those cat-eye frames, invest in some Aqua-Net, and see just what Mom went through to make those beehives stay upright. Whatever your sex, you should stay off the stool at the far right end of the bar—it belongs to Marianna, an old gal who's been drinking here since somewhere in the late '60s. If multiple changes of ownership, a gay strip club, two wars, and a cocktail resurgence haven't budged Marianna from that bar stool, then neither should you.

Best reggae: *Irie*, mon, and all that. The **Red Sea** *(318 S.W. Third Ave., 503/241–5450)* is an Ethiopian restaurant most of the week, but when the music plays on Thursday through Saturday (live at least one night), this is the place to go for reggae and worldbeat. You'll find about as multicultural an array of folks as Portland can muster here, from Ghanaians to stoned collegiate trust-afarians. During the summer, a small courtyard is opened up, providing a surprisingly nice outdoorsy feel to a place right in the heart of downtown. Best pickup line overheard at the Red Sea: "Heh, baby, I'm from Afreeka."

Best gay dance club: When it comes to queer dance floors, there's one club in Portland that has been around long enough to qualify as a landmark—the **Embers** *(110 N.W. Broadway, 503/222–3082)*. It's no longer the only big gay nightclub in town, but it does maintain a pleasant reputation as the Queer Old Dean of Portland's omnisexual hangouts. The place is plenty breeder-friendly, to the point that at times some of the regulars feel overrun. The drag stage remains one of the best budget camp trips in town, and one night with the Embers' in-your-face queens and transsexuals will make a proud straight man rethink his, er, trajectory. The disco remains one of the hottest floors in town, with boys and girls of all interests and persuasions convulsing to Satan's boogie beat until 4 A.M. on weekends.

bars

Best brewpubs: Portland has the great fortune of being a major grain port with very clean drinking water, close to the nation's premier hop-growing region. Consequently, there are more breweries (great and small) in Portland than in any other city in the world. Craft-brewed beers represent ten percent of the market in Oregon, and microbrewing's hold on the regional palate is so tenacious that even the scurviest dock-worker dives have at least one gourmet beer on tap. So, the question of where to go for a good beer is almost like asking what sort of atmosphere one likes. Nevertheless, it's always fun to check out what the breweries are up to, and the best way to experience new experimental beers is to visit the companies' brewpubs and tap rooms. The **Widmer Bros. Brewing Co.** *(955 N. Russell St., 503/281–3333)* maintains the Gasthaus on the premises of its substantial (too big to be called "micro" anymore) brewery. The atmosphere at this yearling pub is still a bit sterile, but it may loosen up a little in time. **Portland Brewing Co.** maintains two brewpubs, a German-themed hall at its big brewery *(2730 N.W. 31st Ave., 503/228–5269)* and an English-themed pub at its original brewery in the Pearl District *(1339 N.W. Flanders St., 503/222–5910)*. The latter is a better bet, having more of that "well-broken-in shoe" feel. The company's new brewmaster is shaking things up a little, and tries out a few new brews at its pubs every month. While the **Pilsner Room** *(0309 S.W. Montgomery, 503/220–1865)* is a bit toney and crawling with yuppies, it's cheek by jowl with **Full Sail**'s pilot brewery, the **Harborside** *(304 S. Montgomery, 503/220–1865)*. Consequently, it has first crack at the fruits of Full Sail's John Harris, one of the most innovative brewers in the state, and who masterminded the ubiquitous McMenamins Hammerhead ESB and most of Deschutes's brews (including Black Butte Porter) before he joined Full Sail.

Best microbrew pub: If true microbreweries are more to your liking, check out such cozy little brewpubs as the **Lucky Labrador** *(915 S.E. Hawthorne Blvd., 503/236–3555)*, the **Alameda Brewhouse** *(4765 N.E. Fremont St., 503/460–9025)*, the **Old Market Pub and Brewery** *(6959*

SW Garden Home Rd. 503/244–0450), or any of the numerous brew-pubs in the McMenamins chain, which has seven-barrel breweries set up all around the state.

Best invention since the VCR: It's a movie theater *and* it's a bar! The McMenamins have combined two of America's favorite diversions— beer and movies—at the **Bagdad** *(3702 S.E. Hawthorne Blvd., 503/230–0895)* and the **Mission** *(1624 N.W. Glisan St., 503/223–4031)*. These theater-cum-pubs charge only a buck admission for second-run features, and they don't force you to drink if you don't want to. When vis-itors hear about this nifty arrangement, their jaws drop in anticipation of nightly mayhem and rioting. But Portlanders can generally be trusted to get a little schwanamachered at a movie without carving their initials into either the seats or each other.

Best dark lounge hideout: Without a doubt, Portland's best gloomy lounge adjoins the restaurant known as (yes, really) **Hung Far Low** *(112 N.W. 4th Ave., 503/223–8686)*. The lounge is small, and you can barely make out the Buddha in the corner through the low light and the ciga-rette smoke. It's also conveniently located at the geographic midpoint of numerous downtown rock clubs. This is where Portland's rock scene goes to get sauced up on the cheap before and after their sets.

Best place where people know your name: Portland loves **Dots Cafe** *(2521 S.E. Clinton St., 503/235–0203)*, a fun little restaurant-cum-tavern on a hopping little strip of cafes and restaurants in Southeast. The decor is power-kitschy, with funky art on every wall and odd trinkets in every corner, including a small menagerie of sock monkeys. The food's pretty good, the micro beers are poured tall, and the Ranier pounders are cheap. The waitresses take no shit, and everybody is totally cool. It's no meat market—gals can have a relaxed night out with-out being routinely propositioned—and local musicians like to hang out here simply because the scene is so very low-key. It's the closest thing a Gen Xer will get to "Cheers."

Best Tiki lounge: Hands down, the **Alibi** *(4024 N. Interstate Blvd., 503/287–5335)* is the premier spot in Portland to recall your days at sea in the South Pacific, dropping anchor in exotic ports o' call, greeting friendly natives, and getting soused on fruity cocktails. The Alibi's casi-nolike marquee is totally epic, and the internal decor is full-on 3-D trop-ical. The drinks are okay, but the bartenders are a bit at sea when it comes to truly exotic drink requests—they usually have those little umbrellas handy, but they lack the log vessels and coconut-shell mugs. Hey, nobody's perfect.

Best Irish pub: If the only thing that will get you to release your steely grip from the throat of your Maggie Thatcher punching clown is a cool (but not cold) pint of Guinness, then **Biddy McGraw's** *(3518 S.W. Hawthorne Blvd., 503/233-1178)* is the Irish pub for you. There's well-poured Guinness on certified-by-Guinness nitrogen taps, peanut shells on the floor, and yes, the entire premises is a smoking zone. The walls are festooned with pictures of IRA stalwarts and unflattering depictions of "Bloody Maggie" Thatcher. The skinhead contingent, which arrives on many nights of the week, is largely well-behaved and anti-Nazi. The live Irish music can be top-notch. Just don't talk religion or politics, and everything will be just fine.

Best honest pint: "Real Ale" purists knock themselves out to make sure that a pint of beer measures a full British imperial pint. That's 19.2 American ounces, with room in the glass left over for a real head. Most places will pour you about 14.5 ounces of beer and 1.5 ounces of foam. But the **BridgePort Brewing Co.** *(1313 N.W. Marshall, 503/241-7179)* serves up full British imperial pints, and then some. BridgePort charges $2.85 for one of these monsters—not bad. Catch BridgePort on Tuesday evenings at 6 P.M., when it "unveils its firkins." This means you get to watch some lesser dignitary (usually someone BridgePort wants to sell on a wholesale account) tap into a small keg called a firkin. The beer that issues forth is a live-cultured "cask-conditioned" ale, which costs a little more but is utterly worth it.

Best Spanish Coffee: In every city, there is one drink all locals know not to trifle with. In Portland, that drink is the Spanish Coffee at **Huber's Cafe** *(411 S.W. Third Ave., 503/228-5686)*. The drink is made at your table, and the show alone is worth the price of the drink—sort of an alcoholic Benihana of Tokyo. To start with, lime and sugar are put on the rim, and then come the liquids: flaming 151, Kahlua, triple sec, and coffee. After the waiter pours the coffee, the dang thing's still on fire, so he has to douse it with whipped cream, and then top off the whole mess with a dash of nutmeg. The Spanish Coffee is known to be the preferred aphrodisiac of the Trail Blazers who frequent this, the oldest bar in Portland. Though Huber's is a classy joint, with stained glass on the ceiling, and enough clear wood in it to seem whittled from a single ancient stump, they don't mind if you come in in T-shirt and jeans. This *is* Portland, after all.

food/coffee

Best after-hours: When it gets really late the smart set can frequently be seen gnawin' on gator steaks at **Le Bistro Montage** *(301 S.E. Morrison St., 503/234–1324)*. By conventional measure, this nominally Cajun restaurant is a culinary chamber of horrors. It's located in an old flophouse under a Morrison Bridge on-ramp, the cook frequently appears to be falling out of his pants, the waitstaff moves at a deliberate pace, and the beer list consists of Rainier Red and Rainier Green. When you order an oyster shooter, your waiter will scream "ONE OYSTER SHOOTER!" at the top of his or her lungs. Yet, they pull it off: The cooking is good, cheap, served in generous portions, and you weren't in *that* much of a hurry when you came in at three in the morning anyway, now were you? They don't take credit cards or reservations (after all, they barely even take your order)—so when you show, be prepared with some cash or a checkbook, and don't be surprised if you have to wait some. That's just the way they do it.

Best vegetarian: The good news for herbivores is that Portland is a veggie-friendly town, so almost every restaurant has a vegetarian item or two on the menu. Some of the Asian places are still a bit unclear on the concept and will sneak chicken broth into veggie dishes every now and again, so it pays to ask. One place that knows the vegetarian ropes, however, is **Old Wives Tales** *(1300 E. Burnside St., 503/238–0470)*, which calls its cuisine "eclectic and multi-ethnic." It earns big p.c. points for having a children's play area that is *not* known for its extensive selection of war toys.

Runner-up: Veggie breakfasts are best at the **Paradox Palace Cafe** *(3439 S.E. Belmont St., 503/232–7508)*, a little hole-in-the-wall in the funky stretch of Belmont, good for a low-animal-content breakfast (chicken sausage and happy-chicken eggs are available).

Best barbecue: There is no better way to get your digits greasy than at **Tennessee Red's Bar-B-Que** *(2133 S.E. 11th Ave., 503/231–1710)*. The barbecue at this inner-Southeast storefront is sweet, tangy, falls off the bone, and is an excellent deal to boot. And Red, a former minor-league ballplayer, is not content to rest on his meat cred either, whipping up good greens, beans and rice, and cornbread to go along with the ribs, chicken, and sausages. Plus, Red's a fun guy (if you don't get him started on politics).

Best Ethiopian: So you think you like your food *hot*, do you? Well, mosey on down to **Jarra's Ethiopian Restaurant** *(1435 S.E. Hawthorne Blvd., 503/230–8990)*, and order up a piping hot plate of *Yebeug Wat* lamb, with sides of lentils, coleslaw, and cottage cheese, all which help cool the fires within. A spongy bed of *injara* bread doubles as your utensil. (Don't touch your face until you've washed your hands). Merely spicy dishes are also available for those in your dinner party with nothing to prove.

Best poetry cafe: Ground zero for Portland's poetry scene is **Cafe Lena** *(2239 S.E. Hawthorne Blvd., 503/238–7087)*. It serves odd dishes, coffee, beer, and vino, but the main attraction most nights of the week is the guy ranting in verse in the corner. Open-mike Tuesdays can sometimes feel like a trip to the nuthouse, while on other nights, you can see Portland's latest Great Slam Hope emitting a riveting torrent of verbiage. Either way, if you bring the right attitude, you'll have a good time.

shopping

records

Best rock paraphernalia: When two local rock shops, the Ooze and the Outer Limits combined, the **Ozone** *(1036 W. Burnside St., 503/226–0249 or 800/396–1975)* was born. The old proprietors still work hard at their indie emporium, and they have an excellent indie-rock, local, and alternative record selection, a friendly, knowledgeable staff of hipsters, and the best T-shirts of any record shop in town, including odd and rude designs that you formerly had to travel to San Francisco to buy. If you're into posters of Kurt or Courtney, you'll like their selection.

Best used discs: One of the major points of debarcation for Portland's trade in second-hand and promo records is **Django's** *(1111 S.W. Stark St., 503/227–4381)*. Sure, the proprietors can be hard-nosed, but that's why they've been in business since 1973 without any help from the majors. They will loosen up a little if you're trading rather than going for cash. In addition to having more (and far more interesting) discs than your average corporate "new records only" shop, Django's has the best poster selection in town. You want a Buster Keaton poster? Which one?

Best local acts: If you want to hear your friend's band, be it blues, rap, rock, reggae, or cocktail-lounge torch singing, **Locals Only Records** *(61 S.W. Second Ave., 503/227–5000)* is your best bet. These masters of consignment aren't picky about format, genre, or even quality: If it comes from Portland (or its outlying areas), the shop will stock it.

books

Best monster bookstore: Powell's Books *(1005 W. Burnside St., 503/228–4651)* is to bookstores what the Borg are to New Trek. It's a giant, and only getting larger. Its minions roam the country "assimilating" smaller bookstores. At this point, Powell's takes up an entire city block (not counting its technical bookstore, with another zillion titles, a block and a half away from the Mother Ship). If you want a book, Powell's will find it; if it's not in stock, it can usually be found for you. And if it can't be found, perhaps you should be talking to Sotheby's instead. If you can't find your twin-spirit flame in Metaphysics, Cooking, Poetry, Small Press, Sci-Fi, or Gay and Lesbian Lit, you can always head back to the **Anne Hughes Coffee Room** and strike up a conversation with someone over a cuppa Joe and your favorite periodical. The classic Portland pick-up line: "So, what have you been reading lately?"

Best alternative-press emporium: If you need to get hold of an obscure collection of saucy art photos, a Feral House release, some Molly Keily comics, or the newest edition of *Gun Fag Manifesto*, there's no better art, comic, zine, and highbrow smut shopping than **Reading Frenzy** *(921 S.W. Oak St., 503/274–1449)*. Well-read proprietrix Chloe Eudaly stocks more than 1,000 titles in this packed storefront around the corner from Powell's. If "they" don't, won't, or can't carry it, she wants it. "We don't carry SPIN," she says, admonishing not to call her store a "zine shop." Fun fact: Everybody in Portland of both major sexes has had a huge crush on Chloe at least once.

clothes

Best used-clothes boutique: As most boys know, thrift shopping is a terrifying experience, fraught with pitfalls and bad fits. **Retread Threads** *(2700 S.E. 26th Ave., 503/230–8042)* will take the edge off of your shopping with help that actually helps, bringing boutique-quality customer service to second-hand shopping. Proprietor Sarah Shaoul will fuss over you just as hard as she would over such celebrity thrift-shoppers as Michael

Stipe and Winona Ryder, both of whom, in fact, have power-shopped in this store. If you're bringing in your used clothes for barter, Sarah drives a hard bargain. But you'll no doubt find something you want to trade for.

Best junk shop with clothes: Larger, more established, and distinguished by the vintage funkiness that only an owner who survived the '60s can impart, **Avalon Antiques** *(318 S.W. 6th Ave., 503/224–7156)* is the anchor tenant of "Retro Row," a downtown plexus of odd antique, vintage, and collectible shops. Where Retread is small and strictly clothing-oriented, Avalon has good clothes and is great for vintage boy and girl accessories, like hip flasks, brooches, tortoiseshell combs, and pocket watches. The owner is a lot more vintage than the one at Retread's, as well, with a historian's sensibility and an eye for quality amidst the slag.

Best serious thrifting: For raw and unmediated thrifting, there's no better place than the **Goodwill** bins *(1943 S.E. Sixth Ave., 503/238–6165)*. God knows what will turn up here, but if you find a score in the bins, you can buy it with the rest of your junk, paid for *by the pound*. If you're diligent, have fast hands, and can ward off the ruthless gauntlet of sharp-eyed babushkas, you can land some outrageous items here—polyester monstrosities that are so out they're in, bell bottoms that only stopped being hip here the first time around about ten years ago. Invariably, when you see a tremendous sartorial display in Portland and find yourself asking, "Where?," the answer will be, "The bins."

Runner-up: A contingent of Portland thrifters swear by the bins at the more-monied suburban **Beaverton Goodwill** *(4700 S.W. Griffith Dr., 503/643–6099)*.

body alterations

Best tattoos: Most of the tattoo parlors in Portland are solid, reputable organizations. And just to make sure of it, there's now a law on the books, composed by tattooists, which ensures that any tattooist you visit will be sanitary, trained, and autoclave-equipped. Though it's hard to go wrong, you should definitely work with a classic, and Terry "International" Tweed of the **Deluxe Tattoo Parlor** *(8333 S.E. Powell Blvd., 503/774–8477)* gets the nod from tattoo artists and aficionados around town as the best old-school artist in Portland. He's a veteran of the classic American/Lyle Tuttle school, and specializes in broad-stroke work. Just remember: If it's good enough for a B-17's nose, it's good enough for your biceps.

Best place to get pierced: While the inked masses will debate the merits of local artists until they (and their tats) turn blue, everyone agrees that there's only one body-modification shop in town: **Attitudes** *(1017 S.W. Morrison St., 503/224–0050)*. Ahna Edwards opened this shop in '89, and she's been piercing since '84—yes, long before RE/Search put the primitive into modern. She's a grandma now, has a partner and an apprentice, and a shop that's one of the most respected in the industry. They make their own line of gold and surgical steel jewelry, and will cheerfully drive a sharp needle through any part of your body which can be safely and legally pierced (except the clitoris). Ahna spearheaded state legislation, passed in '96, that placed piercing under the jurisdiction of the same board that licenses and certifies tattoo artists.

Best barber shop: Admit it, boys, sometimes a man's gotta do what a man's gotta do, and that means a shave and a cut, a beer, a seegar, and a shoe shine. Well, Portland's got a place to satisfy all your he-manly hair-cuttin' needs, the **Old Portland Tonsorial Parlor** *(923 S.W. Washington St., 503/222–3717)*. There's no beating on drums here to heal your inner warrior, but there is a perfect pocket billiards table, a beer bar, and a big enough cigar selection to let you choose your poison in style. Located in the historic Pittock Block, it's the only barbershop/saloon combo in the state. It's 20 bucks for a cut, 15 for a shave, and 30 for the works. Hey, champ, you're *worth* it.

hotel/motel

Best cheap rock motel: While some of us dream of trashing four-star hotel rooms, most working musicians will gladly settle for a good night's sleep, with the assurance that their gear won't be kyped. And when musicians stay in Portland, the rock 'n' roll motel of choice is the **Portland Central ThriftLodge** *(949 E. Burnside St., 503/234–8411)*. It's cheap, clean, centrally located, and has a swimming pool. More important for rockers who stay here, it knows how to take care of bands, even running interference with pesky media types. Doubles start at $49.

Best low-budget bed: Portland's only AYH-affiliated youth hostel is the **Portland International Hostel** *(3031 S.E. Hawthorne Blvd., 503/236–3380)*. This hostel is strategically located across the street from an Asian grocery, about three blocks from Safeway, a couple of blocks from the Haight-ish shopping district on Hawthorne Boulevard, and right on a bus line (the #14), which runs straight into downtown Portland. As with all hostels, there's a midday slack period, when they kick you out into the world and catch up on the sleep they lost to that last batch of rowdy Australians. Because of this, call from 7:30 to 11:00 A.M. or after 6:00 P.M. to make reservations (VISA or MasterCard required). Reservations are advised year-round but essential during the summer months (June 16 to September 15), when it's so crowded that non-members of AYH/Youth Hostels International might be bumped. It's 13 bucks a night for members, and 16 bucks for nonmembers all year round.

Best cool old motel: If you're travelling on a greater-than-hostel budget, the **The Mallory Motor Hotel** *(729 S.W. 15th Ave., 503/223–6311 or 800/228–8657)* is a fave spot for out-of-towners who are in the know. A classy old building, it has some European-style shared washrooms, a knickknack shop on the ground floor, a good dining room known for Sunday brunch, and the coolest little lounge, called the Driftwood Room, on the main floor. While the big hotels along Sixth Ave. and Broadway will ding you 15 bucks a night for parking, the Mal has free parking for your chariot. On the west side light-rail route, it's an easy walk to downtown, and close enough to the Civic Stadium that you can get a contact-high when the Rockies (Portland's Class AA minor league baseball team) are playing. Queen-size rooms are 70 to 80 bucks a night, and suites with private baths go for $110. Brush with Greatness: Gregg Allman was once seen drinking at the Driftwood Room when he was on tour.

local wonders

Best skate park: Portland's crowning glory of hip is known simply as **Burnside**. It's likely the best skate park on the West Coast—and, therefore, in the world—a scattering of smooth mounds and depressions among the east side's warehouses, cobblestoned streets, and railroad tracks under the Burnside Bridge. It's been built totally by skaters, with their own time, energy, and money. It costs nothing to use, though some of the skaters will shake you down to pay for fresh concrete and upkeep. Strangely, City Hall has allowed the Burnside park to flourish on a city right-of-way. The park is world-class, with multiple verts and bowls, extra rails, bumps, dips—you name it.

Best natural-disaster area: If you've ever wanted to check out an H-bomb blast but were bothered by all that pesky nuclear fallout, the **Mt. St. Helens blast zone** presents you with your best non-radioactive alternative to the Club Med Bikini Atoll vacation. If you've got a summer day (the road isn't plowed in the winter) and a full tank of hydrocarbons to burn (it's about 130 or so road miles out of Portland), head north on I-5 into Washington until you get to U.S. Route 12, and then go east to Randle. From Randle, hang a right onto State Road 131 to the mountain. To say that it's an impressive sight is a bit of an understatement. When the top of the mountain blew off, it leveled every tree for miles around (most of these were pretty big trees, too), tearing them up by the roots or snapping them off like matchsticks. A few wadded-up cars have been left along the way, just to clue you in as to what a few megatons of explosive power can do. It's enough to put your band problems into perspective.

transmissions

Best college radio: KPSU (104.5 AM) is the only college station in Portland you can actually receive. By day, it's Benson High School's KBPS, featuring artists such as Raffi and Barney the Purple Dinosaur. From about five in the afternoon until midnight, it turns into KPSU, during which time you're likely to hear anything from Goth to techno, from cookie-cutter alternative to really old jazz and blues 78s.

Runner-up: Reed College's student outlet, **KRRC (104.1 FM)**, broadcasts at 10,000 milliwatts of dental-work-warping power, good enough to be heard as far away as five blocks from the Southeast Portland campus when the ionosphere lines up right.

providence

by Robert Reynolds

"Providence is one of the least likely places in America. It's all wrong and undiscovered."
— **Michael "The Millionaire" Cudahy,**
Combustible Edison Orchestra

Providence will forever be a minor American city, and it is all the better for it. In this twisted little town, Wrock and Wroll thrives alongside tales of lobster-eating mobsters and quiet streets, bargain basement smack bags, and idle teen gang gunplay. The capital of the union's smallest and strangest state, Providence is home to both more paranormal activity per capita than almost any other American city (second overall only to New Orleans) *and* to a mayor who also happens to be a convicted felon famous for his indictment for assault with a cigarette, an ashtray, and a fireplace log, as well as for his delicious marinara sauce. Satanic rites occur on the banks of the Seekonk River, witches fly overhead at twilight, and the undead open certain East Side doorways and glow…. Let us leave these treasures to the experts, of whom Providence has had no shortage. Edgar Allan Poe called it home away from home for a spell, and H. P. Lovecraft, author of super-fantastic specu-lative fiction, shelved his collection of occult books and esoteric knowledge here and feverishly wandered the nameless lanes of the East Side.

Don't count on the kindness of strangers in this city. Long-struggling, hatchet-faced brothers and sisters of Providence often glower rude and mean with sharp, witless, and wordless fuck-yous. Visitors won't feel that big-city "mean…but fair" shtick they might expect from a Chicago butcher or Brooklyn tough, and this gives Providence an edge. Add a limping service-based economy, tensions created by radical, lurking economic disparity, and a five-year urban-renewal blitz with no apparent industry to support it, and you get that go-for-broke feeling of a man deeply in debt, but ever the lucky fella, determined to have the good time he deserves.

Ambitious locals, jive-talking big-city expats, and apologists for obscurity might try to convince you that Providence is emerging as the next great arts mecca. Ethnic, racial, class, and artistic diversity offer many handles, many stories, and no single message. Like the best rock 'n' roll shows that take place in the eight or so clubs in town, Providence feels like a surprising find. Most important for so-called underground music, Rhode Island School of Design (RISD), Brown University, Providence College, Johnson and Wales College, nearby Southern Massachusetts University (SMU), and University of Rhode Island (URI) flush tens of thousands of kids out into the big world each year, only to be replaced by doe-eyed new meat with cash to burn each September. Some drop out, some move on, while those who stay enter the scavenger class and capitalize on Providence's relative obscurity and cavernous low-rent spaces (the loot from deceased textile, brewing, and jewelry industries), enjoying the shadows, clubs, bars, restaurants, and local oddities made possible by a massive transient student population.

No stranger to the underground, Mayor Vincent "Buddy" Cianci is quick to clown that the city doesn't just support the many clubs recently developed in the still spooky downtown arts district ..."we own them!" (Well, almost.) The awe-inspiring excesses of Buddy's first term as mayor of Providence—which led to a prison term—are lived down daily through his furious efforts to revitalize the city with projects such as granite- and marble-lined downtown canals, generous financial support for the public arts center AS220, and tax incentives that indirectly benefit more conventional venues like Lupo's Heartbreak Hotel, the Met Cafe, and the Strand Theatre (see Clubs). As one Providence impresario says of him: "Buddy loves this town!"

If you dig art but desire vice, Providence's unlikely but inspiring urban renewal need not strike fear in your pants: A nervy, druggie, rough and tumble cruising scene still blossoms in Downtown. Skin-mag shops, battery-op one-stops, peep booths, multiple erotic dancing bars, and the indelible trades that have Providence kickin' it with maximum scary flavor flower on. Just the same, it feels like the city is being set up for transformation down the road into one great big casino.

A more than marginal music scene has flourished in Providence since the death of arena rock, belching out a surprising number of good bands for a city of its size; and, as has always been the case in Providence, the number of phat bands far exceeds the audience to watch them. David Byrne and two of four Talking Heads were RISD artists manqué, only to become underground (then pop) superstars. Rubber Rodeo was an arty early-'80s country-and-western pastiche.

Recent Providence dropouts include Stax maniac Jon Spencer, who started his florid career by filming Julia Cappritz defecating in a blender for the Brown semiotics department, hit the harder stuff with Pussy Galore, and now throws down with the Blues Explosion. Cohorts Dig Dat Hole later became Cop Shoot Cop. Jon Moritsugu, maker of hilarious 16mm teen-gressive movies staged now-legendary train-tunnel pagan barbecue "Incest Fests" with players from these bands. More recently, John Davis of the Folk Implosion, and the mopey Will Oldham of Palace, have passed through. Not all rockers build up charge only to leave town, however. Though the world is a bit kinder with Belly no longer together, Tanya Donnely and rok goddess Gail Greenwood both live in the area. Providence seems to be a magnet for creative bands, the most interesting of which include Emergency Broadcast Network (EBN), Combustible Edison, Scarce, soda-fountain hipsters Velvet Crush, and appliance-wielding visionary rokbots Six Finger Satellite.

The scarcity of local labels, and the accessibility of Boston and New York, have made it necessary for Providence bands to look elsewhere for deals. One notable exception on the do-it-yourself front is Providence's deadpan boy-next-door, Ben Mckosker, whose emerging LOAD RECORDs ("a hot handful of fun") is recording totally interesting up-and-coming acts. Killer diverse compilations include bands like Thee Hydrogen Terrors, Arab On Radar, and the Royal Crowns, among others, who record at top-notch local studios the Parlour and Station 7. Meanwhile, Medicine Ball, the Laurels, and Mother Jefferson are each good and hardworking bands in search of an audience—just like the rest of us. Much respect to those bands practicing away in obscurity and purity. May they all explode.

lay of the land

Like a dog with six heads, Providence has different personalities in each of its neighborhoods and radically different faces at each of the exits off I-95 and I-195 (which branches east from Providence toward Newport). Rock clubs are generally within walking distance of **Downtown** near Kennedy Plaza, and the city's major arteries work away from Downtown like bent spokes of a warped wheel. Atwells Avenue leads west to **Federal Hill**, an Italian-American neighborhood, the site of great food shops and restaurants, the best tattoo artist in town, and the odd surgical supply store (latex gloves!). Follow Atwells further to **Olneyville**, site of alternative spaces and galleries such as the Renegade Gallery, Fort Thunder, Station 7 Recording Studio, and Mexico Restaurant. To the east of Downtown, College Street leads up the aptly named **College Hill** to RISD, Brown University, and East Side attractions, including **Thayer Street**, which is basically a student-oriented shopping mall with good record stores, skate marts, and food huts. Bordering the south side of College Hill is Wickenden Street, where a few restaurants, bars, and one hardware store cater to Brown and RISD runoff. Not just a fictitious city immortalized in salacious limericks, **Pawtucket** looms like a palsied northern cousin, just past the East Side, and is worth the trip if only to see a typical New England mill town; or stop by Korb's (see Dining) for a meat loaf sandwich, or the too-good Curtis Mayfield soundtrack at Luke's Record Exchange (see Shopping).

getting from a to b

Think of the city as two lungs separated by the polluted Providence River. Don't look for a grid; Providence rose in booms and busts, constantly recentering around different industries, first shipping, then textiles, jewelry, and brewing (Rhode Island is birthplace of the particularly hearty malt, Haffenreffer Private Stock, a.k.a. "Green Death"), the remnants of which can all be found in different areas. Combine this architectural hodgepodge with the meandering deep reaches of Narragansett Bay and the hilly terrain, and Providence can be one hard town to get around in. Within neighborhoods, there is order and there are direct streets, but try getting from the East Side across Downtown to Federal Hill? Fuhgeddaboudit! If you are planning to explore, no subways and limited bus service make a car essential, especially to access the deep recesses. You can walk from the Amtrak Station downtown to most of the music venues through the recently reconstructed waterfront park, and if you are patient, bus service is available.

sources

The *Providence Phoenix* is a good first stop for information on music events, radio, and arts in the area. (The *Phoenix* is free and can be picked up at cafes and stores all over town.) Extensive club listings and newsy left-of-center reportage will give you that "whichever way the wind blows" angle missed by the *Providence Journal* (called the ProJo). Personals include all manner of positions, including: "SWM, 35 well hung seeks stern woman to spank me for being a naughty little girl." Go grrrrrl!

Numerous local fanzines offer a sideways glance at other Providence scenes. Good local coverage makes *FourBall FanZine*, one of the better ways to find out what's going on; it has cool interviews with Providence punks like local supergroup Ashley Von Hurter and the Haters. *Wingnut* is among the most interesting zines: good writing, super-interesting topics and good graphix created by the frenetic creative wizard Wes Wallace. Interviews, descriptions of dreams, and cryptic remarks on Martin Heidegger add a look at another layer of local kult-ure. *Newspeak* and *Paranoia* are both conspiracy-theory zines published by local perp Joan D'Arc. They're politically suspect, but interesting just the same. *Japankore* has on-the-fly layout and good content provided by Brian of Dropdead, featuring reviews of Japanese hardcore releases, and funny interviews with Melt Banana. The best place to find these zines is at Fast Forward Records (see Shopping).

clubs

Best large rock room: Lupo's Heartbreak Hotel *(239 Westminster St., 401/272–5876)* books most tribes—everyone from Motorhead to the Boredoms. Have fun, but not too much … because the bouncers really are consistently unhelpful and occasionally antagonistic. Mind your words and watch your step. Once the lobby of a long-since defunct department store, Lupo's mammoth room fits as many as 1,500 panting fans. Like the late and much mourned Club Babyhead, good sight lines and a wide-open stage make it feel smaller and more intimate than it is. Superior sound, looming green decor, and a strange little balcony make this an interesting place to see (for example, one recent killer double bill) Jesus Lizard play with Providence's finest, Six Finger Satellite. Fronted by Cumberland fishmonger Jeremiah Ryan, Six Finger has devolved into the most tense and inspired sonic machine this side of Baden-Baden. They will punish you like bad orderlies in a psych ward. On the right night, Lupo's has an uncanny, out-of-time ambience that can't quite be placed. The groove changes nightly, and there's always pool. It also runs Thursday night dance parties where the small-town styling of local DJs packs the house.

Best horrible sound system: Right next door to Lupo's (and now owned by Rich Lupo), it booms and hisses, it buzzes and crackles, its head-high speakers will ruin your ears, it's the 400-person **Met Cafe** *(130 Union St., 401/861–2142)*. Just the sort of place to see smaller-drawing out-of-town bands and local artists, the Met Cafe is an old workers' beer hall with 20-foot ceilings and a stanky smell suggesting the good old days when patrons paid union dues and guzzled 25-cent drafts. A mural over the bar immortalizing movie idols and local personalities makes this the place to imagine dead rockers of Providence past while local menace Guy Benoit of Thee Hydrogen Terrors works his all-screwed-down dances and repetitious patter like a methamphetamized Pete Thomas.

Best grand old theater: Baby angels float across the gilded ceiling at the **Strand Theatre** *(79 Washington St., 401/272–0444)*, the venue with the best decor in town. Two blocks from Lupo's and the Met, this classic theater has been converted into a 3,500-person venue for the likes of Iggy, Ziggy, and Sonic Youth. Nick Cave would look right at home beneath the baroque excesses of this cool old hall's massive proscenium. Though seats were torn out, the balcony was left in place and carpeted benches installed, giving it that '70s-era Sodom and Gomorrah feel of a New York disco. Also houses a 200-person venue downstairs.

Best leopard-skin pillbox seat: Specious though it might be to call the **Green Room** *(145 Clifford St., 401/351–7665)* a club, this loft bar has live music, unconvincing '50s-style loungey furniture, and friendly vibes. The small performance area makes the otherwise horrible room worthwhile. Where else can you sit four feet away from bands like Purple Ivy Shadows playing dark and spacey instrumental music or kick back and enjoy the surfy garage rock of Providence historians, the Itchies. Mods and might-be yobs bob their heads to the Archies-style jangle of Honeybunch. If you get bored with the phony "Happy Days" atmosphere, sober up, and then lose your shirt to a 15-year-old pool shark with a wicked Rhode Island accent next door at **Snookers**. Located toward the waterfront, past Jerky's (see Bars), in what is referred to as the Jewelry District.

Best city juke joint: Diagonally across the street from the Green Room and two flights up the stairs from hell, the **Call** *(15 Elbow St., 401/421–7170)* is a basement room featuring blues, roots, and country music with occasional independently promoted shows by Totally Wired Productions (featuring artists like Bikini Kill, Guided by Voices, and Unwound). Leave your goat at home, sawdust ain't fer livestock, and this is a city blues bar; Huddie Ledbetter would be playing here if he weren't dead. Short on atmosphere, this place more than makes up for it by being loser-friendly.

Best utopian-culture bau: At first it seemed like an unlikely courtship of inconvenience, leading to a marriage of sheer will and suspect political motivations. However, **AS220** *(115 Empire St., 401/831–9327)* has emerged as a nearly unbelievable exemplar of community activism, jackass theatrics, and old-fashioned political cronyism. A renovated 22,000-square-foot condemned building, AS220 is the brainchild of a motley crew of several hundred volunteers, capital investors, original fluxus artist/community organizer Bert Crenca, and Mayor Buddy Cianci. With its collaborators, Perishable Theatre and Groundwerx Dance Company, AS220 is the apparent cornerstone of the madly developing arts and entertainment district in downtown Providence, offering nightly music and performance in a cafe with good espresso and cheap sandwiches, along with studio and rehearsal spaces, two galleries, a recording studio, and a darkroom. Past performers have included noise legends Red Bliss, deceased rockers Dungbeetle (for whom the present author played guitar), Diamanda Galas, Elliott Sharp, Caspar Brötzmann, and, most notably, the Tiki Wonder Hour, a campy musical extravaganza orchestrated by Combustible Edison bandleader Michael "The Millionaire" Cudahy.

Best public hideout: As good a place as any in Providence to chill out, the **Renegade Power Lounge** (*Atlantic Mills, 115 Manton St., 401/331–0877*) is housed in a spectacular and empty Olneyville textile mill. Neither club, bar, nor gallery, local weirdo guru Jim Draper's postindustrial space has elements of each, with frequent poster art exhibits by Koop, Robert Williams, Frank Kozik, and area artists Hidden Agenda Press and Matt Brinkman. Hard-luck DJs from the 'burbs throw down background tracks, offering the only quasi-trippy ambient lounge scene in the area, with many comfortable places to sit and babble as incoherently as you like. If you are hungry and feel lucky, you may be able to buy a cucumber sandwich at the bar.

Best suburban-basement noise scene: An example of the do-it-yourself aesthetic in its purest form, Rhode Island's own home-brewed noise scene grew out of the same thing that has inspired most great rock: creative kids getting organized to rage against the carceral nature of daily life. Stuck in the isolated suburb of Woonsocket in 1995, a bunch of teenagers were frustrated that their brand of madness wasn't being booked in Providence clubs. They realized the best place to throw down was in their own backyard (or basement, or living room). Revved up rehearsals soon took on lives of their own, and thirty or so legendary shows later, rok moms still haven't the slightest idea that 40 kids threw guitars and themselves around their family rooms or basements in bands named Bad Carma, Whisper a Threat, the Toss Offs, and Fess. The music was inspired by Japanese noisecore and bands like Rorschach and Neurosis.

Were it not for the intensity of the music, the size of the following, and the sheer isolation of Woonsocket, R.I., this would be an unremarkable scene; but, after all, though noisecore is not a crime, it might be soon. Though some insist that they stay pure, others have made the 25-minute drive down to Providence, and have made a name for themselves. The godfather of Woonsocket noise, Josh Gravel and his band Shot Gun Flu once played six songs in five minutes plus a coda that consisted of the band throwing amps and instruments at each other for an aching 30 minutes. "We got hurt," comments a taciturn Josh. Events have included a blistering six-band lineup for the Woonsocket Octoberfest and shows in VFW Halls and the Woonsocket Elks Lodge. Look for flyers on Thayer and Brook Streets. Remember: "There is no sweeter sound than that of a Marshall stack on 10 in a small carpeted living room."

bars

Best roost: Once an upstairs adjunct to Providence's top nightclub, **Jerky's** *(73 Richmond St., 401/421–1698)* is now all that remains of the sadly missed Club Babyhead. The wreck 'n' roll club that was the best place to see moshy, bouncy heavy music (rap and punk) is a now a commercial disco, but you can still visit Jerky's upstairs. Thanks to loco hero and owner Jeff Ward and his dog, Jerky (breed: "jerkasaurus"), those kids who used to mosh downstairs in the black box of Babyhead can now drink beer, nosh burgers and dogs from the grill (winter only), and enjoy the jukebox—filled with many of the artists who played such great shows downstairs. Occasional small live gigs have included Jewel. The martyred Saint Cobain, Vedder, Melvins, Rollins, Fugazi, and attorneys-at-law have all hung out in this hallowed club, so be insolent, and have the good time you deserve.

Best place to hear a stranger's life story: Day or night, it is always cocktail time in the dimly lit **Safari Lounge** *(10 Union St., near Weybosset St., no phone)* a perfectly reasonable place in which to drink yourself into a low-key stupor, a dollar draft at a time. In this hidden Downtown hooch house, a horseshoe-shaped bar will remind you that you need more than luck in this life. Hustlers, kind but sad people, and the clinically insane seem to congregate here. The fluorescent uplighting almost makes it tolerable that Bill Withers was taken out of the jukebox five years ago.

Best boxing club: Though the original owner of this bar passed away in 1995, **Babe's** *(Wickenden St., no phone)* is a perfectly preserved little beer room on the eastern edge of the East Side. Just up the street from a jumble of restaurants, natural food shops, and coffeehouses, Babe's borders on being a locals-only club. Beautiful pictures of the great boxers of Providence, and knowledge of the fact that boxing matches were held right there in the intimate 400-square foot room (through the '70s), make it worth the stop.

Best creepy rockers: Wake up motherfuckers, it's recovery time! **One Up** (3 Steeple St., Second fl., 401/272–3620) is where tough guys and the men and women who might have crushes on them hang out. If it were 1987, Ratt would be on the jukebox, and flowing hair and stretch jeans would be in effect … but hey, Phil Anselmo has gone authentic. Now he's just keepin' it real like the rest of us. Just the same, the vibes in this place are strange. Dig Pantera on the jukebox, $3 Rocks, and pool. In the same building as **Fast Forward** (see Shopping), on the border of downtown Providence and the East Side.

Best man-to-man conversations: Women are also welcome at **69 Union Street Station** (69 Union St., 401/331–2291), one of eight gay bars in downtown Providence, is perhaps the most easygoing neighborhood gay bar in Providence. Funny lo-tech videos flicker away on monitors, illuminating the hard drinking and scoping taking place seven nights a week. A small stage comes alive each Tuesday in this dark club, as local brawn work it out for the ongoing Mr. Ocean State Leather Competition.

food/coffee

Best spooky all-night diner: Tell 'em Big Red and the Phantom 409 just dropped you not a block away, and patrons and wait staff alike won't bat an eyelash. Happens once a week at **Joanne's Silver Top** (13 Harris Ave., 401/272–2890). This American diner sits like a fossil of a lost era, in a completely desolate post-industrial triangle adjacent to Providence's vegetable and flower market. Open only late at night, produce truckers waiting for loads and rockers on the lam are the most steady clients. Vegans be warned! Though one door down from thousands of pounds of the freshest and finest legumes in the city, the only vegetal matter on the menu board of this Formica and chrome-clad Pullman car is French fries, though you might petition for a green leaf of lettuce on your burger. Prepare your arsenal of comebacks to insults from the jeering waitress. Not recommended for sensitive people, nor for those with a weak stomach, but, nonetheless, absolutely recommended. Look for this diner in Doug Allen's syndicated *Stephen* comix.

Best veal and peppers: Angelo's Civita Farnese Restaurant *(141 Atwells Ave., 401/621–8171)* is a Federal Hill institution, serving delicious pasta with simple marinara sauce and nightly specials. The photographs on the wall attest to its legacy: Dom DeLuise, Don Knotts, Joey Heatherton, Ernest Borgnine, 20 Italian matinee idols who you might not recognize, and local mama's boy and newscaster Walter Cryan have all been guests. Sit at the large communal enameled tables, elbow to elbow with local families and students, and find out why inexpensive carafes of Chianti and inattention to overrated qualities like intimate lighting and cozy atmosphere make this a ruling, inexpensive place to eat. Many alleged mobsters were slain here in a gangland-style execution some years ago—the restaurant has since been remodeled. Many (happier) customers swear by the veal and peppers ($4.85), though the eggplant parmigiana ($3.55) and fried smelts ($2.95) are very good. The blinding fluorescent lights give it a memorable glow.

Runner-up: **Mike's** *(9170 Randall St., Cranston, 401/946–5320)* can be found five nights a week at the TaborFranchie Post of the Veterans of Foreign Wars located in Cranston. Mike was well known for his creamy polenta in the Knightsville section of Cranston, and the director of the VFW hall hired him to be resident chef. On weekends, Mike's becomes a huge family-style restaurant, and, if the truth be known, it serves the best creamy polenta in the world and should not be missed. Also of note: *rabes* and stuffed artichokes. Call for directions (it's extremely difficult to find) and to confirm whether it's open or not (lest you get stuck, hungry, playing bingo.) Open Mondays, Wednesdays through Saturdays (lunch: 1:30 to 3 P.M.; dinner: 5 to 8:30 P.M.).

Best summer meal: Fresh vegetables and good, light sauces make the Cambodian fare at **Apsara** *(716 Public St., 401/785–1490)* one of the best and least expensive meals in town. For a meal you construct on the spot, try one of the beef dishes served on a bed of lettuce, with cilantro and mint. *Nime chao* (summer rolls with shrimp) and *nime nheung* (grilled chicken with lettuce, rice noodle, mint, and sprouts) are the best choices on the menu. Two can eat like swine for $10, 20 can eat like horses for $100.

Best meatless meal: In a city where Italian sausages dangle in Federal Hill deli windows and menacing chorizo is on every Portuguese butcher's rack, vegetarian restaurants are few and far between. **Garden Grill** *(727 East Ave., 401/726–2826)* is the only vegan joint in town, and it is barely in town at that. It sits on the Providence/Pawtucket line (diagonally across the street from the front portal to the Swan Point Cemetery). Healthy sweet potato pie and the house specialty Boca Burger are at the core of the 87 percent vegan menu. The healthy clientele here does not mind that most people in Providence would prefer two dogs all the way. The Grill has original art, a post-hippie handpainted menu, and full juice bar.

Wurst of Providence: When starving in Providence after the witching hour, **Haven Brothers** *(City Hall Plaza, 401/861–7777)* is one of your only options for hot food. An ignominious Providence institution, this chrome-plated truck mysteriously appears in Downtown sometime before dusk, and throughout the night dredges the city of hungry bottom feeders from every possible class. Whether it's leather-clad bikers pining for the spring's first kill, drunk and angry URI kids in a Mustang, or perplexed Brown semiotics students in white robes, the crowd is always edgy inside the truck. But the burgers, dogs, and fries deliver. Say two dogs all the way, or, if you are with a crowd, order twelve up-the-arm and the wurstelman running the grill will think you have lived here all your life. Just don't look horrified when you see what you get. All the sodium nitrite you can eat for under $2.

Best Mexican: In Olneyville, **Mexico Restaurant** *(964 Atwells Ave., 401/331–4985)*, serves the best-tasting meal that tastes back: *lengua* (that's cow tongue). If you prefer shredded goat, order the *barbacoa*. It's great food, low prices, and authentic Mexican cooking with delicious fatty sauces and good simple tacos. Hearty, if you like hearty, and the people who run it are extremely nice.

Runner-up: **Taco Mexico** *(250 Brook St., 401/521–7191)* is more nouveau, but also good, especially if you must have a burrito and are trapped on the East Side.

Best pizza: At **Fellini's Pizzeria** *(166 Wickenden St., 401/751–6737)*, "the secret is in the crust." No really, it is—the crust is razor-thin, the sauce delicious. The pizza really *is* good, but when Diana Ross came here she ate the muffaletta sandwich. Fellini's also has a cafe in the back serving cannoli, coffee, and ice cream; it is a friendly place and encourages its clients to loiter, offering games to play and magazines to read. During warm weather, the tables out front are a good perch.

Runner-up: Across town on Federal Hill, **Casserta Pizzeria** *(121 Spruce St., 401/272–3618)* serves mammoth rectangular pies with thick, doughy crusts to big sit-down crowds, making it pretty much the opposite of Fellini's; but the pizza is tasty and considered among the best in the area. The secret, it too says, is in the crust.

Best meat loaf sandwich: Korb's Bakery *(540 Pawtucket Ave., Pawtucket, 401/726-4422)* is a bakery with a nice kosher deli. If you are headed to Pawtucket to hit Luke's Record Exchange (see Shopping), or are hightailing it for the highway and need to eat meat, you must stop. Order it with ketchup.

Best grinders: OUR HANDS ARE IN YOUR FOOD! So the sign reads, and it is true, each sandwich at **Geoff's** *(163 Benefit St., 401/751–2248)* is assembled with mirth by the paint-spattered hands and nimble fingers of cheeky Brown and RISD students. Geoff's is covered in a panoply of funny cartoons, making it the post–*Freak Brothers* 'Pistine Chapel of delis. Sandwiches are built to the specs of very demanding Epicureans and gluttons alike, and have funny, appropriate, and disgusting names. Consider the Elvis Presley: crushed banana and peanut butter grilled in one pound of oleo margarine. Then there's the Hammy Davis Junior, the Pearl Bailey, the Buddy Cianci, or have it your way and special order whatever your heart desires. Knock yourself out on free dill pickles from a barrel by the front door while-u-wait.

Best place to black out on neurotransmitters: Who wants to get wired? The owners of **Coffee Exchange** *(207 Wickenden St., 401/273-1198)* have built a great business on the ashes of the industrial revolution. Now that people work in small or home offices and generally have more leisure time than in the 1800s, the very coffee brought in from Sumatra, Nicaragua, and points south to increase productivity now enhances leisure time. People formerly pressing widgets in the factory 18 hours a day today freely scribble wild stream-of-consciousness prose-poems at the crowded tables in this cozy coffeehouse. From sunrise well into the night, the coffee is extremely fresh, the house special Narragansett blend is great, and people are unnervingly alert.

shopping

records

Best hard-to-find tracks: Providence is unusual in its wide selection of used and new vinyl, and **Fast Forward** *(5 Steeple St., 401/272–8866)* should be your first stop for new, hard-to-find, and off-the-grid CDs and vinyl. Run by Ron Marinick and Judy Holmes, it's one of the few places in Providence that offers ambient and trance electronic music and the only place that deals in black metal and grind-, speed-, or deathcores with any depth. Fast Forward is also home to Judy's mail-order business, **Consume, Be Silent, Die**, which deals in domestic and import grindcore, Blak and Deth Metal, and general mayhem. Her growing catalog features titles from Amen to Zionide. The CDs, LPs, and 7-inches are also available at the storefront, a nice place to sit and enjoy the good graces of Ron and Judy, check out some local fanzines, and play with the dog.

Best sugar pop: Part of a several-store retail chain, **In Your Ear** *(286 Thayer St., 401/861–1515)* has a nice big room full of music, mags, and rock ephemera, making it the cornerstone of Thayer Street music shopping for some. Good songs play on the hi-fi, and there are thousands of CDs, new and used records, and zines to fondle, as well as the odd collector's disk. Doc Pomus's credo "Never Hip a Square!" is in full effect at this store, and the workers here are hip. (Guess what that makes you.) But they are also nice on a good day, and know a lot about music, so don't hesitate to ask a stupid question, because you can never know enough about rekkids. Pick up titles from Boss Fuel, Velvet Crush, the Royal Crowns, or Medicine Ball, and guess who to pester for an autograph … they all work here, and they will all give you a hard time for asking, square.

Best selection of local seven-inch records: Right next door to a terrifically bad taco stand is the ever-interesting **Tom's Tracks** *(281 Thayer St., 401/274–0820)*, run by the stern, but just, Tom Tracks. A good selection of local bands and soon-to-be national artists makes this the third important stop for any Providence record orgy—plus, Tom can happily special order titles for you. This time ask for any Sourpuss, Lazy Eye, or Mother Jefferson—they clerk here. Mother Jefferson has a great '60s Texas garage sound, and at their best are comparable to the Sonics. Don't know who the Sonics are? You have come to the right store. Ask at the counter, and one of the nice clerks will show you to the section where you will find three Sonics titles. Try *Maintaining My Cool* in glorious mono, with a smokin' version of "Psycho" for $12.95.

Worst record store for compulsive shoppers: Luckily **Luke's Record Exchange** *(393 Broadway, Pawtucket, 401/725-7156)* is in Pawtucket, hard to find, and out of the way. Great cutout bins, low prices, and zillions of out-of-print LPs make this a must-stop for the vinyl fetishist. Some recent finds: an unscathed copy of Neil Young's oddball masterwork *Hawks and Doves* ($4.99); a ragged copy of the legendary compilation *This Is Boston not L.A.!* ($8.00); and Ezzio Pinza's *You Do Strange Things to Me* ($1.00). Not convinced? How about a pristine copy of the theramin-infused *Pet Sounds* ($15.00), or *Gettin Off* ($8.99) by genius of relentless arch disco, Hamilton Bohannon? *Journey Through the Secret Life of Plants* by Stevie Wonder for $5.00!?

books

Best dog-eared books: Right in the heart of downtown, **Cellar Stories Books** *(190 Mathewson St., 401/521–2655)* is filled with surprises, a musty, expansive shop. From *Moby Dick* to *Dirty Dick's Cocktail Book*, owner Michael Chandly has built an extensive collection of used printed matter from what began 20 years ago as a swelling private bookshelf and lending library for friends. This author found a reprint of *Houdini* by Harry Houdini (ghostwritten by Providence's own H. P. Lovecraft) for $20, and a well-loved copy of Greil Marcus's *In the Fascist Bathroom* for $8.50.

Best gift shop for the unenlightened fascist: You won't be a dummy forever if you start shopping now at the **College Hill Bookstore** *(252 Thayer St., 401/751–6404)*, a semiprogressive book store that does a huge business off textbook sales to Brown students. It tends to the left of center, addressing the queer of gender. It has essential stocking stuffers for the unenlightened: Capitalist pig? *What Is to Be Done?* by Vladimir Lenin. Sexist? *This Body Which Is Not One* by Luce Irrigaray. Antisemite or racist? *Race Matters* by Cornel West. Also a must for that potential reactionary who might be enlightened by the *Prison Notebooks* of Antonio Gramsci or Che Guevara's ride to political activism and revolutionary struggle, *The Motorcycle Diaries of Che Guevara*.

clothing

Best expensive junky clothing: Two stores in the same Thayer Street building near Brown University cater to today's slumming yet fashion-alert children. Though the clothing at **Thayer Street Subterraneans** *(287 Thayer St., 401/274–1484)* all looks pretty much like standard-issue boojy white-trash cast-offs, if you buy it a few sizes too small you might look like an East German kid in the '70s, which, after the ROTC look, is the totally happening style right now. Adidas warm-up jackets ($40), Nordic-looking ski sweaters ($40–$50), and black leather car coats ($40–$120) make the subculture seem kind of expensive these days. Across the hall at **Yellow Submarine Designs/Foreign Affair European Clothing** *(287 Thayer St., 401/274–1484)*, you'll find pretty much the same sort of stuff, except that it is not as well sifted. Hard to say why it is called "European Clothing," except that in a weird way it has captured that European passion for worn-out American clothes from '78 to '80.

Best rockwear: In the days of anything goes, the rocker of tomorrow buys yesterday's clothes at stone-age prices. And where better than the **Salvation Army** *(201 Pitman St., 401/421–5270)*. Shopping list: one blue crash helmet with bubble visor, one black vinyl pullout couch, one broken juicer, one Morris Day and the Time record, two pair Levi's corduroys, one Van Halen T-shirt (OU812 Tour!). Total: $15. That's not a look, it's a lifestyle.

Deepest style for fashion giants: Are you man enough? **Morris Clothes Shop** *(101 Richmond St., 401/421–1290)* next to Jerky's (see Bars) is definitely the coolest clothes shop in town, with totally fly browns, baby blues, yellows, and oranges in fabrics that don't wrinkle. It sells crazy dope '70s cuts, tailor on premises. Outtasight. Keeping it real with Sta-Prest and Sansabelt.

et cetera

Best flea market: Weekends are really the best time to shop for anything in Providence thanks to the flea market, where people dump their unwanted and misbegotten objects on the world at low prices. The **Olneyville flea market** *(585 Atwells Ave.–75 Eagle St., no phone)* is open on Saturdays and Sundays, and is filled with a truly nerve-racking array of tchotchkes with virtually no exchange value. Loved to death or just plain chewed up, the stuff in this junk-mart has hit the end of the line. Most of these objects will not even make so much as a blip on the radar of human desire in this universe, ever again. So be warned: If objects of this sort fill you with sadness or anxiety, stay at home. If you are brave, callous, or just need some vinyl boots, come here.

body alterations

Best tattoos anywhere: There are several tattoo joints on Atwells Avenue, but **Modern Primitives** *(148 Atwells Ave., 401/861–1338)* is the top choice. Thanks to blue laws in Massachusetts and tattoo prohibitions in New York City, Providence has long been a place to get that rendering of a giant squid attacking a whale on your butt cheeks, a scary clown on your arm, or for the real killer, a tattooed tear on your cheek. Now that tattoos have become the brute chic of an aspiring underground, certain artists have taken traditional designs and rendered them as they have never been seen before. Vibrant colors, super-intense shading, and intricate, precise patterns are all within the range of Modern Primitives resident Paul Slifer, who is fast becoming one of the best dye men in the states.

Best candidate to pierce your perineum: "We're not underground anymore!" boasts super-friendly skater Dede. In fact, she points out, "I don't even wear most of my visible piercing anymore, and we dress really square now that *they* have adopted our styles." As always with fashion, so it goes, it's them, they, those people who have co-opted real underground style—squares. Well, if it could be adopted so easily, maybe it wasn't so tough to begin with…. At **Luna Sea** *(286 Thayer St., 401/272–5862)*, the town's top skate and sneaker shop, yes, you can get pierced; the poser kids in town have a good source for Vans and nose rings, while the *real* skaters look like ROTC candidates, or *cholos*, or snowboarders. Actually, as Dede points out, one might be surprised who has piercings, and where they have them. (Across the hall from In Your Ear, see above.)

hotel/motel

Best out-of-town no-tel: Watch yourself sleep! Just across the Massachusetts border on the way to Fall River, the **Shangri-La Motel** *(1495 Fall River Ave., Rte. 6 East, Seekonk, MA, 508/336–8540)* features mirrored canopy beds, color TVs, AM/FM radios, free in-room movies, and WATERBEDS! Five miles from Providence, via the I-195, it's very cheap, and no one will know your name. Wear a false beard and mirrored sunglasses for extra stealth. It's $25 plus tax per night; $32 plus tax per night for WATERBEDS!

Best Downtown digs: Where did Sammy Davis Jr. stay in Providence? The **Providence Biltmore** *(Kennedy Plaza, 401/421–0700)*.

Which hotel has a gilded lobby and a strange, lingering smell of lemons? You got it, the Biltmore, the deee-lux accommodations (from $99 to $1,200 a night) in the heart of Downtown. Outdone by the new competition from the Westin Hotel a few blocks away, this joint is less expensive than it once was. Still, it's a neat old building. Even if you don't stay here, drop by to ride the glass elevator for a truly banal Providence experience.

Best cheap bed downtown: In the rectory of what was once a Downtown church, the **Sportsmen's Inn** *(122 Fountain St., 401/751–1143)* has rooms for $39.95 a night and up (free movies), with crazed erotic dancing going 20 hours a day in the bar downstairs. That pulsing sound coming from the jukebox? Jethro Tull. Have you ever seen an erotic dancer gyrate to "Aqualung"?

local wonders

Best tour of the hidden monuments of Providence: If you spend a few nights in Providence, you might pick up on the uncanny feeling that haunted prodigal son H. P. Lovecraft and famous visitor Edgar Allan Poe. In 1848, Poe came to Providence and fell madly in love with a much younger transcendentalist poet named Sarah Whitman. The author of *The Fall of the House of Usher* stayed in a resident hotel downtown off and on for two years, drinking himself into a stupor regularly; and though Whitman feigned interest in his overtures, she confessed in her journal great relief when he finally beat it. Visiting the favorite haunts of Poe and Lovecraft will take you on a good tour of the East Side. Begin at **Whitman's home**, *(88 Benefit St.)* near Charlesfield, just down the street from the RISD campus. As the story goes, Poe spent several nights lurking outside this typical mid-19th-century bourgeois home, crying out into the night. To his dismay, Whitman saw only "darkness and despair" in his eyes. Continue walking up Benefit Street to the home of **Ellias Whipple** *(No. 144)*, a character in Lovecraft's short story "Shunned House." Lovecraft was obsessed with esoteric knowledge and the occult. He dabbled in astronomy and translated a version of the dread *Necronomicon*. Though all of his residences were either condemned or demolished (no one has a good explanation for this), the narrow, nameless streets and alleys of the East Side were his turf, and, as you walk down Benefit Street toward the St. John's Church Cemetery (where Poe and Whitman courted), you might understand why it was an inspiring setting for him. Stop at 161 Benefit Street and bear left, climb the hill to Prospect Street, bear left again, and go to **Prospect Park**. A gigantic hidden statue of libertarian hero and Providence founder, Roger Williams, is frozen in a pose that looks like any great dance of the ages, the Twist, the Mashed Potato, the Shag, the Hustle, the Macarena. From the hillside there is a great view of the towers of Downtown Providence and beautiful sunsets.

Best tour, part 2: A separate tour begins several miles north of the East Side campus area on Hope Street. Use wheels if you have them; bear right on Observatory Lane next to 475 Hope. The **Ladd Observatory** is the sight of an early solar clock, probably a great source of inspiration to Lovecraft, who had full access. Continue down Hope to **Swan Point Cemetery** (Hope and Blackstone streets). Adjacent to Dunkin' Donuts sits a vacant lot where Lovecraft's house was demolished. Local folklore says that cars left after sundown will be burned by Satan's mortal helpers, who run wild in the cemetery at night. Enter the main gates; Lovecraft is buried here—you must find the small headstone on your own. (Hint: Lovecraft pilgrims leave offerings graveside.) A romantic date will end in the rear of the cemetery on the banks of the **Seekonk River** ... look for traces of ritual sacrifice.

Best adrenaline rush for five bucks: Grassroots auto racing will invigorate the soul. On summertime Saturday evenings, total mayhem erupts at the **Seekonk Speedway** *(1710 Seekonk Ave., Seekonk, MA, 508/336–8488)*, on an oval track built behind a chicken ranch in 1946. Proximity to the cars and the low-budget, pedal-to-the-metal/balls-to-the-wall approach of the worst drivers add an unpredictable element to the action. Headbangers will delight in the monthly 100 Car Demolition Derby. You'll tear at your own flesh during Figure Eight Races, and may run out to the parking lot for the family wagon to participate in Spectator Drags. Fourteen-time Class-1 oval-track champion Bobby Le Clerc shared his secret for success at Seekonk in a recent interview: "Go out there and drive like ten motherfuckers." Outtasight, man. Catch "Speedtalk" on WALE (990 AM) starting in April.

transmissions

Best independent radio: WSMU (91.1 FM) has good college radio broadcasting from the coolest-looking college campus on this earth, Southeastern Massachusetts University. Daily programming includes the standard palate of national 45s, hard-to-get and difficult-to-hear demos, as well as admirable commitment to local heroes such as Arab on Radar, Thee Hydrogen Terrors, and other fiends. Great hardcore shows and good metal, avant krud, and ambient programs are on at all different times. Truly freeform radio. Check the *Providence Phoenix* for listings.

Best Sunday morning reggae: Based in Kingston, R.I., appropriately enough, University of Rhode Island's station **WRIU (90.3 FM)** has an *irie* Sunday morning reggae show, featuring contemporary artists like Beenie Man, Marcia Griffiths, and Peter Dante.

san diego
by Brian Alexander

"San Diego is definitely a leisure town, a place where
people go to retire and die. It's kind of like paradise."
— **Speedo, *Rocket From the Crypt***

San Diego is to underground what Herbal Ecstasy is to PCP.
They'll both kill ya, but sheesh. There's a reason the
Republicans picked the city to hold their 1996 convention.

Long a bastion of John Birchers and anti-immigration
rabble-rousers, this leisure town is far to the right—even by California
standards—and seems to foster a Far West do-it-yourself ethic. Hippie
dropouts and soft-core survivalists can be indistinguishable in the
inland hill communities. San Diego is also a Navy town, and though
every port has its seamy side, its reputation as a computer and biotech
center has recently drawn a fringier crowd with cash to burn. Add the
three major universities in the city (the University of California at San
Diego, San Diego State University, and the University of San Diego—
that's 40,000 kids who need to party!), and there's a sizable audience
that keeps open some of the town's choice small clubs.

San Diego is at the apex of SoCal surf-and-skate culture. This border
town helped invent California's sunny beach life in the '30s and '40s. In the
heady surf's-up days of Hang 10, San Diego gave the world surf attire. So,
when San Diego's music scene came together in the '90s, it was not surprisingly made up of past and future skaterats and surfers. The local label
Goldenrod Records—which puts out 7-inches with local bands like fluf,
Chinchilla and Speedo's Army—is actually a subsidiary of a huge local
skateboard manufacturer, Foundation. Today, the surf at famous spots like
Windansea still attracts ecstatic naturalists and locals-only nazis alike.

The music underground runs the gamut from the kitschy rock of the
Rugburns ("Hitchhiker Joe") to A.J. Croce's bluesy piano to Stevie

Salas' hard-rock guitar slinging. Local heroes Rocket From the Crypt, blink 182, Unwritten Law, and fluf ventured onto higher-profile stages during summer 1996 by appearing on Vans' Warped Tour. San Diego's Chune was booked on the first half of Lollapalooza. This was all an affirmation that San Diego has its own sound, a cross between grungy Sponge riffs and the slightly groovier tones of Blind Melon. One new group, the Planets, is making a more soulful rock 'n' folk music.

San Diego is also a rockabilly, blues, and Tex-Mex refuge. Check out the Paladins and Billy Bacon and the Forbidden Pigs. There used to be a strong rave scene, but when the city became a hotbed of methamphetamine production thanks to ether from Tijuana, a lot of crank was passed around at warehouse and outdoor raves. After body counts grew, due to overdoses and speed-psychotic violence, police cracked down. Now raves are mostly high-tech productions in legitimate clubs, with an occasional outdoor party in vacant lots.

lay of the land

San Diego can be divided into three distinct regions. The city sits on a large bay whose mouth consists of Point Loma on the north and Coronado on the south. The first major area, **Center City**, roughly abuts the bay, curving from the northern **Uptown** (a yuppie-ish residential area which includes the largely gay **Hillcrest**), to the southern **Downtown**, which is mainly business and financial but also has the **Gas Lamp Quarter**, where a lot of clubs and restaurants have made it an urban renewal case study. Fifth Avenue is a central artery, which you can take from downtown all the way to Hillcrest. To the west of Fifth, **Middletown** is poorer, with a Italian and Portugese populations and the excellent rock club, the **Casbah** (see Clubs). Balboa Park, home of the world-famous San Diego Zoo, runs from downtown to uptown.

The beaches lay to the west and north of center city, starting on Point Loma and running up to La Jolla, and are home to good bars and hanging out, especially **Ocean Beach**, where residents refuse to admit the '60s died. You'll see bumper stickers in O.B. declaring the area the People's Republic of Ocean Beach. Most folks shop at the local organic-food co-op People's Market. Tie-dye is everywhere, and ganja is always in the air.

Go east of the city and enter the teenage wastelands of **La Mesa** and **El Cajon**, suburbs that go hot and dusty in summer, places where mall rats in *The Punisher* T-shirts roam aimlessly. Mom and dad work in town, most likely, and moved to the valleys to escape the dangers of people different to themselves, only to wind up with alienated hesher children.

getting from a to b

Hey, this is Southern California, the kingdom of the car, so you will be much better off if you have access to wheels. Unlike, say, New York, where the subway whisks you wherever you need to go in minutes, San Diego is a little tougher to navigate. However, the San Diego trolley can take you from downtown to the Mexican border, north to the Old Town area, and east through Mission Valley by the stadium and into El Cajon. Buses cover the city. If you want to stay in one place and walk to your destination, stay downtown.

sources

The local alternative weekly, *The Reader*, has good listings but has lost touch with anything remotely street level. Entire cover stories may focus on the lifespan of a flea. Surprisingly, the ridiculously conservative daily paper, the *San Diego Union-Tribune*, has excellent listings and music reviews in its Thursday "Night and Day" section. Columnist Karla Perterson is especially good on music. Two freebies, *SLAMM* and *Revolt in Style*, are passed out at record stores, coffeehouses, and on college campuses. *SLAMM* is the more authentic: It's good on local bands and has good listings, announcements of club dates, raves, and new releases. *Revolt in Style* does not seem to think its title is an oxymoron. Articles tend to follow whatever ads are in the paper. Don't be fooled.

clubs

Best San Diego club, period: If you've heard a long-distance buzz about, say, the Godrays or Nancy Boy, you'll catch their first San Diego show at the **Casbah** *(2501 Kettner Blvd., 619/232–4355)*. Booker Tim Mays has a nose for what's happening before it happens. Any worthwhile band that plays San Diego is likely to stop here—including big acts like Cibo Matto, Jon Spencer, and Social Distortion. A small club right under the airport flight path, the Casbah is home stage for the recent crop of bands who have put this town on the map. All the San Diego hardcore hang out here, and it's still a great place to catch the gasolined-up, glitzy rock of Rocket From the Crypt. With the audience crammed into the tight main barroom, it gets hot, sweaty, and downright miserable. You can escape into the back poolroom, which has a small bar and (lest you forget you're in a beach town) Tiki decor.

Best big acts: Slicker than the Casbah and located in a tract-house deadzone the city has taken to calling Bay Park, **SOMA Live** *(5305 Metro*

St., 619/239–7682) still boasts a strong lineup and a few more creature comforts than the Casbah. You'll catch bands like the Goo Goo Dolls, the Nixons and Garbage at SOMA. The club is like a small Moose lodge with a bar in the back of the room, a few dancing lights, and a prettier crowd than the Casbah—that is, if you like jock punks and college frat jar-heads. You might actually get a date at SOMA, though you will certainly have to communicate by sign language. The place gets LOUD. For some reason, perhaps its proximity to middle-class neighborhoods, SOMA attracts cruising patrol cars, so roaming around the sidewalks trying to get that buzz out of your ears is likely to draw some attention. The neighborhood being like it is, try not to freak the locals and you'll be fine.

Best headbangers: There's a reason why **Ministry** is where it is *(3595 Sports Arena Blvd., 619/685–7550)*. The Sports Arena district is a city-planning snafu fit only for the sports arena and a row of bars, strip clubs and chain stores all serving the nearby U.S. Navy base. So you can count on seeing more than a few sailors fresh from Nebraska trying valiantly to blend into civilian life for a few hours. Ministry is a small-town wet dream of black industrial motifs and metal, with heavy skull-and-devil imagery. The acts are mostly local heshers, with occasional sets by up-and-comers or slumming big names like Linda Lasabre (Thrill Kill Kult). Ministry is for the strictly under-25 crowd and teenagers with really good fake IDs.

Best roots music: Okay, so the **Belly Up Tavern** *(143 S. Cedros Ave., 619/481–9022)* isn't exactly in San Diego—it sits near the beach 15 miles north, in the town of Encinitas—but it is easily the best venue to see national blues and roots acts like Gatemouth Brown, Buckwheat Zydeco, and Koko Taylor. Local favorites the Paladins play rootsy rockabilly at the BUT about once a month, and sometimes an act like Horton Heat will play. The club is constantly feuding with upscale neighbors over the noise coming from this old Quonset hut, so there is no ear-splitting rock on the menu. Inside, the dance floor is generous for a club, but watch out for ducktailed swing dancers who congregate for Paladins and Forbidden Pigs shows. Local art hangs on the wooden walls. The crowd is heavy on the surf-dude side.

Best after-hours: Rave might be the wrong word, but that's how it began in the late '80s. Now, **Romper Room** *(526 Market St., 619/526–7529)* battles luxe condo dwellers nearby to stage its Saturday night parties from midnight to 6 A.M.. Mainly for the 18-and-over set,

Romper Room is a DJ-driven hip-hop, house, and disco remix scene for the guys and gals attracting each other through shared sweat stains. Because it's downtown, you can stop in at a sidewalk restaurant like Pane Vino or Croce's (see below) for some good food and a couple of preclub drinks. After watching the people walk by and after carbo loading, you might stroll to Romper Room just about the time most of the downtown party crowd is heading for home.

Best DJ lounge scene: Nightly DJs can be found at Downtown's **Green Circle Bar** (827 F St., 619/232–8080), spinning trip-hop, drum 'n' bass, and acid jazz. Acid jazz mainstay DJ Grayboy got his start here and occasionally brings out his jazzy funk band, the Grayboy All Stars.

Best jazz: When Jim Croce's widow, Ingrid, opened a small restaurant on a downtown corner next to an adult bookstore, a new era dawned in central San Diego. Used to be you could shoot a cannon off down Fifth Avenue and risk hitting three drunken sailors, a tattoo parlor, a peepshow palace, and two hookers. Stores were closed, there were no good restaurants, and certainly no bars you'd want to venture into without armed escorts. Now the place is chock-full of restaurants, clubs, and bars, and parking is a nightmare. Ingrid Croce has half the block, and her jazz bar **Croce's** (802 Fifth Ave., 619/232–4338) gets excellent regional and a few national acts, like her son A.J. The only problem is there's often a heavy cover and the place is always packed, albeit for good reason. The food is good, the drinks are healthy, and the brick-and-wood atmosphere seems built for jazz.

Runner-up: The **Horton Grand Hotel** (311 Island Ave., 619/544–1886) is much more sedate, often uncrowded, and rarely beefs up the cover to the point where you are tempted to just go get the CD instead. The acts are often on a par with anything at Croce's, though usually it's more trad jazz.

bars

Best jukebox: The number one watering hole for San Diego music scenesters who hang out at the Casbah (see Clubs) is Uptown's **Live Wire** (2103 El Cajon Blvd., 619/291–7450), a roomy dive with 23 beers on tap. With chili-pepper lights on the ceiling, tables, booths, and a pool table in back, it's an intimate, homey place to hang out and listen to the very hip juke (Fugazi, Jawbreaker, Drive Like Jehu, Zep—all that fun stuff). DJs spin loungey beats several nights a week, and the occasional Saturday night punk gigs have included Blink, Inch, Rust, and Three-Mile Pilot.

Best lounge bar: Just up the street from Live Wire is the **Red Fox Room** *(2223 El Cajon Blvd., 619/297–1313)*, a piano bar where an antique wood bar and table set the cocktail hour speed for both young punks searching for retro kicks and their older counterparts. A piano-horn combo packs 'em in Wednesday through Saturday with hopping jazz and show tunes. Other nights is just a piano singer, with a mellower crowd.

Best dyke bar: The one and only the **Flame** *(3780 Park Blvd., 619/295–4163)* is easily the best lesbian bar in San Diego, one so good, in fact, that gay men, straight men, and straight women have been crashing the party. The Planets played some of their early gigs here. There are two sides to the bar: The traditional unadorned long bar near the entrance seems to attract butch women, while the dance floor and stage to the rear is more often populated by glammier femmes. Once a neighborhood dive, it hasn't lost touch with its humble origins. There's no real decor to speak of but lately, the Flame has been pushing a retro lounge scene by stressing martinis, cigars, and highballs. Still, if you're sitting up front, be ready with good weightlifting anecdotes.

Best dive: Just on the east side of the city's Hillcrest neighborhood, across the street from a McDonald's and next to an adult bookstore, there's a gem called the **Alibi** *(1403 University Ave., 619/295–0881)*. Inside, you'll find an odd mix of grizzled old guys drinking cheap bourbon, and students from San Diego State University sucking on Becks. A pool table and a television stuck on ESPN are the only entertainment. But if you have lost your girl, lost your job, or wrecked your car, there's no better place to go.

Best surfari lounge: The **Pacific Shores** *(4927 Newport Ave., 619/223–7549)* has been in Ocean Beach for decades, and despite a switch in management a few years ago it still owns some of the best neon lounge decor in town. As you walk in the door, you'll see neon palm trees, blue neon waves, and fish. Old banquettes still line one wall to your right, the bar is to your left, and the floor in between is always crowded. A TV monitor now plays MTV, rock is piped in, and the owners have hired a couple of chain-smoking female Goths as bartenders, but everything else is the way it could have been in 1957. The result is the best late-night drinking in the city. The bar is always crowded, mainly with surf rats, white Jell-O–dreadlocked rastas, and failed poets. Count yourself lucky to grab a booth. If you do, order drinks by twos since you may not see your harried waitress again until closing.

Best darts: The guys who own **Shakespeare's Pub** *(3701 India St., 619/299–0230)* first worked at a nearby pub called Princess of Wales in order to get their green cards. Now they have their own place, and while it's not strictly speaking a darts palace, the atmosphere is excellent, the food good (for English fare), the beer selection wide, and the boards and darts in good condition. About half the patrons are British expats. They get pretty boisterous, but nothing like the fellas they left at home. If you're unsure of scoring or the rotation around the board, don't get into a game—the regulars have no patience.

Best martini: There are about a dozen places in San Diego that advertise "best martini" and wish they could come close to the **Laurel**'s *(corner of Laurel St. and Fifth Ave., 619/239–2222)*. This new restaurant is very upscale, with a kind of Gaudi-esque decor, handmade bar lamps, a fairly hip crowd, and a house signature martini that amounts to a double. Better yet, the well booze is brands you have actually heard of. Bar snacks run to items like salmon carpaccio and things with *aoli*.

Best rock 'n' roll bar: Is **Bodie's** *(528 F St., 619/236–8988)* a bar or a club? From the outside, the place looks like a hole-in-the-wall. Inside, it looks like one too. It's got a bar, a few round tables, and a tiny stage. Located downtown a block up from the main drag of Fifth Avenue, Bodie's attracts some of the best local rock acts and even a few from L.A. You'll fit in best at Bodie's if you've got big hair and a studded leather wristband. Even when a few bikers drop by, this place is peaceful. If you give Bodie's a shot, be ready for blasting volume. The bar is small, but don't tell that to the ham-fisted rockers on stage.

Best beer orgy: The brick interior and blond wood of **Karl Strauss's Brewery and Grill** *(1157 Columbia St., 619/234–2739)* call to mind a fern bar and attract patrons to match. However, if you overlook the decor, you'll get the best beer in the city. Strauss's (formerly Columbia Brewery) was the first microbrewery in the city, and still does beer better with favorites like Karl Strauss's Amber Lager and Light.

Best bar, period: Best here means a real live old-fashioned bar, where the bartenders know their drinks, you can get half a dozen or more single malts, and they spot you a drink if you're a regular. **Dobson's** *(956 Broadway Circle, 619/231–6771)* is perhaps the only place of its ilk in town. This is primarily a businessman's bar and restaurant, but it feels like an old overcoat on a cold day. The bar has tiled floors, dark wood, a mirror behind the bar, wooden stools, and brass plaques with the regulars' names on them by their favorite chairs. The owner, Paul Dobson, is a local restaurateur of some repute, but this signature spot is his best by far.

food/coffee

Best cheap meal: During the lean times when you've barely got enough money to last through the next few hours, head for **Ichiban** *(1449 University Ave., 619/299–7203, and 1441 Garnet Ave., 619/270–5755).* You'll wind up sitting at a picnic table outside with a stranger who may be just as broke, and the food comes in funky plastic compartmentalized cafeteria trays, but hey, for five dollars, you can get one of the specials, which include noodles, some chopped lettuce with ginger dressing, fortune cookies, rice and, for example, pork tonkatsu or teriyaki chicken. It's probably best not to ask what part of the chicken the meat came from, but the food really tastes great.

Best breakfasts: The pancakes at **Big Kitchen** *(3003 Grape St., 619/234–5789)* are so big it can take over an hour to eat. Judy Forman, the owner, is a generous soul—in many ways. The Big Kitchen makes a habit of hiring struggling actors, musicians, artists and down-on-their-luck folks, which is how Whoopi Goldberg wound up working there back in her own lean days. The habitués of the Big Kitchen range from local journalists to gay and lesbian activists to wealthy homeowners who live in the neighborhood around Balboa Park. The chorizo omelettes are a must.

Runner-up: Also worthwhile, if you're Downtown, is **Cafe 222** *(222 Island Ave., 619/236–9902)*, where winning pumpkin waffles, an endless cup, and friendly service make it a favorite with today's rawk kids.

Best 24-hour meal: Although it has been in San Diego forever, **Rudford's** *(2900 El Cajon Blvd., 619/282–8423)* was rediscovered a few years ago by late-night partiers who realized they could get the most filling meal imaginable at 4 A.M. here. Rudford's is one of those Formica-ized spots with hardened waitresses, carrot chunks in the meat loaf, and gravy that oozes slowly down the mashed potatoes. If you can get a window seat, you can look out on El Cajon Boulevard, the city's streetwalker route of choice.

Runner-up: In Hillcrest, the standard white-bread diner **Topsy's** *(1451 Washinton St., 619/296–8268)* fills up between two and three in the morning with local queers and hipsters, making a fun late-night scene.

Best cheap Mexican: San Diego has better Mexican food than Mexico, if you're looking for the plate-o'-beans and burrito variety. And the best spot in the city is **El Indio**, especially the original location *(3695 India St., 619/299–0333)*. You walk in, place your order at the counter, walk across the street to the outdoor patio (an island in the middle of India Street), and grab your picnic table. When your number is called, pick up your order—and be sure to get extra flour tortillas, which are made fresh daily and also make a great, on-the-run comfort-food breakfast. Order half-a-dozen with butter.

Runners-up: Two other top-notch taco stands are **Valentine's** *(844 Market St., 619/234–8256; and 1810 W. Washington St., 619/542–0062)*, which serve outstanding cheese-rolled tacos, and Uptown's **El Cuervo** *(110 W. Washington St., 619/295–9713)*.

Best burgers: It can be a little cruisy, but the **Crest Cafe** *(425 Robinson Ave., 619/295–2510)*, located in the heart of Hillcrest's gay neighborhood, has been a longtime favorite of locals. The 90214 burger, for example, is a cheesy sloppy mess that requires a post-burger shower. The milk shakes are good, too. Recently, the Cafe expanded into pastas and other slightly more trendy items, but it doesn't do them as well as the burgers.

Best vegetarian: Tabbouleh, carrot cake, and a thousand uses for tofu make **Kung Food** *(2949 Fifth Ave., 619/298–7302)* the vegan's diner of choice. This place is pure vegan—don't bother going in here if you can't I.D. Ram Dass or Deepak Chopra. Located between Hillcrest and Banker's Hill on Fifth, Kung Food attracts dedicated vegetarians as well as a few businesspeople trying to eat healthy one day a week. The restaurant is snugly fit inside a wood-frame structure and surrounded by nothing very interesting except, ironically, a nearby cheesecake bakery.

Best coffeehouse: If you're feeling disillusioned with the postindustrial world, go to **Java Joe's** *(4994 Newport Ave., 619/523–0356)*. As soon as you walk into this corner coffeehouse, you'll notice the incense, the aging hippies, and the grain muffins. Java Joe's is in Ocean Beach, so you won't be alone if you think the world oughta be a better place. It has scattered tables and chairs, a wooden floor and some beaten-up pool tables. The rest of the floor is a performing space. Joe has become known for offering a very eclectic mix of music: everything from the Planets to a bizarre percussion duo.

Runner-up: In Middletown, right next door to the Mexican stand El Indio is **Gelato Vera** *(3753 India St., 619/295–9267)*, where coffee, muffins, and croissants are cheap, and local scenesters rev their Vespa engines out front.

shopping

records

Best record store south of L.A.: If it's obscure and if your friends have never heard of it and doubt its existence, you'll prove them wrong by dragging them to **Lou's** *(434 N. Highway 101, Encinitas, 619/753–1382)*. It's a 25-minute drive north of San Diego but well worth it. Called one of the best record stores in the country by Speedo of Rocket From the Crypt, among others, it's got 40,000 new titles plus 20,000 to 30,000 more used. Specialties include reggae (the complete works of King Tubby and Lee Scratch Perry) and indie-label punk (Trans Am and the Swinging Utters), but it's got everything from dance 12 inches to folk. Looking for an old Lookout! 7 inch? Don't miss this place.

Runner-up: In San Diego, **Off the Record** *(3849 Fifth Ave., 619/298–4755)* has great used bins with out-of-print vinyl. Need a back-stage pass to a 1973 ABBA concert? You'll find it here. Know-it-all clerks can be intimidating but ultimately helpful. Off the Record is also one the better spots to find out about the raves, unlicensed clubs, and quickie shows going-on around town. It also carries zines.

Best place to find "Mack the Knife": If you need to locate an old Bobby Darin record or maybe "Wipeout" by the Surfaris, try **Nostalgia Records** *(3750 30th St., 619/543–9930)*. This storefront operation has a pretty good selection of old 45s, LPs, and even a few CDs. It also trades in autographs and memorabilia, mostly from the '50s and '60s, but there is a smattering of new stuff, too.

books

Best used books: There's no guarantee you'll find what you are looking for, but **Wahrenbrock's Book House** *(726 Broadway, 619/232–*

0132) is a great place to lose yourself. A musty odor rises from the seemingly haphazard stacks and piles. Mixed with the dreck are treasures—everything from turn-of-the-century travelogues to last year's Booker Prize winner. Overflow from the packed shelves is stacked in corners, on the floor, and on tabletops. Happy hunting!

Best comics: San Diego is a comic-book mecca. The nation's largest comic-book convention is held here every summer. About a dozen top comic-book artists live in the city, and two or three publishers do business in San Diego. So it's hard to go wrong picking a store, but if you want both underground and mainstream comics, try **On Comic Ground** *(1629 University Ave., 619/683–7879).*

clothes

Best vintage: It may be on the pricey side, but **Wear It Again Sam** *(3922 Park Blvd., 619/299–0185)* is THE place for extra-sweet gabardine shirts for the boys, '40s and '50s babydoll dresses for the ladies, and old shoes and cardigans for everybody.

Best plastic clothes: A clothing store without a shred of natural fabric, **Gamma Gamma** *(3847 Fifth Ave., 619/295–8374)* is the emporium of choice if you're looking for that special neoprene turtleneck. Most of Gamma Gamma's clothing is actually fairly mainstream, just made of plastic. But they do carry a small selection of rather scary fetish items and lingerie. Nosebleed platforms highlight the shoe and boot choices. A few cross-dressers buy their stuff here.

Best shoes: With brands like Fluevog, Fly London, and Georgia Boots, **Catwalk** *(706 Sixth Ave., 619/696–9786)* has the largest alternative shoe and boot selection in town—as long as you like black or purple.

Best East Village outpost: Lulu Boutique *(762 Fifth Ave., 619/238–5673)* is run by a group of young women who must make lots of trips back east to stock their store with the boutique designs of Product's SoHo store. Lulu is about the only place in San Diego where women can find clothes for the groovy, skinny, drugged-out look; this is where you get PVC pants and double-knit polyester jackets ... at a price. Lulu's stock ain't cheap and, if you're not a slave to style, you might wonder why a vinyl miniskirt costs $150.

et cetera

Best surf shop: There are dozens of surf shops in San Diego, predictably enough, but most of them are really tourist souvenir shops or stores for wannabes selling overpriced boards and wetsuits and racks and racks of stupid T-shirts. Beware of surf shops where the sales staff actually look like surfers and ever use the words "dude," "epic," or "whoa." None of which occurs at **Mitch's Surf Shop** *(631 Pearl St., 619/459–5933)*. Mitch, who's about 45, is a longtime surfer who knows what it's like to need a winter wetsuit and not have much money. He keeps prices a little lower than everybody else and doesn't mind if you hang out in his shop looking at surf and skate mags. Regular customers were worried when Mitch expanded to include some snowboard and skate accessories, but he seems to have kept his philosophy the same as when his shop amounted to a hole-in-the-wall next to a fish market. Surfboard rentals are $15 per day.

Best flea market: For sheer junk-o-rama impact, nothing beats the **Kobey Swap Meet**, held nearly every weekend at the San Diego Sports Arena parking lot. The mind reels to see how many garage artisans actually exist in the small world of San Diego County. See the amazing fastest painter in the world make an objet d'art in less than one minute. Boggle at the array of women's underwear imported from Third World countries.

Best neck collars: Gamma Gamma (see above) is tame compared to **CLAW** *(705 Sixth Ave., 619/239–3246)*. This store is serious, godammit, so kneel and be disciplined! Steel-ring belts, spike neck collars, and a wide array of body-piercing applications are on display for your intimidation. They'll pierce you right on the premises. This is as hard-core as San Diego gets.

Best neon-blue condoms: For a celebration of the latex industry, there's no better place than **Condoms Plus** *(1220 University Ave., 619/291–7400)*. Big ones, little ones, rainbow-hued ones, even jet-black ones. The store itself is a little sterile—with a yellow fluorescent sign outside and spare steel wallracks inside—but there are a few toys to go with the condoms; so if you're looking for that special vibrator and don't want to venture into a greasy store full of blowup dolls, you might try this one.

body alterations

Best sailor tattoos: Before Downtown became gentrified, **Tiger Jimmy** *(519 Broadway, 619/234–9419)* was there, placing anchors and devil dogs on military guys. They are doing it still. This place may very well possess the best topless Polynesian hula dancer in the tattoo world. The crowd here is a tad on the rough side, with sailors trying to look badder than Leroy Brown. So if it's white trash you want, come wallow.

Best spike through your tongue: Like tattooing, body piercing is raging in San Diego. Everybody from surfers to street scroungers spend a fair amount of time trying to figure out what to pierce next, like the guy near the Ocean Beach Pier who had two steel rings inserted into his bald scalp and then tied a little braided hair from the back of his neck to them. Anyway, **Dr. Jefe's Body Piercing** *(4944 B Newport Ave., 619/223–1771)* is a kind of temple to the cult. Young grungers sit outside on the sidewalk comparing their latest additions, and more than a few runaways and foreign backpackers from the hostel across the street try to make semipermanent homes on the bench outside Dr. Jefe's door.

hotel/motel

Best cheap, clean bed: The **Golden West Hotel** *(720 Fourth Ave., 619/233–7594)* has seen better golden days, but it is still relatively safe and clean—and with rooms starting at just $16.95 plus a $2 key deposit, you can't be too picky. This place has the added advantage of being in the heart of downtown within easy walking distance to a lot of what's in this list, and not far from the airport, train, and bus stations.

Best beach hotel: Not best as in finest, but best as in cheapest rates and good location. Try the **Beachcomber Shores** *(907 Turquoise St., 619/488–4442)*. Rates start at about $35 per day, which is as good as you can do near the beaches. Since some units have tiny kitchenettes, you can save a little money by stocking up on eggs and cheese and eating omelettes for a few bucks instead of eating out. The beach is within walking distance and so is the bar and shopping district of Pacific Beach. Be aware, though: This section of Pacific Beach probably sees more crime than the rest of the neighborhood. A lot of it is just guys getting drunk and acting like jerks, but there have been more rapes and robberies here than in some other beach sections.

local wonders

Best immortal surf spot: This is a matter of debate and how much you are willing to risk with surf nazi locals. **Windansea** between Pacific Beach and La Jolla is the most famous break in the city, thanks largely to Tom Wolfe's "Pump House Gang" article. This is a reef break off a point, identifiable by the giant rock in the water, with ferocious lefts and rights. Some guys out there, though, believe they own the break, so be careful or be really good.

Runner-up: San Diego's second most epic surf spot is probably **Ocean Beach Pier**. To get to Ocean Beach, a sand spit on the north end of the Point Loma peninsula, take I-8 (the Alvarado Freeway) west to the Sunset Cliff exit; go left to Ocean Beach, where almost any right turn will take you to the beach itself (Newport Avenue is a main drag).

Best casual surf spot: You still have to observe etiquette at the foot of **Tourmaline Street** in **Pacific Beach**, but the waves are fairly easy and they don't call a section of this break "Old Man's" for nothing. Surfers here are out for a fun time in the waves, not a hassle with other surfers. A group of regulars keeps the place well patrolled, so nobody gets out of hand. Pacific Beach is at the end of I-8, west of Sea World. It begins at Pacific Boulevard, north of Mission Beach.

Runner-up: **Sunset Cliffs** is casual in attitude but has challenging waves. On Point Loma, you take Ladera Street to the end, walk down an old rickety staircase to the rocks at the base of the cliff and jump in (with your board underneath you, hopefully). An old-school longboarding spot is Imperial Beach, south of San Diego, near the Mexican border. Unfortunately, it's often closed due to sewage.

Best beaches: The best private, secluded beach to swim from is near the **Sunset Cliffs** off **Point Loma**. Located about 50 yards south of the surf spot, it is accessible only by climbing down the cliff via rope or walking over the rocks from the north at low tide. The little crescent beach is rarely crowded and the sunsets are incredible. Surf's not bad here, either. **Mission Beach** is where they hold the Miss Mission Beach contest every year, the winner of which usually has the best boob job. This is where people with great bodies go to get picked up. No kidding. If you're insecure, don't try to find a date here. People scrutinize each other ferociously. And because of this, Mission Beach at about 3 P.M. on a hot summer day is a place to avoid. Too many frustrated guys, no parking, and lots of beer equals trouble. On the other hand, the crowd at **Ocean Beach** doesn't give a hoot if you lift weights. In fact, women there might find it repulsive. Better to know some poetry, how to surf, or how to cook eggplant. The beach at O.B. is not as nice as Mission Beach, but the crowd is generally mellower and has lots of white people with dreadlocks.

Best Frisbee-golf links in the USA: There's a reason why Frisbee fanatics flock to San Diego. Some of the best throwers in the world live here, and they take the sport very seriously. The sprawling **Balboa Park** *(gen. info. 619/239–0512)* is also home to perhaps the best public Frisbee golf links, a course winding up and down the canyons on the east side of the park just off Pershing Street the main drive through the park. Marginally employed guys with full quivers of disks can be found wondering the links from sunup to sundown, and there are frequent regional and national tournaments staged throughout the year.

Best skate ramp: San Diego's city government has an uneasy relationship with skate culture, which is surprising, since the city is a skating epicenter. Some parts of town have banned skateboards altogether. The only real skate park with a half-pipe is at **Missile Park**, part of a YMCA *(5505 Friars Rd., 619/298–3576)*.

transmissions

Best jazz: Despite the generally awful state of San Diego's radio, the good news is that **KSDS (88.3 FM)**, the station affiliated with San Diego City College, is a true jazz-lover's station, with a seemingly unlimited playlist ranging from the '20s to today. The bad news is the signal is weak. Figures.

san francisco

by Silke Tudor

"San Francisco encourages experimentation like nowhere else. Take advantage, take a risk, wear something daring, have a go at gay sex, open your mind, man. Nobody's watching, but everybody's paying attention."
— **Roddy Bottum,** *Faith No More* and *Imperial Teen*

There is no other city in the world like San Francisco—those who visit rarely return home unchanged (or unscathed, depending on how you see it). Ever since beats Allen Ginsberg, Jack Kerouac, and Gary Snyder practiced "yabyum" in the bungalows of Berkeley, every American counterculture of consequence, from the Black Panthers to the SF Skinz, has taken root in the Bay Area. And in this beautiful city of hills, fog, and views of the endless blue Pacific, several generations of freaks and sexual outlaws have found something to make them happy. Feedback and trash cans filled with Koolaid and LSD? Poppers and golden showers in the Castro? Setting off stationary sonic rockets in Golden Gate Park with Survival Research Laboratories? Or just riding your motorcycle through the Marin headlands at dawn with the Sunday Morning Ride crew?

San Francisco is always up for a good time. If the kick is a little creepy, edgy, or annoying to outsiders, all the better. With the rampant hedonism and shock-value high jinks that are second nature in the Bay Area come certain side effects, like neurological damage for Deadheads and speed psychosis for gutterpunks. San Francisco is as far West geographically and mentally as you can get, and if you don't succumb to the drugs and nightclubs, you may—as have so many of the Bay Area's well-adjusted vegans, lesbians, Dumpster divers, bike messengers, drag queens, health nuts, fetishists, and scooter boys—find that this is the town where you'll shed your small-town roots once and for all and find a happy second skin. Because in San Francisco, whatever you are into, you can rest assured that somebody else is further out.

It's no small wonder, then, that San Francisco is blessed with a strange and exceptional music community. It takes brilliant freaks like acid-jazz guitarist Charlie Hunter to turn jazz on its collective ear. Or like Lawrence Livermore, president of Lookout! Records—the little East Bay indie that gave Green Day the go-ahead—to think punk rock could become a nationwide phenomenon. Or like Spearhead's Michael Franti to use West Coast hip-hop as a means of uniting rather than ghettoizing people. Or like the founders of the Incredibly Strange Wrestling group to see the beauty of coupling masked Mexican wrestlers with surf and punk rock. Or like Paula Frazer of Tarnation and J. Byrd Hosch of the Kuntry Kunts to prove that there's more to country than Garth Brooks. This city puts stock in the belief that nothing worth mentioning has ever grown out of the status quo. San Francisco *makes* its artists (flakes, cranks, and R. Crumb alike), just as its artists make San Francisco. Either way, remember to tip the bartender.

In San Francisco anything goes, like it or not. For some, the often-humorless hippie regimen of recycling, organic produce, wheatgrass juice, and haute political correctness is oppressive. However, who can't help smile when they see San Francisco come out in its wiggy freaky best for Halloween in the Castro? Even if you don't move here, you need to do some time in this city, one of America's best. Just don't call it Frisco.

lay of the land

San Francisco's neighborhoods are all culturally distinctive and worth exploring, but for music there are a few central locations. While **North Beach** is still home to City Lights book store (see Shopping) and old beatnik haunts like Vesuvios, it turns into a big, rowdy military and bridge-and-tunnel party zone on weekends—thanks to the many strip clubs. The **Upper Haight**, where flower children went amok in '67, has since been overrun by suburbanites, so locals turned their attention east. The **Lower Haight**, which was once a good place to get mugged, is now a jumping night spot with more than a dozen restaurants, bars, shops, and clubs crammed into a two-block radius near Fillmore Street. A district of converted warehouses, **SOMA** (South of Market) is still home to all the largest dance clubs and the most well-established rock clubs, such as Slim's and the Paradise Lounge. For uncut urban squalor, the **Tenderloin** is filled with dive bars, streetwalkers, and stickup artists. Enter at your own risk.

The **Mission District** has emerged as an excellent neighborhood—both to live in (thanks to decent rents) and to simply skulk about (thanks to excellent Mexican food, coffee shops, record stores, Santeria shops, a vibrator museum and other run-of-the-mill S.F. fare). In the '90s, this largely Latino neighborhood underwent a dramatic face-lift when the rockers, scenesters, modern primitives, and trust-fund drug fiends moved in. Now, the area is a nightlife mecca with trendy bars, several nightclubs, and restaurants of every ethnicity. Despite, or because of, the continuing presence of junkies, pushers, and aggressive panhandlers, it is the first stop for people looking for cocktails, live music, and trouble with an urban edge. With a new business license being posted every weekend, it is only a matter of time before the neighborhood is completely gentrified and transformed into the city's new entertainment center.

getting from a to b

Considering the cosmopolitan nature of San Francisco, it is a surprisingly small city. This can be a joy for pedestrians and bicyclists who don't mind steep hills, but can be of little help after midnight when the fog has rolled in and you have just got a tip on an Survival Research Laboratories performance that promises modified jet engines and a slew of fornicating robots that explode in flames after battling a cyborg bulldog. Luckily, few neighborhoods are more than a 15-minute drive away. Unluckily, in any neighborhood worth going to, parking is a bitch (one urban myth claims that in Chinatown, parking spots are passed down from generation to generation, guarded by highly trained street gangs). If you don't mind traveling with strangers, the San Francisco public transportation system can probably get you where you want to go. We won't discuss cable cars, since they should only be used by tourists going to Fisherman's Wharf or suits heading for their offices in the Financial District. The MUNI (Municipal Railway) consists of ground buses (mostly electric ones that frequently slip off of their power lines and stall for a minimum of ten minutes) and a fleet of somewhat sleeker, faster trains that travel both above and below ground. Apparently neither has a schedule. BART (Bay Area Rapid Transit), on the other hand, has a schedule that it rigidly adheres to—most of the time. It is a speedy underground train (20 minutes will get you across the Bay into Berkeley or Oakland) that serves a limited number of stops in each city. This brings us to taxis. Fares rarely exceed ten dollars, but there are too many companies and never enough cabs. Hailing is almost always more effective than calling, but if you insist on phoning first, **Yellow Cab** *(415/626–2345)* and **De Soto** *(415/673–1414)* are two of the more popular companies. If you're lucky, you will be picked up by a limo driver who is trolling for fares while his real client is eating dinner. This is a widespread but completely unregulated form of transportation that should not be used by lone passengers. However, for groups, it's a fabulous way to start your evening in high style.

sources

San Francisco has been called a two-paper town. In 1997, it is doubtful that anyone still says this in reference to the laughable dailies. More than likely, they are referring to the two free weeklies, the *San Francisco Bay Guardian* and the *SF Weekly*, whose competitive media war has benefited the public with ever-expanding entertainment listings. For a well-rounded look at the week ahead, it is best to use the papers in conjunction with each other. Web sites like the List (klinzhai.evolve. com/fal-con/thelist.html#schedule) and Yahoo! (sfbay.yahoo.com) can help. The List, which used to be circulated by hand at live gigs, has expanded into one of the finest resources for funk, punk, thrash, and ska club calendars, warehouse parties, radio shows, and magnets. Yahoo! is more general but a useful resource for raves and lesbian, gay, and bisexual events. For those who want their info spoon-fed, KITS 105.3 FM's What Line lists commercial alternative events of all kinds (415/357–WHAT), and KUSF 90.3 FM gives tips on more obscure and street-level goings-on (415/221–2636). Still, despite technology and its wonders, for last-minute shows and truly underground events, it is always best to keep your ears open and read street fliers (check out Upper and Lower Haight Street, 11th Street, and Valencia Street in the Mission). Often a scrap of paper attached to a telephone pole will lead you to the most deliciously clandestine adventure of your life.

clubs

Best noise bands: Located in a former firehouse, the **Kilowatt** *(3160 16th St., 415/861–2595)* is the club that transformed 16th & Valencia from junkie central to home of the Mission noise scene. On weekends, the neighborhood bar rolls back its pool tables to make room for goa-teed rock 'n' rollers, who pack the club for the next-big-thing in garage rock or the loudest-thing-ever-imaginable in Japanoise rock. Clearly undaunted by big noise, the management also likes equally large-scale art. The bar boasts an impressive collection of metal sculptures by local artist Mondo Peña: a life-size hammerhead, a giant octopus, and a Great White hang from the high ceiling, ominously eyeing the free-range club kids below.

Best club night: Snake charmers, Twister boards, go-go dancers, and leis are just some of the perks that come with the **downhear Lounge**, a weekly night offered by **Cafe Du Nord** *(2170 Market St., 415/861–5016)*. The Du Nord, which resides in the basement of the Swedish American

Building, has always been a classy number, with blood-red walls and a carved mahogany bar, but the downhear folks don't give a damn. Committed to music, not social cliques, downhear's focus changes from week to week. Tiki, exotica, disco, funk, ambient, techno, and rock are just some of the musical themes which can be explored on any given Wednesday night. Call ahead to dress accordingly.

Best unknown garage bands: North Beach's **Purple Onion** *(140 Columbus Ave., 415/389–1485)* is cramped, round, purple, and smokey. End of story. Well, not quite. The owner, Tom Guido, is notorious in the Bay Area music scene for riding around town on his skateboard, talking about media conspiracies, and yanking the sound at his club whenever a band looks at him wrong. Sure, he's a little high-maintenance, but damn if he doesn't have an ear! Guido manages to find the best upstart garage and punk bands in the country, giving 'em a shake a full year before anyone else even has a clue.

Best swanky big-band lounge: Bimbo's **365 Club** *(1025 Columbus Ave., 415/474–0365)* has been around since the early '30s, when it was a Prohibition gin joint, and despite the back-to-the-future retro cocktail scene (which has spawned numerous imitators), is still the absolute cream of the crop. Awash in thick carpets and a gold and deep-red color scheme, Bimbo's has two bars, a luscious foyer, a beautiful ballroom, an intimate lounge, and exquisite bathrooms. The new owner is Bimbo's grandson, and he has brought an eclectic edge to booking, adding surf and Britpop to the crowd-pleasing big-band roster.

Best early morning groove: Known by every late-night maven in town for its 6 A.M. Sunday tea dance, the **End Up** *(Sixth St. and Harrison St., 415/896–1075)* in SOMA is, fittingly, the place where every clubber ends up after another delirious night on the town. It draws young, glam, druggy crews who like trance music. Watch out. For six in the morning, the kids at the End Up look *really* good. Whether boogeying to hi-NRG house, playing pool by the cozy fireplace, or lounging next to the water-fall on the sunny outdoor patio, this intimate club is the most comfort-able place for sleepless clubbers to greet the new day. The bar reopens for inebriation at six.

Best hip-hop riddims: The only club in town dedicated to hip-hop, **Deco** *(510 Larkin St., 415/441–4007)* is women-run and, thanks to special promotions aimed at the ladies, draws a good mix sexually—as well as racially. The hottest DJs in town spin blends of soul, dancehall, reggae, and hip-hop. Some names to look for are the Baroness, DJ Pause, Rolo 1-3, Winnie B, Q-Bert, and Short Kut. Despite hip-hop clubs' bad reputation in San Francisco, Deco has never had any gang-related trouble. Unfortunately, you still have to arrive early (like 10:30 P.M.) in order to avoid long lines caused by the prerequisite pat-down scene.

Best place to play Ping-Pong: The Mission District's fave hole-in-the-wall, the **Chameleon** *(853 Valencia St., 415/821–1891)* is a total dump (in a good way) and home away from home for lowlife bike messengers and gutterpunks. Offering up an eclectic combination of thrash rock (Tuesday–Saturday), spoken word (Mondays), and "Simpsons" viewing (Sundays), this place is unique, if nothing else. Black-velvet paintings of E.T., Snoopy, unicorns, busty ladies, and clowns hang from the walls. A trashed-out basement rec room features a Ping-Pong table, a couch, and a broken pinball machine—just like your very own basement back home. Take all this and an open-mike host who grew up in a cult, and you've got some fantastic airport stories.

Best jazz-spot sightings: If you are in the market for shaved heads, baggy clothes, and tiny lip beards, the Mission's slick, design-forward **Elbo Room** *(647 Valencia St., 415/552–7788)* is just the place for you. Featuring a spacious downstairs bar area, several pool tables, and an intimate stage setting with tables and waitress service, the Elbo Room is at the forefront of the new acid jazz scene. A very popular photo booth keeps the kids entertained between sets. Fortunately for the fashion-challenged, the high caliber of music keeps the Elbo Room real. Occasional DJ nights.

Best girls' spot: The **End Up** *(Sixth and Harrison, 415/896–1075)* now hosts the **G-Spot**. This sexually charged girls' night makes full use of the club's black-light room (3-D glasses are provided), rooftop patio, Gothic lounge, indoor balcony, and sunken dance floor—the height of dancing comfort. Lipstick lesbians, hard-core leather dykes, and anyone else who wants to groove to the house pulse are welcome.

Best boys' disco: For wall-to-wall shirtless muscle boys throbbing to 100-plus b.p.m.s, you can't beat **Club Townsend** *(177 Townsend St., 415/974–6020)*—the highest of high-tech clubs, with the biggest dance floor and the best sound-and-light system in town. Though most of the 2,000 patrons who dance into the wee hours are wax-chested gym hounds, no one should feel intimidated. Townsend books some of the greatest dance divas in the world, and the genius of the house DJs would be wasted if you didn't shake your groove thing. Just don't take off your shirt.

Best place to find a victim: The only sex club that specializes in B&D, S&M, fetish, and kinky fun, the **Power Exchange** *(960 Harrison St., 415/974–1460)* is the perfect underground spot to look for a spanking partner or a love slave who will fulfill your every whim. Straight, bi, gay, lesbian, and transgender are all welcomed with open arms and hard paddles.

Best p.c. punk club: Completely volunteer run, Berkeley's **924 Gilman** *(924 Gilman St., Berkeley, 510/525–9926)* is the last bastion of purist punk, a no-frills warehouse for every underage punker in the Bay Area. Before bands are allowed to take the stage, the staff scrutinizes demo tapes and lyric sheets for misogynist, racist, and homophobic lyrics. No major-label acts need apply—such offenses violate the Gilman manifesto. To gain admittance to the club, a punk fan must be a card-carrying member (membership costs $2 and can be purchased on the way in), but shows are never more than $5 and are often worth the hassle. Both Green Day and Rancid claim Gilman as their alma mater, but locals know it best as the place where Jello Biafra had a leg broken outside for being a "sellout." A warning to future Gilman graduates: Stay in touch.

Best sushi and jazz: Real jazz aficionados make the trek across the Bay for a taste of **Yoshi's** *(6030 Claremont Ave., Oakland, 510/652–9200)* fresh fish and steaming artists. Last year saw the intimate supper club play host to Betty Carter, Bradford Marsalis, Clarence "Gatemouth" Brown, and Allen Toussaint, just to name a few. The impeccable reputation of the staff and setting has drawn more than a few heavy hitters out of retirement for "Generation Shows," which feature five icons from five different generations doing what they do best. Smoking is frowned upon, but this is a trifle in the presence of greatness.

bars

Best Polynesian wicker bar: Trader Sam's *(6150 Geary Blvd., 415/221–0773)* has been blending high-octane tropical drinks since the late '30s at prices any sailor can afford. While clearly a dive masquerading as exotica, Sam's has been known to take on a Tahitian glow after the first couple of Mai Tais. Hunker down in one of the plush wicker-and-cushion love seats, squint your eyes, and you may just see Deborah Kerr and Burt Lancaster cozying in a corner. Island favorites include the Blue Hawaii, PT-39, Singapore Sling and the dreaded scorpion bowl. The bar also boasts an eclectic juke and pinball, along with straight booze and beer for the more timid traveller.

Best bike-messenger hangout: A former country & western bar, the **Covered Wagon** *(917 Folsom St., 415/974–1585)* has become a prerequisite pit stop for the city's bike messengers. Pouring in after a long day of dodging potholes and delivery trucks, these modern-day Mercurys talk over the day's dangers while sucking on cold pints and shooting pool. If you stick around past happy hour, you may catch a few die-hard stragglers singing "Gotta Be Me" at the karaoke bar.

Best Bloody Mary: This is not a cocktail. The Upper Haight jazz club **Deluxe** *(1511 Haight St., 415/552–6949)* serves a Bloody Mary that's a piece of art—or, at the very least, a meal. Stuffed with carrots, celery, olives, radishes, and, yes, prawns, and spicy enough to put hair on your chest, this drink is a choice bridge between last night's hangover and tonight's debauch. While any of the well-pressed-tie, clipped bartenders can do the job, Vise Grip, the debonair singer for local swing mavericks the New Morty Show, is the reigning king of the Bloody Mary.

Best British pub: As far as most San Franciscans are concerned, there is only one British pub. The Lower Haight's **Mad Dog in the Fog** *(530 Haight St., 415/626–7270)* is a landing pad for expats easing into America. British-owned and -operated, the Dog features a huge variety of beers on tap, from Guinness to seasonal specials like apricot wheat and oatmeal stout, a beer garden, a substantial pub-grub menu, and several televisions for viewing football matches (soccer to you, boy-o). Tapping into the more competitive side of our beer-swilling natures, the Dog also supports its own softball and football teams, as well as two intensely competitive pub quizzes every week—with mind-benders like, "What was the original name of Paraguay?"

Best transvestite bar: Thousands of little Christmas lights shimmer year-round in the dusky recesses of **Motherlode** *(1002 Post St., 415/928–6006)*. As any well-versed transvestite will attest, the correct lighting can make or break an evening. Catering to transvestites, cross-dressers, transsexuals, and those who love them, this Tenderloin dive lingers somewhere between subtle and seedy. There are plenty of shadowy corners, and the pervasive rose-colored glow does wonders for even the worst complexion. Billowing dry-ice fog doesn't hurt either.

Best place for a first date: Quiet and off the beaten path, the **Lone Palm** *(3394 22nd St., 415/648–0109)* is an intimate bar with subtle lighting and elegant '30s decor. The huge selection of top-shelf liquor and sincerely friendly staff make for a classy but casual environment, which eases even the most awkward of silences. The Manhattans are renowned for taking the chill out of a foggy San Francisco night.

Best tequila challenge: Bartender Julio Bermejo, whose father opened **Tommy's** *(5929 Geary Blvd., 415/387–4747)* more than three decades ago, pedals the largest selection of 100-percent blue-agave tequilas in the city—including a chili-laced variety and its distant coffee-tinted cousin. During his frequent trips to Mexico to taste-test new shipments, Bermejo always picks up one or two bottles which are too, um, special to sell over the counter. If he should take a shine to you or, God forbid, you boast some sort of masterful tequila stamina, you may get treated to one of these alcoholic rarities on the house. Careful: Marines have been reduced to tears by a single whiff of the "spicy" tequila.

Best long-hair holdout: It's dark, it's dingy, and it has a distinctive odor. So does the crowd, but that's not a bad thing. The **Midtown** *(582 Haight St., 415/558–8019)* is one of the last holdouts for the long-haired, black-leathered, motorcycle-riding modern primitive. It's very late-'80s/early-'90s, but that's not necessarily a bad thing either. Some of us aren't ready to embrace the fact that brown is the black of the '90s. Some of us don't like being in the sun. Some of us just want to drink and be left alone, all right! Has pool table.

Best place to feel like Bing: Once owned by Bing Crosby, the **Gold Dust Lounge** *(247 Powell St., 415/397–1695)* looks like a coupling between a faux Western bar at Disneyland and a real-life whorehouse in Reno. It hasn't been remodeled since the '50s, which seems too good to be true. Located near Union Square, this bar is full of foreigners who keep to themselves. It's the perfect place to have a cocktail and listen to live Dixieland jazz without bumping into anyone you know. Chuck Davis, the bartender, looks like he could be a lounge singer and he's got a wicked sense of humor.

Best places to sit 'n' spin: In a town obsessed with fun, it's no surprise that laundry has become a recreational activity. At the **Doo Wash Cafe** *(817 Columbus Ave., 415/885–1222)*, you can catch a flick in the TV room, shoot some pool, play some pinball, or munch on a cornedbeef sandwich while lounging on a comfy couch—all before the spin cycle. **Brain Wash** *(1122 Folsom St., 415/255–4866)* is the perfect refuge for grimy bands who have been cramped in a tour bus all week. Play some music on the acoustic stage, get your laundry done, and have a meal and a pint in the cafe. Not a bad deal.

food/coffee

Best Sunday constitutional: Every Sunday evening at seven, **Biscuits & Blues** *(401 Mason St., 415/292–BLUE)* serves up "Fried Chicken & Gospel," a sublime evening of food and music that's sure to cure whatever ails you. The East Bay's own Gospel Hummingbirds supply the spirituals while the kitchen sends out steaming plates of comfort food—ribs, chicken, grits, corn bread, mash, and okra. If the food and music don't cheer your heathen heart, the warm basement setting and the cozy candlelit atmosphere will at least soothe jangled nerves.

Best rock barbecue: It may be the only club in the Portrero Hill area, but it's one of the best in the city. The **Bottom of the Hill** *(1235 17th St., 415/621–4455)*, with its intimate stage and little patio, has played host—mostly on the sly—to a number of big names, including the Beastie Boys, Alanis Morisette, and Weezer, but it is best known for its gracious handling of local talent and its fantastic Sunday barbecues. Starting at 4:30 P.M., the Bottom of the Hill kitchen serves up an all-you-can-eat spread of chicken, pasta, hot dogs, burgers, and potato salad. For a measly three bucks, you can chow down in a big way, and—if you decide to hang out and shoot pool—there's always the Sunday matinee: three or four bands to grease your music-lovin' soul for the work week.

Best cocktail-nation restaurant: When it comes to late-night dining, it doesn't get much more *haute* than **Bruno's** *(2389 Mission St., 415/550–7455)*. A hugely popular supper club in the late '40s, this is one of the Mission's oldest restaurants. Although it lost customers in the '70s, a face-lift and some innovative booking has turned it into a happening Mission hangout. Complete with two stages and bars, it has a piano trio in a center room and also books a wide variety of lounge-style grooves, like Toledo and El Cameno Cha Cha Orchestra. Bruno's offers the height in fine dining and cocktail-nation entertainment, drawing club kids and visitors like Jim Jarmusch and Tom Waits.

Best Mission taquerias: When you visit San Francisco, you *need* to try a Mission burrito—not just because these hefty Mexican monsters have inspired imitators across the country, but because they are knock-outs (in more ways than one). Available for less than five bucks in the Mission, the real thing comes with fresh sliced avocado, tasty salsa, whole pinto beans, and your choice of meat, from *carnitas* (shredded marinated pork) to *carne asada* (seasoned strips of steak). Every scenester has his or her favorite taco stand, but two places you can't go wrong—despite the often seedy and rough late night clientele—are **Farolito's Taqueria** *(2779 Mission St., 415/824–7877)* near 24th Street, which stays open till 3:45 weekends, and **Cancun Restaurant** *(2288 Mission St., 415/252–9560)* near 19th Street. Also good are the *tacos al carbon*. Chase your feast with the strawberry or watermelon juices.

Best late-night Mexican nosh: It's a rule that if you are a San Fran-ciscan, you must embrace any establishment which displays Christmas lights and tinsel year-round. For a steaming plate of enchiladas at three o'clock in the morning there is no better than **La Rondalla** *(901 Valencia St., 415/647–7474)* in the Mission. The staff is downright motherly. If you look a bit tipsy, the large smiling waitresses offer enormous pitchers of ice water to aid rehydration. A guitarist serenades the irregular crowd of Hispanic families, couples on dates, rockers, club kids, and if every-body's in high spirits, it turns into a freewheeling sing-along.

Best late-night burger: The food at **Hamburger Mary's** *(1582 Fol-som St., 415/626–5767)* is good enough to pull even the most devoted disco bunny out of the club for a quick bite. Voted the best burger in town on more than one occasion, Mary's specializes in the very large and sloppy. For those noncarnivores, there is a wide selection of vegetarian items, and the Mary malted is to die for. The ambiance is something akin to a rummage sale held in the Twilight Zone with traffic signs, clocks, baby dolls, transformers, masks, lunch pails, gumball machines, and the odd picture. Check out the rear bar for its excellent pinball machines.

Best musical sushi: There is nothing quite like a wasabi-induced tear-ing jag accompanied by the soothing sounds of the Bay City Rollers. **Fly-ing Kamikaze's Rock 'n' Roll Sushi** *(3339 Steiner St., 415/567–4900)* may be the only restaurant in the known universe to attempt this strange, yet savory combination. Thanks to a unique menu, which includes tapas-style items like pot stickers stuffed with *ahí*, and an honest-to-goodness bar at which you might consume alcohol while pondering your fresh-fish intake, Kamikaze's has made a lasting mark in a town where sushi is more common than oxygen. The music selection—Beatles, Pink Floyd, and the like—could use some updating, but the fish is delicious.

Best vampire den: The other side of midnight can be a frustrating time for those craving some of the common daytime amenities in San Francisco. That's what makes **Big Heart Cafe** *(5700 Geary Blvd., 415/668–2919)* such an indispensable dawn-patrol treasure. Twenty-four-seven you can count on this diner for video rentals and modest malt-shop cuisine. Multiple TV screens show round-the-clock action classics to keep the glaze on your eyes, and—just so you don't look too rested come daybreak—you can bring titles home for noncommunal viewing. The video catalog is geared toward limited attention spans, with a concentration on martial arts and slasher flicks—which is to say nothing of the actual zombies who roam this place at odd hours.

Best hot *coppa* on a hard roll: The long-standing wet or dry sandwich debate continues at **Dominic's Original Genova Delicatessen** *(4937 Telegraph Ave., 510/652–7401)* in Oakland. Pick out your own seeded, sour, rosemary, whole wheat, or Dutch crunch roll from the vast bread trough. Hand it over the counter to any of eight old-school technicians, and they will load it to your specs with a staggering variety of meats, cheeses, veggies and condiments. For 70 years, Genova has been delivering the goods to Oakland's racially and economically diverse community of appetites in an earnest and affordable fashion. One sandwich provides a picnic for two, and may be augmented with a variety of salads and wines as well as homemade raviolis and pastas, made fresh daily. First-date warning: The spicy salami or mortadella could forfeit the kiss.

Best Mission coffeehouses: In a city that seems to spend most of its waking hours hanging out in coffeehouses, it can be hard to find something to do besides from drink coffee. There are so many pleasant variations on the coffee experience, it's possible to visit a new coffeehouse every time your mood shifts, seven days a week, 24 hours a day. Three Mission options on Valencia are a good place to start. Right near the punk headquarters Epicenter at 16th is **Muddy Waters** *(521 Valencia St., 415/863–8006)*, where local rock stars recover from last night's gig and the coffee is always strong: a good place to find flyers for upcoming shows. At the far end of the Mission at 24th Street, **Muddy's** *(1304 Valencia St., 415/647–7994)* offers a slightly more upscale, politically-aware, world-beat vibe, as befits its proximity to the yuppie-ish Noe Valley. In between the two, across from the Chameleon near 20th Street, is the end-of-the-line soul-searching station, **The Club Coffeehouse** *(920 Valencia St., 415/821–7112)*, where you go when you can't get in a band and just want to be left alone, man.

shopping

records

Best soulful vinyl: Don't you dare ask for a CD or refer to an album as (shudder) a disc. You gotta call it like it is, and what it is is a record, fool. The **Groove Merchant** *(687 Haight St., 415/252–5766)* deals in vinyl and vinyl only—and it deals specifically in music that sounds best on vinyl—soul, funk, and rare groove. Here you'll find hip-hop and reggae DJs browsing for a mix alongside ska kids who are looking forward by looking back to that '60s-soul sound.

Best punk headquarters: Right around the corner from Kilowatt (see Clubs) and up a rickety staircase is the anarchist community clubhouse **Epicenter** *(475 Valencia St., 16th St., 415/431–2725)*. It has a huge selection of new and used indie punk rock—from old Gun Club to the Redskins and the latest from Lookout!—as well as a fully stocked zine library, pool tables, and a bulletin board that features all the best underground happenings, like sewer tours, soapbox races, warehouse parties, rallies, and meetings. Epicenter also squeezes in a live gig every once in a while just to get the kids really riled up.

Runner-up: For the less rabid indie-label shopper, take a look at the time-honored **Aquarius Records** *(1055 Valencia St., 415/647–2272)* new Mission location, where the help never makes you feel stupid for asking questions.

Best DJ do-it-yourself kits: Used by professional DJs, **Zebra Records** *(475 Haight, 415/626–9145)* has everything you need to turn your warehouse gathering into an event. State-of-the-art mixers and turntables can be purchased or rented for a few ducats, and if you are really unprepared, there's a large assortment of 12-inches to choose from. Acid jazz, hip-hop, jungle, Latin house: You want it, they got it.

Best place to sell used records: If you have a grandmother who still insists on buying you random gifts of music because "the band kind of dresses like you, dear," then you need to make a trip over the mighty Bay Bridge to **Amoeba** *(2455 Telegraph Ave., Berkeley, 510/549–1125)*. This is a tremendous music store that will buy anything—*anything*—unless it's scratched. Trade is the way to go here, though, because there is no doubt that you will find something of interest, whether it's psychobilly compilations, R&B, or Tuvan throat singing.

books

Best pocket pulp: You almost need a map to navigate the multiple levels of **Green Apple Books** *(506 Clement St., 415/387–2272)*, but it is well worth it—for selection and trade-in value, there is no finer. In fact, Green Apple has such a hefty reputation, having won readers' polls in every local newspaper, that people who would never step foot in the Richmond district otherwise find themselves drooling in bookish anticipation at the chance. The staff, though often overtaxed by the crowds, are extremely well informed, and they take pride in their hard-to-find items, including a huge vintage pulp-pocketbook selection.

Best book store: Lawrence Ferlinghetti's **City Lights** *(261 Columbus Ave., 415/362–8193)* has been home to generations of the most revolutionary of San Francisco's renegade authors, publishers, and editors. This is the place to go if you are looking for a manifesto written by that crazy guy on the street corner. It is also the place to go if you are looking for a rare reissue of John Fante, William S. Burroughs, or Charles Bukowski—or a university press edition of the French theorist du jour. It is not, however, the place to ask for advice or a job. There is a waiting list three years long for the position of cashier.

Best zine newsstand: While Jackie Chan kicks butt on a large television screen, you can join neighborhood locals in a hunt for the perfect foreign film or cult classic, or you can finger through a huge selection of local and international zines. For those far from home, the Lower Haight's **Naked Eye News & Video** *(533 Haight St., 415/864–2985)* always has the most current issue of the *Village Voice* or the *Tattler*, as well as more serious periodicals like *Bananafish* and *Asian Trash Cinema*.

Runner-up: **Leather Tongue** *(714 Valencia St., 415/552–2900)* is the Mission's equivalent one-stop shop for today's cultural extremist.

clothes

Best clothes by the pound: The key is not to buy Levi's. Pants and jackets weigh a lot, but for summer shifts, dress shirts, thermals, scarves, and T-shirts, you've hit the jackpot. The staff at **Clothes Contact** *(473 Valencia St., 415/621–3212)* is very funky and most of their clothes are too, but when you find that very special item—say, an embroidered silk kimono—you know you're getting the steal of the century. Luckily, if you do fall madly in love with a floor-length wool coat, the cashier is not above bartering.

Best fail-safe vintage fashions: Offering an award-winning window display and the most discriminating buying staff this side of a gem dealer, **Wasteland** *(1660 Haight St., 415/863–3150)* is the perfect vintage-clothing store for both the ultimate trendoid or the self-conscious shopper. There is no need to worry whether a sweater ensemble is so orange that it's cool or whether even Mary Tyler Moore would reject it. If it's on a hanger at Wasteland, it is guaranteed to be in immaculate condition and at the very height of retro fashion.

Best street buzz: Celebrating the connection between music and fashion, **Behind the Post Office** *(1550 Haight St., 415/861–2507)* is a laid-back environment for local designers to sell boutique versions of the latest street fashions, while some of the town's most popular acid jazz and hip-hop DJs spin the steel wheels. Threads here tend to the knit, loose-fitting end of the spectrum. Don't forget to ask for a rundown on the city's most happening events, including Behind the Post Office club nights.

Best kinderwhore shopping: No need to pay $30 for a baby-T when **Foxy Lady** *(2644 Mission St., 415/285–4980)* stocks Taiwan-made knockoffs of trendy clothes. It may last you only three weeks, but at these prices, who's arguing? Six bucks will get you a little shirt with all the curtsey-cute decals you could possibly want. Eight bucks will get you a satin micro-miniskirt to go with it. Wading through racks of hideously sequined prom dresses doesn't seem all that bad when you're saving the cold green.

Best fetish gear: While customizing is crucial to any true fetish junkie, the casual fashion kitten can find what she needs at **Stormy Leather** *(1158 Howard, 415/626–1672)*, from leather jockstraps with studs to cat-o'-nine-tails. If they don't have it, they know where you can get it.

et cetera

Best way to build a Farrah Fawcett altar: Call it Mission spiritualism. The holy nature of this tiny, cramped Mission store forbids **381 Guerrero** *(381 Guerrero St., 415/621–3830)* from having an official name. Beyond its iron-work gate are fetish cult items worthy of only the most pious Mission hipsters: votive candles bearing the aspects of Brad Pitt, David Cassidy, Cher, Dolly Parton, ABBA, Liberace, and Charlie's Angels; enamel key chains and lighters in the form of Jesus Christ Our Savior; voodoo dolls complete with pins and guidance; eight balls that tell your future with a couple of well-chosen phrases; and lunch boxes and Zippos. The local, holy five-and-dime.

Best guitar shop: Located directly across the street from the gaping cavity that was Guitar Center in Berkeley, **Univibe Musical Instruments** *(3299 Adeline St., Berkeley, 510/420-0302)* offers a wide array of vintage and used guitars, basses, drums, and accessories for both discriminating musicians and scrounging hacks. While there are few saints in music retail, owner-proprietor William Charman may soon be anointed by the legions of Bay Area bands and musicians who rely on this establishment. Straight-up deals are complemented by humane service: no ponytails, no keyboard ties, and no "Let me go talk to my manager" (retail code for "Cig break"). Customers are encouraged to handle the merch, free from the blistering scrutiny of the embittered heshers who staff many other music stores. The clientele runs the gamut from the crustiest gutterpunk to the most seasoned pro, and there's even a pool table if you need a quick game of stick to get your mojo going. Bear in mind: the "No Stairway" clause is in full effect.

Best vintage vibrators: Masturbation during the Victorian era must have been a strange experience if the dildos at **Good Vibrations** *(1210 Valencia St., 415/974–8980)* are any indication. Though this large yet discreet lesbian-run store (no sign, painted windows) is famous for its vibrator museum, it is actually worth visiting for its contemporary retail devices as well—most notably its special silicone dildo collection. A large selection of female-approved porno, sex books, erotic comics, and body oils rounds out the merchandise. Devotedly sex-positive Good Vibrations hosts classes, seminars, and readings and is a benchmark of enlightened San Francisco.

body alterations

Best piercers: For some people, *who* pierces their flesh is as important as *how* it is pierced. Among the very first piercing studios in San Francisco, **Body Manipulations** *(3234 16th St., 621–0408)* has a reputation that is beyond reproach. Always on the cutting edge of new techniques and trends, Body M also has an uncanny eye for trendy neighborhoods. The original shop shared a building with Erno Tattoo in the Lower Haight. When that area became too hip, Body M picked up and moved to a much more spacious location in the Mission district, where—you guessed it— its strip of 16th Street became ground zero for '90s youth action.

Best corsets: The most likely spot to see body-manipulation sage Fakir Musafar is **Dark Garden Corsetry** *(551 Hayes St., 415/626–6264)*. Known for its exquisite custom-made corsets, Dark Garden wants to bring said underappreciated undergarment back into high fashion. Each year, the lovely proprietors throw a number of fashion shows, which feature models with waists as small as 17 inches. Corsetry tip #27: Overlacing can result in internal complications and vomiting. Consult a professional.

Best tattoo museum: Fascinated with all things tattoo related but afraid to commit to anything too permanent? That's okay, you're more than welcome to wander through **Lyle Tuttle's** *(841 Columbus Ave., 415/775–4991)* tattoo museum. The history of tattooing—ancient flashes, antique machines, newspaper clippings, and priceless photos of sailors and circus freaks—can be found on these legendary walls. And if you hang out a while, you're bound to catch some real-life inking.

Best tattoos: There are nearly 30 tattoo shops in San Francisco alone, making this one of the better cities for ink, but pretty confusing for the tattoo virgin. To find the right artists for you, talk to people you see whose work you like. Visit several shops, and examine everyone's flash before you make a decision. A few suggestions to get you started: If you are looking for biomechanical or modern tribal work, try Nala at **Ed Hardy's Tattoo City** *(722 Columbus Ave., 415/433–9437)*; for traditional tribal, try Greg Kulz at **Erno Tattoo** *(252 Fillmore St., 415/861–9206)*; for portraits, try Henry Goldfield at **Goldfield's Tattoo Studio** *(404 Montgomery St., 415/433–0558)*; for pinup girls, try Patrick at **Everlasting Tattoo** *(1939 McAllister St., 415/928–6244)*; for Japanese traditional, try Freddy Corbin at **Tattoo City**; for aliens and monsters, try Patrick Ethington at Erno Tattoo or Aaron Cain at Everlasting; for biker slop, try anybody at **Anibus Worpis** *(1525 Haight St., 415/431–2218)*. Call ahead, as most of these inkers are booked weeks in advance.

hotel/motel

Best cheap SOMA bed: Warm and brightly painted, **Interclub Globe Hostel** *(10 Hallam Pl., 415/431–0540)* has fewer rules than most hostels, although you will need a passport (U.S. or other) to stay. The rooms sleep four, but who wants sleep when you have an entire city to explore? A helpful bulletin board gives directions to all the most happening cafes, bars, clubs, and restaurants. A pool table and a sun deck with an impressive view are just a couple more amenities. Rates run $10 to $16 a bed, and there's an entire floor for nonsmokers.

Best Haight hideout: Decorated with loving care by owner Sami Sunchild, the **Red Victorian Bed & Breakfast** *(1665 Haight St., 415/864–1978)* is one of Haight Street's most beloved relics. Each room offers its own idiosyncratic trip. For less than $100, you can taste this city's past by staying in the extravagant "Summer of Love Room," furnished with a tie-dye canopy and a collection of '60s rock posters. Then again, there's always the "Japanese Tea Garden Room" or the "Teddy Bear Room."

Best girls' sleepover: This women-only guest house is so comfortable and sex-positive that you may never want to leave. The folks who run **House O'Chicks** *(2162 15th St., 415/861–9849)* live on the premises—it doesn't get much more homey than that—and if they dig you, you can have access to their large collection of films, including a plethora of lesbian porn. Each room has a stereo, a TV, and a custom-made mattress—custom-made for what, you'll just have to wait and see. Rates run from $50 to $75 except during the Gay, Lesbian, Bisexual, Transgender Freedom Parade weekend—well, you can imagine.

Best rock hotel: This is where the rock stars stay—and party. That's right, it is very possible that Dave Navarro has plunged into the black-tiled swimming pool at the **Phoenix Hotel** *(601 Larkin St., 415/776–1380)*. The always-popular Civic Center/Tenderloin stop offers in-room massage and bodywork, and California cuisine can be had at **Backflip**, which used to be the famously groovy restaurant Miss Pearl's Jam House. Rates run about $90 but can go as low as $20 in the winter.

local wonders

Best soapbox races: One of the best views in town is also the site of San Francisco's harrowing, semifrequent boxcar races. On most summer Sundays, **Twin Peaks**, our lovely towering hills just west of the Castro District become overrun with *Gearhead*-obsessed lunatics, who will race anything from a claw-footed bathtub to a lawnmower attached to a pushcart, all for the glory of a six-pack of Black Label.

Best Mission grave site: The oldest building in San Francisco is also one of the last remaining grave sites within city limits. Folks at the **Mission Dolores** *(3321 Sixteenth St., 415/621–8203)* are sweet as pie and more than happy to answer any question. The enclosed graveyard offers a pleasant retreat in the city, complete with a citrus grove and stone benches. The gift shop has quite a lot of papal paraphernalia left over from when the Pope visited.

transmissions

Best radio station: Hands down, the best radio station in town is college-run **KUSF (90.3 FM)**. With a slew of DJs who are in the know, the station plays the very latest in everything from East Indian surf music to Latin jazz to trance, hardcore, blues, rock, and punk. The progressiveness of the programming is largely due to the fact that so many of the DJs are actively involved in shaping the music scene from a grassroots level. Terrible Ted, who was recently named "Best DJ" by the *SF Weekly*, has worked at Slim's for a number of years; Bonnie Simmons works as a club DJ, a band manager, and one of the producers of SFO3, San Francisco's annual music convention; Sep Ghadishah runs Lipp Service Promotions and also spins at the community-run KPFA as well as at local clubs.

Best blues DJ: As laid back as they come, **Big Bones** *(Wednesday 9–12 P.M.;* **KPOO 89.5 FM***)* plays it like a man who knows. Down with the local blues groove (he plays an unforgettable harmonica for Preacher Boy & the Natural Blues) and up on his blues lore, Bones promises to treat you to a splattering of that Chicago-style lovin' while keeping you up to date on all the upcoming shows and events

—additional contributions to this chapter by Blake Schwarzenbach

seattle

by Brooke Holmes

"Seattle's a horrible place. It rains all the time, the streets
are full of dead fish, and we're all hopelessly provincial and
backward. Please don't move here."
— **Dave Dederer, *Presidents of the USA***

Mudhoney's 1991 track off the *Singles* album says it blunt-
ly: "Everybody loves us, everybody loves our town..."
Well, everyone in Seattle is sick of hearing about Seattle.
But with local brands at the top of their fields in software
(Microsoft), coffee (Starbucks), indie rock (Sub Pop), and underground
comix (Fantagraphics), Seattle *is* what pundits say the 21st century
needs: The Ultimate Content Provider. Though the sweaty, dirty club,
the Off Ramp, where giants like Nirvana, Soundgarden, and Pearl Jam
once walked the earth, has closed, Seattle grunge lives on in many
guises—it's hard to argue with good content. Even Seattle scenesters
have given up on arguing over which members of the primordial alternative band Green River sold out first.

More recent Seattle rockers seem haunted by the heady memory of
MTV prime time—making some bands at once overconfident and self-
conscious. But a few bad moments haven't eclipsed the city's trademark
innovation or energy. Even though Sub Pop's comprehensive and slick-
looking store off First Avenue has landed on the tourist map of Seattle's
downtown and mournful teenagers still gather on the street in front of
Kurt Cobain's suicide site, Seattle is not about nostalgia. Bands seem
to follow a pattern: Local gems build up an enthusiastic following in the
area's excellent midsize clubs, and then, bolstered by strong local labels
and the support of their hometown fans, they hit the road. Recently acts
like the Presidents of the United States of America, Muzzle, and Critters
Buggin' have begun this cycle and been dubbed Seattle's second wave,
and their absence (as well as the absence of a handful of other promis-

ing groups) has once more created a void that tons of new bands are eager to fill. So, don't write Seattle off. Not too long from now you may be bragging about having seen Mavis Piggott at Moe way back in '97.

Locals took the grunge hubbub well; they only got really pissy when things like Planet Hollywood moved in. Everybody from Birkenstock-wearing do-it-yourself types to snowboarding skate rats and post-grunge rockers (identifiable by dirty T-shirts minus the flannel, shorter hair, and more piercings) lives here; the unifying trait is a laid-back, accepting attitude that borders on lobotomized. "Herb-friendly" tags in the personals of the weekly *Stranger* seem redundant. Who isn't? In the last five years, the gay scene, centered on Capitol Hill, has grown to become a huge part of the community (from the annual Gay Pride Parade to the AIDS support group, the Chicken Soup Brigade). The scene's kingpin—*Stranger* sex columnist, radio talk show host, and sometime social critic—Dan Savage is a living local treasure.

lay of the land

The hilly heart of Seattle is surrounded by water, Elliot Bay to the west, Lake Union to the north, and Lake Washington to the east. The Evergreen Point Floating Bridge crosses Lake Washington, heading out to the East-side suburbs of Bellevue and Redmond, home of the Microsoft campus. I-5 runs up the middle of the Seattle; on its east side is Capitol Hill and First Hill (called Pill Hill due to its many hospitals). **Capitol Hill** has survived the erratic shiftings of youth culture to remain the 'hood with the most action; its main thoroughfare, Broadway Avenue, is still lined with surly punks hitting up passersby for beer money at all hours, and tipsy Urban Outfitter princesses fill the sidewalk as happy hour begins at Broadway's numerous restaurants. If you want to skip franchises like Ben & Jerry's, head over to Pine and Pike on the west slope of the hill, where off-beat stores and nightspots are thriving. The **park behind Seattle Central Community College** on 11th Avenue has a mix of dog-walkers and young drifters—think of it as a very clean and presentable version of New York's Tompkins Square Park. On 15th Ave. near the Group Health building, an irregular clutch of cafes, independent groceries, and specialty stores caters to the residents' eclecticism and general freakishness, and has more of a neighborhood feel than Broadway. If you're feeling bored on a summer night, head down to the **Miller Community Center** *(301 20th E., 206/684–4753)* on 19th Ave. for an all-ages punk bash.

Pine and Pike streets run all the west across town to Downtown and Elliot Bay. Situated between the Seattle Center, where you'll see the Space Needle, and the Downtown retail zone, **Belltown** may feel like a residential neighborhood during the day, but come sundown the night owls come out to play, crossing paths briefly with the beer-seeking post-work yuppies. To the north of the Seattle Center is the residential Queen Anne Hill. Heading up across Lake Union, **Fremont,** with its oh-so-wacky public art (a sculpture of a big monster eats a VW bug under-neath a bridge) and oodles of vintage toasters, is a proud enclave of '60s right-thinkin' and right-livin', supporting a huge hemp mercantile store and several food co-ops. To the east, also above Lake Union, the **U-District** is thronged with students year-round. Known locally as U-Dub, the University of Washington has a campus larger than most sub-urbs, and its major stretch of sidewalk, the Avenue, boasts a number of boutiques—everything from African art to used CDs—that cater to the collegiate-at-heart. Finally, south of the city, there are miles of ware-houses and industry, and eventually the city of Tacoma.

getting from a to b

Seattle has a complex bus system that, for the most part, runs smooth-ly. During nonpeak hours it's $.85 to ride anywhere in the city and $1.10 anywhere in the county. Peak prices are $1.10 and $1.35 respectively. Transfers are good for about three hours after you get off the bus and can be used for round-trips. The buses discontinue service for two or three hours late at night, though schedules vary from line to line. Call the Metro Rider Line at 206/553–3000, or pick up a schedule, available at colleges, libraries, malls, and Metro outposts (like the Metro Tunnel downtown). Recently there's been a campaign to extend the Monorail, but currently it only shuttles between Seattle Center and Westlake Mall, making it more a novelty than anything else. Cabs are reasonable, clean, and the only option during the witching hours. Yellow Cabs are most dependable. Call 206/622–6500 for the Seattle dispatcher if you're traveling within the city; 206/455–4999 for the Eastside dispatcher for destinations in Bellevue or Redmond; and 206/872–5600 for the King County dispatcher, if you're traveling to other points in the county like Tacoma. Don't rely on flagging cabs on the street.

sources

For the best coverage of the local scene and the most intriguing person-als, check out *The Stranger*, a free weekly that comes out Thursdays and can be found at most cafes and trendy stores. Columns like "I Love Televi-sion," "Pop Paralysis," and Dan Savage's syndicated "Savage Love" con-sistently deliver dead-on commentary with a healthy dose of humor. *The Stranger* also regularly features in-depth reporting on everything from alleged homophobia at the *Seattle Times* to the pitfalls of business improvement districts. The other major free weekly is the *Seattle Weekly*, geared to a slightly older, highbrow crowd. Though they're a bit tamer, the features are unpredictable, treating everything from local murders to neighborhood revivals. *The Rocket* is a biweekly paper for the Portland and Seattle music scenes and harder to find; try a record store or a college campus first.

clubs

Best hangout: Sure, the **OK Hotel** *(212 Alaskan Way S, 206/621–7903)* served as Java Joe's in the movie *Singles*, but that's not the reason to visit—the OK stands on its own merits. During business hours, when it's not too crowded, you can get cheap food, drink coffee, and shoot pool for 50 cents a game. By night, it's one of the only rock clubs in the Pioneer Square neighborhood, an area known for blues joints. Quality alt.rock acts (from Screaming Trees to Critters Buggin' to Soundgarden frontman Chris Cornell) play most nights in the back ballroom; the OK has also got the strongest avant-garde jazz lineup in the city, with shows by Charles Gale as well as John Zorn's sometime collaborator Wayne Horvitz. To top it off, there are poetry slams in the lounge at least once a week, making it one of the city's most eclectic clubs. Along with the goateed college set and grim 30ish scenesters in Pumas, you'll run into hangin'-on-by-a-thread hippies and second-generation flower children.

Best Seattle rawk: Even though the days of unannounced Pearl Jam and Soundgarden gigs have gone the way of the old Kingdome ceiling, the **Crocodile Cafe** *(2200 Second Ave., 206/441–5611)* still wins top-dog status among local clubs. It's the first pick for both rising local bands and major alternative touring acts, despite newcomers like Moe (see below) and the recently renovated Showbox. The Croc's in the heart of Belltown, and owner Stephanie Dorgan (wife of R.E.M. guitarist Peter Buck, who occasionally stops by and plays surprise acoustic sets) has kept up with the post-grunge scene, even adding a Wednesday night acid jazz party and a Sunday night karaoke slam (this city thrives on kitsch). It's got incredible acoustics—and an adjacent cafe, busy during the day.

Best cocktail-lounge parties: Moe's Mo'roc'n Cafe *(925 E. Pike St., 206/324–2406)* has come to rival the Crocodile Cafe as the core

Seattle club, drawing major indie acts. An adjoining diner has nifty curving lime-green booths. Drop by late in the afternoon and you'll find aging, pockmarked rockers sharing french fries and talking shit about the scene. If you prefer a little twist with your conversation, be sure not to miss the Shaken not Stirred parties, currently on Tuesdays and Thursdays: camp evenings of Value Village chiffon and feathers, Singapore Slings, and the *Pink Panther*–theme man Henry Mancini. They're such a hit that the owners enlisted a Seattle Repertory Theater designer to create the second-floor Moonlight Lounge, complete with tin ceiling, etched windows that create strange lighting, and faux Corinthian leather wainscoting. Regular DJ Riz Rollins is a Seattle household name, a big fish in a small pond.

Runner-up: Another Pioneer Square club, **Zasu** *(608 First Ave., 206/682–1200)* has DJ Terrence Gunn on Wednesdays, making elevator music the breather of choice between weekends of cranked-up amps.

Best Laundromat hoedowns: At first, it was just a cool place to nurse a big cup of java and vent some capitalist ambition on a game of Monopoly while you waited for your laundry. But then the funky Belltown Laundromat-cum-juice bar **Sit 'n' Spin** *(2219 Fourth Ave., 206/441–9484)* began booking bands, and Seattle gained yet another quirky venue for its talents. Everyone from local jazz outfits like BeBop & Destruction to harder hitting alt.rockers plays here, drawing impressive crowds of twenty-somethings with pierced tongues and vintage T-shirts, who table-hop and suck down concoctions from the juice bar between shows. Location scouts take note.

Best dance club: Kid Mohair *(1207 Pine St., 206/625–4444)* is one of the newer operations on the west slope of Capitol Hill in the Pike and Pine area, but it's already established itself quite nicely. First, its owners skipped urban decay themes and decor; Kid Mohair is, if you can believe it, tasteful with a capital T, taking design cues from the **Sorrento Hotel** (see Hotel/motel) with long velvet drapes and mohair banquettes. Kid Mohair pulls out all stops when it comes to late-night parties. While it caters to a gay crowd, boasting regular drag shows and the Wednesday night Wall-to-Wall Girls on Girls party, the delineation isn't clear-cut. The crowd's likely to be mixed for mellower jazz nights; a wine bar hops early in the evening.

Runner-up: To see the best after-hours divas, in a just about breeder-free environment, head up Pine to Broadway and the club **Neighbours** *(1509 Broadway Ave., 206/324–5358)*, where "I Will Survive" still reigns supreme over Seattle's sweatiest all-night male scene.

bars

Best Pike Place Market hideaway: With the Seattle Film Festival's rising prestige and Seattle's new life as a Hollywood movie backdrop, it's only appropriate that Tom Skerritt and Rob Morrow should open a wine bar in the bowels of Pike Place Market, right? Though it's tragic to see the previous tenant, Bugsy's Pizzeria, move out, the **Alibi Room** *(85 Pike St., 206/623–3180)* is a refreshingly refined—that is, not a dive—addition to the youth drinking scene. Located in the Post-Alley of the Market, it's set off from all the shops in a mazelike warren of nooks and crannies. With a wood-and-plant decor, staff in crisp white aprons, and well-dressed if chatty drinkers in black, it feels like Manhattan on Puget Sound. Thanks to a between-the-buildings view of Elliot Bay and the smart vibe, it's a prime place to flee faux Nordic metal bands and relax a little—or try to meet that special someone. Lunch offers a daily menu with fresh fish from the Market across the street.

Best bar with DJs: BIGOTS STAY AWAY reads the sign on the door to the cheery **Re-Bar** *(1114 Howell St., 206/233–9873)*. At this Belltown anything-goes spot the regulars are open to everything, as long as it involves a good time. This sometime club (DJ Riz spins here twice a week, though resident mixologist MC Queen Lucky also packs 'em in with her danceable Janet Jackson remixes and other revival faves) and perennial meat market best represents Seattle's nightlife: easygoing, accepting, but never dull. Shlumpy REI shoppers knock back shots with frat boys, leather dykes, and flaming queens and nobody blinks. The crowd ranges in age from those who just became legal to thirty-something barflies, though most are prime Gen Xers. Stylewise anything goes, so you'll see punks and Allen Ginsberg groupies alike. People dance here whether they can or can't (most can't).

Best pub: While Fremont Avenue's **Red Door Alehouse** *(3401 Fremont Ave. N, 206/547–7521)* is a meat market in its own right, this mellow, comfortable beer and wine bar is also one of the best places around to smoke a pack of cigarettes with a long-lost friend, nurse a drink, and rehash the salad days. Don't let the yuppies scare you off—nobody's trying to impress anyone here—and enough Fremont locals spice things up. The dark, smoky but clean spot has sturdy wooden tables, old pictures on the wall (which lend faux alehouse authenticity), and a long bench that runs along one wall. In the summertime, the cluttered patio opens up.

Runner-up: If you like the mood at the Red Door but want to change the setting later in the evening, head on over to the **Triangle Tavern** *(3507 Fremont Ave. N, 206/632–0880)*, a low-key bar down the street that draws more of the I-just-became-legal drinking crowd. Like the Red Door, this bar closes up pretty early (midnight during the week) so the best time to stop by is around 9 or 10.

Best friendly dive: It's true some people might call **Linda's** *(707 E. Pine St., 206/325–1220)* a dive, but they'd say it affectionately, like the way you might call *Melrose* "trash TV." It's the official neighborhood bar for Broadway thrift-store hipsters, offering the requisite cheap pitchers and cutthroat pool. The bartenders will indifferently pour you a glass of wine and immediately go back to talking to their friends (all enjoying free beer) at the other end of the bar, but this is good. Linda's is a tad cramped.

Best biker bar: You're trying to get the bartender's attention in a packed room and inadvertently jostle someone behind you. Turning, you face a burly, sweating Hell's Angels lifer. If it was a road movie, you'd be eating his fist, but if you're at the **Buckaroo** *(4201 Fremont Ave. N, 206/634–3161)* in Fremont, he'll contritely say, "Excuse me." The neon bucking cowboy out front sets the tone for the friendliest biker bar in the West. Inside, there's standard pub grub, and darkly stained wooden booths, well-worn pool tables, and almost every Northwest microbrew.

food/coffee

Best low-key brasserie: It's not just **Cafe Septieme's** *(214 Broadway Ave. E, 206/860–8858)* new, ultraslick cocktail lounge and the strategically placed sidewalk seating (in the middle of one of Broadway's busiest blocks) that makes it a top dinner bet: The food is really good. Vegetarian lasagna (lunches only), Caesar salad, and pasta variations—try beet pasta—defy the limitations of cafe food, making Septieme's move from Belltown to Capitol Hill extremely welcome. Cafe Septieme strives to create a Parisian bistro setting, but the locals' mellow left-coast attitude shines through. It's an ideal place to linger and see and be seen—especially if you want to ogle drop-ins like Melanie Griffith and Antonio Banderas.

Runner-up: Also check out the cafe that moved into Septieme's old space in Belltown, **Good Chow** *(2331 Second Ave., 206/443–5833)*, a new shabby-chic restaurant that recently opened to deserved rave reviews for its updated continental cuisine and salads that the results of an inspired forage in the woods. Prices are on the low end of upscale.

Best people watching: Finding parking on the backstreets of Capitol Hill is a near-impossible feat. The airy and relaxed **TestaRossa** *(210 Broadway Ave. E, 206/328–0878)* is the answer, with hassle-free validated parking (and you can shop in Broadway thrift stores and hang out later with no worries), along with great Italian lunch deals and a roomful of everybody from dapper gym dandies to Seattle art gallery hounds. Try the deliciously fattening stuffed pizzas (not for the lactose-intolerant) or the daily soups (usually creative) and light pasta dishes.

Best greasy fries at 2 A.M.: Greenlake area's **Beth's Cafe** *(7311 Aurora Ave. N, 206/782–5588)* could've invented the "Best Dive" and "Best Greasy Spoon" categories it always snags in local polls. From the fake wood-paneled walls to the mini-pinball arcade, Beth's has it all. It's cramped, the sound of the grease on the grill echoes through the room, and even if you're not smoking, you feel as if you've finished off a pack by the time you leave. There's almost always a few tables of greasy bikers or punks, whose crayon masterpieces (materials available at the tables) cover the walls.

Best juice bar in a mall: An indoor mall like the **Broadway Market** should not be the hepcat mecca that it is. Yet the home of Seattle's Urban Outfitters also has dozens of little jewelry and magnet stands, tables of homemade candles and pipes shaped like the Starship Enterprise, along with table upon table of Capitol Hill scenesters just chillin' out, man. Some street urchins seem to live out of here, using the bathrooms and public phones. One of the Market's hippest places to look bored is **Gravity Bar** *(415 Broadway Ave. E, 206/325–7186; downtown, 113 Virginia Ave., 206/448–8826)*, a juice bar and vegetarian restaurant with a *Jetsons*-era look. It has the old health food standbys—like hummus and garden burgers—as well as more creative entrees like Bathing Rama (peanut sauce with tofu, spinach, and red cabbage) or Ginger Mushroom Tempeh. If you're stopping by for an afternoon pick-me-up, try the Dennis Hopper, a drink made of carrot, beet, garlic, and wheat grass that tastes like nuclear waste.

Best vegetarian sandwiches: After a lazy day of poking around in Fremont junk shops, there's only one place to go and collect your wits: the **Still Life in Fremont Coffeehouse** *(709 N. 35th St., 206/547–9850).*

The Seattle Folklife Festival meets the Velvet Underground here—and that's just the background music. This is where Fremont gathers, in all its transgenerational, counterculture glory. Fortyish yoga regulars dine next to patchouli-drenched girls with cornrows. The Still Life has delicious, meticulously prepared, always-fresh sandwiches that, thankfully, don't taste like health food sandwiches. Almost always a line at the counter and the prime outdoor tables are hard to come by.

Best coffeehouse: Guess what? Seattle takes its coffee seriously. Seattle espresso jerks who think they should be rock stars and hate their boss have been known to ignore customers when asked giveaway soft-core questions like "Are you sure that's nonfat?" A cup of good black coffee still garners the most respect here. It's hard to pin down the best cup, but **Espresso Roma** in U District *(4201 University Way, 206/632–6001; Capitol Hill, 202 Broadway Ave. E, 206/324–1866)*, is the pit stop of choice for both U-Dub students and post-grad dropouts. The U-District cafe has huge windows (for a comparatively sordid view of the lumpen proles, skate rats, and runaways who line the Avenue) and plenty of earth-toned spartan tables, while the Capitol Hill one is smaller but brighter.

Best late-night espresso: If Espresso Roma is perfect for lounging about in the late afternoon, **Bauhaus Books & Coffee** *(301 E. Pine St., 206/625–1600)* is the only choice for caffeine vampires looking for after-hours fixes—late night in Seattle meaning one in the morning. Big on candles and Portishead tapes for nodding out, Bauhaus has plenty of seating in the loft area over the espresso bar, along the windows that look out on Pine and Bellevue and on the outside tables (which are often packed during summer). A wall of books with a sliding ladder reminds everyone that Bauhaus is also a used bookstore, though the cafe definitely dominates. The crowd ranges from laptop-toting loners to groups of Capitol Hill scenesters to the de rigueur Seattle REI types. Even Yoko Ono's been sighted here.

Best 24-hour living room: Whether you're crammed into a motel room that reeks of fungus and cheap cigars, or you're curled up on a couple of pillows in the corner of your friend's studio apartment, the **Book and Bean Company** *(1635½ Olive Way E., 206/325–1139)* is the living room that all budget travelers need, open 24 hours. The armchairs are well-worn and don't match, and the two main rooms (there's also a computer room with Internet access) are small enough to be cozy. The little espresso setup in the corner is the only clue that this is a business, though it reminds you of when your younger brother used to play grocery store in the dining room. No food.

Best Internet cafe: Even if you think cafes are completely incompatible with computer freaks who need to pretend they're being social, it's worth staying openminded long enough to take a trip to the **Speakeasy Cafe** *(2304 Second Ave., 206/728–9770).* This Belltown hangout singlehandedly justifies the marriage of modems and macciatos. The emphasis here isn't all on the PCs scattered throughout the garagelike room with bare wood floors; the Speakeasy also has a local arts scene, with everything from open-mike poetry readings to silent films to original local theater. While the nearby **Crocodile Cafe** (see Clubs) often draws tourists eager for star sightings and surprise shows, the Speakeasy is mostly for locals.

shopping

records

Best place to trust the staff's picks: For all their requisite surliness, the maladjusted youth of Seattle are the mellowest in the country ... at least the ones who work at the U-District's **Cellophane Square** *(4538 University Way NE, 206/634–2280).* So what if the guy who checked your backpack looks blankly at you when you ask for it back. He'll find it eventually, and at least he's smiling. Besides, the floor staff has encyclopedic knowledge of music, and if you're looking for a bootleg or something else Cellophane doesn't carry, the staffers will tell you where to go or who to order it from. A few years ago Cell Square moved to its current, larger location; its old store, five or six blocks down the street, still houses the vinyl collection. Packed with a wide selection of imports and local gems, the main store includes recordings of area music festivals (like a CD of the Kill Rock Stars Olympia show five years ago, with Nirvana, 7 Year Bitch, and Bikini Kill) and I-was-playing-the-Off Ramp-when-Eddie Vedder-was-still-in-California bands, as well as stuff from the *Billboard* charts.

Best used CDs: Even though Cell Square's stock outnumbers it by thousands of CDs, **Wall of Sound** *(2237 Second Ave., 206/441–9880)* in Belltown gets by on charm and selectivity. Almost half its collection is obscure world music (both worldbeat and folk and tribal music), though the other side of the store boasts impeccably arranged ambient, acid jazz, trip-hop, jazz, noise, and what they call eclectic sections (meaning everything from Belly to Laurie Anderson), and a lot of obscure electronic stuff. They also have a whole room of vinyl worth checking out.

Best vinyl: Retrospect Records *(1524 E. Olive Way, 206/329–1077)* smells like it's been around since the invention of vinyl, though that could just be the kids flipping through the used GWAR. It resembles a garage with migraine-inducing fluorescent lights. While Retrospect has a respectable selection of new and reasonably priced used CDs, its record collection is what makes the trek down from Broadway worth it. It has both new and used vinyl, which is well-organized and tends to center around mainstream and alternative rock; it also carries turntables, guitar accessories, and other run-of-the-mill record store stuff.

Best experimental noise: If you're searching for a store where William S. Burroughs is the closest thing to mainstream, **OHM** *(1510 E. Olive Way, 206/323–8669)* is a dream come true. This small, four-year-old CD and record store has got the best collection of music that's beyond "alternative" in Seattle: underground, experimental, electronic, ambient, and good old Gothic. Though it's only open from 1 to 7 P.M., Tuesday through Saturday, what it lacks in convenience and size it makes up for in quality. While it can be humbling to wander in and recognize only a handful of the hundreds of artists, OHM is a good place to push the boundaries of your taste. John Cage would be proud.

books

Best place to buy Emma Goldman's complete works: Left Bank Books *(92 Pike St., 206/622–0195)* is a true mecca for old-school leftists, their student counterparts, and yurt-dwelling tree spikers. The store is cramped, and the selection admirable, with extensive women's studies, philosophy, religion, eco-theory, and political theory sections (it carries all of Noam Chomsky). It also has the most impressive bumper-sticker collection in the Northwest, and bears responsibility for all the KILL YOUR TELEVISION and LOBOTOMIES FOR REPUBLICANS: IT'S THE LAW stickers visible on every politically overt car from here to Canada.

Best used books: Magus Bookstore in the U-District *(1408 N.E. 42nd, 206/633–1800)* is a bibliophile's dream of high shelves and narrow passageways. It's a great place to browse in the early evening. After a few minutes in the towering stacks, you forget the outside world exists. The selection goes high and low; there's a lot of Louis L'Amour paperbacks to balance out the metaphysics. The coffee-table art books are often bargains.

Best browsing: If you're under the impression that Seattle had no culture before Sub Pop and Starbucks, drop by **Elliot Bay Books** *(101 South Main, 206/624–6600).* The multilevel, densely packed bookstore, firmly planted downtown in Pioneer Square, is a testament to Seattle's long-standing obsession with strong coffee and good books (the weather inspires such hobbies). You can spend time in Elliot Bay without spending a dime, the result being that it is a community hangout. There are couches and armchairs everywhere; downstairs is a cafeteria with a surprisingly well-rounded selection of vegetarian dishes, health food, and even more books.

clothes

Best place for women to comb the vintage racks: While the store's buyers sometimes seem to confuse biker-bar cocktail waitress chic with clothes you'd actually wear, **Retro Viva** *(the U-District, 4515 University Way NE, 206/635–8886; Capitol Hill, 215 Broadway Ave. E, 206/328–7451; downtown, 1511 First Ave., 206/624–2529)* is still the vintage store of choice for most women gearing up to go out on the town (its men's selection isn't worth it). Retro Viva combs Seattle's thrift stores (which don't get picked over too badly if you're up to the task yourself—try Value Village or Goodwill), and stocks loads of genuine '50s cocktail dresses and fake-fur minis, plus, for the less bold, plenty of basics like simple dresses, tiny cashmere sweaters, and hip-huggers.

Best vinyl club clothes: When that Special K–inspired moment of creativity hits and you're ready to splurge on a new baby-blue vinyl mini, **Paragon** *(2300 First Ave., 206/448–4048)* is ready for you, sister. The high-end trendy club clothes are more over-the-top here than at other Seattle boutiques, which tend to play it safe with retro eccentricities. And if you're feeling thrifty, Paragon also has racks of cheaper synthetic basics reminiscent of New York's lower Broadway street stands. The staff can be a tad overbearing; go shopping with a friend whose taste you trust: When the salesgirl gasps "that's so fierce!" you feel she'd be saying the same thing if you were Cher on a I'm-still-21 fashion kick. Paragon's best at outfitting women, though it does have a few racks of men's clothes (higher-end items like leather jackets).

Best secondhand threads: Goodwill *(1400 S. Lake St., 206/329–1000)* is the place for hard-core thrift shoppers. If you're not ready for the mounds of '70s castaways (not everything from that era is worth reviving) or if you tire easily, stick to the stores where "thrift store" clothes miraculously transform into "vintage"-wear. Part of the reason this Goodwill, by far the biggest branch in the area, can be the source of great finds is its size. In the warehouse-size rooms you'll find racks of old varsity soccer sweatshirts and SOMEONE IN TUCSON LOVES ME T-shirts, cheap cords, army/navy surplus, as well as bric-a-brac, paperbacks, records, and everything else under the sun. The best buys require time.

Runners-up: For shops where the buyers do your work for you, try **Nine Lives** *(1656 E. Olive Way, 206/325–6530)*, which goes for the wilder, costume-type outfits, or **Jet City** *(2200 First Ave., 206/728–7118)*, a tiny place in Belltown that picks out wearable yet trendy secondhand stuff.

et cetera

Best lucky monkey paw: From the moment you confront the plaster wheelchair-bound Vincent Price at the door and hear the opera singers shrieking inside, you know **Ah Nuts** *(601 N. 35th St., 206/633–0664)* is not your average junk shop. How could it be? It sits under the Fremont rocket, a 53-foot "monument" on top of the Bitters Building which, according to its accompanying plaque, symbolizes Fremont as an "artistically eccentric community," the equivalent of "Seattle's Left Bank." For all the self-congratulations, Fremont really is a wild place, with a bustling Sunday flea market (a statue of Lenin ensures equitable trading) and unusual street art. From the ceiling inlayed with vintage lunch boxes to the set of Nazi poker chips to the antique, though still usable, child's coffin (price: $250), Ah Nuts is a haven for truly bizarre and macabre junk. For a mere 30 bucks, the monkey paw really can be yours, along with a guarantee of three wishes. Don't come to us for a refund, suckah.

Best beginner's handcuffs: If you want an enlightened adult toy store, try **Toys in Babeland** *(711 E. Pike St., 206/328–2914)*. The store came about after one of the current owners had a difficult time shopping for lubricant at a run-of-the-mill First Avenue sex shop; Toys in Babeland wants to make buying sex toys a hassle-free experience. The informative and attentive staff—mostly graying lesbians with closely cropped hair—screens video selections, making notes for customers like "bondage scenes on the violent side."

Best condom gift packs: the **Rubber Rainbow Condom Company** *(1515 First Ave., 206/233–9502)* is a jolly franchise. In Seattle, it has an airy space on the upper level of Pike Place Market (above the Post-Alley) and is popular with the European tourists, but it's still your best bet for Homeboy Rubbers—if you're "livin' large" (so says the packaging)—or cutesy neon condoms. Safe sex is no laughing matter, right?

body alterations

Best body designs: Seattle is home to a number of creative tattoo talents, which makes picking the best a matter of taste. George Long, the resident needler at the Capitol Hill barbershop **Rudy's** *(614 E. Pine St., 206/329–3008)*, has one of the most unique and balanced portfolios around, specializing in Native American designs, though he handles sailor fare just as well. He's careful about keeping things clean and as painless as possible (especially by minimizing the scabbing), and he'll touch up the design for free. Rudy's is also a barbershop for the experimental hair crowd, offering good deals on everything from buzz cuts to the craziest geometric styles. There's usually a bit of a wait, but they've got sprawling space and good CDs by local bands, making the line to the barber chair a scene in itself.

Best piercing: the **Pink Zone** *(211 Broadway Ave. E., Broadway Market, 206/325–0050)* is as much a gay mercantile store as it is a piercing parlor; so, even if you're not facing the needle, you should stop by and check out the erotic pasta, Tired Old Queen board games, and assorted T-shirts and bumper stickers. If you're in the middle of a lunchtime identity crisis and decide that what you need is a nose ring, you can just walk in, but it's usually best to call ahead and make an appointment—they can be pretty busy and booked up by midafternoon. It's 15 bucks for the first five holes in the earlobe and 30 bucks for piercings elsewhere—cash only.

Best high-end haircutter: Though it's not the cutting-edge salon in terms of new hairstyles for the girls on *Friends*, the **Gene Juarez Salon** *(1501 Fifth Ave., 206/628–1405)* can match pictures or verbal descriptions with the best of 'em. If you've finally decided to go for that Jean Seberg-in-*Breathless* look, don't take risks—come here, pay the 50-odd bucks, and avoid the bowl cut by Supercuts. A boutique resident of the Northwest yuppie-darling department store Nordstrom, the place has got its share of perm candidates and spoiled children, but know that you can trust the perfectly coiffed staff. Dye job? Save yourself grief and do it here.

hotel/motel

Best pricey digs: Someone in this building changed the sheets on David Bowie's bed. It's possible David Lynch first imagined the White Lodge's Dancing Man while brushing his teeth at one of these sinks. The **Sorrento Hotel** *(900 Madison Ave. 206/622–6400)* is, overall, Seattle's best high-end hotel. The Sorrento makes you want to believe the old Gatsby myth that you can buy happiness, and there's no denying a plush sofa and an ornate shower are beautiful things to come home to, even if only for one night.

Best dirt cheap room: You can't beat $15 plus tax a night for a view of Elliot Bay and a clean bed in a prime location right below Pike Place Market, **Hosteling International-Seattle** *(84 Union St., 206/622–5443)*. Sure, bunk beds bring back memories of Wonder Woman underwear and you do have to share a bathroom with fellow slummin' travelers, but since you'll only be sleeping a fraction of the time you're in Seattle you should be splurging on other aspects of your vacation. This is the best option for those traveling alone and even in a group—you'll probably have more privacy here than if you were sharing a hotel room with a bunch of friends.

local wonders

Best view of Seattle: If you want to blend in with the natives—thousands of commuters take the ferry every day—pack a lunch (the food onboard is worse than train food) and head out to Bainbridge Island or north to the San Juans for a day trip on the ferry. The ferry leaves from Colman Dock on Pier 52 *(801 Alaskan Way, 206/464–0041 for schedules)*. On weekends you'll be joined by families heading out to their cabins and crunchies playing Bob Dylan songs on the harmonica for spare change. Views of the Olympic Mountains and Mt. Ranier—both are usually visible—and of the city's skyline (gorgeous at sunset) should not be missed.

Best *Twin Peaks* field trip: While most of *Twin Peaks*'s eerie overtones came from David Lynch, the spooky forest backdrop helped. If you don't want to drive all the way up to the Cascades (45 minutes from Seattle) for a look at the trees, you can drive a quick 25 or so minutes on I-90 to **Snoqualmie Falls** (seen in the *Twin Peaks* credits), attempt the four-mile hike straight up the side of **Mount Si** (for a gorgeous view of the area), and top it all off with a slice of cherry pie at the Mar-T Diner that supposedly inspired Agent Cooper's cravings—all in a day. Snoqualmie Falls is privately owned by Puget Power, but most of the area around it is preserved and open to the public during the day. You can walk out to the lookout tower, or, even better, hike down to the bottom and go swimming in the pool at the fall's base. Mount Si, about five miles past Snoqualmie Falls, is a popular hike with locals. Reaching the summit is challenging, and if you plan on making an attempt on the haystack (a large rock) at the summit, make sure to bring plenty of water and suitable climbing gear; you'll be ascending about 1,000 feet per mile. Lots of people go about halfway up and then head down, which is still enough to enjoy the wild huckleberries and cool forest interior. To get to the area, take I-90 east past Issaquah, and there'll be an exit for Snoqualmie Falls. Once off the freeway it's pretty much a straight path, with the falls on one side and Mount Si a little ways past on the other. The diner is right at the corner of the road off the freeway exit and the road that runs to Mount Si and Snoqualmie Falls (plus there's a large sign proclaiming its claim to fame).

Best skate rats: In recent years, Seattle's public officials, like those of most other cities, have had to deal with locating an area to put the local skate rats. Their solution was the construction of some good-sized ramps in the shadow of the Space Needle near **Seattle Center**, and, for the most part, they were successful in providing a centralized place for skate culture (which is large here thanks to the snowboarder crossover). On a nice afternoon the place is packed, a hotbed of poker-faced boasts, gossip, and one-upmanship. If you hang out long enough and try to shed the out-of-towner look, you may just pick up news on house parties around the city, upcoming gigs, and much more than you ever wanted to know about ollies.

transmissions

Best radio 24/7: Quite frankly, it's all about **KCMU (90.3 FM)**. Since it's listener-supported, there are no annoying radio ads and the DJs are all-volunteer, so forget programming consistency. Aretha coexists with wedding music from Mozambique, which gets sandwiched between Bikini Kill and Sky Cries Mary; Marlene Dietrich shares airtime with Beck; the jazz ranges from classic Miles Davis cool to very out, avant-garde stuff. All the DJs love to throw in ambient, acid jazz, and trip-hop tracks. Local celeb DJ Riz Rollins has his own show Thursdays from 10 P.M. to 1 A.M., where you can hear Etta James sandwiched between Dub Narcotic and George Clinton. If you think of yourself as at all musically sophisticated, tune in to KCMU and prepare to reconsider.

Best jazz: KPLU (88.5 FM; also north of Everett, 91.3 FM) is just the sort of radio you need after a long night or a tough day; it's guaranteed to make a sunny morning even better with that perfect Ella track ringing through the kitchen. KPLU, like KCMU, is listener-supported so the only interludes between the jazz are the commentaries by KPLU's DJs. KPLU also has NPR in the afternoons and updates throughout the day.

washington d.c.

by Holly Bass

"D.C. has two things vital for a healthy music scene:
creative people with lots of time on their hands and a high
per capita intake of caffeine."

— **Eli Janney, *Girls Against Boys***

When you think of Washington D.C., you think No Fun. And it's true, D.C. is a serious-minded, self-conscious city in a capital way, full of conservative, dronelike bureaucrats, who come to add a few paragraphs to their resume, then split. You might also be forgiven for thinking D.C. means Danger City, given all the media hype about the town being the "murder capital" of the country due to the high drug-gang mortality rate. And it's also true that Our Nation's Capital has seen better days—the city is basically falling apart in chunks, with city services gone to hell on a Harley under the stewardship of re-elected ex-con Marion "Bitch set me up" Barry. Let's face it: D.C.'s a pretty weird place. And except for the (too-short) spring and fall, the weather sucks. Majorly.

All this makes the fun—when you find it (and believe us, sometimes you really have to ferret it out)—that much more FUN. And because the population is in flux perhaps more than in most other, more stable cities—there's a steady in-and-out flow of students, tourists, international and embassy employees, immigrants and others. The cityscape is constantly changing to reflect and accommodate the transient population, with clubs and restaurants here one season, gone the next. Certain things hang on tenaciously, though: punkers, funkers, go-go-istes, indie rockers, bluegrass/roots-rockers and folkies, and worldbeat worshipers all have established scenes that somehow survive the flushing-out that accompanies the four-year changing of administrations.

Of the homegrown scenes, what the kids locally called harDCore was pound for pound one of the best teenage riots ever. Clean, mean, and lean, bands like Minor Threat, Bad Brains, Government Issue, and Rites of Spring changed the face of music across the country in the early '80s, pounding out three-chord anthems that went straight to the heart of oppression (real or imagined): "We will not do what they want or do what they say. Oh no!" (H.R. of Bad Brains).

Today, hardcore has faded away so much as mutated, continuing on in acts like Fugazi, Girls vs. Boys, and the now-defunct Jawbox with the same innovative, high-octane spirit. Ian "I Will Refuse" MacKaye's Dischord Records has been a model for independent labels nationwide, and now, even though it has plenty of local competition, still records strictly D.C. bands. Like the music scene itself, the company has grown tremendously. Where boxes of records were once skateboarded to different local stores, Dischord now distributes in countries as far-flung as Bahrain and Singapore.

At the same time that harDCore was making nightclubs into human popcorn machines, go-go music—the rootsy R&B audience-participatory spectacles that lasted three or four hours—was becoming more percussion-oriented. It was all about taking a hook and extending it for ten minutes. By 1985, rap artists like Whodini and Doug E. Fresh were making a significant impact on the music. Each band had followings from different neighborhoods and crews, like C.J.'s Uptown Crew, which sometimes led to violent clashes. The scene also created an intense (mostly male) bonding. The artists didn't call it slamming, but there was no difference between the center floor at a go-go show and the pit at a punk gig. Occasionally, the two scenes came together, like in the 1984 "PhUNK Throwdown" that featured Grand Mal, Trouble Funk, and Government Issue. But for the most part people remained as segregated in their music as they were in their daily lives. The same is true today, if not more so—a hard truth for the Chocolate City.

What's happening in D.C. now is more about rebirth than rebellion. Take a walk down U Street—nicknamed "The New U"—to see an (admittedly gradual) renaissance going on. In the '40s, it was the place to be, all jazz and speakeasies. Riots in 1968 ended that—the 14th and U Street corridors, once bustling centers of black street life, were lined with burned-out and boarded-up husks for decades and are finally, slowly being renovated. Some of the city's most adventurous eateries, clubs, and bars, especially on the hip-hop tip, can now be found on the five-block strip of U between 12th and 16th streets.

The three o'clock liquor limit dampens the club scene, but makes happy hour big business. The limit means that illegal after-hours clubs sprout up like magic mushrooms, but the only way to find one is to ask around—most don't linger in one location for more than a few weeks. Some of the best live shows happen in small clubs where DJs spin hip-hop, reggae, or alternative with bands performing once or twice a week.

By the way, don't believe the Danger City hype—and definitely don't let it make you miss out on the after-dark action in this all-too-serious-minded city. Sure, you have to keep your wits about you, stick to the main streets when possible, and watch where and when you're walking, but you should be playing it safe in just about any major city, right? When in doubt, call yourself a cab or hop aboard a nearby Metro.

lay of the land

D.C. is laid out in a circle with four quadrants: Northwest, Northeast, Southwest, and Southeast. At the core of the circle is—at least theoretically—the **U.S. Capitol**, which sits on the east end of the **National Mall**, a three-mile long swath of green that is bordered on the west by the **Potomac River**. FYI, the **White House** is several blocks to the north of the Mall's center at 1600 Pennsylvania Avenue.

Because the streets radiate out from a central circle, and some take a surprising twist or dog-leg, you might find yourself momentarily disoriented. But rest assured, there IS a system. Numbered streets run north-south; alphabet streets run east-west, and the whole system is thrown into disarray by the diagonal slanted avenues, named after states. Intersecting letter and number streets are easy to find: 1504 R Street is going to be on R between 15th and 16th streets (the quadrant will clue you in as to the neighborhood). For avenues, in general, the address number corresponds closely to the number of the letter in the alphabet (skipping the nonexistent J Street): thus, 1025 Connecticut Avenue is near K Street, the eleventh letter of the alphabet.

Get it? Got it? Good—let's go.

Well-meaning people may warn you not to go to Southeast because it's dangerous, but those people have obviously never crossed the river. If you really want to take advantage of D.C.'s rich Southern heritage, the **Anacostia** section of Southeast is the place to go. Most of D.C.'s after-dark action is concentrated in a handful of hip areas in the Northwest quadrant. Start with **Adams Morgan**—the Village-like, pan-ethnic, artsy-to-avant-garde sector, with its plentiful cheap eats and funky boutiques, it's the most exciting and ever-changing neighborhood in town. Nearby, residential **Mt. Pleasant** with its roomy houses, relatively inexpensive rents, and pleasantly run-down bars and shops, is a favorite of local indie bands, who cluster in group houses. In **Georgetown**, well-heeled Euros mix with college kids and Virginia bridge-crossers on the weekend; there's good shopping around Wisconsin and M streets. The true heart of the residential city may be traditionally bohemian **Dupont Circle**, a green central meeting place with an elegant fountain, surrounded by "tribes" of bike messengers, all-day chess players, punk hangers-on and hippie hold-outs, gays, lesbians, transsexuals, and scenemakers in general. Smack in the middle of Connecticut Ave., D.C.'s main drag and shopping strip, Dupont Circle is studded with restaurants, gay bars, and straight cafes. After the lights go out in the **Capitol Hill** offices, the lights go up in the Capitol Hill pubs, where male and female Hillites doff their ties and pearls and dance on the bars to Motown tunes. Downtown doesn't have much flava, but at night the dance club crowd filing into converted banks and warehouses perks up the empty streets lined with old office buildings. **Takoma Park** is crunchy and quaint, with hippie-yuppie vibes, natural healing stores, a weekend farmer's market, and, in the summer, really good street festivals.

getting from a to b

In terms of transportation, D.C.'s got it made. The city center is compact enough to make walking an option. The clean, quiet and virtually graffiti-free Metro subway system, though not as extensive as, say, Manhattan's, will take you to Maryland, Virginia, and the heart of D.C. Fares start at an affordable $1.10 per ride, and you can buy $5 daypasses at the Metro Center stop (13th and F streets NW). Buses go virtually everywhere, and you switch from Metro to bus on one fare—just remember to get a transfer.

The only problem with D.C. public transportation is that, except for a few bus lines, it pretty much shuts down at midnight (if you're planning on being out late and need to rely on Metro or buses, call the Metro Information Center, 202/637–7000). But you can always call a cab. D.C. cabs can be hailed pretty easily on the street (except during bad weather or rush hour) and are generally affordable, thanks to the unusual zoned fare system. There are no meters—the city center and most major tourist attractions are within one low-cost zone, so travel within a single zone should cost about $3, with a $1.25 charge for each additional passenger. The zone system does have some drawbacks—the zoning lines are erratic and zigzag through the outer rings of the city, so if your cab driver doesn't take the most direct route, you might be charged more. Also, cabbies are sometimes reluctant to accept passengers for places off the beaten track, especially to such (perceived dangerous) areas as Southeast. Try Capitol Cab *(202/546–0200)* or Yellow Cab *(202/544–1212)*. For short trips, you might as well just hoof it.

Sure, tour buses are cheesy and strictly for tourists, but get over yourself and get on the **Old Town Trolley** *(301/985–3020)*. The drivers (and the passengers) are funny, and you can disembark at various points around town during the trolley's two-hour loop. Trolleys come around every 30 minutes, so you can hop back on and check out more sights. Think of it as a personalized chauffeur for $18 a day.

sources

The free alt.weekly *Washington City Paper* is the most reliable place for finding out about concerts, clubs, exhibits, and events. It features extensive listings and ads as well as cranky, opinionated critics—music and film reviewers Christopher Porter and Mark Jenkins seem to create the most ire in readers. Also check out the CP's web site at www.washingtoncitypaper.com. In addition to up-to-date listings, you'll find quirky columns like Tina Plottel's inside look at the indie world "Rock Stars Hate Me" and contests like "Spot the Drummer." For gay and lesbian clubs, pick up *Metro Weekly* (MW), a witty, well-designed digest-size tabloid with all the latest happenings, gossip, reviews, and maps. Both papers are free and widely available in most bookstores and bars.

The *Washington Post's* Friday "Weekend" and daily "Style" sections also highlight upcoming events, especially for families and the food-and-wine crowd. *Post* nightlife columnist Eric Brace knows where the action is (he's been a bass player and singer/songwriter in some of the city's best bands, and unlike his colleagues, he actually goes out) and usually has some inside tips and breaking news about clubs and bands.

Check for club flyers and passes next to the doors in most bars and clubs, as well as record stores and used book shops. The cluttered bulletin boards at the crunchy, countercultureish Food for Thought (see Dining) restaurant in Dupont Circle or **TomTom** *(2333 18th St. NW, 202/588–1300)* in Adams Morgan are always interesting reading—you might find a show to see, a place to stay, and a ride to share. A comprehensive music web site is dcpages.ari.net/dcmw/dcmusic.html. There you'll find home pages for punk, ska, go-go, rave, and even Celtic music and zydeco, as well as the Black Cat (see Clubs) and various small labels.

clubs

Best go-go: Most people's familiarity with go-go music begins and ends with E.U.'s 1988 hit "Doin' Da Butt," but the hard-driving, funk-infused syncopated rhythm is an indigenous art form, too often taken for granted. The go-gos are like family gatherings in a way, with each band having its own following. If you don't have family ties, but want to know about the music, your first stop should be **Nico's tape stand** *(corner of F and 12th streets NW, Metro Center subway stop)*. Lots of people sell tapes on the street, but Nico's tapes, made from band-approved originals, are high quality. Plus, your $10 purchase comes with a little history of the music and the inside on where the good jams are happening.

Chuck Brown, revered by most as the godfather of go-go (or grandfather, to the young heads) usually plays at a little joint called **Deno's** *(2335 Bladensburg Rd. NE, 202/526–8880)* in Northeast. Brown's music shows jazz influences and an old-school beat, so he draws a more chilled-out crowd. Young 'uns who follow Rare Essence would go to the **Eastside** *(1824 Half St. SW, 202/582–5907)* before it closed last August. Chances are it will reopen under a new name. The **Ibex** *(5832 Georgia Ave. NW, 202/726–1800)* is the place to see Backyard Band, the preeminent gangster rap/go-go group, or old-school bucket bangers like the Junkyard Band. Fashion profilers tend to favor the balcony, away from the sweat and crowds of the main dance floor. Hoochie mamas in hot pants abound. The pit gets as rowdy as any early punk show, so act like you know. Not for the timid or confrontational.

Best name-brand shows: For 15 years, the dark, dank **9:30 Club** was THE original alternative club in town, the best place to catch up-and-coming (and been-and-went) bands. But owner/concert promoter Seth Hurwitz finally tired of everyone griping about the stink and the sweat of the beloved/detested joint and bought the old WUST Radio Music Hall and spent beaucoup bucks refurbishing it into D.C.'s premier rock showcase. The new 9:30 *(815 V St. NW; 202/393–0930)* is one huge, booming ballroom, with balconies and a movable stage (to adjust house from intimate to arena). You can see everyone from Johnny Cash and Tony Bennett (though not on the same bill—yet) to cultier attractions like Wilco and Luna. Food concession by well-regarded vegetarian restaurant Planet X.

Best place to check out local bands: Black Cat *(1831 14th St. NW, 202/667–7960)* features a mix of post-punk, alt.rock, and the occasional rap group for around $5. High-ticket bills like the Kostars, Velocity Girl, and G Love and Special Sauce often include up-and-coming D.C. groups like Tuscadero, the Make Up, the Delta 72, and the buzz du jour, Trans Am, an instrumental trio of three good-looking guys. The club is owned by former punk kid Dante Ferrando (Iron Cross, Gray Matter).

Ever since his eponymous restaurant (and inevitable late-night end-up) closed in '96, the scene has moved to the **Red Room**, a side bar to the Black Cat. It's favored by locals because there's no cover, six pool tables, and an eclectic jukebox with music ranging from Peggy Lee to Black Sabbath.

Best rave romper room: The **Capitol Ballroom** *(1015 Half St. SE, (202/828–1984)* is a warehouse-size concert venue that features every-one from the Fugees to the Misfits to the Rev. Horton Heat, but every Friday it becomes a techno extravaganza known as **Buzz**, hyped with the most eye-popping fliers in town. The crowd ranges from space cadets in "Jetson"-esque outfits to standard club kids wearing those ubiquitous baby backpacks and pacifiers to Midwestern types in sweat-drenched T-shirts and jeans. In the summer, the Ballroom sets up huge outdoor tents and pumps jungle tracks into the notoriously steamy D.C. air. It's crazy packed, and when the heat gets to be too much people park it on benches outside. Ages 18 and over.

Best dance music: Tracks *(80 M St. SE, 202/488–3320)* should get an award for club longevity. For more than ten years, the megadisco has drawn serious house heads and dancers with its lineup of top DJs. Every night draws a different crowd, but (discoid) Saturdays and (house-heavy) Sundays may be your best bet. There are plenty of pretty boys looking to show off (and peel off) their fashions, but most come to sweat. In between extended remixes, you might want to check out the volleyball court outside for fresh air and maybe a quick match.

Runner-up: On most Saturday nights at **Red** *(1802 Jefferson Place NW, 202/466–3475)*, Sam "The Man" Burns or Baltimore's Basement Boys burn up the wax; Wednesday is trance night. A basement joint, the club is small but the vibe is live. Ages 18 and up. Midnight to 6 A.M.

Best DJs: Despite the club's Russian decor, **State of the Union** *(1357 U St. NW, 202/588–8926)* is far from austere. The looming figure of Rasputin stares you down as you enter the U Street club. A mural of Harlem, done in glowing fluorescent paint, adorns the back wall by the DJ booth. On any given night you may find poetry read to live jazz in the back room, a mellow acid-jazz groove, or a rap show getting the heads nodding up front (the homemade vodka helps, too). The city's most adventurous DJs—the Deep Dish Boys, Lofty Love, Neal Becton, and Frank Rosario—spin here regularly, attracting a racially mixed crowd. Club manager David Kasdan and owner Stewart Woodroffe, along with musician Peter Fraize, recently started Union Records, a label that records unsigned local artists who perform live at the club.

Best new club zone: It's a jungle in there—the newest thing in town is a thicket of jungle/drum 'n' bass clubs on Connecticut Avenue, just south of Dupont Circle. Formerly the Roxy, gay club **Ozone** *(1639 R St. NW, 202/293–0303)* operates a jungle night once a week; and right next door and down the stairs, the Italian restaurant **Sesto Senso** *(1214 18th St. NW, 202/785–9525)* turns into a pounding rhythm palace on weekend nights. Also a heartbeat away are the **18th St. Lounge** (see below) and **Red** (see above), also on the groovy techno jungle trip. And just across the street is **Planet Fred** *(1221 Connecticut Ave., 202/331–3733)*, a bar working an extraterrestrial theme, that books white-boy funk bands-to-watch like Sampson and Citizen Cope (think what Beck would sound like if he lost his sense of irony).

Best acid-groove living room: The novelty has definitely worn off since its peak in '95, but the **18th Street Lounge** *(1212 18th St. NW, 202/466–3922)* is still a comfortable place to dance a bit or chill out listening to ambient vibes. The Dupont Circle club doesn't advertise and there's no name on the door. Look for the "1212" and head up the red-carpeted stairs. Except for the long bar, the Lounge could easily be someone's uptown apartment; it's just three rooms with framed photos of jazz greats lining the walls and votive candles adding to the warm/cool atmosphere. The main bar has a few tables and chairs, along with some comfy sofas. The club's owners (and regular DJs) are the same studio minds behind acid jazz outputs by the Exodus Quartet and Thievery Corporation. And DJ Spen from the Baltimore-based Basement Boys (as a producer/remixer, he put Crystal Waters and Ultra Nate on the map) takes the turntables alternating Saturdays. Upstairs is another bar with a more intimate vibe where the house band, the Originals, performs acid jazz on weekends. On any given night, the music swings between trip hop and funk to bossa nova and soul. The crowd ranges from monochromatically attired hipsters to cheerful young kids grooving endlessly.

Best live jazz: One Step Down *(2517 Pennsylvania Ave. NW, 202/331–8863)* offers great music in a relaxed atmosphere with low cover charges. The long, narrow club seats just under 70 people. During the week (except Tuesdays when it's closed), top D.C.-based musicians like Steve Novacell (former bass player for Rahsaan Roland Kirk) and pianist

Lawrence Wheatley gig. Saturday and Sunday afternoons from 3:30 to 7:30 there's a jam session followed by performances by out-of-towners. Late greats like Sonny Stitt and Chet Baker played here. Recent headliners have included Shirley Horne, Roy Haines, Benny Carter, and a long-time member of Ella Fitzgerald's band, bassist Keter Betts.

Runners-up: **Vicki's** *(1928 Ninth St. NW, 202/265–2889)* is a juke-style joint with jazz and blues. Midweek is best for straight-ahead jazz and low covers. **Twins Lounge** *(5516 Colorado Ave. NW, 202/882–2523)* sometimes has a steep cover and drink minimum, but a truly intimate arrangement and good players like Gary Bartz and Fred Foss make it worthwhile.

Best African diaspora: Jamaicans, Ethiopians, and Americans mix it up at **Erico** *(1334 U St. NW, 202/265–1911)*, an intimate club featuring live reggae several times a week and DJs playing world music on other nights. The mood gets spiritual when the Benjamin brothers take the stage with their roots reggae band, Midnight. Downstairs, you can grab some cheap eats at **Cafe Nema** *(202/667–3215)*, which combines Middle Eastern and East African cuisines to good effect.

Best gay club: Newt Gingrich and his pals don't want you to know this, but, girlfriend, D.C. is one of the gayest cities in the U.S. of A., with a gay/lesbian population estimated at more than 200,000. Queers here tend to be assimilated, integrated, and almost invisible, as many of them hold suit-and-tie government jobs. You'll spot the more stylized gay guys and girls around such traditional bohemian pockets of town as Dupont Circle, Logan Circle, and yes, Capitol Hill. But the boy-loving-boys (and girl-loving-girls) know how to party. What sets the **Circle** *(1629 Connecticut Ave. NW, 202/462–5575)* apart from other D.C. gay bars is that it's a fairly racially mixed scene—partly because it's known that you can safely satisfy your jungle-fever jones here, and partly because it's just a cool vibe. In this trilevel complex with bar, restaurant and dance club (with outdoor deck) in the heart of tres gay Dupont Circle, house remixes blare from the speakers with accompanying music videos shown on televisions around the dimly lit bar. Sundays the bar hosts a tea dance, but people come mostly for the drink specials and to hang out on the balcony overlooking Dupont Circle.

Runner-up: Coolest newcomer on the gay club scene is **Cobalt** *(1639 R St. NW, 202/232–6965)*, which has a live DJ in the bar from 5 P.M. till close every night, and on weekends it opens the upstairs dance floor, vibrating to the latest tweaky, thumpy, jungley beats.

Best lesbian parties: Traditionally, there's never been as many exclusively lesbian bars as gay bars in town, although the **Hung Jury** *(1819 H St. NW, 202/279–3212)* draws an all-gal crowd that loves to dance to songs they know (dyke DJs are different from their more experimental gay-club brethren—the women will clear the floor if they're not familiar with the music). The social scene for women revolves around parties, and the biggest and best are produced by local party promoter and independent publisher Sheila Reed, who started **Women in the Life** *(202/483–6786)* around four years ago. The name came from a series of parties her friends used to throw in New York. Once their series ended, she adopted the name for her own affairs. The loosely formed organization hosts dance parties, cabarets, and open mikes at various venues around the city, like the **District of Columbia Arts Center** *(2438 18th St. NW, 202/462–7833)*. Pick up a copy of the monthly newsletter at sites like **Sisterspace and Books** *(1359 U St. NW, 202/332–3433)* and the lesbian-centric **Lammas Women's Bookstore** *(1426 21st St. NW, 202/775–8218)*, or call the hot line for details on upcoming events.

Best split personality: At **Club Heaven and Hell** *(2327 18th St. NW, no phone)* you can have it both ways. In the basement-level Hell, you'll find cheap drinks, open mike poetry on Sundays, and an appropriately Boschian atmosphere. (Hmmm—sounds suspiciously heavenly.) The second-floor Club Heaven isn't necessarily better-lit than its downstairs counterpart, but has a decidedly livelier outlook (in between is an Italian-Ethiopian restaurant that some wiseacres have nicknamed "Purgatory"). Heaven's '80s dance party on Thursdays is not to be missed (although it can get hellishly hot up there dancing to Duran Duran and Heaven 17). On other nights dancing ranges from hi-NRG and worldbeat to alternative and the doomiest, most tragic techno-Goth.

bars

Best ancient dive bar: The pleasantly nondescript the **Raven** *(3125 Mt. Pleasant St. NW, no phone)* has been around since the '30s, and some of the bartenders and regulars have put in almost as many years at this neighborhood institution. Mt. Pleasant is one of those working-class neighborhoods that no one has gotten around to gentrifying, so there's still lots of businesses from the '50s and before, like crusty Heller's Bakery down the street, welcoming generation after generation with nary a nod to the latest interior decorating trends. The only recent change to the neighborhood is the wave of Salvadoran immigrants in the last ten years, which added Latin American grocers and the Spanish language to the otherwise Beaver Cleaver streets. Circling the Raven's bar are booths, each equipped with a mini-jukebox, all of which are broken, but the management keeps the mood flowing with an oldies soundtrack. Metrobus workers mingle with punk kids and pickled booze hounds, all basically looking for a good drink. All-female groups may find the atmosphere a tad oppressive, so it's best to bring male company or come before peak late-night hours.

Runners-up: Good times and bad times, **Mr. Eagan's** *(1343 Connecticut Ave. NW, 202/331–9768)* has seen them all, and my dear, he's still here. A subterranean pub just south of Dupont Circle, Mr. Eagan's is just plain paradise for those holdouts who like to smoke and drink. The free popcorn keeps you drinkin'. The **Tune Inn** *(331½ Pennsylvania Ave. SE)*, just a few blocks from the Capitol building, has been called "the best restaurant in the U.S." and "best dive in D.C." The latter is closer to the mark. The hallmarks of the Capitol Hill hole-in-the-wall: cheap beer, greasy burgers, cranky waitresses, dead animals on the wall, a great jukebox, and generations of Hill history.

Best beer blast: Despite being doors away from several gay bars and minutes away from Georgetown U, the crowd at the **Brickskeller** *(1523 22nd St. NW, 202/293–1885)* is pretty ordinary. The selection of beers, however, is far from typical. With over 900 selections from 50 different countries, you can get everything from Ngomatogo Pills to good old all-Amurican Bud. The servers actually have to go to "beer school" before they begin work. You'll appreciate their expertise once you try to narrow down your field of choices. The food isn't bad either.

Best year-round outdoor tables: Pop Stop *(1513 17th St. NW, 202/328–0880)* is a favorite hangout for gay boys making the rounds on the 17th Street strip, D.C.'s one-street answer to New York's Chelsea neighborhood or California's Castro and West Hollywood, although all are welcome. If they can handle the attention and the A-T-T-I-T-U-D-E. The coffee is good and the selection of pastries is decent if small. But the real draw is the people-watching (that's putting it mildly—the glances and glares you'll get at this place can have X-ray intensity). During the winter, the outdoor tables come equipped with massive electric heaters, so you and your pals can grab a cuppa joe and converse outside as if it were spring. It's perfect for those drab days when you're tired of being cooped up. In summer, big umbrellas replace the heaters, so it's even good for those hot humid days when you're tired of being in the sun.

Best coffee bar with liquor: Newly refurbished to resemble a dark cave with glowing stalactites, **Kaffa House** *(1212 U St. NW, 202/ 462–1212)* is where you'll find a working mix of hip-hopping, yuppie happy hours, funk nights, fashion events, art openings, readings, live reggae, chess games, and alternative dance parties. It started as a coffee bar but now serves alcohol, so lots of different scenes flow through here. The Freestyle Union *(hot line 202/466–1638)*, D.C.'s premier hip-hop collective, holds not-to-be-missed monthly ciphers at Kaffa. No written rhymes are allowed, and anyone can join in. Beyond-imagination lyrics emanate from the young improvisers, under the direction of Union president Toni Blackman.

food

Best Tokyo rock sushi: The dyed-hair crowd joins expatriate businessmen for sushi and beer at **Cafe Japone** *(2032 P St. NW, 202/ 223–1573)* in Dupont Circle. Swirls of neon light accent the restaurant's black walls and dark plum furnishings. Every night is karaoke night with a mostly Japanese contingent working the mike once the sake starts flowin'. A couple of times a week a live jazz band provides sounds for the early evening. The sushi is good and moderately priced ($3 to $4 for maki, $2 for most hand rolls). The teriyaki and tempura dishes are tasty, too.

Best (and only) raw vegetarian: No meat, no dairy, and no heat, but the eats at **Delights of the Garden** *(2616 Georgia Ave. NW, 202/319–8747)* still have plenty of flavor. The veggie tuna has caused many to scratch their heads in wonderment at how carrots can taste like fruit of the sea. The Cajun-spiced Seaweed Greens is another favorite, along with hummus and a tabbouleh-like dish called Kush. The desserts might not pass the test if you're not accustomed to unrefined sweeteners, but with Delight's low prices you might as well be adventurous.

Runners-up: For those who like their vegetables cooked, nearby **Soul Vegetarian** *(2602 Georgia Ave. NW, 202/328–7685)* offers inspired food like Garveyburgers. And **Food for Thought** *(1738 Connecticut Ave. NW, 202/797–1095)* adds a few meat selections to the menu, some folk singers, and the best bulletin board in the city for apartment hunters and concertgoers.

Best fill-up station: Here's where to find home-style victuals at '50s prices. Don't be put off by the word "colonial." During the Depression you could find Sholl's Colonial Cafeterias all over downtown D.C., but now only one remains. Tucked into one of downtown's many nondescript office buildings, **Sholl's** *(1990 K St. NW, 202/296–3065)* is not the kind of place you'd stumble on accidentally. Harry Truman used to frequent the cafeterias during his vice presidency, and the red-and-green carpet, faux marble tables and orange-cushioned straightback chairs look as if they could have been around during his administration. The elderly loners who frequent Sholl's don't seem to mind a little color-clash with the cuisine, and punks come here for that look. The menu here is all familiar comfort food—from roast chicken to meat loaf—cooked by a staff of matronly types dressed in hospital white. Normally, it would not be advisable to eat ethnic entrees in an American diner, but with half the staff made up of Salvadoran *abuelitas*, any Latin American dishes on the daily changing menu are heartily recommended. It serves a righteous flan—the custard is smooth, the caramel just right. And prices start at $.35 for side dishes, $1.95 for a full breakfast, and an easy five bucks for lunch.

Best late-night eats: At **Kramerbooks & Afterwords Cafe** *(1517 Connecticut Ave. NW; 202/387–1400)*, a combination bookstore-cafe and D.C. must-see in Dupont Circle, you can dig into delicious (if a bit pricy) food while devouring the latest by David Sedaris or David Foster Wallace. Kramerbooks is open round the clock on Friday and Saturday.

Runner-up: If you're in a *Grease*-y mood, cruise into the brightly lit 24-hour **American City Diner** *(5532 Connecticut Ave. NW, 202/244–1949)*, a neat-o place to grab a burger and fries in an *American Graffiti* atmosphere. And can always head for D.C.'s Chinatown (H St. NW between 6th and 7th streets), where you can take your pick of more than a dozen restaurants that stay open 'til 2 a.m and beyond.

Best late-night burgers: Before all the trendy bars and cute cafes opened on U Street there was **Ben's Chili Bowl** *(1213 U St. NW, 202/667–0909)*. And Ben's will still be there long after those disappear. This family-owned venue survived '60s riots as well as '90s redevelopment. Red glitter vinyl barstools line the faux marble counter where you can watch the food grilled to greasy perfection before your eyes. Soul classics play on the jukebox. Oblivious to fads, Ben's sticks to staples like chili, burgers, dogs, and fries. Its only nod to the '90s is the addition of turkey and veggie burgers, which, incredibly, taste every bit as good as their dead cow counterparts. Its Southern-style breakfast of grits, eggs, sausage, and bacon is a good morning option. Open 'til 4 A.M. on weekends and 2 A.M. other nights except Sunday, when it closes early.

Best soul food cafeteria: After a day in Southeast's Anacostia visiting the local Smithsonian Anacostia Museum *(1901 Fort Place SE, 202/ 357–1300)* or Frederick Douglass's house *(1411 W St. SE, 202/ 426–5960)*, fortify yourself at **Imani Cafe** *(1918 Martin Luther King, Jr. Ave. SE, 202/678–4890)* a ten-minute walk from the Anacostia Metro. The low-priced menu changes daily but always features a fish of the day and chicken, served fried or baked. Sometimes ribs make an appearance. The side dishes are divine, from black-eyed peas to macaroni-and-cheese. Save room for peach cobbler, and have a glass of sweet tea punch while you're at it. P.S.: Check out the **World's Biggest Chair** one block away—a good spot for taking photos for the folks back home.

Best Ethiopian food: D.C. has a gazillion Ethiopian joints, and the packed restaurant row of Adams Morgan has at least one dozen within a three-block strip, but there's no need to work yourself up into an inde-cisive frenzy. Go to **Meskerem** *(2434 18th St. NW, 202/462–4100)*, a peerless establishment. Food is served family-style on one large piece of *injera*, a sourdough flat bread that serves as a plate, with extra pieces for scooping up food. Standout dishes include the spicy *watt* stews, the green-chili seasoned potato salad, and the various lentil dishes.

Best Caribbean getaway for two, under $50: Eating at **Hibiscus Cafe** *(3401 K St. NW, 202/965–7170)* is a full sensory experi-ence. Unlike actually going to the islands, there's no chance of hurri-canes or vexing vendors. Neon art, African masks, brightly colored murals, and eclectic modish furnishings provide the atmospherics; fans simulate ocean breezes, and mellow worldbeat plays in the background. Traditional items like jerk chicken, curried shrimp, and perfectly done fried calamari join nouvelle items like shark in fried bread pockets with fresh pineapple chutney and unique soups like butternut ginger bisque. Definitely try the homemade passion fruit punch.

Runner-up: What the **Islander** *(1762 Columbia Rd. NW, 202/234– 4955)* lacks in atmosphere is more than compensated for by the food this Trinidadian establishment serves, especially its *roti* and whole fried fish.

shopping

records

Best DJ tracks: 12″ Dance Records *(2010 P St. NW, 202/659–2010)* is the place the DJs go to find the hottest club tracks and to talk shop.

That's because the place is stocked and staffed by DJs, and there's always someone spinning live while you shop. While the store has CDs, that's not what you come here for. The name says it all—whether it's house, go-go, rap, or alternative, domestic or import, if it's a got a beat that makes your head nod or hips swing, you'll find it here. The store also offers DJ accessories and record maintenance supplies.

Runner-up: For ambient, techno, and jungle sounds, a good spot to check out is **Music Now** *(3209 M St. NW, 202/338–5638)* in Georgetown, which offers listening stations and a broad selection, although mainly in CD form.

Best discs, new and used: Flying Saucer Discs *(2318 18th St. NW, 202/265–DISC)* has an excellent selection at prices lower than any of the chains. Its business card boasts a "non-irritating staff" and it's true. The store has an especially good selection of acid jazz and lounge. Of the three listening stations, the best is in the back with a rattan sofa, right next to shrines to Billie Holliday and Patsy Cline. The used CDs are in the case, so you can listen to your heart's content without having to constantly ask for help.

Runner-up: **Phantasmagoria** *(11319 Elkin St., 301/949–8886)* in Wheaton, Maryland, has the unique advantage of having a live music stage onsite. It features all-ages shows almost every night with bands ranging from ska and punk to folk and bluegrass. It's walking distance from the Wheaton Metro. The store sells vinyl, CDs, and cassettes, and has another branch (retail only) in D.C. *(1719 Connecticut Ave. NW, 202/462–8886)*.

books

Best small indie shop: It doesn't have the large selection of the city's chain bookstores or the quirky charm of a used bookstore, but what **Vertigo Books** *(1337 Connecticut Ave. NW, 202/429–9272)* in Dupont Circle does have is a wide selection of excellent multicultural literature and a reverence for writers. Vertigo is the place to go for readings by emerging or established writers. Last year novelists Ntozake Shange and Walter Mosely, academic bell hooks, and Nuyorican poet Willie Perdomo, to name a few, came by to promote their new books. Check the store's calendar in the window, but don't forget to buy something too.

Best used books: The posters of musical icons John Coltrane, Sid Vicious, and Frank Sinatra that decorate **Second Story Books** *(2000 P*

St. NW, 202/659–8884) let you know right away the store isn't stuffy or pretentious. It offers an eclectic and, for a used bookstore, surprisingly well-organized selection of books. It also has a small selection of used CDs and records. Open till 10 every night.

Best open mike poetry: For the past three years, D.C. poetry diva Toni Lightfoot has presided over the city's most consistently strong open reading series, which has moved into a new venue. Every Tuesday from 8 to 11 P.M., all manner of poetical types head to **Mango's** *(2017 14th St. NW, near U St., 202/232–2104)*, a restaurant serving a Caribbean-based fusion of cuisines. First-timers, affectionately called "virgins," are greeted with overwhelming applause before they even begin to read. The second hour is often dedicated to a specific theme, such as haiku, politics, or O.P.P. (other people's poetry). When a poet reads, no one talks or moves around. Respect is key. Styles range wildly—political and lyrical to hip hop influenced, academic to black nationalist. Of course, there's always unfunny standup comedians and Hallmark entries, but there's a lot of good work too.

clothes

Best '40s to '70s vintage: Out of the plethora of shops plying used threads, **Uniform** *(2407 18th St. NW, 202/483–4577)* offers clothes in excellent condition at a price just about anyone can afford. It's also a good place to look for club invites. Last year's finds included a straw porkpie hat for $20; a funky, sheer, '70s wide-collared button-down shirt for $8; a pair of prescription '50s shades for $10; and a '40s-era, wool skirt suit, $30 for the set. It offers clothes for men and women in a good range of sizes, as well as accessories and a select amount of home furnishings.

Runner-up: **Mood Indigo** *(1214 U St. NW, 202/256–6366)* provides all the fashions and accessories to make your black-and-white movie fantasies come to life, from Bette Davis to Claudette Colbert. Clothes hang on an electric conveyor rack left over from the store's former life as a dry cleaner. Good finds have included a pink chiffon '50s party dress for $30; a five-piece set of mint condition '30s suitcases for $325; a men's sage-green leisure shirt for $15; and '40s suits for around $80 apiece.

Best B-boy/girl outfitter: All the young 'uns, from hip-hop heads to rave kids, go to the four-store chain **Up Against the Wall** *(main branch: 3219 M St. NW, 202/337–9316)* to find the new styles. On the male side of the store, the smallest size is XL. On the female side, tiny tops, big jeans, and short skirts dominate. A lot of the stuff is made of temporal fabrics (thin cotton and rayon/polyester blends sewn together dubiously), but regulars here aren't looking for stuff to last. Be sure to check the store's **Wearhouse** *(1749 Columbia Rd. NW, 202/328–8627)* for exceptional bargains.

Best shoes: The **Bootlegger** *(1420 Wisconsin Ave. NW, 202/333–0373)* offers high-quality shoes for all manner of people—punks, mods, hippies, and homeboys—and the prices are usually a little less than what you would pay at a department store. It's also surrounded by plenty of clothing stores, so after you've paid for your yellow Dr Martens, you can start looking for a matching outfit at **Commander Salamander** next door *(1420 Wisconsin Ave. NW, 202/337–2265)* or **Betsey Johnson** *(1319 Wisconsin Ave. NW, 202/338–4090)*.

et cetera

Best retro everything: You can furnish your entire house and wardrobe and meet all your entertainment needs with stuff from **Millennium** *(1528 U St. NW, 202/483–1218)*. An upscale, multidealer garage sale offering what it calls "20th Century Antiques," it's a great place to browse. Recent finds: a '50s Columbia record player with auxiliary speaker; trashy '60s novels; classically styled modern furniture by Heywood-Wakefield; cardigan sweaters for $12; a '50s pink Formica table with six matching chairs for $295; dishes for under $5; chrome appliances; Bakelite silverware; obsolete kitchen utensils; jewelry; a '70s orange vinyl/wood paneled bar with stool for $99; dresses; hats; poker caddies; cookie cutters. And more.

Best flea market: If you look hard enough you can probably find anything you need at **Eastern Market** *(225 7th St. SE)* and, if you haggle well enough, at a cheap price. The market is open every day except Monday; on weekends vendors spill out of the historic red-brick building onto the sidewalks and adjacent parking lot. Local farmers come by to sell produce. Antique dealers hawking jazz 78s or old-fashioned milkshake machines and seltzer bottles set up shop next to local artisans who'll gladly explain their technique and trade, whether it's photography, jewelry, or custom-made candles.

Best fantasy/fetish store: The thing that makes **Exotic Pleasures Boutique** *(1356 U St. NW, 202/256–3806)* so excellent isn't that it has a larger stock than stores like **Dream Dresser** *(1042 Wisconsin Ave. NW, 202/625–0373)* or **Pleasure Place** *(1710 Connecticut Ave. NW,*

202/483–3297; or 1063 Wisconsin Ave. NW, 202/333–8570) but that it has an owner like Portia Morgan. The statuesque diva is at turns as bawdy as an old-time bordello madam or as sensitive as a mother. She and her staff are well-informed about the products and give their very honest opinions on whatever matter is at hand. If all the sex shopping works up an appetite, Portia also owns **Morgan's**, a cybercafe next door serving breakfast 'til 4 A.M. on weekends.

body alterations

Best braids, twists, knots, and dreads: Twist-N-Turns *(7416 Georgia Ave. NW, 202/882–2309)* specializes in chemical-free natural hair care. Owner Sharon Abney focuses on the health of the hair, rather than just appearances, so customers are asked to come in for a consultation before their appointments. The salon also offers classes on styling and natural hair care. A basic shampoo and trim starts at $15; double-strand twists at $40 and individual braids with extensions start at $150. The cost of dreads varies depending on the technique used and the person's hair texture.

Runner-up: **Cornrows and Co.** *(5401 14th St. NW, 202/723–1827)* salon owner Pamela Ferrell did the hairstyling for the film *Daughters of the Dust*. With the large clientele, you may need to call a month or more in advance for an appointment.

Best fades: Brothers in need of a good shape-up and camaraderie head to the **Underground** *(1110 Eighth St. SE, 202/546–0473)*. Cuts range from $8 to $10. Appointments cost a little more, but walk-ins are welcome. While you're waiting, enjoying the temperature-controlled air, you can check your e-mail on the Underground's computer, play checkers, chess, or spades, and peruse the fine selection of T-shirts and baseball caps in the display case. There's always some interesting conversation happening, or sometimes everyone will watch a movie and kick it for a while.

Best Old World hair singeing: Don't try this at home, kids. It takes years of practice and training. For the last 25 years, Pietro Santoro of **Pietro Hair Salon** *(16th and K streets NW, in the Capitol Hilton, 202/342–1052)* has been using a styling method he learned in his native Sicily. With a spaghetti-thin dripless candle and a small comb, he burns the ends of his male clients' hair for $26 a pop. There's no research to back him up, but he'll tell you that it keeps male hair from thinning out.

It certainly gives the hair great body and sheen. Motion picture *macher* Jack Valenti swears by him, and his hair is Hollywood-perfect. Pietro Hair Salon also does women's hair and offers full salon services.

hotel/motel

Best cheap sleep: At the **Washington International Student Center** *(2452 18th St. NW; 202/265–6555)*, there's no sign on the door. Just the address. That's because this Adams Morgan hostel charges newcomers to D.C. just $15 per night. There's a catch: there are only three clean but cramped rooms, and registration is limited to out-of-state and international visitors.

Runner-up: If you can't get in at the WISC, try the **Washington International Hostel** *(1009 11th St. NW; 202/737–2333)*, where you can get a bed in an air-conditioned, dorm-style room for just $17 a night. The young, hip staff is a plus, and you'll meet people from all scenes and all parts of the globe.

Best no-frills beds: Simpkins' Bed and Breakfast *(Dupont Circle, 202/387–1328)* offers a clean place to sleep in a family atmosphere. A passport (including U.S.) or professional license will get you a discount. At basic rates, private rooms start at $40 a night and non-privates at $20. Add tax and $5 for bedding. Breakfast is simple—make your own toast and coffee or tea—and be sure to clean up after yourself when you're done. It takes credit-card reservations and recommends at least two weeks' notice for summer travel.

Best swanky sleep: When money isn't such an object, you can't do better than the quirky, comforting, and luxurious **Tabard Inn** *(1739 N St. NW, 202/785–1277)*. Named after the hostel in Chaucer's *Canterbury Tales*, the Inn features mismatched antique furniture in its many lounges, a lovely brick courtyard, and a restaurant offering organic food and nice but ditzy servers. Each of the 42 rooms in the three connected Victorian townhouses is unique in its design and decor. Rooms with a private bath start at $99 and those with a shared bath range from $59 to $79. The complimentary breakfast features delicious homemade muffins and fresh fruit, or you can order items like cinnamon-orange French toast and Virginia grits with applewood-smoked bacon from the main menu.

local wonders

Best city view: When you don't feel like waiting in line to go up to the top of the Washington Monument (or "the brick prick" as some locals call it), the **Old Post Office Pavilion** *(Pennsylvania Ave. and 12th St. NW, 202/289–4224)* offers a self-guided tour of the bell tower without the lines you find at the Monument. It's open from 10 A.M. 'til 9 P.M. (Sundays, 12 to 8 P.M.) in the summer, and, at 315 feet, it's the second highest point in D.C. At the top, all four sides offer breathtaking views, especially at dusk. The windows are strung with wires that let the cool breezes in. Downstairs you can look at the Congressional Bells, huge bronze things made in England for this country's bicentennial in 1976.

Best bonsai trees: The 400-acre **National Arboretum** *(3501 New York Ave. NE, 202/245–2726)* does Central Park one better with its bonsai exhibits. It's best to enter at 24th and R streets NE, off of Bladensburg Road, to view them. The Chinese, Japanese, and North American bonsai pavilions all have a slightly different character, but each is extremely beautiful and meditative. You'll forget you're in the city as you walk by the extensive herb garden, various flower beds, and the water lily pond with the biggest goldfish you've ever seen. The **National Capitol Columns** are a surreal scene—22 sandstone pillars (from the original Capitol building) in the middle of an empty field. On weekdays, the Arboretum is less crowded, but even on weekends it's so huge you can always find a secluded area for picnicking or napping.

transmissions

Best jazz: WDCU "Jazz 90" and WPFW (89.3 FM) are neighbors on the FM dial and in fierce competition. WDCU's slogan is "Washington's Jazz Station," which the local Pacifica network outlet WPFW counters with its slogan "Where the REAL Jazz Is." Both stations are member-supported. Both have politics-oriented talk shows in the morning and gospel and blues on the weekend. WPFW has more world music segments—reggae, Brazilian, soca, etc. WDCU is run by the University of the District of Columbia. While both stations have their lite jazz lapses, depending on the DJ, for the most part they provide good straight-ahead sounds.

Best hip-hop: Flipping back and forth between **WPGC (95.5 FM)** and **WKYS (93.9 FM)** on any given night is like witnessing a battle of the DJs as each station presents their live mixing and hip-hop programs. WPGC features the *Flava Sunday* hip-hop show with DJ Flexxx from 10 P.M. 'til midnight, while WKYS offers *Caught in the Webb* with basketball player Chris Webber as host and Jayski on the turntables from 7 to 10 P.M. WPGC presents *Club 95* weeknights from 9 to 10 P.M., featuring a half-hour of go-go. Then Fridays and Saturdays the mix goes from 7 P.M. 'til 3 in the morning. WKYS breaks their mixes into smaller meals—the Old School Mix at noon, the five o'clock Traffic Jam, and then the Live Squad from 9 to 10 P.M. On Saturday, Celo mixes from 7 to 10 P.M.

—additional contributions to this chapter by Joe Brown

contributors' notes

Fourteen-year Portland resident **William Abernathy** writes about beer for *Willamette Week* and about music for several online publications.

Brian Alexander surfs Tourmaline and eats Mexican food at El Indio. His most recent book is *Green Cathedrals: A Wayward Traveler in the Rain Forest*.

Todd Anthony reviews film and nightlife for the *Miami Herald*. He clubhops and plays in a band.

Matt Ashare is a staff music writer at Boston's *Phoenix*, and he contributes to *Musician, Guitar Player*, and *Warp*, as well as the web site Sonicnet (http://son icnet.com). He can often be found drinking Newcastle at the Middle East in Cambridge.

Freelance writer and performance poet **Holly Bass** covers arts and entertainment for the *Washington City Paper* and the *Washington Post*.

Joe Brown is author of *San Francisco by Night*.

Sometime DJ **Jeff Clark** has written for *Details* and *Pulse!* Born and raised in Atlanta, he edits the Atlanta-based music magazine *Stomp and Stammer*.

A co-author of *Generation Ecch*, **Jason Cohen** is a contributing editor at *Texas Monthly* and has also written about music, movies, books, and hockey for such publications as *Rolling Stone, RayGun*, and SPIN.

Writer and critic **Matthew DeBord** is co-author of *Manhattan by Night* and contributed to the *Irreverent Guide to Manhattan*.

Robert Gordon is the author of *It Came from Memphis* and producer of the companion CD of the same name.

Brooke Holmes grew up outside Seattle and attends Columbia University.

Ron House is the lead singer of the Thomas Jefferson Slave Apartments. He sells his CD for seven dollars when it comes in used at the store where he works, Used Kids Records.

Chris Iovenko is a writer and filmmaker who lives in Louisville, Kentucky.

Cara Jepsen is a Chicago-based freelance writer and sometimes waitress whose work regularly appears in the *Chicago Reader*.

Chris Lawrence lives in Manhattan and is a researcher at *Vanity Fair*.

Though not born in Memphis, **Andria Lisle** considers herself a native. She manages Shangri-La Records and contributes to the Sugar Ditch Action Condition, a seven-inch recording label.

Tara McAdams, a native of Philadelphia, hates Memphis except for the listings in this book.

Mac McCaughan plays in the rock bands Superchunk and Portastatic and co-owns Merge Records.

A contributing editor at *Motorbooty*, **Dave Merline** is a freelance writer and graphic artist who has yet to leave Detroit for the greener pastures of anywhere else.

Kerry Murphy works in the music industry and has a small label, Atomic Gimlet. She has lived in Los Angeles all her life.

Andrea Reusing is a caterer in Chapel Hill, North Carolina.

Robert Reynolds is an artist and writer living in New York.

Blake Schwarzenbach plays music and writes in Brooklyn, New York.

Robert Sietsema is currently *Village Voice* restaurant critic and also edits *Down the Hatch*, the nation's first food zine. He grew up in the Midwest and came to New York 20 years ago, where he took up the cause of ethnic food.

Terri Sutton writes regularly for *SPIN*, the *Village Voice*, and *Minneapolis' City Pages*. She moved to the Twin Cities from San Francisco a decade ago and has learned to admire the weather.

Since he was kicked out of a zydeco group a decade ago, **Michael Tisserand** has been writing about Louisiana culture and events for various publications, including the *Washington Post*, *USA TODAY*, and *Billboard*. He is author of *New Orleans by Night* and *The Kingdom of Zydeco*.

SF Weekly correspondent **Silke Tudor** writes three weekly columns about the culture of San Francisco nightlife and the ins and outs of the local music scene.

Hollywood native **Daniel Weizmann** has two spoken jazz CDs, *The Wet Dog Shakes* and *Hollywoodland*, and is in the band Double D Nose. He is also a children's book editor at Price Stern Sloan and the author of several children's titles, including *The Adventures of SuperGonzo!*

Gary Panter won three Emmy Awards for his production design of "Pee Wee's Playhouse" on CBS. He lives in Brooklyn with his wife and daughter.

index

412 index

Acknowledgments

SPIN would like to thank the following artists for sharing their hometown spirit: Andre and Big Boi of OutKast; Junior Brown, Tanya Donelly, Lou Barlow of Sebadoh; Eric Bachmann of Archers of Loaf; Chris Holmes of Yum-Yum; Marcy Mays of Scrawl; Vinnie Dombroski of Sponge; Carla Bozulich of the Geraldine Fibbers; Rob Zabrecky of Possum Dixon; David Grubbs and Scott Taylor of the Grifters; Raul Malo of the Mavericks; Slim Dunlap, James Hall, Moby, and Corin Tucker of Sleater-Kinney; Michael Cudahy of Combustible Edison Orchestra; Speedo of Rocket From the Crypt; Roddy Bottum of Faith No More and Imperial Teen; Dave Dederer of the Presidents of the USA; and Johnny Temple and Eli Janney of Girls Against Boys.

Thanks are also due to their publicists and managers, especially Lorraine Sanabria at LaFace, Janie Osborne and Nancy Russell at Force, Gary Smith and Dan Gilliam at Fort Apache, Cece Stelljes at Sub Pop, Jill Hagara at Alias, Bobbie Gale at Tag, Jodi Smith at Elektra, Lisa Lashley at Columbia, John Mathiason at Susan Silver Management, Cindy Greer at Virgin, Juli Cotta at Larrikin Management, Jennie Boddy and Curtis Smith at Interscope, Orna Banarie at Pacific Management Services, Michelle Roche at Restless, Olivia Cottrell and Dennis Dennehy at Geffen, Shelby Meade at Nasty Little Man, Julie Butterfield at 24, Regina Joskow-Drenton at London, and Aaron Blitzstein at Gold Mountain.

Finally, this book wouldn't have happened without the hard work and enthusiasm of our friends at Balliett & Fitzgerald and Vintage, especially Sarah Burnes, Tom Dyja, Edward Kastenmeier and, of course, Duncan Bock, the editor. Thanks, Duncan; you're the best.

Editor's Acknowledgments

My thanks go to all the writers for giving away the best secrets of their cities and also for their perseverance and good humor as this book unexpectedly grew in size and scope.

I am grateful to Craig Marks for setting this book on course and for his on-target suggestions throughout. I would like to give special acknowledgment to Susan Hobson for all her time, commitment, and ideas in making the book better; and to Sarah Burnes for her guidance and help. And thanks to Fred McIntyre for smooth leadership.

Several music aficionados lent me their expertise, and their knowledge was indispensable. I am grateful to Ben Cooley, Bruce McGuire, Anthony Newman, and Andy Goldman for their advice and good tips. Thanks also go to Tom Dyja for handling the Last Detail.

My wife Samantha Gillison helped with her time, insight, ideas, motivation, encouragement, and support; she made the book happen without knowing it.

AVAILABLE FROM

VINTAGE BOOKS

SPIN ALTERNATIVE
RECORD GUIDE

edited by Eric Weisbard with Craig Marks

America's premier alternative music magazine presents a book of outrageously opinionated reviews of the essential albums of punk, new wave, indie rock, grunge, and rap. The **SPIN** *Alternative Record Guide* explores this music scene in all its variety by providing in-depth and informative record reviews and discussions of such phenomena as the New Zealand Sound, techno, and the secret history of women in punk. The book also includes a listing of the top 100 albums of all time, selected by the editors of **SPIN**, and top ten lists from such artists as Courtney Love and Joey Ramone.

A Vintage Original
Music/0-679-75574-8

Available at your local bookstore, or call toll-free to order:
1-800-793-2665 (credit cards only).